~ *Epic Revisionism*

~ Epic Revisionism

Russian History and Literature as
Stalinist Propaganda

Kevin M. F. Platt and David Brandenberger, editors

THE UNIVERSITY OF WISCONSIN PRESS

The University of Wisconsin Press
1930 Monroe Street
Madison, Wisconsin 53711

www.wisc.edu/wisconsinpress/

3 Henrietta Street
London WC2E 8LU, England

Copyright © 2006
The Board of Regents of the University of Wisconsin System
All rights reserved

5 4 3 2 1

Library of Congress Cataloging-in-Publication Data
Epic revisionism : Russian history and literature as Stalinist propaganda /
   Kevin M. F. Platt and David Brandenberger, editors.
   p. cm.
   Includes index.
   ISBN 0-299-21500-8 (cloth alk. paper)—ISBN 0-299-21504-0 (pbk.: alk. paper)
   1. Popular culture—Soviet Union—Political aspects. 2. Russian literature—
History and criticism. 3. History in literature. 4. Propaganda, Soviet—History—
20th century. 5. Russian literature—Political aspects. 6. Communism and
literature. 7. Ideology and literature. I. Platt, Kevin M. F., 1967–
II. Brandenberger, David.
DK266.4.E66   2005
891.709'358—dc22   2005011172

This book was published with the support of a grant from the
Research Foundation of the University of Pennsylvania.

Contents

Illustrations	ix
Acknowledgements	xi
A Note on Conventions	xiii
Terms and Acronyms	xv

Introduction: Tsarist-Era Heroes in Stalinist Mass Culture
and Propaganda   3
    David Brandenberger and Kevin M. F. Platt

Lev Tolstoi

1. Tolstoi in 1928: In the Mirror of the Revolution   17
    William Nickell

2. Press Commentary on the Tolstoi Centenary Celebration   39
    Novus, "Do We Know How to Celebrate Jubilees?"
    Chitatel' i pisatel', 7 November 1928

Peter the Great

3. Rehabilitation and Afterimage: Aleksei Tolstoi's Many Returns
to Peter the Great   47
    Kevin M. F. Platt

4. Aleksei Tolstoi's Remarks on the Film *Peter I*   69
    Anatolii Danat, "At Aleksei Tolstoi's," *Skorokhodovskii
rabochii*, 15 September 1937

The Epic Heroes

5. Chronicle of a Poet's Downfall: Dem'ian Bednyi, Russian History, and *The Epic Heroes* — 77
   A. M. Dubrovsky

6. The Reaction of Writers and Artists to the Banning of D. Bednyi's Comic Opera — 99
   NKVD Report, 1936

Nikolai Leskov

7. The Adventures of a Leskov Story in Soviet Russia, or the Socialist Realist Opera That Wasn't — 117
   Andrew B. Wachtel

8. The Official Denunciation of Shostakovich's *Lady Macbeth of Mtsensk District* — 135
   [P. M. Kerzhentsev], "Muddle Instead of Music," *Pravda*, 28 January 1936

Ivan the Terrible

9. The Terrible Tsar as Comic Hero: Mikhail Bulgakov's *Ivan Vasil'evich* — 143
   Maureen Perrie

10. Terribly Pragmatic: Rewriting the History of Ivan IV's Reign, 1937–1956 — 157
    David Brandenberger and Kevin M. F. Platt

11. Internal Debate within the Party Hierarchy about the Rehabilitation of Ivan the Terrible — 179
    A. S. Shcherbakov, "Memorandum to Stalin concerning A. N. Tolstoi's Play *Ivan the Terrible*," 1941–1943

Aleksandr Pushkin

12. The 1937 Pushkin Jubilee as Epic Trauma — 193
    Stephanie Sandler

13. Editorial Eulogy of A. S. Pushkin — 214
    "The Glory of the Russian People," *Pravda*, 10 February 1937

Contents	vii

14. The Pushkin Jubilee as Farce — 220
   Mikhail Zoshchenko, "What I Would Like to Say about the Late Poet," *Krokodil* 5 (1937); "A Speech Given during the Pushkin Days at a Meeting of the Tenants' Cooperative on Malaia Perinnaia, No. 7," *Krokodil* 5 (1937)

Aleksandr Nevskii

15. The Popular Reception of S. M. Eisenstein's *Aleksandr Nevskii* — 233
    David Brandenberger
16. Aleksander Nevskii as Russian Patriot — 253
    Mikhail Kol'tsov, "An Epic Hero-People," *Pravda*, 7 November 1938

Ivan Susanin

17. Reinventing the Enemy: The Villains of Glinka's Opera *Ivan Susanin* on the Soviet Stage — 261
    Susan Beam Eggers
18. Official Praise for *Ivan Susanin* — 276
    B. A. Mordvinov, "*Ivan Susanin* on the Stage of the Bolshoi Theater," *Pravda*, 7 February 1939

Mikhail Lermontov

19. Fashioning "Our Lermontov": Canonization and Conflict in the Stalinist 1930s — 283
    David Powelstock
20. A Rare Voice of Caution — 308
    A. Ragozin, "In the Poet's Defense," *Pravda*, 25 August 1939

Epilogue

21. An Internationalist's Complaint to Stalin and the Ensuing Scandal — 315
    V. I. Blium, 31 January 1939; V. Stepanov, 16 February 1939

Conclusion: Epic Revisionism and the Crafting of a Soviet Public — 325
  James von Geldern

Archival Repository Abbreviations — 341

Contributors — 343

Index — 347

Illustrations

Figure 1. Cartoon by N. Lebedev depicting Tolstoi under "cross-examination" 22

Figure 2. Cover art from the collection *Lenin i Tolstoi* 27

Figure 3. Cartoon entitled "L. N. Tolstoi's Works in Our Day" 29

Figure 4. Ia. O. Maliutin as Peter the Great 52

Figure 5. N. K. Cherkasov as Peter the Great 58

Figure 6. D. N. Goberman and M. O. Gol'dshtein's poster advertising V. M. Petrov's *Peter I* (part 1) 71

Figure 7. Detail from cover art of D. Bednyi's book *O pisatel'skom trude* 78

Figure 8. B. M. Kustodiev, *A Beauty* 122

Figure 9. B. M. Kustodiev, *Au Bain (Vénus russe)* 123

Figures 10–12. Title page and Kustodiev's illustrations from N. S. Leskov's *Lady Macbeth of Mtsensk District* 125

Figures 13–15. Kustodiev's illustrations from N. S. Leskov's *Lady Macbeth of Mtsensk District* 126

Figure 16. Katerina Izmailova, one of Kustodiev's illustrations from N. S. Leskov's *Lady Macbeth of Mtsensk District* 127

Figure 17. Kustodiev, untitled depiction of a merchant's wife 127

Figure 18. M. F. Larionov, *Katsap Venus*   129

Figure 19. M. F. Larionov, *Venus*   129

Figure 20. Paul Gauguin, *The King's Wife*   130

Figure 21. M. O. Dlugach's 1945 poster advertising Eisenstein's *Ivan the Terrible* (part 1)   163

Figure 22. N. K. Cherkasov as Ivan the Terrible   164

Figure 23. N. K. Cherkasov as the older Ivan the Terrible   167

Figure 24. Autographed picture of N. K. Cherkasov as Ivan the Terrible given to A. A. Zhdanov   181

Figure 25. L. G. Brodata's cover for *Krokodil* 3   197

Figure 26. A. P. Bel'skii's poster advertising Eisenstein and Pavlenko's *Aleksandr Nevskii*   237

Figure 27. N. K. Cherkasov as the eponymous hero of Eisenstein and Pavlenko's *Aleksandr Nevskii*   239

Acknowledgments

The origins of this volume date back to a routine electronic discussion group inquiry in 1997 about representations of Ivan the Terrible during the Soviet period. This chance intersection sparked a wide-ranging "virtual" discussion on the subject between the editors of this volume, located at the time at opposite ends of the globe in Claremont, California, and central Moscow. Our shared interests developed over the course of the following year in Cambridge, Massachusetts, while we were both in residence at Harvard University. Late-night debates, an atmosphere of intellectual ferment, and a willingness to put other projects on hold led to interdisciplinary cross-fertilization, several jointly prepared presentations, and a co-authored article in the *Russian Review*. Sensing that there was more to the topic of historical revisionism than just Ivan the Terrible, we then decided to assemble a diverse team of specialists from the United States, Great Britain, and Russia to develop a collection of case studies, which is contained in the present volume.

From the very start of this collaboration, we have benefited from the advice and criticism of a large number of friends and colleagues. First and foremost, we must thank the contributors to this volume, who not only have shared their time, work, and expertise, but who have proven willing to work closely with us in order to fine tune their pieces to fit the overall project. Others read parts or all of the manuscript at various stages and significantly influenced its overall framing and composition. For this, we owe thanks to Benjamin Nathans, Katia Dianina, Catharine T. Nepomnyashchy, Ronald Grigor Suny, and Danny Walkowitz. Still others have contributed to individual pieces contained in this volume, and their assistance is credited at the beginning of the endnotes to each chapter.

We also owe a debt of gratitude to a number of institutions that have supported us in our research, writing, and editorial activities. These include Pomona College, the Davis Center for Russian and Eurasian Studies at Harvard University, the Amherst College Center for Russian Culture, the Stanford Humanities Center, and the University of Pennsylvania. Research for several chapters was supported in part by grants to the editors from the International Research & Exchanges Board (IREX), with funds provided by the National Endowment for the Humanities and the United States Department of State, which administers the Russian, Eurasian, and East European Research Program (Title VIII). Support was also provided by a fellowship from the National Council for Eurasian and East European Research, under the authority of a Title VIII Grant from the U.S. Department of State.

The editors have contacted the copyright holders of all the protected material contained in this volume and would like to express gratitude to a number of organizations and institutions for their permission to publish or republish important documents and illustrations. A. N. Iakovlev's International "Demokratiia" Foundation provided permission for the publication of the document in chapter 7, as did the Russian State Archive of Social and Political History for the document and illustration in chapter 11; the Russian State Library granted permission for the use of poster art in chapters 3, 10, and 15. The book's cover illustration is used with permission of the estate of V. B. Koretskii (RAO, Moscow; VAGA, New York).

Finally, we are grateful to David Bethea of the University of Wisconsin for shepherding this project toward publication and to Steve Salemson, Gwen Walker, Adam Mehring, Erin Holman, Carla Aspelmeier, and Jane Curran of the University of Wisconsin Press for their editorial advice, patience, and unflagging support.

A Note on Conventions

The transliteration of terms, titles, surnames, and geographic locations in this volume follows a modified form of the standard practiced by the Library of Congress. Exceptions occur in quotations taken from other sources and in the relatively rare instances when contradicting existing practice would create unnecessary ambiguity (Eisenstein, not Eizenshtein; Meyerhold, not Meierkhol'd; etc.). In order to improve readability, frequent terms like "the Party" and "Communist" and "Fascist" are not capitalized in the text. For similar reasons, French calques like "etatist" and English constructions like "party hierarchy" are used instead of anglicizing Russian colloquialisms like *gosudarstvennik* and *partiinaia verkhushka*.

The translation of the primary sources contained in many of the chapters that follow, as well as their annotation and introductory commentary, has been performed by the volume editors. William Nickell, Susan Beam Eggers, and David Powelstock made substantial contributions to the introductions and translations in chapters 2, 18, and 20, respectively.

Terms and Acronyms

For a complete list of the terms, historical events, and personalities referred to in this volume, see the index.

ACP(b)	All-Union Communist Party (Bolsheviks)
Agitprop	Central Committee Directorate of Agitation and Propaganda
boyar/boiarynia	nobleman / noblewoman
Glaviskusstvo	Main Directorate for Literary and Artistic Affairs, the censor for the arts
Glavrepertkom	Main Repertory Committee, the theatrical censor at Glaviskusstvo
KDI	All-Union Committee for Artistic Affairs
Komsomol	communist youth league
kulak	"rich" peasant
MKhAT	Moscow Art Theater
Narkompros	People's Commissariat of Education
NKVD	People's Commissariat of Internal Affairs, the secret police
Orgburo	Central Committee Organizational Bureau

Politburo	Central Committee Political Bureau
RAPP	Russian Association of Proletarian Writers
RSFSR	Russian Soviet Federation of Socialist Republics
Sovnarkom	All-Union Council of People's Commissars
strel'tsy	seventeenth- to eighteenth-century musketeers

∾ *Epic Revisionism*

Introduction

Tsarist-Era Heroes in Stalinist Mass Culture and Propaganda

∾ David Brandenberger and Kevin M. F. Platt

In late 1931, the popular German biographer Emil Ludwig conducted an interview with Joseph Stalin that drew attention to a rather unorthodox dimension of the party's Marxist-Leninist ideology. Aware of the general secretary's respect for a broad array of "historic individuals" from V. I. Lenin to Peter the Great, Ludwig asked how such beliefs could be reconciled with the tenets of historical materialism. Their subsequent conversation prefigured a gradual evolution of Bolshevik views on the past that would return the "great men of history" to center stage by the end of the 1930s:

> LUDWIG: Marxism denies the leading role of personality in history. Don't you see a contradiction between a materialist understanding of history and the fact that you nevertheless recognize a leading role for historic personalities?
>
> STALIN: No, there is no contradiction. . . . Every generation is met with certain conditions that already exist in their present form as that generation comes into the world. Great people are worth something only insofar as they are able to understand correctly these conditions and what is necessary to alter them. . . .
>
> LUDWIG: Some thirty years ago when I was studying at university, a large number of German professors who considered themselves to be adherents of the materialist understanding of history assured us that Marxism denies the role of heroes and the role of heroic personalities in history.
>
> STALIN: They were vulgarizers of Marxism. Marxism has never denied the role of heroes. To the contrary, it gives them a significant role, albeit in line with the conditions that I have just described.

In perhaps their most famous exchange, Ludwig asked Stalin if he recognized a parallel between himself and Peter the Great. Did he consider himself a latter-day Peter or a continuer of his work? "Not by any means," Stalin replied, dismissing all historical parallels as "risky" and a waste of time. Of course, it was true that Peter had "done a great deal" within the context of the eighteenth century and deserved recognition for his accomplishments. Yet Stalin scoffed at the idea that the tsar might serve as a role model for the twentieth century. Instead, he declared, "I am a pupil of Lenin," adding for good measure that "Peter the Great . . . is a drop in the ocean, whereas Lenin is the ocean itself."[1]

Stalin's refusal to consider himself a continuer of Peter's work is neither surprising nor remarkable. After all, it is entirely possible to have respect for the past without anachronistically identifying with distant ancestors or outmoded precedents. But Stalin's characteristic self-assurance notwithstanding, in the years leading up to the Ludwig interview, Soviet ideologists, historians, and other public figures wrestled over the role of the individual in historical events. On one hand, Marxism's focus on materialism, anonymous social forces, and class struggle had given rise to an understanding of history as a mass phenomenon, a vision captured in S. M. Eisenstein's "heroless" films *Strike* and *October* and M. N. Pokrovskii's "sociological" school of historiography. On the other hand, the mythologization of the October 1917 Revolution had led to a rash of accounts foregrounding heroic individuals, ranging from D. M. Furmanov's celebrated novel *Chapaev* (1923) to the myriad of works associated with Lenin's developing cult of personality.[2] "Revolutionaries" from the tsarist past, from the Decembrists to Stepan Razin, Emil'ian Pugachev, and the Imam Shamil', were similarly mythologized. Ludwig's line of questioning in 1931 focused precisely on this conceptual disagreement over the proper role of the hero in history.

Yet Stalin's pat answers to Ludwig's questions suggest that a resolution to this tension was already beginning to take shape in Soviet public life by the early 1930s. Within a few years' time, heroes and heroism would come to stand at the center of a series of Soviet propaganda drives that were designed to promote a newly populist vision of the USSR's "usable past."[3] Between 1929 and 1935, a heroic pantheon was constructed from the ranks of the society's most famous Old Bolsheviks, Red Army commanders, industrial shock workers, and champion agricultural laborers. Even Arctic explorers found representation on the Soviet Olympus.[4] These celebrities, in turn, were joined during the second half of the decade by an array of mainstream historic figures from the pre-revolutionary period—famous individuals like Aleksandr Nevskii, Minin and Pozharskii, Ivan Susanin, Suvorov, Kutuzov, Lomonosov, Pushkin, and so on.

If Stalin had been vague in 1931 when Ludwig asked him about Peter the Great's historical significance, it is revealing to note that just six years later, on the eve of the twentieth anniversary of the revolution, a major motion picture about Russia's first emperor dominated Soviet movie house screens. Peter and other themes drawn from the Russian national past also loomed large in a new generation of public school history textbooks released during the fall of that year.[5] As the contents of this volume indicate, such themes became ubiquitous in Soviet mass culture during the late 1930s, throughout popular literature, the press, film, opera, and theater.

This growing prominence of names and reputations from the Russian national past at times threatened to eclipse the celebration of more recent Soviet heroes, sparking protest from veteran leftists. The literary critic V. I. Blium expressed particular disdain for productions like Eisenstein's film *Aleksandr Nevskii*, A. E. Korneichuk's play *Bogdan Khmel'nitskii*, and the revival of M. I. Glinka's opera *Ivan Susanin*, even complaining in a letter to Stalin that "Soviet patriotism nowadays is sometimes coming to resemble racist nationalism." Although hyperbolic, Blium's analysis was also quite perceptive. Propaganda based on Russian princes, tsars, and generals seemed iconoclastic and perhaps even counter-revolutionary in a society fashioned according to a revolutionary and proletarian internationalist aesthetic. Blium's protests effectively ended his career (see chapter 21), yet the question that the critic posed remains valid to the present day: how did heroes from the Russian national past come to figure so prominently in Stalinist public culture?

The authors of this volume propose to resolve this question by examining the circumstances under which heroes drawn from the annals of medieval Rus', Muscovy, and imperial Russia were mobilized to serve the Soviet state during the 1930s and 1940s. Many have dismissed the rehabilitation of figures such as Peter the Great, Aleksandr Nevskii, and Ivan the Terrible during this time as either a component of Stalin's burgeoning personality cult or one of the more marginal, prosaic aspects of the party's ideological "Great Retreat."[6] Others ignore the phenomenon entirely, apparently considering it to have been an aberration within an otherwise orthodox socialist political culture.[7] We, however, believe that the Soviet rehabilitation of the tsarist past deserves a more serious investigation. As the present collection demonstrates, the Stalinist revival of great names from Russian history was a defining feature of Soviet public life during the 1930s. Not only do these rehabilitations reflect a growing sense of populism, russocentrism, and etatism over the course of the decade, but they also anticipate the direction taken by the most effective genres of wartime propaganda between 1941 and 1945.[8] Consideration of the era's "epic revisionism" reveals a significant and hitherto understudied aspect of Soviet ideology during the Stalin era.

Responding to a growing body of recent literature concerning the idiosyncratic nature of the USSR's interwar "search for a usable past,"[9] the case studies assembled here approach the rehabilitation of the Russian past from a variety of angles. Several contributions examine figures whose rehabilitations exemplify the Soviet enthusiasm for elaborate "jubilee" celebrations. Thus William Nickell investigates one of the first Soviet experiments with this genre of public life, the Tolstoi centenary of 1928, providing insight into the formation of a pattern of official culture that would become dominant during the following decade. In her contribution, Stephanie Sandler examines the traumatic subconscious of Soviet public discourse surrounding what was perhaps the most prominent cultural event of the 1930s, the Pushkin commemoration of 1937. David Powelstock complements both of these chapters with analysis of the debates surrounding the Soviet canonization of the notoriously "difficult" poet Mikhail Lermontov in connection with his 1939 and 1941 jubilee years.

Other chapters of the volume examine the rehabilitation campaigns themselves. David Brandenberger and Kevin M. F. Platt offer a comprehensive account of the Soviet reinvention of Ivan the Terrible, which details the tension between official intent and historical contingency that ultimately led the entire endeavor into stalemate. In a separate contribution, Platt investigates the political and textual strategies employed by Aleksei Tolstoi in his contributions to the rehabilitation of Peter the Great, revealing that the novelist possessed a remarkable degree of political savvy during the turmoil of the interwar period. Brandenberger surveys public and private reactions to a similarly pioneering work, S. M. Eisenstein's epic film *Aleksandr Nevskii*, offering insight into the broader popular reception of Soviet historical propaganda as a whole.

Still other chapters provide counterpoint to the revival of Russian historical and cultural figures by examining the backlash, scandal, and "reverse rehabilitation" that accompanied the official campaigns. A. M. Dubrovsky chronicles the downfall of Dem'ian Bednyi, a radical poet who struggled unsuccessfully to adjust to the new Soviet attitude toward Russian history. Maureen Perrie details a similar case involving Mikhail Bulgakov, observing how the playwright's comedic treatment of Ivan the Terrible during the mid-1930s failed to anticipate Soviet officialdom's evolving views concerning this controversial figure. Andrew Wachtel provides a fascinating account of the devastating effect that an earlier revival of Nikolai Leskov's "Lady Macbeth of Mtsensk District" had on Dmitrii Shostakovich's operatic version of the story—one that nearly cost the composer his career. Finally, Susan Beam Eggers investigates the reverse rehabilitation (i.e., vilification) of the Polish invaders of the seventeenth century "Time of Troubles" in her treatment of the Soviet revival of M. I. Glinka's opera *A Life for the Tsar*. According to Eggers, this opera's indictment of the Poles took on epic proportions in the late 1930s in order to provide Soviet society with a convenient allegory for the rising threat of German fascism. Adding to the depth of the collection, each of these case studies is complemented by the translation of a primary source—either a contemporary newspaper article, short story or unpublished archival document—in order to enrich the discussion at hand. This combination of primary and secondary sources provides students of the period with an unusually subtle and nuanced understanding of the context and "texture" of Stalinist historical propaganda.

Unlike many loosely assembled collections of conference proceedings, *Epic Revisionism* is a focused, multi-author investigation of the role played by Russian history and literature in Stalinist public discourse. The diversity of the volume's contributors—representing three countries, two academic disciplines and a range of professional advancement—has resulted in a remarkably varied set of approaches and conclusions regarding the subject at hand. While some chapters reflect a largely "top-down" conception of the Stalinist state's management of public life (Dubrovsky, Eggers), others focus on the extent to which the revival of figures from the Russian past was driven by the political strivings and creative energies of individual artists (Platt) or other, more historically contingent factors (Nickell, Perrie, Brandenberger and Platt). Another set of productive tensions among the volume's chapters may be drawn between those authors who focus on conflicts between official discourse and atypical or dissenting voices (Sandler, Wachtel, Dubrovsky), and those who investigate internal divisions within the official discourse itself (Nickell, Platt, Brandenberger, Platt and Brandenberger, Powelstock). Finally, a variety of disciplinary affiliations provides the volume with a wide array of methodological approaches, ranging from a cultural-historical analysis of individual texts (Sandler, Platt) to broader surveys of journalism (Powelstock) and mass media as a whole (Nickell). Biographically based analysis also plays a role in the volume

(Dubrovsky, Perrie), as does work that focuses tightly on individual components of the overall campaign (Wachtel, Brandenberger, Eggers).

In aggregate, these studies capitalize on the multi-author format to generate a coherent, yet internally diverse account of the intent, design and impact of the Stalinist rehabilitation of the Russian national past. As James von Geldern observes in his conclusion to the volume, this coordinated effort also allows us to comment more broadly on the elusive nature of "public culture" in the USSR during the most repressive years of the Soviet era. But beyond the collection's relevance to the study of the Stalinist period, it would seem to have considerable contemporary application as well. Russian political life today is turning increasingly to the myths, imagery and iconography of the tsarist past in a search for authority and legitimacy. Many of the watchwords and catch phrases of present-day mythmaking were last deployed as politically significant symbols under Stalin. Today's enthusiasts of the pre-revolutionary past no doubt imagine themselves to be reaching back to the roots of the Russian political tradition—to a "true" wellspring of Russian national pride that predates the Soviet era. Yet in reality, this dialogue with the past—ostensibly conducted "over the heads" of seven decades of Soviet history—borrows heavily from the cultural norms of the Stalin period. In many cases, works being reissued today as part of the current "rediscovery" of the Russian past were last printed between the 1930s and the 1950s.[10] Clearly, the Stalinist celebration of the Russian national past must be seen as an important link in the genealogy of current nationalist rhetoric. In this sense, the chapters that follow make a valuable contribution to our understanding of contemporary political culture in Russia as well.

∽

Before turning to the case studies themselves, a brief overview of general trends in interwar Soviet mass culture is necessary in order to set the stage for the detailed accounts that follow. Of central importance to our discussion is the rise of Socialist Realism during the early 1930s. According to Katerina Clark's now widely accepted view, official endorsement of this mode of literary, artistic, and cultural expression between 1932 and 1934 led to the abandonment of the previous decade's avant-garde and revolutionary cultural movements. In contrast to the experimentalist writing associated with the many literary groups of the 1920s (the Left Front in Art, or LEF, Novyi lef, VAPP, Kuznetsy, etc.), Socialist Realism was characterized by a simple, traditional style of description derived from the realist prose of the nineteenth century. Thematically, this new mode of expression promoted everyday tales of valor in which heroic individuals struggled for the greater societal good. Engineered for mass appeal, many of this new mode's plot elements and narrative devices had much in common with epic and folkloric traditions.[11]

Elaborating on Clark's analysis, Evgenii Dobrenko has argued more recently that Socialist Realism emerged as a populist corrective to the often arcane and inaccessible literature of the 1920s. Aware that the cultural innovations of the first fifteen years of Soviet rule had failed to win the hearts and minds of the poorly educated mass audience, writers and Soviet authorities alike moved to embrace more conventional forms of literary expression toward the end of the first Five-Year Plan.[12] Within only a few years, the new canon of Socialist Realism had eclipsed the challenging, often intentionally obscure writing of the 1920s with an elaborate pageantry of memorable protagonists and dramatic (if also formulaic) story lines, celebrating heroes from the civil war and the on-going socialist construction.

This explanatory model can be generalized in many ways to describe Soviet mass culture as a whole during the early to mid-1930s. Complementing trends in official literature, attempts were made in the early 1930s to enhance the mobilizational potential of Soviet propaganda on the mass level by means of a populist emphasis on contemporary heroism. This approach had been championed already during the late 1920s by A. M. Gor'kii and others who contended that contemporary heroes could be used to inspire and rally "by example." At the same time that mass journalism was shifting its focus to accessible, popular themes, prominent multivolume series like Gor'kii's *History of Plants and Factories* and *The History of the Civil War in the USSR* were launched as a way of developing a new pantheon of Soviet heroes, socialist myths, and modern-day fables. Focusing on shock workers in industry and agriculture, this "search for a usable past" also lavished attention on prominent Old Bolshevik revolutionaries, industrial planners, party leaders, Komsomol officials, Comintern activists, Red Army heroes, non-Russians from the republican party organizations, and even famous members of the secret police. These populist, heroic tales were to provide a common narrative—a story of identity—that the entire society could relate to. Reflecting a new emphasis on patriotism and russocentrism in the press after the mid-1930s, these heroes were to be a rallying call with greater mass appeal than the preceding decade's narrow and impersonal materialist focus on social forces and class struggle.[13]

Interest in individual heroes, patriotism, and the "usable past"—referred to at the time as "pragmatic history"—led some propagandists in the direction of folkloric themes and imagery.[14] Others concluded that additional members of the newly forming Soviet pantheon of heroes might be drawn from the annals of the pre-revolutionary history of the USSR. Although rehabilitating representatives of the old regime was a politically difficult undertaking, during the second half of the 1930s classic cultural icons like A. S. Pushkin were revived in tandem with a few selectively chosen state-builders like Peter the Great. Such figures were expected to bolster the regime's legitimacy, with Pushkin lending credibility to Soviet literature while Peter's radical reforms would serve as a precedent for Stalin's breakneck industrialization. Among those historical reputations rehabilitated during the second half of the 1930s were famous names such as Nevskii, Donskoi, Minin, Pozharskii, Susanin, Lomonosov, Suvorov, Kutuzov, and Lermontov. Concurrently, one observes a noticeable decline in official enthusiasm for peasant rebels like Razin, Pugachev, and Shamil'.[15] A reflection of the emergent etatist and russocentric tendencies of the day, these moves were purely instrumental, the party hierarchy apparently believing that the Soviet Olympus could be hybridized to allow its Peters and Pushkins to stand shoulder to shoulder alongside contemporary shock workers (e.g., A. Stakhanov), Old Bolsheviks (A. S. Enukidze), prominent industrialists (Iu. L. Piatakov), Komsomol activists (A. V. Kosarev), Red Army commanders (A. I. Egorov), republican party leaders (F. Khodzhaev), and members of the secret police (N. I. Ezhov). By 1936, these heroes stood at the center of countless productions designed for the stage, screen, and public library reading room. Stalinist propagandists' peculiar willingness to line up the heroes of the present with those of the distant past certainly constitutes one of the most surprising developments in the history of Soviet public life. Indeed, the contributions to this volume suggest that many of the most distinctive features of the Soviet rehabilitation of the Russian national past stem from the difficulty of reconciling the contradictions inherent to these campaigns. At base, this tension indicates that, while the Soviet establishment clearly attempted to harness "tried and true" historical myths for its own purposes, this investment in tsarist historical propaganda should not be mistaken for a simple repetition of imperial mythmaking.[16]

Although the deployment of tsarist heroes was initially quite modest and selective (focusing largely on both Russian and non-Russian artists and scientists), these pre-revolutionary names and reputations were augmented by so many Russian military and political figures after 1937 that they came to dominate the new Soviet pantheon by the end of the decade. This peculiar turn of events was likely the result of both official direction and historical contingency. Beginning in the fall of 1936, the Great Terror devastated the party, state bureaucracy, the military high command, and the national republics, crippling the new heroic Olympus as the rolling waves of the purge swept away the leading lights of Soviet society. Agitational efforts at the grassroots level likely appeared close to collapse as the Enukidzes, Piatakovs, Kosarevs, Egorovs, and Ezhovs were consumed in the bloodletting. One may imagine how propagandists on the local level must have panicked over materials that turned out to be littered with the names of recently exposed "enemies of the people." At times, it must have seemed as if only Socialist Realism's *fictional* heroes—Pavel Korchagin, Gleb Chumalov, and others—did not risk arrest.[17]

As this cruel winnowing process stripped the Soviet Olympus of its party activists and Red Army commanders, the prominence of the pantheon's constituents from the Russian national past rose dramatically.[18] Not only were the Peters and Pushkins arguably more familiar to average Soviet citizens than the Frunzes, Shchors, and other Bolshevik heroes who were colorless enough to survive the purges, but they were far easier to propagandize (in part because there was little risk that they might be exposed one day as fascist spies or Trotskyites).[19] In other words, the party's pragmatic willingness to hybridize its pantheon of heroes, compounded by the purges' destruction of many of the available Soviet heroes, led to an increasing reliance on pre-revolutionary Russian reputations in Soviet propaganda during the mid- to late 1930s.

To many, this substitution may have seemed quite unremarkable in light of the growing conservatism of Stalinist culture. As party propaganda became increasingly russocentric and populist toward the end of the 1930s, it seemed quite natural for the USSR to lay a claim to the political and cultural heritage of tsarist Russia. That said, one fundamental problem could not be denied—these newly discovered "Soviet" heroes were, in the final analysis, a group of nobles, tsarist generals, emperors, and princes, whose status as exemplary figures within the Soviet pantheon of heroes could never be fully reconciled with the reigning revolutionary ethic of Marxism-Leninism. The following case studies examine the inevitable tensions that resulted, detailing some of the most curious dimensions of the Stalinist regime's "epic revisionism."

Notes

1. "Beseda s nemetskim pisatelem Emilem Liudvigom," *Bol'shevik* 8 (1932): 33. Stalin's view is reminiscent of Hegel's—see G. Hegel, *The Philosophy of History*, trans. J. Sibree (New York: Dover, 1956), 30.

2. Stalin set the general tone with his treatment of Lenin in 1924: "When I've compared him with the other leaders of our party, it's always seemed to me that Lenin stood head and shoulders above his comrades-in-arms—Plekhanov, Martov, Aksel'rod and others—and that in comparison with them, Lenin was not simply one of the leaders, but a leader of the highest sort, a mountain eagle, who did not know fear in battle and who bravely led the party ahead along the unknown paths of the Russian revolutionary movement." I. V. Stalin, *O Lenine i o leninizme* (Moscow: Gosudarstvennoe izdatel'stvo, 1924), 8. Generally, see Nina Tumarkin, *Lenin Lives! The Lenin Cult in Soviet Russia* (Cambridge, Mass.: Harvard University Press, 1983); Frederick Corney, *Telling October: Memory and the Making of the Bolshevik Revolution* (Ithaca, N.Y.: Cornell University Press, 2004).

3. On the revival of individual actors in Soviet ideology, see Leo Yaresh, "The Role of the Individual in History," in *Rewriting Russian History: Soviet Interpretations of Russia's Past*, ed. C. E. Black (New York: Praeger, 1956), 78–106. The "usable past" expression was coined in 1918 by Van Wyk Brooks and made something of a commonplace by Henry Steele Commager. See Van Wyk Brooks, "On Creating a Usable Past," *Dial* 64 (1918): 337–41; Henry Steele Commager, *The Search for a Usable Past and Other Essays in Historiography* (New York: Knopf, 1967), 3–27.

4. See John McCannon's account of the campaign surrounding the far north: *Red Arctic: Polar Exploration and the Myth of the North in the Soviet Union, 1932–1939* (Oxford: Oxford University Press, 1998).

5. See Iu. Olesha, "Petr I," *Izvestiia*, 2 September 1937, 4; *Kratkii kurs istorii SSSR*, ed. A. V. Shestakov (Moscow: Gos. uchebno-pedagog. izd-vo, 1937).

6. See, for instance, Richard Taylor, "Red Stars, Positive Heroes and Personality Cults," in *Stalinism and Soviet Cinema*, ed. Richard Taylor and Derek Spring (London: Routledge, 1993), 88; Sheila Fitzpatrick, "Introduction: On Power and Culture," in *The Cultural Front: Power and Culture in Revolutionary Russia* (Ithaca, N.Y.: Cornell University Press, 1992), 9–11; Nicholas Timasheff, *The Great Retreat: The Growth and Decline of Communism in Russia* (New York: E. P. Dutton, 1947), 167–81. Timasheff's "Great Retreat" thesis fails to explain this propaganda campaign's selectivity, politicization, or goal of reinforcing party and state legitimacy. That said, such suspicions were not uncommon among members of the left-leaning Soviet intelligentsia—see chapter 21.

7. Stephen Kotkin ignores the high profile of films such as *Peter I* in his epic study of Stalinist "civilization" in Magnitogorsk despite the fact that one of his primary informants, John Scott, described seeing one of them in his memoirs. Compare Stephen Kotkin, *Magnetic Mountain: Stalinism as a Civilization* (Berkeley: University of California Press, 1995); and John Scott, *Behind the Urals: An American Worker in Russia's City of Steel*, ed. Stephen Kotkin (Bloomington: Indiana University Press, 1989), 236. David Hoffmann more readily acknowledges the degree to which the advancement of such heroes called into question the USSR's commitment to class consciousness and internationalism—see his *Stalinist Values: The Cultural Norms of Soviet Modernity, 1917–1941* (Ithaca, N.Y.: Cornell University Press, 2003), 163–66.

8. Many have overlooked this emphasis on russocentric myths, imagery, and iconography during the late 1930s, linking it instead to 1941's exigencies of war. See Harold Swayze, *Political Control of Literature in the USSR, 1946–1959* (Cambridge, Mass.: Harvard University Press, 1962), 28; Lowell Tillet, *The Great Friendship: Soviet Historians on the Non-Russian Nationalities* (Chapel Hill: University of North Carolina Press, 1969), 49–61; Christel Lane, *The Rites of Rulers: Ritual in Industrial Society—The Soviet Case* (Cambridge: Cambridge University Press, 1981), 181; Alexander Werth, *Russia at War, 1941–1945* (New York: Carroll & Graf, 1984), 120, 249–50; Vera Dunham, *In Stalin's Time: Middleclass Values in Soviet Fiction*, 2nd ed. (Durham, N.C.: Duke University Press, 1990), 12, 17, 41, 66; Stephen Carter, *Russian Nationalism: Yesterday, Today, Tomorrow* (London: Pinter, 1990), 51; John Barber and Mark Harrison, *The Soviet Home Front, 1941–1945: A Social and Economic History of the USSR in World War II* (London: Longman, 1991), 69; Nina Tumarkin, *The Living and the Dead: The Rise and Fall of the Cult of World War II in Russia* (New York: Basic, 1994), 63; Victoria Bonnell, *Iconography of Power: Soviet Political Posters under Lenin and Stalin* (Berkeley: University of California Press, 1997), 255–57; E. Iu. Zubkova, "Mir mnenii sovetskogo cheloveka, 1945–1948: po materialam TsK VKP(b)," *Otechestvennaia istoriia* 3 (1998): 34.

9. A. M. Dubrovskii, "Kak Dem'ian Bednyi ideologicheskuiu oshibku sovershil," in *Otechestvennaia kul'tura i istoricheskaia nauka XVIII–XX vekov: Sbornik statei* (Briansk: BGPU, 1996): 143–51; Maureen Perrie, "Nationalism and History: The Cult of Ivan the Terrible in Stalin's Russia," in *Russian Nationalism Past and Present*, ed. Geoffrey Hosking and Robert Service (New York: St. Martin's, 1998), 107–28; Kevin Platt and David Brandenberger, "Terribly Romantic, Terribly Progressive or Terribly Tragic? Rehabilitating Ivan IV under I. V. Stalin, 1937–1953," *Russian Review* 58, no. 4 (1999): 635–54; Stephen Moeller-Sally, "'Klassicheskoe nasledie' v epokhu sotsrealizma, ili pokhozhdeniia Gogolia v strane bol'shevikov," in *Sotsrealisticheskii kanon*, ed. Hans Günther and Evgenii Dobrenko (St. Petersburg: Akademicheskii proekt, 2000), 509–22; Serhy Yekelchyk, "*Diktat* and Dialogue in Stalinist Culture: Staging Patriotic Historical Opera in Soviet Ukraine (1936–1954)," *Slavic Review* 59, no. 3 (2000): 597–624; Joan Neuberger, "The Politics of Bewilderment: 'Ivan the Terrible' in 1945," in *Eisenstein at 100: A Reconsideration*, ed. Al LaValley and Barry Scherr (New Brunswick, N.J.: Rutgers University Press, 2001), 227–52; Maureen Perrie, *The Cult of Ivan the Terrible in Stalin's Russia* (New York: Palgrave, 2002); David Brandenberger, *National Bolshevism: Stalinist Mass Culture and the Formation of Modern Russian National Identity, 1931–1956* (Cambridge, Mass.: Harvard University Press, 2002); Stephen Moeller-Sally, *Gogol's Afterlife: The Evolution of a Classic in Imperial and Soviet Russia* (Evanston, Ill.: Northwestern University Press, 2002); Serhy Yekelchyk, *Stalin's Empire of Memory: Russian-Ukrainian Relations in the Soviet Historical Imagination* (Toronto: Toronto University Press, 2004).

10. For a detailed examination of the assimilation of Stalinist texts on tsarist history to current conditions, see Kevin M. F. Platt, "History, Inertia and the Unexpected: Recycling Russia's Despots," *Common Knowledge* 10, no. 1 (2004): 130–50.

11. See Katerina Clark, *The Soviet Novel: History as Ritual* (Chicago: University of Chicago Press, 1980), 34–35, 72, 119, 136–55, 148, 8–10; idem, "Little Heroes and Big Deeds: Literature Responds to the First Five-Year Plan," in *Cultural Revolution in Russia, 1928–1931*, ed. Sheila Fitzpatrick (Bloomington: Indiana University Press, 1978), 205–6.

12. Evgenii Dobrenko, "The Disaster of Middlebrow Taste; or, Who 'Invented' Socialist Realism?" in *Socialist Realism without Shores*, ed. Thomas Lahusen and Evgeny Dobrenko (Durham, N.C.: Duke University Press, 1997), 153–64; idem, *The Making of the State Reader*, trans. Jesse M. Savage (Stanford, Calif.: Stanford University Press, 1997), esp. chap. 3.

13. On the emergence of russocentrism and the heroic in Soviet propaganda, see Brandenberger, *National Bolshevism*, chaps. 2–3, 5.

14. D. L. Brandenberger and A. M. Dubrovsky, "'The People Need a Tsar': The Emergence of National Bolshevism as Stalinist Ideology, 1931–1941," *Europe-Asia Studies* 50, no. 5 (1998): 875–76; Frank Miller, *Folklore for Stalin: Folklore and Pseudofolklore of the Stalin Era* (Armonk, N.Y.: M. E. Sharpe, 1990).

15. A. A. Zhdanov toned down triumphalist commentary on peasant rebellions while re-editing Shestakov's seminal textbook on the history of the USSR—see pages 20, 45, 55, 64, 73, 93–94, 104 and 134 of the text's June 1937 page proofs, stored at RGASPI, f. 77, op. 1, d. 854.

16. For a rather schematic discussion of the rehabilitations as the party's "endorsement of the high culture of the [pre-revolutionary] intelligentsia," see Fitzpatrick, "Introduction: On Power and Culture," 9–11; Timasheff, *The Great Retreat*, 167–81.

17. In a sense, of course, they did. Although the classics of Socialist Realism were never removed from circulation, virtually all were savaged by the censor during the period—see Herman Ermolaev, *Censorship in Soviet Literature, 1917–1991* (Lanham, Md.: Rowman and Littlefield, 1997), 51–140. Korchagin and Chumalov were the heroes of N. Ostrovskii's *How the Steel was Forged* and F. Gladkov's *Cement*, respectively.

18. Fear of non-Russian nationalism—a major motivating factor for the Great Terror in the national republics—may provide part of the explanation for why the rehabilitation campaign on the all-union level focused almost exclusively on Russian heroes after 1937. Some republics did promote their own historical heroes during the late 1930s, but these rehabilitations were explicitly subbordinated to the russocentric vision that dominated historical propoaganda on the all-union level. Further evidence of the russocentrism that underscored this campaign is visible in the fact that non-Russian heroes were seldom celebrated outside of their respective republics with anything close to the attention afforded to the Peters and Pushkins of the Russian tradition.

19. Linda Colley discusses the political usefulness of long-dead heroes in *Britons: Forging the Nation, 1707–1837* (New Haven, Conn.: Yale University Press, 1992), 168–69.

Lev Tolstoi

1
Tolstoi in 1928

In the Mirror of the Revolution

☙ WILLIAM NICKELL

> To Tolstoi the writer: peace,
> But to Tolstoi the prophet: war!
> —*Vlast' truda*, 1928

The one-hundredth anniversary of Tolstoi's birth, in September 1928, was the first large-scale, government-sponsored event during the Soviet era celebrating a pre-revolutionary writer. Tolstoi was feted throughout the year and throughout the country, from the rural peasant reading hut to the capital, where a seven-hour ceremony at the Bolshoi Theater inaugurated a whole Tolstoi week of cultural events.[1] Postage stamps were issued, documentary films were produced, and three separate editions of the author's collected works were published, including the beginning volumes of a ninety-volume "jubilee" edition. Yet the anniversary was hardly an unequivocal celebration; rather, it was marked by an ambivalence that characterized the official Soviet attitude toward Tolstoi. On one hand, Tolstoi's artistic talents were openly acknowledged, and Soviet writers were already at that time being enjoined to learn from Tolstoi—Iurii Libedinskii, in fact, used him as his primary literary model in the platform for the RAPP Plenum of May 1928.[2] On the other hand, other aspects of Tolstoi—his religiosity and his theory of nonviolence, as well as the Tolstoian movement that they educed—elicited a great deal of caution, distrust, and, at times, open hostility. Although it was asserted that the anniversary opened a new era in the study of Tolstoi that reflected the tremendous social progress of the previous ten years, there was also a great deal of concern that it would lend legitimacy to those dangerous elements in his legacy. Worse still, Tolstoi's artful writing could obscure the dangers of his backward ideas, requiring that the novelist be read with heightened ideological vigilance.

Thus it was with considerable anxiety that the Soviet authorities acknowledged the national significance of Tolstoi and directed the public to celebrate his holiday. Even as they promoted Tolstoi's centennial, they sought to diminish the adulation that surrounded him and limit his influence on Soviet readers. An elaborate interpretive apparatus was produced to accompany the anniversary celebration, forming a sort of protective supertext that would prevent readers from being infected by Tolstoi's way of thinking. The public was carefully instructed as to how to read Tolstoi and was provided with lists of recommended works as well as Marxist critical treatments.[3] The editorial board of the jubilee edition was fortified with staunch party ideologues, and editions of Tolstoi's works were bracketed with communist exegeses—introductions and commentary that clarified class contradictions and countered Tolstoian "theses" with Marxist antitheses.[4] Anthologies of Marxist Tolstoi criticism were printed in cheap editions, including separate editions of Lenin's and Plekhanov's well-known articles on the subject.[5] Whole guidebooks on the proper observation of the holiday were also published, offering instructions on setting up displays, organizing evenings, and lending Tolstoi's books in libraries (including recommendations for alternative authors).[6] A Glaviskusstvo piece called "Theses for Lecturers at Cultural-Educational Establishments and Schools" appeared in both *Pravda* and *Izvestiia* three days before the anniversary, describing methods of counteracting the dangers of Tolstoi.[7]

These precautions added a particularly Soviet flavor to ritual practices inherited from the pre-revolutionary cult of literature in Russia. Under the old regime, quarter centuries and even decades were regularly observed milestones in the afterlives of major Russian writers, with their centennials becoming full-blown national holidays. Already in the late nineteenth century these events had become richly coded moments of public discourse, in which the legacy of an author was used to promote cultural ideas and archetypes. Thus while the Pushkin anniversary of 1879/1880 was a landmark in establishing the poet's cult, it is most vividly remembered for the way in which Dostoevskii's rousing panegyric used Pushkin to define Russia itself. Subsequent Pushkin anniversaries produced new collective identities as diverse as the times in which they occurred (in keeping with Apollon Grigor'ev's equation "Pushkin is our everything!").[8] Insofar as the democratic tendencies of nineteenth-century Russian literature gave voice to political positions that conflicted with the ideologies of the Russian state, the literary holiday could become a political event, as the Russian public seized the day of an anniversary or funeral to express their sympathy for whatever subversive agendas the author might represent. By the beginning of the twentieth century this mixture of remembrance and protest had become quite overt: when tsarist authorities attempted to limit commemoration of Tolstoi's death in 1910, the public responded with widespread strikes and demonstrations that expressed both sympathy for Tolstoi and antipathy toward the government.[9]

The official statement by Nicholas II on Tolstoi's death had recognized him only as the author of *War and Peace*, abdicating considerable rhetorical power to others who could make much more effective identifications with Tolstoi's legacy. For Lenin, a Russia that could identify so intensely with Tolstoi was a nation on the verge of revolution. This approach became a model for the post-revolutionary period, when the Soviets exploited literary holidays for their own agitational work. The literary calendar now provided occasion for the redefinition of pre-revolutionary literary history and the celebration of new collective identities, but also for the articulation of a new set of political agendas. The 1928 Tolstoi anniversary became a focal point in the campaign to reorient Soviet literature away from its avant garde tendencies toward the accessible tradition of the "classics"; it was also used to illustrate the need for collectivization by characterizing the peasant population in terms of Tolstoi's passivity and religiosity. As Soviet critics asserted their ideological hegemony over Tolstoi, they also demonstrated a model for cultural revolution: as one critic explained, the revolution supplied "those essential clarifications that will help the contemporary reader gain an understanding of the work of Tolstoi after it has passed through the prism of Marxist analysis."[10]

This refraction was not always precise, however, as those who engineered it confronted the ambiguities not only of Tolstoi but of early Soviet cultural practices as well. The months leading up to the Tolstoi anniversary have been recognized as a period of "confusion and uncertainty in party alignments." Stalin was consolidating power, defeating rivals first on the left and then on the right. L. D. Trotskii and his political retinue were expelled from Moscow in January 1928; N. I. Bukharin also came under attack; a speech printed in *Pravda* during the Tolstoi anniversary week has been cited as his last appearance as major spokesman for the party. The campaign against Trotskii and his supporters continued throughout the year, and another round of arrests was made in October, following a September decree by V. M. Molotov.[11] These conflicts caused confusion among rank-and-file party members, who found it difficult to identify various enemies and their positions relative to the general line. The censure of former ideological authorities for transgressions that were not clearly defined made party members unsure of their own positions and allegiances.[12]

The party's struggle to define itself in relation to these "deviations" had the net effect of forcing the Tolstoi anniversary toward the ideological center represented by Lenin's writings on Tolstoi. These pieces provided a reassuring lodestar by which to navigate the anniversary and a means of orientation toward the course of ideological orthodoxy and political viability. Although many important works of literary criticism on Tolstoi also appeared during the centennial, including seminal volumes by Formalists Victor Shklovskii and Boris Eikhenbaum, they were largely overshadowed in the press by the work of leading Marxists like P. S. Kogan, V. M. Friche, and F. Raskol'nikov. These latter authorities were themselves superseded by revolutionary forebears like Luxembourg, Plekhanov, and, ultimately, Lenin. The discussion below explores the dynamics behind this centrism and describes more fully the debates that characterized the Soviet celebration of the Tolstoi centennial. The picture of increasing ideological deference that it presents not only reflects contemporary developments in the broader political spectrum but also anticipates the course of Soviet cultural policy into the 1930s.

∼

In an often-cited passage from Gor'kii's memoirs, Lenin holds up a volume of Tolstoi's works and exclaims, "Who in Europe can compare to him? No one."[13] Lenin's attitude supported a certain institutional respect toward Tolstoi on the part of the Soviet establishment, deriving from a cultish veneration of a national icon that transcended the politics of Soviet culture. Gor'kii, the anointed godfather of the new Soviet literature, shared Lenin's admiration and did much to memorialize it in his reminiscences of Tolstoi.[14] The participation of Soviet elites in the broad currents of mass enthusiasm for this world-renowned writer made the Tolstoi centennial an event of great political importance—one that challenged the new Soviet society to define its attitude toward a powerful cultural figure representing ideas and beliefs that directly contradicted Marxist and Bolshevik ideology.

The conflict of interests around Tolstoi is attested by comparison of his anniversary celebration with others occurring during that same year. Nikolai Chernyshevskii's centennial, coming just six weeks prior to Tolstoi's, offered much more fertile ground for the celebration of Bolshevik values but proved to be much less momentous than that of his more storied contemporary. The relative lack of fanfare for the Chernyshevskii event was decried in the Bolshevik press, but efforts to redress this imbalance proved ineffective, and at the year's end a rather awkward victory on the ideological front was conceded to Tolstoi.[15] Other important anniversaries were also marked that year, including the tenth commemoration of Plekhanov's death and Gor'kii's sixtieth birthday celebration. The latter event was perhaps the closest equivalent in popular appeal to the Tolstoi centennial, particularly as it occasioned Gor'kii's triumphal return to Soviet Russia from Italy, but none of these events attracted the sustained attention and animated discussion that surrounded the Tolstoi celebration.

The looming presence of Tolstoi was not just a problem of residual affection for a hero of the past, however. In spite of the Bolsheviks' rise to power in 1917, Tolstoian philosophy remained a viable alternative, or threat, to Bolshevism into the late 1920s. Tolstoian communes still existed, and their adherents still proselytized the Tolstoian gospel. Many first-generation Tolstoian disciples were still actively publishing and popularizing his views, and the anniversary offered them an opportunity to appeal to a larger audience. There was a particularly active group of Tolstoians in Moscow, who spent much of the year preparing commemorative publications, speaking at public events, and organizing anniversary celebrations.[16]

Soviet anxiety about Tolstoianism was undoubtedly heightened by the latter's historical contiguity with Bolshevism. It was not uncommon for aspiring revolutionaries to go through "Tolstoian episodes" in their journey toward Marxism.[17] Nadezhda Krupskaia was a friend of Tolstoian publicist Ivan Gorbunov-Posadov and published in his journal *Svobodnoe vospitanie* before the Revolution. Lenin's personal secretary, Vladimir Bonch-Bruevich, was a student of Russian sectarianism and had accompanied a group of Dukhobors in their Tolstoi-sponsored emigration to Canada in 1899; he also worked with Tolstoi's publishing house, *Posrednik*. His wife, Vera Velichkina, had worked with Tolstoi in the Riazan' famine relief project of 1892, and her memoirs about the experience were published during the anniversary year with an introduction by her husband.[18] While her book ridiculed the dreamy idealism that motivated many who were drawn to the movement, it nonetheless pointed to an uncomfortable ideological proximity to Bolshevism. The veneration of Tolstoi's heroic aspect by Bolshevik god-builders like Gor'kii, Lunacharskii, and even Lenin set an awkward example for new Bolshevik converts, one that needed to be rigorously qualified by repeated criticism of Tolstoi's ideological fallacies. Militant organizations like the Society of Old Bolsheviks and the League of the Godless mounted a propaganda campaign against Tolstoi's moral philosophy only

Figure 1. Cartoon by N. Lebedev depicting Tolstoi under the "cross-examination" of contemporary critics at a public forum. From left to right, A. N. Lunacharskii sheds light on Tolstoi's exposure of hypocrisy in *War and Peace;* L. Ortodoks-Aksel'rod examines the limits of the author's concern for the peasantry; and M. Ol'minskii critically illuminates Tolstoi's belief in passive resistance in *Resurrection.* The captions surrounding Tolstoi's bust in the center read "Resist not evil" and "I cannot remain silent." The forum is "moderated" by F. Raskol'nikov. From *Chitatel' i pisatel',* 28 April 1928.

slightly less strident than the attacks that had been launched by the Orthodox Church some thirty years earlier. And much as Nicholas II had done, the Bolsheviks rigorously differentiated the writer from the social philosopher. It was generally accepted that Tolstoi could serve as a model for writers in terms of form, but in terms of content numerous caveats applied: his critique of Orthodoxy and economic inequality were good, but his belief in God, nonviolence, and the virtues of poverty were not. Often these distinctions blurred, however, and Plekhanov's notion that Tolstoi could be accepted "only so far" ("*otsiuda i dosiuda*") became the operative slogan describing this ill-defined middle ground.[19]

The scope of the efforts made to limit Tolstoi's influence attest to his abiding appeal among proletarian and peasant readers. Surveys of Red Army soldiers in 1921 had shown Tolstoi far outpacing other writers in popularity, and throughout the 1920s he continued to top contemporary Soviet authors in terms of mass readership and library circulation. Some analysts suggested that this popularity was higher among women and older (i.e., more "passive, backward") readers, but other surveys showed that even among workers he was one of the most widely read authors.[20] This broad circulation among rank-and-file proletarians required that their reading be informed by an appropriate level of class consciousness. Some argued that such consciousness would make workers "immune" to the negative effects of bourgeois literature. Viacheslav Polonskii, a leading spokesperson for this immunity theory, pointed in particular to Lenin's approval of the publication of Tolstoi's works and said that any danger in literature could be exposed and neutralized by criticism—not only that of Marxist theorists, but also that of the masses themselves. The goal of class struggle in literature was precisely this sort of awakening of the proletarian reader's critical capacities.[21]

Others viewed this notion with considerable skepticism. Leopold Averbakh saw the theory of immunity as "fatalistic, thoroughly passivist rubbish."[22] This more puritanical view considered the literary text as a point of potential infiltration for bourgeois values into proletarian consciousness. Tolstoi's prodigious talent as a writer might enable him to deceive and seduce the proletarian reader, necessitating extreme vigilance and control over the publication and presentation of his works. This position was articulated clearly in a letter of the Society of Old Bolsheviks to Stalin in early 1928, which listed a series of preemptive measures that should be taken to protect Soviet readers. Tolstoi's complete works should be published only in an academic version and accompanied with appropriate Marxist criticism; popular editions should omit works that the government considered ideologically inappropriate, while those published were to be accompanied by commentary "paralyzing" pernicious Tolstoian social philosophy; Marxist brochures on Tolstoi should also be issued, and the editorial staff of the jubilee edition should be augmented with senior party members.[23]

This sort of vigilance was believed to be particularly necessary in protecting the more impressionable Soviet readers to be found among the youth and peasantry.[24] The Komsomol and its newspaper, *Komsomol'skaia pravda*, were among the most outspoken critics of the Tolstoi centennial. The newspaper spoke out against the party's expenditures on the anniversary celebrations and questioned its leniency in dealing with *tolstovstvo*, as the categorical embrace of Tolstoian philosophy was known. Bolshevik atheist organizations joined in this attack with particular vehemence, producing books and special issues of their journals devoted to the Tolstoian "heresy."[25]

These various attitudes toward Tolstoi reveal a spectrum of opinions on the legacy of pre-revolutionary culture—a spectrum that in early 1928 was still fairly broad but beginning to narrow. The loss of polemical breadth that characterized the discussion of Tolstoi over the course of that year reflects changes that would dramatically alter the USSR's political and cultural landscape. While those changes have been described in greater detail elsewhere, they will emerge here in a different light, one that draws organizing metaphors of the 1928–1932 Great Break and Cultural Revolution into particularly sharp focus.

∼

With all of these forces allied against the centennial, it is fair to assume that the anniversary would not have been such a major event in 1928 had it not been for the particular attention that Lenin had paid to Tolstoi. Tolstoi's eightieth birthday and his death had both been significant political events in Russia, to which Lenin had responded with seven articles in pre-revolutionary Bolshevik newspapers that were smuggled into Russia from abroad.[26] Though perhaps motivated on some level by Lenin's admiration for Tolstoi, these articles were intended to diminish Tolstoi's influence as a social and political philosopher, which was heightened at these moments of focused public attention. To borrow a metaphor from the most widely known of these pieces, "Lev Tolstoi as a Mirror of the Russian Revolution," Lenin attempted to cash in on Tolstoi's political capital by "reflecting" attention from the writer onto the revolutionary movement as a whole. This agenda made Lenin's articles particularly expedient models for dealing with the 1928 anniversary, which brought similar dynamics into play.

Lenin's "Mirror" article, in fact, became a sort of keynote for the 1928 anniversary, providing the proper formula for the interpretation of Tolstoi. Lenin's text, marking its own twentieth anniversary at the time, was probably quoted more frequently than any single work by Tolstoi himself. Lenin's Tolstoi was tremendously gifted as a writer, but weak and ineffectual as a political philosopher. He had the ability to discern and express the unconscious rebellion of the peasants as a class—reflecting like a mirror Russia's undeveloped revolutionary consciousness. Yet like a mirror he was passive and lacked the political insight necessary to solve these problems. The Russian proletariat, Lenin argued, would one day resolve the contradictions inherent in Tolstoi's work. They would show the way, not toward Tolstoi's goal of spiritual enlightenment, but instead toward the political enlightenment that would truly change their conditions.

Though Lenin often dealt rather harshly with Tolstoi in these articles, ridiculing his vegetarianism, pacifism, and religiosity, it was nonetheless clear that he believed Tolstoi had a place in the post-revolutionary canon. Lenin predicted that Tolstoi's works would be fully appreciated only when the yoke of tsarist oppression was lifted, and did his part to see that this happened after 1917. As the public heard many times during the anniversary celebration in 1928, Lenin had personally helped to plan the ninety-volume jubilee edition of Tolstoi's works, which was to contain all of his writings, including works that had been censored under the old regime as well as those that reflected his backward religious and political views.[27]

Lenin's encouragement of the jubilee edition, juxtaposed with his critique of Tolstoi's social philosophy, struck a tenuous balance that proved difficult to maintain amidst the ideological tempest of 1928. Political deviations to the left and right were viewed with suspicious scrutiny. In its directives regarding the 1928 anniversary, we find the party steering critics to acknowledge both Tolstoi's ideological shortcomings and his accomplishments as an artist and critic. To lose sight of either aspect of Tolstoi, according to this centrist view, would be to misunderstand his legacy.[28] As Lenin's interpretation provided the primary model for this approach, the anniversary became an exercise in reading not only Tolstoi but also Lenin.

A great deal of the discussion of the 1928 anniversary was thus focused on the correct understanding of Lenin's interpretation of Tolstoi. Two episodes from early in the anniversary year illustrate how the debate came to be centered within the margins of Lenin's critique. The central figure in the first of these was M. Ol'minskii, one of the oldest surviving Bolsheviks and an editor of *Na literaturnom postu*, who charged onto the anniversary scene with an editorial entitled "Our Attitude toward Tolstoi," stating boldly that Tolstoi's works held no interest among revolutionaries of his generation. Ol'minskii had read *War and Peace* as a teenager, and then *Anna Karenina* while in prison, and had come to the conclusion that he had wasted his time reading such counter-revolutionary works.[29] Ol'minskii's aversion to Tolstoi found other expression as well. Large ads for Tolstoi editions that were appearing in newspapers and journals prompted him to begin a campaign against what he called the "extraordinary advertising of, and the possible infatuation with, the works of Tolstoi." The ads in question, he wrote, had a "purely American character" and were the sort of thing that one might expect to find in a bourgeois country "in an ad for cosmetics or insect repellant."³⁰ On 4 February, in a *Pravda* editorial entitled "Lenin or Lev Tolstoi?" he complained of the inadequate presentation of Lenin's works on Tolstoi in an advertisement that had appeared in *Pravda* two days earlier. Ol'minskii was glad that Gosizdat was at least including these texts in its Tolstoi ads but was dismayed to see that the description of the Lenin texts appeared in the corner of the ad, and in very small print. The Lenin text was too little, but also too late: the government publishing house, Ol'minskii argued, should have published Lenin's works about Tolstoi first, and then Tolstoi's works in their wake.

As odd as this assertion might sound to us, it speaks to an agenda that was gradually realized over the course of the anniversary year. As one writer declared, "Our basic aim in connection to the anniversary of L. N. Tolstoi is to make known, to disseminate widely, and to clarify the views of V. I. Lenin on Tolstoi."³¹ This goal seems to have largely been fulfilled: you couldn't spill coffee on a piece about Tolstoi from 1928 without soiling Lenin's name or some of his holy words. But Ol'minskii's comment that revolutionaries had had no time to read Tolstoi had gone too far, and he backed down when it was pointed out to him that his antagonism was itself in disagreement with the Leninist view he so self-righteously supported.³² In answer to his critics, Ol'minskii explained that he had been writing in a memoiristic vein—the "our attitude" of his title referred to himself and his fellow revolutionaries and was not meant to be programmatic in any way. He clearly understood, judging by his criticism of the Tolstoi ads, that this program was provided by Lenin, and in spite of his own errors he was one of the most vocal defenders of Leninist orthodoxy during the rest of the anniversary year.

Anatolii Lunacharskii, the commissar of education who headed the government's anniversary committee and the jubilee edition editorial board and who could be described as the official ideological steward of the Tolstoi anniversary, was among those who criticized Ol'minskii's extremism.³³ Lunacharskii, however, provoked a second and even more rancorous episode illustrating the ideological infighting around Lenin and Tolstoi in 1928. A twenty-four volume edition of Tolstoi's collected works, published by *Ogonek,* began appearing early in the year and, in a sense, inaugurated the anniversary celebration. Lunacharskii authored the introduction to the edition and concluded with the following lines, which were presented as a paraphrase of Lenin's view of Tolstoi: "You are the prophet of our peasants, their ideologue, with all of their great positive traits, and all of their negative ones too."³⁴

Figure 2. Cover art from the collection *Lenin i Tolstoi* (Moscow, 1928), illustrating the superiority of Lenin, aggressively postured and associated with the working class, to the bucolic Tolstoi and his passive response to rural exploitation.

This description of Tolstoi quickly drew fire, as critics hastened to point out Lunacharskii's distortion of Lenin's position: where Lenin had ascribed to Tolstoi the passive role of "mouthpiece of the ideas and moods" of the peasants, Lunacharskii called him an "ideologue" and a "prophet." Still worse, Lenin's sharply defined historical periodization of Tolstoi's influence—from 1861 to 1905, was expanded in Lunacharskii's formulation to include the peasants of the present day.[35] Furthermore, Lunacharskii had failed to recognize the distinction that Lenin had made between Tolstoi the artist and Tolstoi the political philosopher and moral educator (praising the former, but always denouncing the latter). The horror of his error was in his representation not only of Tolstoi but also of Lenin. "You not only cannot distort Lenin," one writer objected, "but you also cannot 'improve' his thoughts, add to them or circumscribe them—for this is also a distortion of Lenin." And how, the same writer asked, had Lunacharskii dared to suggest that Tolstoi was just as ingenious as Lenin but had expressed his genius artistically, rather than politically? He closed by asking incredulously how this "anti-Leninist" interpretation of Lenin could have appeared as the preface to the first edition of Tolstoi's collected works to be published by a Soviet government press.[36]

In his response to these attacks, Lunacharskii admitted that communists should not distort the views of their teachers, but insisted that they have "the right to certain nuances in relation to the main course of party thinking."[37] Suggesting that Lenin's view of Tolstoi was balanced, and that others were excessive in their praise or criticism of Tolstoi (here he cited Ol'minskii), Lunacharskii did not doubt that, under the influence of Lenin, they would find the proper tone. If there were slight variations, he argued, no harm was done.[38]

But what was the "proper" Leninist tone? In the context of the developing Cultural Revolution, many felt that it should be decidedly more confrontational. *Na literaturnom postu* argued that: "We need the sort of celebration of the Tolstoi anniversary in which anti-Tolstoianism will conquer the masses, and the masses will conquer Tolstoi."[39] Although the political center tended to soften this rhetoric, it seconded the call for a critical reassessment on the mass level of society. An article appearing in *Pravda* on the day after the anniversary illustrates this tendency. It concerned a letter by a group of demobilized soldiers, who had written the paper asking why the government was spending so much money on Tolstoi's anniversary when they were forced to live in squalid barracks. The authors of the *Pravda* article endorsed the anniversary itself but also hailed the reversal

Figure 3. Cartoon entitled "L. N. Tolstoi's Works in Our Day" that ironically adapts Tolstoian morality to contemporary society. *Master and Man* serves as a title for a contract dispute; *What Men Live By* is applied to a depiction of a payday; *The Fruits of Enlightenment* is inscribed below a scene of street violence outside a theater showing violent films; *Resurrection* is travestied in a picture showing how people spend their "Sundays" (almost a homonym for resurrection in Russian); and *The Power of Darkness* is made to refer to the enduring power of the church. From *Vecherniaia Moskva*, 13 February 1928.

in consciousness signaled by the soldiers' letter: while workers had taken to the street in 1910 to honor Tolstoi and criticize the government, now they were criticizing Tolstoi and had a lot that they could teach the pre-revolutionary author.[40]

This reversal seems to have been particularly expedient in the countryside, where ideological deviations were seen as a great danger. Special guidebooks were produced addressing the concerns and objectives for organization of anniversary celebrations in local "reading huts." Displays were to include data on the exploitation of the peasants and a section devoted to Lenin's writings on Tolstoi; it was also suggested that village readers should exercise their own authority over Tolstoi's works by putting them "on trial." Tolstoi's play *The Power of Darkness*, for instance, could be presented in a version of agitational theater called a "lit-trial," in which the audience questioned the characters in order to better understand class conflict and the contradictions in Tolstoi's ideas. Meetings and lectures in the villages were supposed to show attending peasants how their own everyday experience revealed Tolstoi's errors.[41]

A ceremony at Iasnaia Poliana two days after the anniversary was brought forth in the pages of *Izvestiia* to illustrate not only these errors but also the abiding ideological dangers of Tolstoi's influence in the countryside. One of the main events marking the anniversary at the estate had been the opening of a new school organized according to his pedagogical principles.

It was mentioned during a tour of the school that the students were also being taught according to Tolstoi's beliefs, including his teachings about the existence of God; Lunacharskii, who was presiding over the ceremony, explained that the government was not worried about this regimen, which was allowed out of respect for Tolstoi, because experience would show the children the superiority of the Soviet way. The report on this event in *Izvestiia*, however, offered a less sanguine view of the school. Entitled "A Monument to Tolstoi, or to Tolstoianism?" the article described an evening concert, at which children from the Iasnaia Poliana school sang a hymn to Tolstoi (with its own eerie echo of the Lenin cult: "No, he hasn't died, he's alive"). Yet the effects of the continued "life" of a Tolstoian education were immediately clear to the correspondent: the "quiet, thin, weak little boys with no light in their eyes, and girls with the timidity of boarding school girls and the sadness of nuns in their eyes" sang hesitantly, looking to Tolstoi's daughter Aleksandra for prompting when they were unsure of the words. According to *Izvestiia*, they were so different from the party's young pioneers, who were "lively, jolly, full of joy and true faith in the future." Was it right, the author asked, that these children were being deprived of the joys of the typical Soviet school child?[42]

∼

We can only wonder how radiantly many Soviet literary critics looked toward the future when it came time for them to sing their own paeans to Tolstoi on the occasion of his anniversary. "It would be a shame," Lunacharskii wrote, "if our party, in its relation to such a genius as Tolstoi, were to sing in monotonous unison." Lenin had written just a few short articles on Tolstoi, and "it would be absurd," he wrote, "if we took those articles as something . . . limiting the study of Tolstoi, and began to fear—and there are such people among us—making even one step to the right or to the left."[43] Despite such an ostensibly tolerant point of view, Lunacharskii felt compelled to spend much of 1928 attempting to prove that his views on Tolstoi did, in fact, "correspond absolutely accurately" to those of Lenin.[44] Thus Lunacharskii, too, joined a chorus that indeed often sang in one voice, taking its cues from Lenin and looking hesitatingly to him for reassurance.[45] Lunacharskii summed up the prospects for any sort of critical polyphony by expressing his confidence that Marxists would mark the holiday "in our own way, in Lenin's way."[46]

Discussion of the anniversary in its aftermath hints that Lunacharskii's confidence was not entirely justified. The author of a *Chitatel' i pisatel'* article titled "Do We Know How to Celebrate Anniversaries?" argued that the new proletarian culture had failed the "exam" represented by the anniversary. On a positive note, the party had succeeded in preventing the Tolstoians from making the holiday their own and had widely publicized its own views on Tolstoi. But although new Marxist writings had generally followed a line defined by Plekhanov and Lenin, they had not always produced the proper "tone." In an obvious rebuke of Lunacharskii, the author noted that a leading orator's speech had struck a false note; worse still, he complained, in the provinces "a whole aria from a completely different opera" had been performed. As evidence he cited an article from an Orel newspaper describing the great respect that the Iasnaia Poliana peasants held for Tolstoi and the religious atmosphere surrounding the celebration of the holiday at the estate. *Chitatel' i pisatel'* ridiculed the pathetic, reverent tone of the piece and then revealed the most sobering fact of all—that its author was a member of the Komsomol.[47]

Throughout the fall of 1928 there were consequences for singing out of tune with the party line as the literary heterogeneity of the NEP period hardened into the orthodoxy of RAPP.[48] In October *Krasnaia nov'* was attacked for the "eclecticism" of its special Tolstoi issue (for, among other things, reprinting Lunacharskii's debate with one of his critics, Raskol'nikov), and a *Na literaturnom postu* editorial complained that the Tolstoi anniversary had revealed "an inability to effectively organize resistance against petty-bourgeois elements."[49] In December, the Central Committee issued new directives for literature, demanding that it play a larger role in class warfare; a *Pravda* editorial on the 25th of that month declared that class warfare was just beginning in art and attacked Lunacharskii for being lax on ideological questions.[50] The following year, 1929, saw the arrest of former *Krasnaia nov'* editor Aleksandr Voronskii as a Trotskyite and the removal of Lunacharskii from his post as commissar of education. It was around this time that the demographic center of the Tolstoian movement began to shift radically to the east, as Tolstoian communes were liquidated and their members deported to special settlements in Siberia.[51] In these circumstances, it is no wonder that we find critics huddled in the Leninist center.

In 1928, then, we could say that Tolstoi was still a mirror of the Revolution: when Soviet readers looked at Tolstoi, after all, they saw Lenin. However, readers were enjoined to view Tolstoi through the "corrective lens" of Lenin, in order to see clearly the contradictions and errors that riddle the classic author's works. These reading glasses would correct ideological myopia, the very nearsightedness that had prevented Tolstoi from understanding the future. Readers were promised "a new Tolstoi, comprehensible to all and free of the contradictions, pacifism and unctuousness" that had shaded his life and work.[52] Thus the passive Tolstoi, who merely reflected his age and all of its contradictions as a mirror, was to be refracted through Lenin, who showed the way to actively resolve those contradictions, and through whom Tolstoi's works could reveal truths that Tolstoi himself had not foreseen.

This scheme, coupling the passive Tolstoian/peasant/reader with the active Leninist/worker/critic, resembles the fabled alliance (*smychka*) of workers and peasants of the first Five-Year Plan. In the restraining of Tolstoi's spontaneous, "reactionary" realism with Lenin's revolutionary consciousness, we can recognize elements of the master narrative of a Socialist Realist aesthetic that was already beginning to shape Soviet culture, long before its official articulation in the early 1930s. Lenin emerges in the obvious role of father figure, first in relation to Tolstoi, whose unconscious, ineffectual, and passive "Iasnaia Polianism," as it was called (we can read 'Pollyanna-ism), was reshaped by the resolute, sagacious Lenin.[53] Soviet readers were reminded more than once that Tolstoi offered a barren ideology, while Lenin had fathered the Revolution.[54] But Lenin also played this role for the Soviet critics who found themselves uncertain of their own authority to shape the collective responses to Tolstoi's works. As the literary establishment entered an era in which they were called upon to take a larger role than ever in shaping Soviet collective consciousness, this deference to a single, central authority becomes rather ominous. It resonates with Stalin's rise to power and also suggests why RAPP would be short-lived, to be replaced by a Writers' Union that was structured around its own strong father figure, Maksim Gor'kii.

Likewise, the formation of a militant "center" was a strategy in many ideological confrontations both literary and political in subsequent years, when accusations of "deviation from the correct Leninist line" became the operative words of attack. "Knowing how to celebrate jubilees" was a matter not of literary expertise, after all, but of political savvy. Viacheslav Polonskii wrote that the discussion of the Tolstoi centennial "couldn't be more timely," because it "allowed Marxist criticism to try its weapons on first-class material."[55] More often than not, however, these imperious ambitions were frustrated as the critics in question turned their weapons on each other.[56] The intolerant, strident tone of their debate reflects their inability to navigate the rhetorical narrows that they themselves had created. As they attempted to follow a party line that could thin to the point of inscrutability, Marxist critics found themselves struggling less with Tolstoi's legacy than with Lenin's. In demonstrating how to conquer the former, they surrendered a great deal of their own authority to the latter. Thus during his centennial year Tolstoi proved to be a mirror of the Revolution as he had been in 1908; now, however, he reflected a new set of contradictions, and a new stripe of passivism. Although the 1928 centennial was a rather benign, "vegetarian" affair when compared with what was to come in the 1930s, it provides a valuable perspective on the way new, Stalinist identities were shaped around rituals of confrontation, acquiescence, and conformity.

Notes

The author wishes to acknowledge the State Tolstoi Museum in Moscow for access to the unpaginated newspaper materials cited below, and for the invaluable assistance the museum's archivists provided in gathering material for this study.

1. The Bolshoi event included numerous speeches, a concert, and a keynote address by A. V. Lunacharskii. Numerous foreign dignitaries were invited to attend, including Thomas Edison and Mahatma Gandhi. Other events included the opening of an exhibition at the Museum of Fine Arts, a meeting of the Union of the Lovers of the Russian Word, an evening at the Experimental Theater sponsored by the Commissariat of Education, and a special performance at the Conservatory.

2. Iurii Libedinskii, "Khudozhestvennaia platforma RAPP," *Na literaturnom postu* 19 (1928): 9–19. RAPP, the Russian Association of Proletarian Writers, began in 1920 as a militant proletarian movement calling for working-class hegemony over culture. It tempered these demands somewhat in the late 1920s amid growing respect for nineteenth-century realism but never fully abandoned the practice of critiquing literary works according to their authors' social origins. Within a few years of RAPP's closure in 1932, this approach to literary criticism was condemned as "vulgar sociology."

3. See, for example, *Lev Tolstoi, 1828–1928*, ed. B. S. Ol'khovii (Moscow: Rabotnik prosveshcheniia, 1928); N. Piksanov, "Chto chitat' o Tolstom," *Biulleten' gosudarstvennogo izdatel'stva* 30 (1928): 13–15. The newspaper archive at the Tolstoi Museum contains numerous articles entitled "What to Read about Tolstoi" from provincial newspapers throughout the country. The Czech émigré journal *Volia Rossii* pointed out the incompleteness of the Tolstoi who was being presented to the Russian reading public, noting that, among other things, his writings against the death penalty were not being published. See S. Postnikov, "Strakh pered Tolstym," *Volia Rossii* 7, no. 8 (1928): 34–42.

4. The editorial board formed in 1925 was dominated by Tolstoians. Joining it now were M. N. Pokrovskii, I. I. Skvortsov-Stepanov, and Vladimir Bonch-Bruevich. Pokrovskii was the deputy commissar of education and had organized the Communist Academy and Institute of Red Professors. Skvortsov-Stepanov was an editor at *Izvestiia* and Gosizdat, served on the Central Committee, headed the Lenin Institute, and was an active anti-religious propagandist.

5. *Lenin i Tolstoi* (Moscow: Kommunisticheskaia akademiia, 1928) and *Plekhanov i Tolstoi* (Moscow: Kommunisticheskaia akademiia, 1928) were larger, scholarly editions. Numerous smaller editions of Lenin's writing on Tolstoi also appeared, as well as larger scholarly anthologies of Marxist criticism—see especially *O Tolstom*, ed. V. Friche (Moscow: Gosizdat, 1928).

6. One guidebook provided a list of works with Marxist and atheist orientations that could be recommended to readers as they borrowed Tolstoi's books: N. Maslennikov, *V izbe-chital'ne: stoletie Tolstogo* (Moscow: Glavpolitprosvet, 1928), 15.

7. Tolstoi's "reactionary-utopian non-resistance to evil" was the main ideological problem. The theses conclude with a list of works that were appropriate *in their form* as models for beginning writers. See "L. N. Tolstoi—Tezisy dlia dokladchikov i kul'turno-prosvetitel'nykh uchrezhdenii i shkol," *Pravda*, 7 September 1928. Glaviskusstvo was the main literary censor.

8. See Marcus C. Levitt, *Russian Literary Politics and the Pushkin Celebration of 1880* (Ithaca, N.Y.: Cornell University Press, 1989).

9. Funerals were particularly valuable in this regard: as a sacred rite of the Orthodox Church, they provided a state-sanctioned occasion for public gatherings that drew attention to literary achievements, but also to political and social ideals. For discussion of this tradition see William Nickell, "Smert' Tolstogo i zhanr publichnykh pokhoron v Rossii," *Novoe literaturnoe obozrenie* 44, no. 4 (2000): 43–61.

10. A. Stavrovskii, "Lenin i Tolstoi," *Biulleten' gosudarstvennogo izdatel'stva* 30 (1928): 12.

11. E. H. Carr, *Foundations of a Planned Economy*, 3 vols. (Middlesex, UK: Penguin, 1976), 2:58, 78.

12. For an account of this confusion among Bolshevik intellectuals, see Michael David-Fox, *Revolution of the Mind: Bolshevik Higher Learning, 1919–1928* (Ithaca, N.Y.: Cornell University Press, 1997), 186–87.

13. M. Gor'kii, "V. I. Lenin," in *Sobranie sochinenii v tridtsati tomakh*, 30 vols. (Moscow: Gos. izd-vo khudozh. lit-ry, 1949–1955), 17:39.

14. Gor'kii's widely read memoir "Lev Tolstoi" ends with his observation that the novelist was "like a god." Ibid., 14:300.

15. See especially V. M. Friche, "L. N. Tolstoi i N. G. Chernyshevskii," *Krasnaia nov'* 8, no. 9 (1928), reprinted in his *L. N. Tolstoi* (Moscow: Kommunisticheskaia akademiia, 1929), 122–41; A. V. Lunacharskii, "Chernyshevskii i Tolstoi," *Vecherniaia Moskva*, 19 July 1928; "V pochti zabytom iubilee," *Pravda*, 25 March 1928.

16. For discussion of Tolstoian activity at the time, see Mark Popovskii, *Russkie muzhiki rasskazyvaiut . . . Posledovateli L. N. Tolstogo v Sovetskom Soiuze* (London:

Overseas Publications Interchange, 1983). Also see *Vospominaniia krest'ian-tolstovtsev: 1910–1930-e gody,* ed. T. V. Gromov (Moscow: Kniga, 1989). For an image of the anniversary from a more Tolstoian point of view, see *K stoletiiu L. N. Tolstogo: Sbornik komissii po oznamenovaniiu 100-letiia so dnia rozhdeniia L. N. Tolstogo* (Moscow: Krasnyi pechatnik, 1927).

17. For a discussion of relations between the Tolstoians and Bolsheviks, see Popovskii, *Russkie muzhiki rasskazyvaiut,* 42–59.

18. Vera Velichkina, *V golodnyi god s L'vom Tolstym: Vospominaniia* (Moscow: Gos. izd-vo, 1928).

19. G. V. Plekhanov, "Zametki publitsista: 'Otsiuda i dosiuda,'" in *Plekhanov i Tolstoi,* 25–38.

20. D. A. Bondarev, *Tolstoi i sovremennost'* (Moscow: Gosizdat, 1928), 6. State officials took another approach to show that interest in Tolstoi was diminishing: admitting that he had been the most widely read author before the revolution, they pointed to recent statistics showing a slide in Tolstoi's popularity among certain groups of workers. A. Bek, "Romany Tolstogo i rabochii chitatel'," *Biulleten' gosudarstvennogo izdatel'stva* 30 (1928): 7–10.

21. V. Polonskii, "K voprosu o nashikh literaturnykh raznoglasiiakh," *Iz literaturnykh sporov poslednikh let* (Moscow: Gosizdat, 1927), 47–49.

22. L. Averbakh, "O kul'turnoi preemstvennosti i proletarskoi kul'ture," *Krasnaia nov'* 6 (1929): 178.

23. RGALI, f. 611, op. 1, d. 399, 11. 5–6.

24. In 1928 the combined membership of the Baptist Bapsomol and Mennonite Mensomol was higher than that of the Komsomol. See Sheila Fitzpatrick, "Cultural Revolution as Class War," in *Cultural Revolution in Russia, 1928–1931,* ed. Sheila Fitzpatrick (Bloomington: Indiana University Press, 1978), 20.

25. See, e.g., *Antireligioznik* 7 (1928); *O L. N. Tolstom i "tolstovtsakh,"* ed. E. Iaroslavskii (Moscow: Bezbozhnik, 1928).

26. Lenin's articles, concerned with Tolstoi less as an author than as a social institution, came to serve as a model for the Soviet attitude not only toward Tolstoi but toward all pre-revolutionary literature. The pre-modernist literary tastes of many Bolshevik leaders made the correct Marxist reading of the classics especially important.

27. A. V. Lunacharskii, "Po povodu iubileinogo izdaniia sochinenii L. N. Tolstogo," *Pravda,* 10 February 1928; Vladimir Bonch-Bruevich, "Lenin i Tolstoi," *Pravda,* 19 November 1935, 4, cited in "O polnom sobranii sochinenii Tolstogo ('iubileinom')," *Literaturnoe nasledstvo* 69, no. 2 (1961): 430.

28. Even such strident authorities as the Bezbozhnik Publishing House adopted this "centrist" rhetoric. They criticized those who denigrated Tolstoi's talent as an author, but they also censured Lunacharskii for glorifying Tolstoi beyond measure. See *O L. N. Tolstom i o "tolstovtsakh,"* 24–25.

29. M. Ol'minskii, "Nashe otnoshenie k L. N. Tolstomu," *Na literaturnom postu* 3 (1928): 4–5.

30. Ol'minskii, "Lenin ili Lev Tolstoi?" *Pravda,* 4 February 1928, 3. It should be

noted that the ads had the same format as Gosizdat's announcements for Gor'kii's works later that year.

31. Bondarev, *Tolstoi i sovremennost'*, 9.

32. Ol'minskii at first defended himself against this criticism—see "O L. N. Tolstom," *Pravda*, 31 January 1928, reprinted as "Po povodu primechaniia *Ogon'ka*," *Na literaturnom postu* 3 (1928): 6–7; also "Otvet tov. Lunacharskomu," *Pravda*, 16 February 1928. He subsequently backed down in "O stat'e Raskol'nikova," *Na literaturnom postu* 11–12 (1928): 126–27.

33. Lunacharskii wrote thirty-five articles and lectures on Tolstoi; he was entrusted with most of the keynote addresses in connection with the anniversary and became a spokesperson for the official attitude toward Tolstoi. He viewed Ol'minskii as "a vehement enemy of Tolstoianism, in his vehemence exceeding all bounds of reason and directly contradicting Lenin's views on Tolstoi." A. Lunacharskii, "Lenin i Raskol'nikov o Tolstom," *Krasnaia nov'* 8, no. 9 (1928): 274.

34. A. Lunacharskii, "Predislovie," in Lev Tolstoi, *Polnoe sobranie khudozhestvennykh proizvedenii*, 15 vols. (Moscow: Gos. izd-vo, 1928–1930), 1:20.

35. Lunacharskii's hubris was famously satirized by F. Raskol'nikov in this imaginary dialogue with Lenin:

> "Tolstoi is the voice of the ideas and moods," says Lenin.
>
> "No, the ideologue and prophet," Lunacharskii corrects him.
>
> "—of the Russian peasantry," continues Lenin.
>
> "No, part of the revolutionary peasantry," Lunacharskii again inserts a correction.
>
> ". . . of the narrow historical period from 1861–1905," Lenin concludes his formulation.
>
> "No, of the peasantry in general, including the contemporary peasantry of the USSR," continues Comrade Lunacharskii.

F. Raskol'nikov, "Lenin o Tolstom," *Na literaturnom postu* 10 (1928). The September issue of *Krasnaia nov'* carried a continuation of the dispute, with a response by Lunacharskii and a rebuttal by Raskol'nikov. See "Lenin i Raskol'nikov o Tolstom," "Eshche o Tolstom (Otvet t. Lunacharskomu)" *Krasnaia nov'* 8, no. 9 (1928) 274–89. The tension surrounding the debate was such that *Krasnaia nov'* was criticized for publishing Lunacharskii's half of this polemic, even though the editors had printed an apologetic explanation that the text was being published "as a basis for discussion." See V. Lominadze, "*Krasnaia nov'* v 1928-om godu," *Molodaia gvardiia* 10 (1928): 216–23, and the response: V. Vasil'evskii, "Protiv bezotvetstvennogo frazerstva," *Krasnaia nov'* 8, no. 11 (1928): 208–12. Ol'minskii had also taken issue with Lunacharskii's interpretation of Lenin's view of Tolstoi in his "O L. N. Tolstom," *Pravda*, 31 January 1928.

36. Boris Volin, "A. V. Lunacharskii o Tolstom," *Na literaturnom postu* 6 (1928): 12. Volin was something of a specialist on Lenin's view of Tolstoi—see his *Lev Tolstoi v otsenke V. I. Lenina* (Moscow: Gosizdat, 1928); also *Na literaturnom postu* 5

(1928): 39–48. The debate was joined by others as well—see, for instance, Dmitrii Bondarev, *Lev Tolstoi i sovremennost'* (Moscow: Glavpolitprosvet, 1928), 93.

37. Lunacharskii, "Lenin i Raskol'nikov o Tolstom," 274.

38. Ibid., 281. In defending his own "variations," Lunacharskii referred to the "duplicitous nature" of the peasants, who were especially susceptible to Tolstoi's influence. This was why Tolstoi was still their ideologue, and why it was necessary to struggle against his ideology. He defended calling Tolstoi a prophet with the same logic—he was the sort of "revolutionary" represented by the biblical prophets, but he was not a prophet of the revolution.

39. Lunacharskii at times adopted this more aggressive stance. At a Moscow Komsomol evening celebrating the Tolstoi anniversary he warned his audience: "It's not easy to get through Tolstoi, but if you do, you'll be stronger. He'll captivate you with imagery. You must resist." Anyone who unquestioningly accepted all of Tolstoi, Lunacharskii continued, was an "enemy." "Chto my otvergaem u Tolstogo," *Komsomol'skaia pravda*, 21 September 1928.

40. A. Sviderskii, "Dva iubileia," *Pravda*, 11 September 1928. The article compared the anniversaries of Gor'kii and Tolstoi, citing the former for its resonance with genuine proletarian feeling, the latter for the discord demonstrated in the soldiers' letter. The irony implicit in this propaganda campaign should not be lost: the newspapers were filled with citations of Lenin's reading of Tolstoi; when workers parroted these ideas, Lenin was credited with foreseeing their point of view.

41. *V izbe-chital'ne*, 16.

42. M. Zhivov, "Pamiatnik Tolstomu ili tolstovstvu?" *Izvestiia*, 14 September 1928. The newspaper subsequently printed letters from Soviet students objecting to the school's program, as well as a letter in defense of the school from Tolstoi's daughter, to which the editors replied with renewed criticism—see "Prosveshchentsy i uchashchiesia o Iasnopolianskoi shkole," *Izvestiia*, 19 September 1928; A. L. Tolstaia, "Pis'mo v redaktsiiu," *Izvestiia*, 21 September 1928.

43. Lunacharskii, "Lenin i Raskol'nikov," 281.

44. See the preface in the 1928 collection of his writings on Tolstoi: A. V. Lunacharskii, *O Tolstom* (Moscow: Gosizdat, 1928), 3–4. Also see his "O znachenii iubileia L'va Tolstogo," *Krasnaia niva*, 9 September 1928.

45. Often it was simpler to defer completely to Lenin: a particularly striking example is Dmitrii Bondarev's "Tolstoi kak myslitel'," which begins with a nearly four-page quote from Lenin's "Lev Tolstoi kak zerkalo russkoi revoliutsii"—see Bondarev, *Tolstoi i sovremennost'*, 12–15.

46. Lunacharskii, "Lenin i Raskol'nikov," 280.

47. Novus, "Umeem li my prazdnovat' iubilei?" *Chitatel' i pisatel'*, 7 November 1928. For more discussion along this line, see "Na tekushchie temy," *Na literaturnom postu* 20–21 (1928): 1–5.

48. The first RAPP plenum was convened in May of that year.

49. *Krasnaia nov'* had also published Tolstoi's correspondence with I. I. Panaev, as well as family memoirs. The editors answered the charges against them by

explaining that additional selections by R. Luxembourg, Friche, and Raskol'nikov represented the true ideological position of the journal. For the critique of *Krasnaia nov'*, see V. Lominadze, "Krasnaia nov' v 1928 godu," *Molodaia gvardiia* 7, no. 10 (1928): 216–23.

50. Literature was to play a greater role in the fight against bourgeois and petty bourgeois attitudes, and writers were to be more responsible for writing socially useful works—see Edward J. Brown, *The Proletarian Episode in Russian Literature, 1928–1932* (New York: Columbia University Press, 1953), 88–89.

51. Popovskii, *Russkie muzhiki rasskazyvaiut*, 105. The Moscow Vegetarian Society, which had served as a center of Tolstoian activity during the anniversary year, was closed in February 1929 after the government refused to renew their building's lease.

52. Ibid., 12.

53. I. N. Kubikov closed his book on Tolstoi by calling him an "ingenious unmasker" (*oblichitel'*) who *unconsciously* hastened the way of the revolution—see his *Lev Tolstoi* (Moscow: Gos. izd-vo, 1928), 142; republished from "Lev Tolstoi i revoliutsiia," *Krasnaia niva* 37 (1928). Lenin's superior role was similarly underlined in the discussion of Gor'kii's anniversary, as epitomized in the March 29, 1928, *Pravda* headline "Lenin—Gor'kii's Teacher."

54. For Lenin, the Russia that was reflected in Tolstoi's writing was a profoundly duplicitous old woman, as in the lines from Nekrasov's poem "Rus'" that he quoted in "Lev Tolstoi kak zerkalo": "You are both impoverished and bountiful, You are both powerful and impotent, Mother Russia!"

55. V. Polonskii, "Lev Tolstoi i marksistskaia kritika," *Pechat' i revoliutsiia* 6 (1928): 7.

56. Polonskii's article provides a nice overview of the debates surrounding the centennial. See also "V sporakh o Tolstom," *Chitatel' i pisatel'*, 28 April 1928.

2

Press Commentary on the Tolstoi Centenary Celebration

Tolstoi's jubilee in 1928 suffered from a lack of clear direction from the party. Indeed, the event revealed profound confusion over precisely how the great novelist was to be venerated in a revolutionary society. Ten years of iconoclasm in the arts had left many in the party and cultural elite yearning for what M. Gor'kii called a "return to the classics." Yet Tolstoi's potential influence as a competing moral and social philosopher complicated his appropriation into Soviet literary culture.

The following article surveys the accomplishments of the 1928 jubilee celebration, giving the event a decidedly mixed evaluation.[1] To be sure, official involvement in the anniversary had enabled its organizers to stifle discussion in the press of Tolstoi's legacy as it related to religious belief and Tolstoian cultural practices. But the party's near-total control over mass culture also forced officials and members of the creative intelligentsia to be more than vigilant censors and to essentially construct a persuasive case for Tolstoi's Sovietization. This proved to be an ideologically treacherous process, even with Lenin's and Plekhanov's writings on Tolstoi serving as guidelines. Materialist rhetoric resonated rather poorly with many of Tolstoi's readers and Soviet critics found it difficult to redefine "the great writer of the Russian land" in the context of the adulation he recieved during the centennial celebration. In the end, they failed to advance a new Tolstoi who was particularly compelling or politically expedient from a Soviet viewpoint; critics like the one below denounced such efforts as a waste of resources that could have been used to popularize more progressive literary figures.

Novus, "Do We Know How to Celebrate Jubilees?"

Chitatel' i pisatel', 7 November 1928

The eleventh year [of the Revolution] was spent under the rubric of cultural revolution. Among the big cultural campaigns of the year, the events surrounding the jubilee of L. N. Tolstoi were among the most prominent.

This jubilee was a test of our proletarian culture. There were great dangers and difficulties, which were, for the most part, resolved satisfactorily. Among the people, the jubilee had considerable appeal. V. I. Lenin proclaimed that "if his great works are really to be made the possession of all," the "system of society which condemns millions and scores of millions to ignorance, benightedness, drudgery and poverty" will have to be destroyed.[2] And these words have proven true. Enormous editions of Tolstoi's artistic works have for the first time been made available to the general proletarian reader.

The Tolstoians' hope to co-opt the anniversary did not come to pass.

From the very beginning an accurate Leninist evaluation of Tolstoi was taken as the basis of the jubilee. From the very beginning Tolstoi, "the great artist, the genius who has not only drawn incomparable pictures of Russian life, but has made first-class contributions to world literature," Tolstoi, with his "remarkably powerful, forthright and sincere protest against social falsehood and hypocrisy," was sharply distinguished from "the 'Tolstoian,' e.g., the jaded, hysterical sniveler," and from Tolstoianism itself, with its "crackpot preaching of submission, 'resist not evil' with violence."[3]

Everyone who was preparing to drag moth-eaten phrases about "the great seeker after God" out into the light of day was very quickly reminded that these phrases are "false from beginning to end," and those who mouth them don't "believe in Tolstoi's God or sympathize with Tolstoi's criticism of the existing social order." Theirs is simply an attempt "with the din and thunder of claptrap to drown the demand for a straight and clear answer to the question: what are the glaring contradictions of Tolstoianism?"[4]

The Communist Academy and State Publishing House republished works on Tolstoi by Lenin, Plekhanov, and a number of other Marxists.

New Marxist work on Tolstoi has generally proceeded according to the standards set by Lenin and Plekhanov.

In general a correct orientation has been given.

But it must be said that its implementation has not always been successful in every way, that the tone has not always rung true, and that this has led to some distortions in the general line of the jubilee.

If a wrong note slipped into the speech of a leading orator during the celebration of the jubilee days in Moscow,[5] in the provinces it was as if a whole aria from a completely different opera was being performed.

Right here in front of me is a four-column newspaper article entitled "At Tolstoi's Estate." Its author describes the festivities at Iasnaia Poliana on September 12.

Here are two or three quotations:

"I sit expectantly with a policeman on the veranda of Tolstoi's manor house, on an antique wicker divan.

"'All sorts of people have been coming here,' says the policeman. 'From America, Italy, from everywhere. They do great honor to Lev Nikolaevich. There were particularly many last winter. They come to the grave, take off their hats, and stand there. Our Russians don't behave this way: they just turn around and they're gone....'"

It is clear that not all our Russians lag behind their foreign counterparts in honoring Tolstoi, however. This is only a sin of those "depraved" by city culture, a sin displayed by visitors.

In answer to the question: "But what about the Iasnaia Poliana peasants?" the policeman answers: "Ooh ... they're fine.... What else would you expect.... After all, he helped them. He gave one woman a hut and even installed her stove himself.... They respect him. But t'day look how many'll come," the policeman finished thoughtfully. "You'll see!"

And further on the author describes what he saw:

"Tolstoi's grave is quiet, deserted. Somewhere here his favorite horse is buried. How pagan and wonderful.... A great lover of nature has been embraced by the hospitable depths of the earth."

Further on, in just the same "wonderful, pagan" style and tone, is the pathetic conclusion: "This was an unforgettable September 12."

Where was this published? By whom? In an "honorable, democratic" newspaper, by a member of the "honorably democratic" intelligentsia?

No, it was published in *Orel Pravda* on September 16 of this year.

The author of the article is M. Kireev—a member of the Komsomol and VAPP[6] and the head of the "Workers' Life" section of the newspaper.

Evidently we're still not rid of people who consider it necessary to love the whole Tolstoi.

But if Lenin and Plekhanov were dressing down the lovers of the whole Tolstoi in 1910, now the articles of such people are nauseating proletarian readers from Orel.

Two readers—V. D. Lebedev, a former student of the Communist

University of the West, and V. Tiunin, a worker from Orel, wrote letters to the editor that, I hear, were not printed because the editors did not want to undermine their colleague's authority. V. Tiunin complains that from his point of view—that of "a novice reader"—Kireev's article confuses the socio-class characterization of Tolstoi's work given by Lenin in his article "Lev Tolstoi as a Mirror of the Russian Revolution." The reader correctly notes that Comrade M. Kireev pays no regard to Lenin's characterization "either from ignorance, or because the author needed to shame the Russian peasants for their lack of respect. Perhaps he wanted to make them bow and honor Tolstoi for the scythe that some factory owner gave him, or perhaps he wanted to praise the foreigners because they stand for a long time with their hats off over Tolstoi's remains." The former student of the Communist University, armed with Lenin and Plekhanov, inveighs against the author for his glorification of Tolstoi as a life-spirit and wonderful pagan and is astounded that the author did not notice the Komsomol cells at Iasnaia Poliana. Indeed, he notes, there is not a single word of a communist evaluation of Tolstoi in the article at all.

This polemic is significant.

Readers are correcting their newspapers in a Leninist fashion.

Were such corrections needed only in Orel? No, they were needed throughout the whole holiday.

We ought to admit that:

In terms of public attention, the Tolstoi jubilee has eclipsed several of our anniversaries that could have been celebrated with no qualms whatsoever.

Comrade A. Serafimovich's jubilee passed by relatively unnoticed.[7]

Not even the most fanatical champion of proletarian literature would place Serafimovich on a par with Tolstoi. But Serafimovich is one of our most significant and dedicated revolutionary writers so far.

In a year that was spent under the rubric of cultural revolution, this anniversary should have resonated as a more powerful celebration of proletarian culture.

Chernyshevskii's anniversary, too, is in danger of being overlooked.[8] Of course, Chernyshevskii is not Tolstoi in terms of his artistic or even journalistic gifts. But Chernyshevskii was a genius of heroic action and was certainly the genuine revolutionary conscience of his age. He weighed in on the side of the Russian Revolution while the ideas of Tolstoi—according to Lenin—played no small role in the defeat of 1905.[9]

But there's no talk of any mass edition of Chernyshevskii's works. Our publishers republish whomever and whatever they want, but we don't hear anything about a mass edition of the novel *What Is to Be Done?* Our journals even offer serialized installments of Conan Doyle, but not a single journal has thought to popularize Chernyshevskii.

The disparity in scale between the celebrations of Tolstoi and Chernyshevskii is unbelievable.

Tolstoi and Chernyshevskii were both born in 1828.

In the minds of our mass readers, the year of 1928 will be associated only with the Tolstoi centennial. This is our mistake and sin. We must correct this historical injustice.

Notes

1. Novus, "Umeem li my prazdnovat' iubilei?" *Chitatel' i pisatel'*, 7 November 1928.

2. Unattributed Lenin quotation that would have been familiar to many in 1928, drawn from "L. N. Tolstoi," in V. I. Lenin, *Works*, 45 vols. (Moscow: Progress, 1960–1972), 16:323.

3. V. I. Lenin, "Lev Tolstoi as the Mirror of the Russian Revolution," in *Works*, 15:205.

4. Ibid.

5. A. V. Lunacharskii was accused of distorting Lenin's appraisal of Tolstoi during the celebrations—see chapter 1 in this volume.

6. The All-Union Association of Proletarian Writers was formed in 1920; it was later known as RAPP (the Russian Association of Proletarian Writers). Initially a militant proletarian movement, VAPP tempered its demands for working-class hegemony over culture after the mid-1920s amid growing respect for nineteenth-century realism.

7. A. Serafimovich (1863–1949), Bolshevik journalist best known for the revolutionary romanticism epitomized by his 1924 novel *The Iron Flood* (*Zheleznyi potok*).

8. N. G. Chernyshevskii (1828–1889), radical journalist, literary critic, and author known for his 1863 novel *What Is to Be Done?* (*Chto delat'?*).

9. Reference to the "first" Russian revolution of 1905.

Peter the Great

3
Rehabilitation and Afterimage

Aleksei Tolstoi's Many Returns to Peter the Great

◠ Kevin M. F. Platt

> Russians [...] in the course of fifteen years, having been reborn primarily through an act of will, have created a gigantic heavy industry and a mighty defense for the country. They have eliminated illiteracy and, in plain view before the rest of the world, they are leaping thousands of years ahead, building socialism. In the Petrine epoch, although on a different scale, with different goals, and with a different leading class [...], something comparable took place. [...] In this one may see the dialogue of epochs.
>
> —A. N. Tolstoi, "O tom, kak nuzhno obrashchat'sia s ideiami," 1933

> The beginning of work on the novel coincided with the beginning of the realization of the five-year plan. In the main, my work on *Peter* is an entrance into history via the present, understood in a Marxist fashion.
>
> —A. N. Tolstoi, "Marksizm obogatil iskusstvo," 1933

> In every historical phenomenon we must take what is necessary for us, discard what is archaic, and extract that which resonates with our epoch.
>
> —A. N. Tolstoi, "Pisatel' i teatr," 1933

Aleksei Nikolaevich Tolstoi considered the literary investigation of history to be as deeply concerned with the present as with the past. It was this view that brought the former "fellow-traveler" author to the pinnacle of success in Soviet public life by the time of his death in 1945. As the contributions to this volume attest, during the 1930s and 1940s the Soviet political establishment increasingly sought to mobilize popular support by means of a novel, largely russocentric vision of the past, in which the legitimacy of the

Russian empire translated in mystical fashion into the legitimacy of the Soviet Union, and in which the defeat of fascism and the eventual triumph of socialist might in Europe was envisioned as a realization of the epic destiny of the Russian nation itself. Tolstoi's success derived from his willingness and even enthusiasm to devote his talents and energies to raising these new standards "on the cultural front." In 1939 he was elected to the Soviet Academy of Sciences precisely for his historical fiction and other historiographic projects (particularly the publication of Russian folklore, literary histories, and histories of non-Russian Soviet nationalities). In 1941 he received a Stalin prize for his historical novel *Peter I*.

Members of the Soviet establishment, Tolstoi included, presumed that their new vision of history was objective and authoritative, composed of fixed, "scientific" truths revealed by Marxist theory. Yet as I argue below, the rate at which the evaluation of the past evolved during the 1930s worked ironically to render history a moving target and even to relativize historical knowledge. The traces of this dynamic of authority and instability in Tolstoi's works concerning Peter the Great are the subject of the present chapter. In the course of his career Tolstoi wrote an impressive number of works revolving about the person of Russia's first emperor. These include several stories, three versions of a play, the screenplay for a two-part film, a children's novel, and a monumental, unfinished historical novel, written intermittently over two decades. Most of these works, particularly those dating from 1929 on, bear a single title: *Peter I*. This extension of one title to many works motivates my own working method, in which I examine Tolstoi's vision of Peter as a single "work in progress." In my view, throughout his career Tolstoi struggled to creatively extend the earlier installments of his monumental work on Peter in order to save them from political obsolescence. Tolstoi's successive reevaluations of Peter and the corresponding revisions of his works present a case study in the mechanics of historical rehabilitation under Stalin. My investigation of Tolstoi's creative engagement with his political environment sheds new light on the author's biography, adds to our understanding of the Stalinist perspective on the tsarist past, and, finally, suggests new methodological propositions concerning the dynamics of Stalinist historical consciousness.

∽

First, consider the "raw data" of Tolstoi's texts. Over the course of his career Tolstoi's vision of Peter the Great changed frequently and radically, as may be seen from the following passages from the author's works. For clarity of contrast, I have selected comparable moments: depictions of Peter eating and drinking with his entourage. The passages are of some length, since I will return to them several times in the course of this chapter. At the start of the author's work on the tsar, in the story "Peter's Day" of 1917 or 1918, Peter appears as a brutal, cruel, and drunken despot:

> [Peter's] red face, with its fat, round cheeks, wasn't gaining anything in lucidity. He had already pushed away his dish and, resting his elbows on the table, was gnawing on the amber stem of his pipe. As before, the tsar's bulging eyes were glassy, unseeing. And fear began to overcome the guests. Had a courier arrived with bad news from Warsaw? Or was there unrest in Moscow again? Or had someone seated here committed some offense?
>
> Peter pulled the pipe from his mouth, spat under the table, and spoke, grimacing from a belch stuck in his throat: "Come 'ere, Archdeacon. [. . .] I'm not joking with you [. . .]. You're trying too hard, somehow. You've been trying too hard, too hard, that's what! I'm afraid of what they might start saying about you and me. They might say, 'the tsar's fool. . .'"
>
> As often happened, he didn't finish his thought and clenched his teeth, grated them, restraining a grimace.
>
> [. . .] "I'm afraid that by your efforts—yes, yes—your excessive efforts, they might, in an instant, put your cap on my head. . . With its horns. . . They're getting ready to. . . I know. . . They've been talking, talking, you've probably heard. . . A cap with horns might be more suitable for me than a crown. . ."
>
> And again he turned his head to the left, to the right, staring intensely. His incoherent, drunken words with their obscure meaning deepened the sense of fear among the guests.[1]

In contrast to this grotesque image, the first volumes of Tolstoi's novel cast Peter as a complex figure whose progressive aspirations are weighed down by the burden of tradition and the impossibility of controlling the historical process. In a passage from volume 1 of the novel, dating to 1929, Tolstoi wrote:

> At lunch [Peter's] spirits again seemed to rise. Some noticed a new habit in him—a dark, steady gaze. In the middle of discussion or jokes he would suddenly fall silent and begin to stare at someone—impenetrably, inquisitively—with an inhuman gaze. . . . Then he would flare his nostrils, and once again he would chuckle, drink, laugh woodenly . . .

Foreigners—soldiers, sailors, engineers—sat merrily and breathed freely. But for Russians this lunch was a difficult one. Music was playing, and they were waiting for the ladies to arrive for the dances. Aleksashka Men'shikov was looking at Peter's hands lying on the table—they were clenching and unclenching. [...] Suddenly, shrieking at high pitch with his neck extended like a rooster's, Peter jumped up, madly leaning across the table to Shein: "Thief, thief!"

Flinging away his chair, he ran out.[2]

This vision is displaced in turn by yet another image of Russia's first emperor that comes to the fore in the films of 1937 and 1939, and even more so in the unfinished third volume of the novel dating to 1943–1945. Here, Peter appears as a fearless leader, working tirelessly to increase the military, cultural, and political prestige of Russia. Thus in the third volume of the novel we read:

Having eaten, Peter Alekseevich rested his large-wristed hands on the table, their veins enlarged after the bath. He spoke little, listened attentively. His bulging eyes were stern, almost frightening, but when he lowered them—filling his pipe or for some other reason—his round-cheeked face with its small, smiling mouth appeared genial. Go ahead, approach him, clink glasses with him: "Your health, Sir Bombardier!" And he, depending on the individual, of course, would either refrain from answering or would toss his head, throwing back his thin, dark, curly hair. "In the name of Bacchus," he would intone with his bass voice, and he would drink. [...]

Peter Alekseevich was feeling satisfied today that [...] all his people were here sitting around the table and arguing and carrying on about the great matter at hand [the construction of St. Petersburg], not giving a thought to how dangerous it was or whether it would be crowned with success. In particular his heart was gladdened that here, where all his distant thoughts and difficult undertakings came together, everything that he noted down randomly for memory in the fat little writing book that lay in his pocket with the gnawed end of a pencil, his pipe and his tobacco pouch—all of this had been realized in fact. The wind tore at the flag on the tower of the fortress, pilings rose out of the muddy riverbanks, everywhere people were moving to and fro, consumed by their work and cares, and the city already stood as a city—still not a large one, but already in all of its everyday life.

Peter Alekseevich, chewing on the amber of his pipe, listened and did not listen.[3]

The implications of these passages are transparent and strikingly diverse. The first passage presents a revolting caricature of Peter as a despot with neither political will nor historical foresight: his eyes are "unseeing," and his speech is frighteningly incoherent. "Peter's Day" was published in the immediate aftermath of the October Revolution, and its representation of Peter is an outgrowth of late-nineteenth-century views of Russian history, as exemplified in the influential works of V. O. Kliuchevskii and his pupil P. N. Miliukov. For much of the nineteenth century, historians, whether they glorified or denigrated Peter's accomplishments, attributed to him a prescient, almost divine historical vision. Kliuchevskii and Miliukov after him broke with this tradition and declared Peter to have been simply a product of his times—and a brutal, haphazard, and disorganized one at that. In their view, Peter's ruthless methods of rule often undercut the beneficial effects of his reforms.[4]

In keeping with this historical vision, Tolstoi's narrator muses on Peter's lack of control over the historical process: "What happened was never what proud Peter had intended; Russia did not appear, strong and elegant, at the feast of the great powers. Rather, she appeared before her new relatives in a pitiful and unequal state, dragged along by the hair, bloody and half-mad from terror and despair—as a slave."[5] The narrator ends the story with the pathetic summary statement: "And the burden of this day, and of all days past and future, lay like a leaden weight on the shoulders of the individual who had assumed a burden beyond the strength of any man: one for all."[6] The political resonance of Tolstoi's satire is uncertain. On one hand, its vilification of the tsar's despotism capitalizes on new possibilities for denigration of Russian imperial rulers inaugurated by the Revolution (far surpassing Kliuchevskii and Miliukov) and anticipates the wave of historiography and *belle lettres* of the 1920s that, in the spirit of a revolutionary break with tradition, rejected a priori all representatives of the Russian imperial state.[7] Yet Tolstoi's satire on the use of political power to effect radical reform might also be seen as an indictment of the Bolsheviks' own social transformations as well.[8]

In the second passage cited above, written about a decade later in 1929, Peter appears in more positive light. His undertakings are now the object of the reader's sympathy and his motivation is comprehensible (he is angry at Shein for mishandling the rebellion of the strel'tsy). Yet if he has gained the reader's respect, he retains something of the unruliness of the early passage. Although he is capable of decisive action, such as the punishment of rebels and the shaving of his boyars (described just prior to the passage

Figure 4. Ia. O. Maliutin as Peter, from the Pushkin State Academic Drama Theater's 1935 staging of A. N. Tolstoi's *Peter I*. In *Ocherki istorii russkogo sovetskogo dramaticheskogo teatra* (Moscow, 1960).

cited above), his outburst at dinner and his demonic stares demonstrate a certain impotence and even childishness. Peter is clearly serving progressive ends, but it often appears in this volume of the novel that he is the unwitting tool of impersonal historical mechanisms—and that the engine of history moves though the suffering of the lower classes, rather than at the tsar's initiative. Following this passage Tolstoi ends the first book of his novel with a withering deadpan description of Peter's mass tortures and executions of the strel'tsy.[9] Even so, the author's antipathy for Peter as a representative of a hated regime has faded: the eponymous hero of the first volumes of *Peter I* is undoubtedly already a sympathetic character.

This view of Peter is very much in step with the vision of Russian history promulgated by the then-ascendant dean of Soviet Marxist historiography, M. N. Pokrovskii. As discussed in the introduction to this volume, in an attempt to create a materialist science of history, Pokrovskii downplayed the role of individuals, concentrating instead on the economic and social forces that he saw as the true causes of events.[10] In keeping with this Marxist conception of history, in the first volumes of Tolstoi's novel Peter appears to be a product of new institutions rather than their inventor—

instead of being the mastermind of historical progress, he is a symptomatic expression of it. Other characters, such as Sophia's favorite, the unlucky Vasilii Golitsyn, share Peter's sense of the necessary direction of Russia's historical development and the empire's need to expand. Peter is distinguished from such rivals not as a unique and exceptional genius of reform but rather as a skilled leader who accomplishes what the times themselves demand. This impression is confirmed by the presence of proto-capitalist heroes such as the fictional peasant Ivan Borovkin in the first two volumes of the novel, who reflect Pokrovskii's interpretation of the key role of a rising merchant capital economy in the transformations of the Petrine era.[11]

The final passage I cite presents yet a third stage in Tolstoi's vision of Peter. Here, the wise and calm emperor muses about grand affairs of state: the creation of Petersburg and war with envious European enemies. He is surrounded by advisers of a similarly lofty character. Here, finally, he appears to be fully in control of both himself and historical events—listening attentively but without excess passion, thinking with satisfaction about the realization of his conceptions. As has often been noted, this last version of Peter may be read as a eulogistic allegory for Stalin and his transcendent leadership qualities. Wartime propaganda celebrated Peter as an inspirational model of heroism and decisive leadership.[12] As *Pravda* announced in 1941, the present Bolshevik leaders were "the lawful heirs to the Russian people's great and honorable past."[13] As an example of the place of Peter I in Soviet public life during the 1940s, one may adduce the following lyrics that were entered in a wartime competition for the Soviet national anthem:

Хранят великие страницы	Great historical pages may be found
Дела великого Петра.	In the deeds of Peter the Great.
Наполеона из столицы	Napoleon was swept from the capital
Гнала народная метла.	By the broom of the people.
В великом мужестве народа,	In the great courage of the people
В порыве сдохновенных масс—	In an upsurge of the inspired masses—
В огне семнадцатого года	In the fires of 1917
Держава наша поднялась.	Our state arose.
Никогда не сдаемся	We shall never surrender
Мы в жестоком бою,	In cruel battle,
Клянемся	We swear
Клянемся	We swear
Отстаивать землю свою!	To defend our lands.[14]

So in the course of Tolstoi's career, his conception of Peter I ascended steadily, from a nadir of ugly and violent despotism to a zenith of inspired, charismatic leadership.

∼

How does one account for this development of the author's representations of Peter? The most common explanation is that Tolstoi's vision changed in step with dominant Soviet views of the first emperor, in a transparent example of Tolstoi's willingness to cater to the Stalinist regime. Typical of views of Tolstoi as a toady to Soviet officialdom is the article in the *Handbook of Russian Literature*, which begins: "Tolstoi, Aleksei Nikolaevich (1883–1945), a nobleman by birth, has been described as a man 'who towards the end of his life became the most authoritative apologist for the Stalin regime.'"[15] Nicholas Riasanovsky has written that the author's views on Peter evolved "as a parody of the rise and fall of Pokrovskii."[16] Robert Tucker describes Tolstoi's work on Peter quite simply as the fulfillment of Stalin's own literary designs.[17] Of course, there is some merit to this view, as the above summary of Tolstoi's visions of Peter demonstrates. Clearly, the author was oriented toward the needs of the Soviet establishment. Lev Kogan reports that Tolstoi remarked in the early 1930s, "I don't understand why people are afraid of the word 'commission' even in its more literal meaning."[18] Moreover, the evolution of Tolstoi's conception of Peter in the late 1920s appears to correspond to Stalin's own view (expressed through an intermediary) after a preview of the 1929 Moscow Art Theater production of the first version of the play *On the Rack (Na dybe)*: "A splendid play. Only it's a pity that Peter wasn't depicted heroically enough."[19] Tolstoi tended to test the political waters by whatever means he could, and he did not hesitate to consult with Gor'kii and more powerful establishment figures, including Stalin himself, whenever the opportunity arose.[20]

Yet, granting that the overall development of the Petrine theme reflects Tolstoi's conscious efforts at ideological accommodation, this does not really lay to rest the matter of how this development took place. The most glaring shortcoming of such an explanation is the simplistic presupposition that public life during the 1930s was sufficiently monolithic and scripted that one could identify a "party line" and conform to it. In fact, the historical interpretation of Peter never approached a well-defined official view until the very late 1930s. As is well known, as a result of the complexity of the historical-interpretational landscape of the late 1920s and early 1930s, Tolstoi suffered at the hands of RAPP for his overly soft depiction of Peter in the early versions of the play and in the first two volumes of the historical novel. Thus, for example, the RAPP critic I. Bachelis assailed the second version of Tolstoi's play *Peter I* in a 1930 review entitled "And This Is for Whom?": "This play by Aleksei Nikolaevich Tolstoi—a former count, in past years a bard of the bankrupt aristocracy, and currently numbering among the petty bourgeois "fellow travelers"—is the malicious, maddened sortie of a class enemy, covered over with the artful mask of 'historicity.'"[21] In a striking illustration of just how dramatically Soviet historical consciousness was changing in these years, Bachelis saw the central mechanism of Tolstoi's "camouflaged counterrevolutionary attack" as his evocation of a historical analogy between the Petrine and Soviet epochs—precisely the rhetorical device that would govern Stalinist historical discourse by the end of the decade. The degree to which attacks like this affected Tolstoi may be judged by the vehemence with which he would publicly attack RAPP in subsequent years.[22]

Later in the 1930s, the significance of Russian history in Soviet public life began to shift rapidly, as the Politburo denounced the Pokrovskii school's "vulgar sociological" historiography and organized competitions for the creation of new elementary school textbooks that would represent a less abstract view of history, focused on significant names, dates, and events.[23] By 1936 early versions of the textbook that was to be published the following year as the official new version of history were taking shape in a draft co-authored by A. V. Shestakov and a brigade of historians including N. G. Tarasov, N. D. Kuznetsov, D. N. Kuznetsov, and others. As David Brandenberger has observed, this work evolved under A. A. Zhdanov's direction into an etatist and russocentric view of history that "conferred the legitimacy of a thousand-year pedigree upon the Soviet leadership."[24] Peter—described in the textbook as an "intelligent and businesslike young tsar" who "upon his ascent to the throne [. . .] began to introduce a new order"—forms an important part of this pedigree.[25] Brandenberger concludes that the Shestakov text signified "the completion of the party hierarchy's decade-long search for a usable past."[26] Yet as the campaign for a new vision of history was heating up in the middle 1930s, it was still far from clear that this particular version would eventually come to dominate.

Records from jury deliberations in the textbook competition dating from 1936–1937 demonstrate that a variety of historical interpretations were under consideration until just months before the publication of the Shestakov text. Some of these interpretations cast Peter in a decidedly negative light, as an important figure in historical development, but nevertheless as a representative of the nobility (*dvorianstvo*) who achieved social and economic progress at the expense of the lower classes. Consider M. V. Nechkina's elementary school manuscript, drafted in 1935. In her view, Peter's diplomatic mission abroad—which Tolstoi had celebrated in the first volume of his novel as a search for enlightenment—was a self-glorifying adventure in the service of imperial expansion, and one that bled the treasury and therefore cost the Russian peasant dearly. In her concluding paragraph on Peter, Nechkina states:

> Celebrating the formation of the new empire, the serf-owners, naturally, concealed their true intentions under a facade of false phrases. They assured all that the creation of the empire was, primarily, a path of glory for the people, a path leading Russia into the ranks of the great European powers. [. . .] The central concern of the administration of Peter I was the intensification of the oppression of serfdom.[27]

Nechkina's textbook boasted the fact- and personality-driven narrative that the party leadership demanded, yet it retained much of the anti-tsarist bent of earlier Soviet historiography. Several other competition entries, such as one coauthored by N. N. Vanag, B. G. Grekov, A. M. Pankratova, and S. A. Piontkovskii, shared this view of history, which broke with Pokrovskian historiography, albeit less completely than did the Shestakov textbook.[28]

Yet consideration of still another version of Soviet history that surfaced in the textbook competition reveals the extent to which historical interpretation was truly in flux in the mid-1930s. This was an "internationalist" account of the Soviet Union's past, which deemphasized the role of Russia and presented an integrated history of all Soviet nations.[29] Although Nechkina's and Pankratova's draft textbooks were far more critical of Russian imperial figures than the Shestakov work, the proponents of this third view saw these works as excessively *apologetic*. For instance, the critic F. D. Kretov remarked of their portrayal of Peter:

> Undoubtedly, Peter was an outstanding personality. Moreover, Marx says simply that he was a genius. There is much in him that it might even be a good idea to learn from. But the crux is that he was a tsar, that he was a genius of landowners and merchants, that he created and strengthened a national government of exploiters.[30]

Kretov's views undoubtedly represent an extreme in the records of the textbook competition. Yet the presence of such divergent views so close to the center of Soviet institutional life calls into question the teleological notion that a russocentric, etatist vision of history came to dominate Soviet public life in a planned and controlled development. Interpretation of the Russian past, and of Peter in particular, was diverse and contested up until the publication of the Shestakov textbook in September 1937.

How did Tolstoi's Petrine project fare in this unsettled interpretative environment? Continuing into the middle 1930s, Tolstoi faced serious criticism and was forced to engage in political infighting, particularly with regard to the two-part film about Russia's first emperor. The screenplay underwent enormous reworking before it finally went into production, and continued to be revised during the process of shooting. Some characters, such as Feofan Prokopovich, who delivers the triumphant final speech of the original screenplay, were nearly written out of the final version of the films, while the project's ideological underpinnings shifted from Pokrovskian to post-Pokrovskian historiography.[31] Tolstoi's March 1937 press release regarding the final work on part one of the film illustrates the author's "embattled" working conditions:

> A pack of various staff "film theoreticians" descended upon us with a mass of contradictory demands. The wobbly, hysterical Peter which they were pushing on us did not correspond at all to our conceptions. They demanded that we show the ultimate futility and defeat of all of Peter's transformational activity. These demands would have nullified our attempts to show the progressive significance of the Petrine epoch for the subsequent development of Russian history. [. . .] The central idea of our film was and remains our intention to show the power of the great Russian nation, the indomitable nature of its transformational spirit.[32]

Scattered evidence regarding the reception of this first film indicates the extent to which it failed to correspond to any well-established interpretive line, instead confusing its audiences. Its outright celebration of Peter so disturbed some viewers that they asked Shestakov about the film's political correctness in public lectures, while in Magnitogorsk at least one audience member inferred from the film's treatment of Peter that it had been made abroad.[33] The second part of the film was also a target of political intrigue. In May 1937 A. I. Angarov, the deputy director of the Central Committee's Department of Cultural and Educational Work, denounced those at work on the film for criminal negligence with regard to budgetary overruns, chiefly as a result of the continuous rewriting of the screenplay during shooting. Not mentioning Tolstoi by name, Angarov explained that the "gross historical distortions" of the original screenplay made such rewrites necessary. He ends with a recommendation to halt production and to bring those responsible to justice.[34] Perhaps only Angarov's own arrest that summer saved Tolstoi and his films from scandal and ruin.

Given the fluidity of Soviet visions of Peter current in the 1930s and the political infighting that surrounded Tolstoi throughout the period, it is difficult to support the view that the author's changing interpretive stance reflected his straightforward catering to a well-defined "party line" on history. A more accurate view might be that Tolstoi's rehabilitation of Peter extended far ahead of the general curve of Soviet historical revisionism—in short, that he was engaging in a high-stakes political game that he repeatedly won. Tolstoi's aggressive position with regard to Peter exposed him to considerable risk, but he was clever enough (or lucky enough) to outlast his critics in the stormy cultural politics of the era. In sparring with RAPP over his play, he had been saved by Stalin's favor and his enemies' eventual fall from grace. In later political battles, Tolstoi's critics were

Figure 5. N. K. Cherkasov as Peter in V. M. Petrov's two-part film *Peter I* (1937–1939). In N. K. Cherkasov, *Zapiski sovetskogo aktera*, ed. E. Kuznetsov (Moscow, 1953).

swept away by repression before they could effectively undermine party authorities' confidence in the "red count." Rather than being a toady to official interpretive positions proclaimed from on high, Tolstoi was a skilled politician who chose allies well and took risks that paid off. In 1943 at a conference on historical themes in wartime writing A. A. Fadeev explained:

> It is to the greatest credit of our historical novelists that many of them understood these problems [of the importance of historical knowledge in Soviet public life] and posed them in their works when they were still poorly comprehended in broader circles of the intelligentsia. And many of these authors, having created their works, met considerable social resistance and were slapped down. *Peter I*, from my point of view, by now constitutes a classical historical work. But *Peter I* initially provoked an almost physical violence. [. . .] Now, however, it is clear why [. . .] it was necessary to raise the novel *Peter I* up and to place it in the position of honor that it deserves.[35]

As Fadeev's remarks illustrate, Tolstoi's aggressive stance bore fruit. He enjoyed prominence in the 1940s not only by virtue of his undoubted accomplishments in historical *belles lettres* but also because of the stunning timing of these accomplishments, which anticipated with near prescience the unexpected rise of tsarist history to the forefront of Soviet public life.[36]

∼

This retelling of Tolstoi's political trajectory leads to a further line of inquiry. If the political field was contested—leading us to recast the process of accommodation into one of deft negotiation of a dynamic and mobile landscape—one may ask: what strategies did Tolstoi employ in his engagement of the political scene? Many authors adapted their works to the USSR's changing political environment by simply rewriting them. Tolstoi was remarkable for the modest degree to which he resorted to this common practice. He did revise his play several times, improving Peter's image with each new version. Yet surprisingly, despite multiple new editions of the first two volumes of the historical novel, he never made significant changes in this text.[37] So how did Tolstoi engineer the long-term success of his vision of Peter? How was it that in 1941 a Stalin prize could be awarded to a novel that was founded on Pokrovskii's views, which were by then thoroughly discredited?

In our search for answers to these questions, let us return to the three passages from Tolstoi's Petrine works cited above. While my initial reading of this material stressed the distinction between successive representations of Peter, now consider some of the intriguing continuities that link them together. First of all, the shared imagery that runs like an undercurrent through all of these passages is striking: the image of Peter's hands resting on the table, giving hints as to his interior state, which occurs in all three citations; the image of his well-chewed pipe stem, which unites the first with the last; his bulging eyes and penetrating gaze, which are mentioned in each citation. These poetic linkages are matched by continuities in overall architectonics: Peter is characterized by separateness, impenetrability, and an unnerving tendency to take abrupt action. Note that the scene from the novel's third volume, the only one of the three citations that does not end in conflict, subsequently comes into alignment with the other two in this regard as well. After leaving the gathering at Men'shikov's, Peter visits the laborers' barracks and is so outraged at their rotten provisions (shades of Eisenstein's *Battleship Potemkin*) that he returns to the ongoing banquet with a piece of moldy bread and forces the comically apologetic, infantile Men'shikov to eat it as punishment.[38] Thus despite radical changes in the historical-interpretive implications of Tolstoi's image of Peter, some of its features remain constant. These peculiar structural constants are striking enough to suggest that Tolstoi was, in some manner, reworking the same episode—the same elements in his creative conception of Peter—but spinning their historical potential in different directions. Whereas Peter's isolation in the initial fragment reads as distance from servants and advisers—indeed, from reality—in the second it communicates impatience with a historical process that he cannot rush along fast enough, and in the final scene it projects Peter's divine ability to direct events in a superhistorical manner. Similarly the atmosphere of fear around Peter at first reflects the dread inspired by random and incomprehensible beatings. This is replaced first by the terror of those who are unable to fulfill impossible commands, and then by the loving awe inspired by an all-knowing and omnipotent leader.

These reflections are relevant to a broad range of material that is repeatedly deployed in Tolstoi's Petrine works. The emperor's military exploits also appear as successive hypostases of a single compositional vision. For instance, in volume 1 of the novel a telescope is shot out of Peter's hands when he recklessly exposes himself to enemy fire in the Azov campaign. He jumps down into the trenches, visibly shaken, smiling a "parched" smile and cursing "with difficulty."[39] In volume 2, while inspecting battle preparations in the disastrous first battle of Narva, the tsar and his generals come under fire, and while some flinch, "Peter's eyes widened and he clenched his jaws, but he did not bow down to the canonballs."[40] Finally, in volume 3 Peter and his generals are again inspecting the field before the second, ultimately successful siege of the city. Here Peter does not expose himself to fire but watches as the daredevil Men'shikov rides up to the walls of the city to taunt the enemy.[41] This recurrent motif is just one of many that tie the battle scenes together, working to delineate the evolution of the tsar from callow youth to wise leader while retaining a certain peculiar constancy of representation.

Interrogation and torture is yet another recurrent theme, and it also figures prominently in Tolstoi's own creative mythology of work on Petrine history. As he explained in several published discussions, Tolstoi first grasped the essence of early-eighteenth-century linguistic norms by studying original interrogation transcripts from that era:

> Suddenly [...] I saw, felt, comprehended—the Russian language. The scribes and copyists of Muscovite Russia artfully recorded interrogations; their task was constrained and precise: to communicate the stories of those under torture, preserving all the peculiarities of their speech—a literary task, in a way.[42]

Considering Tolstoi's view of interrogation as a mechanism for discovery of the "linguistic" truth, it is curious how malleable the presentation of interrogation became in his works. "Peter's Day" depicts the emperor himself torturing prisoners charged with "word and deed" offenses, with callous indifference to their pain.[43] In the first two volumes of the novel, Peter's personal participation in interrogations, first of the supporters of the Tsaritsa Sof'ia and later of the strel'tsy, is portrayed in a somewhat less prejudicial manner. But now the reader discerns Peter's discomfort with the barbarity of the practice by his overt distress and by his efforts to conceal his participation in this cruelty from foreign emissaries.[44] In the second part of the film (1939) Tolstoi shows Peter's complicity in the torture and execution of the traitorous Tsarevich Aleksei, but also the great pain Peter experiences in sacrificing "the flesh of his flesh" to the defense of Russia against European enemies and to continued progressive social transformation. Tolstoi included a similar treatment of the interrogation of the tsarevich in the final version of the play, and he likely intended to depict this episode in the third volume of the novel as well. Through the evolution of the interrogation scene over the course of Tolstoi's career, we see a gradual exoneration of Peter's bloody methods of rule, as they are minimized, humanized, and legitimated in the context of grand historical imperatives. Yet we also witness once again Tolstoi's remarkable conservative streak, which time and again drew him back to the same basic scenes in Petrine mythology.

In addition to Tolstoi's reliance on recurrent themes and images, one may note other curious patterns of repetition in his Petrine works. He returned many times to a specific set of fictional characters: the members of the boyar Buinosov family and the peasant Borovkin family, who resurface in various works and genres. Finally, as I noted at the start of this chapter, there remains the overriding peculiarity of Tolstoi's stubborn application of a single title, *Peter I*, to all of his treatments of Peter from the late 1920s on. The insistence of these elements of Tolstoi's *poetical* project flies in the face his fluid, dynamic *historical-interpretative* project. If the author were striving simply to recast his vision of Peter in keeping with (or in anticipation of) the changing political line, a more obvious approach would be to strive for distance from all aspects of the earlier Petrine works in the creation of later, more politically acceptable ones.

In this light, it is clear that Tolstoi's did not aspire to replace his earlier conceptions of Peter, so much as he worked to preserve the integrity of his poetical imagination—in particular to preserve his magnum opus, the historical novel. Rather than rewrite his novel, erasing his own compositional accomplishments in the service of the Soviet erasure of outworn historical visions, Tolstoi revised his novel by highly original means. The release of new works in other genres and media on the same topic, using the same characters and bearing the same title, acted to cast a new interpretive net over material already in print: viewers of the movie almost certainly would return to the novel with a very different sense of Peter than was communicated by the printed text alone. The addition of new episodes to the novel, both in these other media and through the appearance of later volumes, afforded an opportunity to recast the interpretive implications of old episodes, nudging readers' perceptions incrementally toward a different understanding of earlier installments in Tolstoi's Petrine project. The most obvious evidence that Tolstoi's compositions of the 1930s reflect an intentional strategy in this regard may be the never-ending task he set for himself and nursed for two decades: that of writing the historical novel itself. By never actually bringing his work to a close he left it open for constructive reconfigurations as new material affected the immanent implications of old.

In effect, the novel was an open-ended bildungsroman—and a bildungsroman is not over until it's over. Thus the second description cited above of Peter at a banquet, from the novel's first volume, must certainly be taken differently in light of the final such description, from the third volume. Rather than seeing the young Peter as impotent before the forces of history, the reader of the work as a whole is tempted to see him as immature, not yet in full control of the historical process that he will eventually master. The interpretive reach of later episodes of the novel back toward earlier ones is perhaps most evident in Tolstoi's treatment of the second siege of Narva. As the tsar inspects the terrain around the city, he explicitly reminds his commanders (and the reader) of the catastrophic losses of the first battle at Narva and of his own decidedly less heroic stature in that engagement, when he was forced to flee the battlefield:

> "Here is where my army perished," he said simply. "Hereabouts King Charles found great glory, but we found strength. Here we learned from which end to eat the radish, and we buried forever the ossified past, which all but brought us to final perdition."[45]

The final capture of the city is overtly staged as a correction of Peter's earlier missteps. It may also be read as a correction of the author's earlier underestimation of Peter's epic magnitude.

Tolstoi's strategy in his Petrine project might be formulated as the harnessing of interpretive looseness in order to outmaneuver a restrictive ideological environment. This looseness preserved the political validity of compositions that changing circumstances would otherwise have rendered obsolete, ensuring the author's safety by leaving him rhetorically maneuverable, able to spin on a dime and recast his tale as the need arose. Undoubtedly, Tolstoi's aim at each stage of his work on the carpenter-tsar was to realize what he viewed as a "correct" image. Yet his strategy of "over-writing" rather than simply "rewriting" his text may have had unintended interpretive consequences. After all, the result of Tolstoi's successive tinkerings is not a consistent, authoritative vision of Peter, but rather a multiple and shifting one. As this reading demonstrates, taken as a whole the novel betrays traces of a range of interpretive options, stacked up like geological strata in a canyon. Ultimately, the syncretic character of Tolstoi's novel—and of the "hypertext" of his many Petrine works taken together—may have undermined the Soviet rehabilitation of Peter that the author was ostensibly serving. Indeed, Tolstoi's own sense of the lingering afterimages of his previous historical conceptions likely motivated his 1944 decision to correct the text of the first two volumes of the novel. Yet the author's restraint in these corrections just as surely demonstrates his squeamishness regarding major revisions of his published works. The novel's success during the 1930s precluded any more extensive revisions of the by then thoroughly canonized Soviet "classic." Ultimately, Tolstoi's relatively minor revisions did not efface the work's complex interpretive structure, leaving Peter's image rather blurred. He is part young turk, part transcendent leader—only one thing is certain: Peter is the focal point for the affective energies of national pride and identity.

The best metaphor for Tolstoi's syncretic works on Peter is that of the palimpsest, where a number of old images and new ones, interpretations and reinterpretations, are accumulated one on top of another, gaining in emotional force by virtue of their overinscribed character, foiling any attempt to retreat to a single interpretive position. By way of conclusion, I would apply this characterization of Tolstoi's writings to the Soviet process of rehabilitation as a whole. As Soviet elites set out in the 1930s to revise tsarist history and so reclaim a valuable repository of national identity, they undoubtedly intended to establish a final, corrected, and "usable" version of the past. Yet the process of rehabilitation was a complex one, both politically and historiographically. Rather than simply replacing past conceptions with fresh ones, the imperfect mechanism of historical revisionism leaves traces of outworn ideas of the past in plain view for those who wish to see them. Furthermore, as my brief account of the rehabilitation of Peter demonstrates, although some have imagined the Soviet rehabilitation of tsarist history as a top-down process in which those in power imposed a new vision of the past in one sweep of revisionist energy, in actuality it was a complex, heavily contested political enterprise. The struggle between multiple explanations of historical events signaled to all actors in this process an interpretative openness directly contradicting the imperative of uncovering a single, politically correct version of the past. On the highest level of abstraction, one might observe that the very mechanism of revision works against the project of erasure, for when one text is calculated to replace another, it may in fact commemorate what it sets out to bury. Rehabilitation, I would offer, tends to destabilize knowledge and interpretive certainty just as much as it works to establish authoritative, official "truths"—delivering afterimages and palimpsests instead of the clean, airbrushed portraits sought by party bosses. Indeed, the contradictory nature of so many of the Stalin era's historical and contemporary heroes—and the abrupt reversals of fortune that they experienced—may be yet another indication that Soviet public life was not as monolithic, as subject to the "total" control of the state, as was once imagined.

Notes

1. A. N. Tolstoi, "Den' Petra," in *Sobranie sochinenii v desiati tomakh*, 10 vols. (Moscow: Khudozhestvennaia literatura, 1982–1986), 3:99. "Peter's Day" was first published in the Petrograd literary almanac *Skrizhal'* in early 1918 and was republished several times during the author's lifetime.

2. A. N. Tolstoi, "Petr I: Kniga pervaia," in *Sobranie sochinenii*, 7:358. The first volume of *Peter I* first appeared in serial form in *Novyi mir* from July 1929 through July 1930. The second appeared in the same journal from February 1933 through April 1934. The first two volumes also appeared in very successful separate editions during the 1930s. The passage I have cited is drawn from chapter 7 and represents the original text of the novel as it appeared in *Novyi mir*.

3. A. N. Tolstoi, "Petr I: Kniga tret'ia," in *Sobranie sochinenii*, 7:701–2. This final volume of *Peter I* was serialized in *Novyi mir* from March 1944 through January 1945, when Tolstoi's death brought the work to a premature conclusion. Since that time, this perennial favorite has been republished many times. The first part of the film premièred on 1 September 1937; the second followed on 7 March 1939.

4. V. O. Kliuchevsky, *A History of Russia*, trans. C. J. Hogarth, 5 vols. (New York: E. P. Dutton, 1911–1931), 4:207–29; Robert Byrnes, *V. O. Kliuchevskii: Historian of Russia* (Bloomington: Indiana University Press, 1995), 198–202; P. A. Miliukov, *Ocherki po istorii russkoi kul'tury*, 2nd ed., 3 vols. (St. Petersburg: I. N. Skorokhodov, 1896–1903), 3, pt. 1:167; Anatole Mazour, *Modern Russian Historiography*, rev. ed. (Westport, Conn.: Greenwood, 1975), 148. On the relationship of Kliuchevskii to subsequent Russian historical thought, see Terence Emmons, "Kliuchevskii's Pupils," in *Historiography of Imperial Russia: The Professional Writing of History in a Multinational State*, ed. Thomas Sanders (Armonk, N.Y.: M. E. Sharpe, 1999), 122–24. For an overview of the reception of Peter I in modern Russia see my "History and Despotism, or: Hayden White vs. Ivan the Terrible and Peter the Great," *Rethinking History* 3, no. 3 (1999): 247–69. In the 1930s, Tolstoi had harsh words for Miliukov's historical works on Peter—see "O tom, kak nuzhno obrashchat'sia s ideiami," in *Sobranie sochinenii*, 10:206.

5. Tolstoi, "Den' Petra," 84.

6. Ibid., 103.

7. Outright villifications of Peter I in the post-revolutionary era, in particular Tolstoi's "Peter's Day" and Boris Pil'niak's "His Majesty Kneeb Piter Komondor" ("Ego velichestvo Kneeb Piter Komondor," 1919), so outraged the eminent historian S. F. Platonov that he produced an explicit refutation of these works in the late 1920s: S. F. Platonov, *Petr Velikii: Lichnost' i deiatel'nost'* (n. p.: Vremia, n. d.).

8. In an interview in 1933 with the journal *Smena*, Tolstoi stated: "This *povest'* was written at the very start of the February revolution. I don't recall what motivated me to write it. Undoubtedly, the *povest'* was written under the influence of Merezhkovskii. It's a weak piece." See "Stenogramma besedy s kollektivom redaktsii zhurnala 'Smena,'" in *Sobranie sochinenii*, 10:207. Tolstoi's connection of this work with the February Revolution likely represents an effort to mask the actual topical relevance of the work to the October Revolution, after which the story was,

in fact, published. Tolstoi's nod toward Merezhkovskii's historical novel of 1905, *Antichrist (Peter and Alexei)*, although not a complete misrepresentation of the grotesque caricature of "Peter's Day," diverts attention from Tolstoi's conception of Peter's significance. Tolstoi's remarks were probably calculated to mask the story's anti-Bolshevik resonance.

9. Robert Tucker sees the novel's first book as unambiguously "optimistic" in *Stalin in Power: The Revolution from Above, 1928–1941* (New York: Norton, 1990), 117–18. Tucker reads the suppression of the strel'tsy at the close of this first volume of the novel as an expression of Peter's sympathies for the working people, rather than the aristocratic classes. In my view, the novel communicates Peter's affinity for the *merchant class*, in keeping with then ascendant Pokrovskyian views of history. The brutal pursuit of "progressive" aims in volume 1 recalls Lenin's remark that Peter used "barbaric means to fight barbarism." V. I. Lenin, "O 'levom' rebiachestve i o melkoburzhuaznosti," in *Polnoe sobranie sochinenii*, 5th ed., 55 vols. (Moscow: Gosudarstvennoe izdatel'stvo politicheskoi literatury, 1958–1970), 36:301.

10. See M. N. Pokrovskii, *Russkaia istoriia v samom szhatom ocherke* (Moscow: Partizdat, 1932), 58–60.

11. Nicholas Riasanovsky, *The Image of Peter the Great in Russian History and Thought* (New York: Oxford University Press, 1985), 280–82.

12. On the valorization of Peter and other tsarist rulers, see Klaus Mehnert, *Stalin versus Marx: The Stalinist Historical Doctrine* (London: G. Allen and Unwin, 1953), 76, 84–86; Lowell Tillet, *The Great Friendship: Soviet Historians on the Non-Russian Nationalities* (Chapel Hill: University of North Carolina Press, 1969), 46, 54; Tucker, *Stalin in Power*, 7, 52, 319, 322, 481–86, 557; Maureen Perrie, "The Tsar, the Emperor, the Leader: Ivan the Terrible, Peter the Great and Anatolii Rybakov's Stalin," in *Stalinism: Its Nature and Aftermath—Essays in Honor of Moshe Lewin*, ed. Nick Lampert and Gábor Rittersporn (London: Macmillan, 1992), 77–100; Platt, "History and Despotism"; David Brandenberger, *National Bolshevism: Stalinist Mass Culture and the Formation of Modern Russian National Identity, 1931–1956* (Cambridge, Mass.: Harvard University Press, 2002).

13. Emel'ian Iaroslavskii, "Bol'sheviki—prodolzhateli luchshikh patrioticheskikh traditsii russkogo naroda," *Pravda*, 27 December 1941, 3.

14. RGASPI, f. 17, op. 125, d. 217, ll. 86–87.

15. Leon I. Twarog, "Tolstoi, Aleksei Nikolaevich," in *A Handbook of Russian Literature*, ed. Victor Terras (New Haven, Conn.: Yale University Press, 1985), 475.

16. Riasanovsky, *The Image of Peter the Great*, 281. See also George Nivat, "Alexis Tolstoi et le Roman Historique," *Lettres Nouvelles* 1 (1977): 183–84.

17. Tucker, *Stalin in Power*, 114.

18. Lev Kogan, in *Vospominaniia ob A. N. Tolstom: Sbornik* (Moscow: Sovetskii pisatel', 1973), 205.

19. R. Ivanov Razumnik, *Pisatel'skie sud'by* (New York: Literaturnyi fond, 1951), 39–43; see also "Kratkaia biografiia," in A. N. Tolstoi, *Polnoe sobranie sochinenii*, 15 vols. (Moscow: Khudozhestvennaia literatura, 1946–1953), 1:87.

20. On Tolstoi's contacts with Gor'kii and on other aspects of his political

maneuvering in the Soviet establishment, see Viktor Petelin, *Sud'ba khudozhnika: zhizn', lichnost', tvorchestvo Alekseia Nikolaevicha Tolstogo* (Moscow: Khudozhestvennaia literatura, 1982), 364–82. Tucker cites anecdotal evidence that Tolstoi consulted frequently with Stalin regarding Peter and even became a "friend" of the Soviet ruler in *Stalin in Power*, 116–18. For Tolstoi's own mention of contact with Stalin, see chapter 4 in this volume.

21. I. Bachelis, "Dlia kogo sie," *Komsomol'skaia pravda*, 2 March 1930, 4. This review, which explicity calls for a press campaign against Tolstoi modeled on the 1929 campaign against Pil'niak, is the most negative public response to the play. Articles in *Pravda* and *Izvestiia* panned the play, calling it "distant from the Soviet audience" and a failure, but refrained from hyperbolic accusations against its author. N. Volkov, "'Petr I,'" *Izvestiia*, 9 March 1930, 4; L. Cherniavskii, "Restavratsiia merezhkovshchiny ('Petr I' v MKhAT)," *Pravda*, 11 March 1930, 6.

22. See in particular Tolstoi's statement of 1937, "Prodolzhim i uglubim samokritiku," in *Sobranie sochinenii*, 10:365–67. Here, Tolstoi "confesses" that he and the Soviet literary establishment as a whole were guilty of insufficiently eradicating RAPPist errors. As always, Tolstoi's rhetorical and political acuity, which turned "self-criticism" into an offensive weapon, is astonishing.

23. Pokrovskii's investment in historical materialism and anonymous social forces, as well as his "unpatriotic" criticism of Peter the Great, tsarist imperialism, and Russian chauvinism, were officially denounced in January 1936—see Anatole G. Mazour, *The Writing of History in the Soviet Union* (Stanford, Calif.: Hoover Institution Press, 1971), 17–23. In 1936, Tolstoi wrote a broadside against Pokrovskii for *Pravda* that remained unpublished—see A. M. Kriukov, *A. N. Tolstoi i russkaia literatura: Tvorcheskaia individual'nost' v literaturnom protsesse* (Moscow: Nauka, 1990), 201.

24. Brandenberger, *National Bolshevism*, 53.

25. *Kratkii kurs istorii SSSR*, ed. A. V. Shestakov (Moscow: Gos. uchebno-pedagog. izd-vo, 1937), 60.

26. Brandenberger, *National Bolshevism*, 62.

27. RGASPI, f. 17, op. 120, d. 357, l. 346.

28. RGASPI, f. 17, op. 120, d. 356, ll. 23–25.

29. RGASPI, f. 17, op. 120, d. 367, l. 10.

30. Ibid., l. 78.

31. Compare a March 1935 version of the screenplay at RGALI, f. 631, op. 3, d. 207, with A. Tolstoi and V. Petrov, "Petr I," in *Izbrannye stsenarii sovetskogo kino*, 6 vols. (Moscow: Goskinoizdat, 1950), 4:5–94.

32. A. N. Tolstoi, "Petr I v kino," in *Sobranie sochinenii*, 10: 349–50.

33. Brandenberger provides a good summary of viewers' responses to the film in *National Bolshevism*, 56, 87–88; see also the letters to the editor printed in *Skorokhodovskii rabochii*, 15 September 1937, 3.

34. RGASPI, f. 17, op. 120, d. 256, l. 103.

35. RGALI, f. 631, op. 15, d. 635, l. 13.

36. See a similar recognition of Tolstoi's achievement in adapting his works on

Peter to a changing political environment in a December 1945 memorandum to G. M. Malenkov from the critic O. S. Reznik, published in *"Literaturnyi front": Istoriia politicheskoi tsenzury, 1932–1946 gg.—sbornik dokumentov,* ed. D. L. Babichenko (Moscow: Entsiklopediia rossiiskikh dereven', 1994), 179.

37. Tolstoi made no significant changes in prewar editions of the novel. While writing the work's third volume during the war years, the author undertook somewhat more involved rewrites of the earlier parts, reaching only chapter 5 of volume 1 before his death. Although some of these corrections were plot adjustments in the interests of consistency, others realign Peter's image in keeping with Tolstoi's later, more heroic vision—eliminating a scene where the young Peter cries from fear during the strel'tsy rebellion, for instance. Yet these changes were in general so minor as to leave original historical-interpretive implications intact. Given Tolstoi's political position and the looser political climate of the war years, one may suggest that these late corrections do not reflect political pressure but rather the aesthetic or ideological decisions of the author. Regarding Tolstoi's corrections, see A. V. Alpatova's commentary in "Petr I," in *Sobranie sochinenii,* 7:850–51.

38. Tolstoi, "Petr I: Kniga tret'ia," 708.

39. Tolstoi, "Petr I: Kniga pervaia," 292.

40. Tolstoi, "Petr I: Kniga vtoraia," 588.

41. Tolstoi, "Petr I: Kniga tret'ia," 736.

42. A. N. Tolstoi, "Kak my pishem," in *Sobranie sochinenii,* 10:141–42. Also see "Stenogramma besedy s kollektivom redaktsii zhurnala 'Smena'," *Sobranie sochinenii,* 10:211–12.

43. Tolstoi, "Den' Petra," 95–96.

44. Tolstoi, "Petr I: Kniga pervaia," 192–97, 360–64.

45. Tolstoi, "Petr I: Kniga tret'ia," 734. Reference is to Charles XII, of Sweden (b. 1682, reign 1697–1718), renowned soldier king, whose rule constituted both the culmination and collapse of Swedish imperial power in northern Europe. He was Peter I's most significant military rival, and his defeat at the battle of Poltava (1709) marked the turning point in the Northern War between Russia and Sweden for predominance in the Baltic region.

4
Aleksei Tolstoi's Remarks on the Film *Peter I*

In early September 1937, as moviehouses all across the USSR were beginning to screen the historical film *Peter I*, a delegation of worker-correspondents from the *Skorokhod Worker* factory newspaper visited Aleksei Tolstoi at his dacha in Pushkin, an elite Leningrad suburb known until that year as Detskoe Selo. The interview that they conducted with Tolstoi illustrates how press releases functioned in Soviet mass culture and provides an example of the stylistic register developed for the lowest common denominator of this poorly educated society.[1]

As in the West, it was standard practice for Soviet authors, directors, and composers to publish essays or grant interviews in order to advertise current projects. Such publications also generated advance publicity for upcoming releases—in this case pointing readers toward the second part of *Peter I*, which would be completed only after many delays in 1939. Yet in the USSR, these publications also functioned to define the propaganda value of the works in question, alerting their audiences to their "correct" interpretations and indicating how they were to be seen within the larger context of the official party line.

In this interview, Tolstoi speaks to the "common Soviet man" in demonstratively simple language, describing the significance of *Peter I* in the most straightforward and understandable of terms. He portrays Peter's epoch as an epic struggle for the Russian people's national independence—a struggle that demanded cultural and technological change in order to rebuff foreign aggression. Peter is seen as a visionary leader who was able to grasp the correct course of action to secure Russia's future. Tolstoi also implies an allegorical relationship between the Petrine epoch and Stalin's day by means of an understated, yet ingenious, step from discussion of the "Russian people" in the body of the interview to evocation of "the great Soviet people" in its conclusion. In short, Tolstoi's account informs readers that the film was about leadership in times of crisis and the exigencies and sacrifices that national defense demands of society—a message that could be expected to resonate well within the larger context of Stalin-era mass culture.

Of course, such publications advanced personal agendas as well. Tolstoi's invectives against various stock enemies of the Soviet historical establishment—fascist stooges, Trotskyites, and former members of RAPP[2]—reveal the extent to which Tolstoi felt that his Petrine project and his career remained vulnerable to attack. In this connection, his demonstrative mention of Stalin's personal involvement in the rehabilitation of Peter was clearly designed to send a message to his critics and rivals about the official sanction that his views enjoyed.

Anatolii Danat, "At Aleksei Tolstoi's"

Skorokhodovskii rabochii, 15 September 1937

We were very excited as we stepped into the home of the famous Soviet writer and talented "engineer of men's souls,"[3] Aleksei Nikolaevich Tolstoi.

His drawing room is striking it its elegance and simplicity. One's gaze is drawn to massive bookshelves made of dark wood. Behind beveled glass doors stand the gold-embossed spines of thousands of books.

Somewhere, a floorboard creaked. A deep male voice could be heard and then the imposing figure of Aleksei Tolstoi appeared in the doorway. He entered the room at a slow, confident pace, puffing at a long pipe. His face was calm and dignified. Aleksei Nikolaevich looks very fit and healthy—just days ago, he returned from a trip abroad and has now plunged back into his complicated literary work. Sizing us up with an attentive, penetrating glance, Aleksei Nikolaevich shook our hands in a friendly manner.

We explained the purpose of our sudden invasion of his quarters. He smiled and said, "Why not? Indeed, let's have a chat."

We sat down at a round table in comfortable, upholstered chairs. Aleksei Nikolaevich spoke slowly and calmly, mulling over every word:

"The idea of making the historical film *Peter I* initially came to me three years ago. In cooperation with the Distinguished Artist of the Republic Vladimir Mikhailovich Petrov, I set about writing the screenplay. We wanted

Figure 6. D. N. Goberman and M. O. Gol'dshtein's poster advertising V. M. Petrov's *Peter I* (part 1). Courtesy of the Russian State Library, Moscow.

to create for the screen the entire epoch of Peter I in three feature-length films: *Peter's Childhood, The Events at Narva,* and *Peter's Struggle for the Transformation of Russia.* Our plans and conceptions were expansive indeed.

Not a single truthful film has ever been made about Russian history until now—neither here nor anywhere else. Several years ago a film called *Peter I* was shown abroad, but it was total nonsense, a false film. So we—Director Petrov and I—decided to make a truthful, Soviet film about the epoch of Peter I.

However, we encountered serious obstacles from the very outset. The Trotskii-Bukharinite scum that had worked its way into the Lenkino[4] management tried to slander and stall our work with every trick in the book. They intentionally delayed the funds budgeted for the film.[5]

Fascist stooges raised a terrible hue and cry about *Peter I.* They attempted to impose on us their anti-Soviet, anti-historical understanding of Russian history, in particular regarding the Petrine epoch. Everywhere, the Trotskyites and their RAPP agents tried to defame my novel *Peter I.* Foaming at the mouth, they argued that Peter I was a malignancy and that his personality had to be stamped out.

The Trotskyites and RAPP critics denied the greatness of the Russian people. Repeating the worst clichés of the Pokrovskii "school,"[6] they simply erased the entirety of the Petrine epoch from history.[7]

It is only thanks to the personal involvement of Comrade Stalin that these Trotskyite intrigues met with utter defeat. As is well known, Comrade Stalin devotes an enormous amount of attention to questions of art and history. The recommendations of Comrades Stalin, Kirov, and Zhdanov on questions of history served as a guiding light for us in our creation of the image of Peter I, and in the correct interpretation of the Petrine period of Russian history.[8]

Iosif Vissarionovich went over our plans very attentively, approved them, and gave us directions, which became the foundation for our work.

In the course of these three years our draft of the screenplay changed dramatically. At first, the Lenkino management categorically refused to make a series of three feature-length films. They suggested that we portray the entire Petrine epoch in one film. This would have resulted in the complete collapse of our expansive conception for a large-scale historical film.

Comrade Petrov and I reworked the screenplay over and over, eliminating everything that was malignant and un-Soviet—everything that the RAPP critics and the Trotskyites had tried to force on us. Finally, we were allowed to make a two-part film. Not without considerable regret, we were forced to abandon our proposals for the first part of the project, *The Youth of Peter I*.[9]

The epoch of Peter I was one of the greatest pages in the history of the Russian people. Virtually the whole Petrine epoch was permeated with the Russian people's heroic struggle for their existence as a nation and independence. Dark, uncultured boyar Rus', with its backward technology and patriarchal beards, would have fallen to foreign invaders in no time. A revolution was necessary within the very life of the country in order to lift Russia up to the level of the cultured European countries. Peter accomplished this, and the Russian people were able to defend their independence.

Having completed and polished the screenplay, we encountered another, no less serious problem: selecting the right actors for the film. Casting the appropriate character type for Peter was especially difficult.

Vladimir Mikhailovich Petrov considered nearly 70,000 individuals before finally selecting the correct actors.[10] And I must say that he fulfilled this task marvelously.

The most difficult role of Peter I was entrusted to N. Simonov; the role of Catherine to People's Artist of the USSR A. Tarasova; the role of

Men'shikov to Distinguished Artist of the Republic M. Zharov; the role of Tsarevich Aleksei to Distinguished Artist of the Republic N. Cherkasov; the role of Sheremet'ev to People's Artist of the USSR M. Tarkhanov; and so on.

Major credit is due to Vladimir Mikhailovich, who spared neither time nor energy in portraying personalities that were true to the Petrine epoch. Individual scenes, episodes, and frames were shot and reshot thirty times over. It took only the smallest hint of falseness or exaggeration in the facial expression, movement, or conversational speech of this or that actor, and Comrade Petrov would order the entire scene to be shot over from the start without the slightest regret.

The battle scenes comprised the most difficult segments of the production, but thanks to the experience of Comrade Petrov, this work was carried out masterfully.

We are now at work on the second film, 35 percent of which has already been shot. A considerably greater number of actors will participate in this film, and a whole new series of characters will be introduced. Thirty-five hundred costumes are being sewn for the actors of part two of *Peter I*. In Kherson twenty Petrine-era ships are being built in order to film a battle at sea.

We aim to complete the second film in September of 1938...."

Aleksei Nikolaevich tapped his fingers on the table thoughtfully. His pipe had gone out. With an unhurried movement, he struck a spark with a piece of flint and, after exhaling a cloud of aromatic smoke, announced aloud to no one in particular:

"I think, all the same, that we will secure the completion and release of the first part of the project, *Peter's Youth*.[11] Patriarchal Rus' was radically transformed during the Petrine era. The great Soviet people should know the true history of their country."

Notes

1. A. Danat, "U Alekseia Tolstogo," *Skorokhodovskii rabochii*, 15 September 1937, 2–3, reprinted as "Beseda s rabochimi fabriki 'Skorokhod,'" in A. N. Tolstoi, *Polnoe sobranie sochinenii*, 15 vols. (Moscow: Khudozhestvennaia literatura, 1946–1953), 13:534–36. This translation is based on the original newspaper publication.

2. Critics associated with RAPP had hounded Tolstoi in the early 1930s. After RAPP was itself discredited and disbanded during the political realignment surrounding the creation of the Soviet Writers' Union, Tolstoi delighted in denouncing the organization in print.

3. Stalin termed Soviet writers the "engineers of men's souls" in October 1932 at a meeting of the organizational committee of the newly formed Soviet Writers' Union. The term had already become something of an official cliché by the 1934 writers' conference, where Central Committee member A. A. Zhdanov invoked it in his keynote address as part of his definition of the official literary method of Socialist Realism. Danat's use of the term to refer specifically to Tolstoi, along with his general obsequiousness and rapt fascination with Tolstoi's elegant dacha, testifies to the journalist's inexperience.

4. The Leningrad Film Studio.

5. This sentence and the one that precedes it were censored in 1949 when the interview was reprinted in Tolstoi's collected works.

6. On the denunciation of Pokrovskyian historiography, see chapter 3 in this volume.

7. In an earlier interview, Tolstoi gave a somewhat different account of the opposition they faced during the film's production: "The most serious and bitter debates concerned the image of Peter himself. A multitude of various staff 'film theoreticians' descended upon us with a pack of contradictory demands. The wobbly, hysterical Peter that they were pushing on us did not correspond at all to our conceptions. They demanded that we show the ultimate futility and defeat of all of Peter's transformational activity." See "Petr i kino," *Literaturnaia gazeta*, 30 March 1937, 6.

8. Stalin, Kirov, and Zhdanov's famous 1934 observations contained little mention of Peter the Great—see I. Stalin, A. Zhdanov, S. Kirov, "Zamechaniia po povodu konspekta uchebnika po 'Istorii SSSR,'" and I. Stalin, S. Kirov, A. Zhdanov, "Zamechaniia o konspekte uchebnika 'Novoi istorii,'" *Pravda*, 27 January 1936, 2; also RGASPI, f. 558, op. 1, dd. 3156, 3157. Tolstoi claimed in an earlier interview that it was actually "the discussion of *The Epic Heroes* that . . . defined the mission of the Soviet writer-historian and disarmed all the vulgarizers in this field of scholarship and art once and for all." Confirming what he would later tell *The Skorokhod Worker*, Tolstoi pointed to the implicit connection between Peter and his epoch: "The central idea of our film was and remains our intention to show the power of the great Russian people and the indomitable nature of their transformational spirit. We have no intention of reviving the trivial, schoolbook image of the 'carpenter on the throne' in our picture, but we also do not want to diminish the significance of a man who towered over his epoch." "Petr i kino," 6.

9. Tolstoi gives a slightly different title here to the first part of the project than he did in the opening paragraph. This first feature-length part of the proposed trilogy was never made.

10. Tolstoi's exaggerated estimate of the number of auditions was apparently borrowed from Petrov—see Vera Bryzgalova, "Beseda s rezhisserom fil'ma 'Petr I' —zasluzhennym artistom respubliki V. M. Petrovym," *Skorokhodovskii rabochii*, 15 September 1937, 3.

11. Here, Tolstoi offers a third, slightly different version of the title.

The Epic Heroes

5
Chronicle of a Poet's Downfall

Dem'ian Bednyi, Russian History, and *The Epic Heroes*

∽ A. M. Dubrovsky

Lenin's well-known appraisal of the Russian people as "a nation of Oblomovs" epitomized the Bolsheviks' views of the USSR's largest ethnic group during the early years of the Soviet "experiment."[1] Yet as the contributions to this volume demonstrate, this view began to fade from fashion early in the 1930s as Stalin gradually freed himself from the weight of the existing party line and its naïve faith in proletarian internationalism and world revolution. Instead, he charted a new course toward an ideology valorizing patriotism and state building, believing that the struggle for socialism and the interests of the country would be best promoted through the creation of a mighty superpower.

This major reorientation demanded a correspondingly new view of state history and the Russian national character. The present chapter examines some of the earliest evidence of Stalin's resolve to reverse early Soviet views on the Russian national past, drawn from the leader's interactions with the "official state poet" Dem'ian Bednyi during the early to mid-1930s. Bednyi's repeated errors in regard to this ideological about-face illustrate the sense of confusion that gripped the creative intelligentsia during these years.[2] Analysis of a number of Bednyi's artistic works, his emotional correspondence with Stalin, and an interview conducted with V. P. Stavskii in 1937 provides a revealing glimpse of how the revival of the Russian national past affected veteran radicals within the early Soviet cultural elite.

∽

A poet with a gift for both art and politics, Bednyi began his professional life writing verses in honor of Nicholas II before crossing over to the social democratic movement and ending up on the side of the victors in 1917. A good relationship with those in power even led Bednyi to live in the Kremlin for a time—an ironically appropriate turn of events for someone born with the last name Pridvorov (lit.: "of the court"). Widespread recognition soon followed, due to Bednyi's distinctive approach to poetry that combined wry wit with a colloquial style borrowed from the fables of I. A. Krylov. Lenin repeatedly extolled the poet's talents, and L. D. Trotskii praised him as no less than "a Bolshevik armed with poetry"[3]—endorsements that made Bednyi one of the leading members of the creative intelligentsia during the early Soviet years. Always ready to blur the line between art and propaganda, he played a prominent role in anti-religious campaigns during the mid-1920s and obediently attacked Trotskii, G. E. Zinov'ev, and their supporters when the time came.[4] It would be an understatement to say that Bednyi was just well-known during the 1920s and early 1930s—he was

Figure 7. Detail from cover art of D. Bednyi's book *O pisatel'skom trude* (Moscow, 1931).

famous. In the eyes of his readership, he was the proletarian poet par excellence, and his work was seen as the party line set to verse.

In a series of newspaper feuilletons during the fall of 1930, Bednyi trained his sights on the Russian national character, which he viewed as a legacy of the "accursed" imperial past. Such a theme was in keeping with the agitational propaganda of the 1920s, and *Pravda* willingly granted Bednyi dozens of column inches in which to pillory the ancien régime. In one piece, provocatively entitled "Get Down Off the Hearth,"[5] he wrote:

Уклон этот жуток,
С ним—совсем не до шуток:
Он—наш кровный, прилипчивый
    свой!
Он—наследие всей дооктябрьской
    культуры!
У нас расслабление всей волевой
    Мускулатуры!
Мы—рванчи:
Мы, рванувши, с надрыва
    шатаемся,
За брюхо хватаемся.
—И соломенные силачи,—
Отпарившись в баньке, храпим на
    печке.
Храпим и сердито бормочем:
—Прорывы на фронте рабочем?
Текучесть . . . ? Нельзя без утечки . . .
Не тяните нас с печки . . . !

Ничего, что в истории русской
    гнилой
Бесконечные рюхи, сплошные
    провалы,—
А на нас посмотрим:
На весь свет самохвалы!
Чудо—богатыри!

This deviation is bruising,
And not at all amusing:
An inheritance passed down the family
    tree!
A pre-revolutionary cultural legacy!
Our will-power is utterly spent
As are our physiques!
We're such creeps:
We teeter at the edge, having gone way
    too far,
Clutching at our guts, as we are.
—Each of us a mighty straw man—
A snooze on the hearth—such is the
    plan.
Loud snoring followed by an angry
    grunt:
—a break-through on the workers'
    front?
Labor turnover . . . ? It's such a
    waste . . .
Don't pull us off the hearth—no need
    for haste . . . !

It's understandable with Russia's
    history of rot
To have endless rips, gaping chasms,
    and whatnot—
Just take a look at us:
Praising ourselves, making such fuss!
Epic heroes—so miraculous![6]

In another column, he developed these themes further while reproaching workers who were apparently responsible for a train accident near the town of Pererva:

Работяги—мигали расейского типа	Menial workers, Russia's darlings of old
Липа!	Mold!
Липа!	Mold!
Зто липа взросла на расейском болоте	This mold was nurtured in Old Russia's murk
У нее есть своя родовая черта:	Passing on a trait that we've retained:
Недобросовестность в каждой работе	Irresponsibility regarding work Turns out to be deeply ingrained.[7]
Испокон сердцевине ее привита.	

Bednyi's pieces met with initial fanfare, especially his denigration of Old Russian traditions and his celebration of the Revolution's break with the past. According to the poet, V. M. Molotov[8] praised his work "to the skies" and urged him to publish "Get Down Off the Hearth" as a pamphlet designed for shock workers.[9] In an elated mood, Bednyi met with Stalin, expecting further compliments, but instead came away from the meeting upset and confused. Later, he described the incident in a letter to the general secretary in the following way: "I expected praise from the man to whom I had always related with the most personal affection.... I expected to be scratched behind the ears. But I got them boxed instead: there's no way in hell 'Get Down Off the Hearth' will do! [*ni k chertu 'Slezai s pechki' ne goditsia*].... I'd been doused with cold water. Worse: I'd been derailed. I was paralyzed. I couldn't write. I was only barely able to scratch something out for November 7th."[10]

Caught off guard by Stalin's reaction, Bednyi struggled to make sense of it. Guessing that "Get Down Off the Hearth" and "Pererva" must have implied too much continuity between the pre- and post-revolutionary eras, he attempted to correct things with a new *feuilleton*—"Without Mercy"—that would be more explicit about the differences between the Russian past and Soviet present. As Bednyi would later confess to Stalin, he was unsure about the proper tone to take in this historical discussion and was dismayed that the editors at *Pravda* failed to offer anything but contradictory advice regarding "Without Mercy":

> I worked as if in a labor camp. It was difficult to write with such self-doubt, compounded as it was by the flu. But I finished it. I turned it in to the press.

> At about 12 midnight, a hitch came up at the editorial offices: Iaroslavskii[11] felt that the introductory portion was too historical and weakened the second, agitational section. Couldn't we get rid of the introductory section? I didn't object, but Iaroslavskii, sensing my disappointed expression and realizing that this would pain me, said, "Oh well, let it go as it is. After all, it is already laid out in type." Iaroslavskii departed [for home]. I was left with mixed emotions. I knew something that Iaroslavskii didn't know: I would have you as my meticulous reader. And what if I would not be able to win over this reader? Having thought it over, I categorically announced to Mekhlis and Savel'ev[12] that I was going to cut the first section out! There was great commotion due to the late hour—now it'd have to be laid out again. Iaroslavskii was informed. He summoned me to the telephone and forcefully told me to "stop being so capricious," as he put it. Let the whole *feuilleton* run. It wasn't hard to talk me into it. And that was that.[13]

Bednyi's letter reveals his sense of complete confusion concerning the proper line to take in this poem. Even more importantly, this passage reveals the poet's attempt to shirk responsibility for its publication—particularly the historical section—knowing that it was this new excursus into the national past that had again succeeded in angering Stalin.

Appearing in print on 5 December 1930, "Without Mercy" elaborated upon "Get Down Off the Hearth" and "Pererva," assailing the pre-revolutionary Russian past with thunder and lightning. Among other things, Bednyi disputed the traditional characterization of Kuz'ma Minin and Dmitrii Pozharskii as defenders of the fatherland during the early seventeenth century. Describing them instead as bribe takers and embezzlers, he wrote: "Patriots for all of eternity / Have been a failure when it comes to the treasury: / Patriotism is inseparable from thievery." Condemning Minin and Pozharskii as the butchers of the Time of Troubles, Bednyi suggested that they had been as reactionary and misguided as the modern White émigré movement abroad or wreckers at home. More generally, "Without Mercy" assailed the widespread misery of the pre-revolutionary era and ridiculed the notion of patriotism through the use of the comical neologism "patri-autism" (*patrevoticheskii*).[14]

Incensed by the content of the column, Stalin subjected the proletarian poet to blistering criticism the next day in a Central Committee Secretariat resolution drafted with Molotov and L. M. Kaganovich. Deeming Bednyi's work provocative and divisive, this censure focused on the poet's claim that "laziness" and "sitting on the hearth" were "Russian national characteristics" and reprimanded him for his failure to understand that "in the past, there had been *two* Russias: a revolutionary Russia and a counter-revolutionary Russia"[15] and for his inability to realize that Soviet power "depends, first and foremost, upon the Russian working class, the most active and revolutionary segment of the worldwide working class."[16]

Such an official, bureaucratic denunciation left the normally savvy Bednyi paralyzed with frustration and fear. Stalin's rebuke seemed arbitrary and undeserved—there had been no mention in the press of a change in the party's view of the tsarist past, and Bednyi had no reason to suspect that such a turnabout was imminent. Unable to grasp the nature of his political error, he concluded that he was the victim of an innocent misunderstanding that had somehow acquired a life of its own. Picking up a pen and paper, he complained bitterly to Stalin:

> a living voice either ought to have complimented my work or, in a friendly and convincing way, pointed out my "distortions" [*krivizna*]. Instead, I received a memo from the Secretariat. This memo highlighted with Bengal fire my isolation and [sense of impending] doom. I was also given a dressing down at *Pravda* and then at *Izvestiia*. I am a failure. After this, I will not be able to publish, not only in these two papers, but everywhere, so the threat goes. . . . For twenty years I've been a cricket in the Bolshevik hearth, but now I'm to get down off of it. My time has come, I guess. [. . .] Perhaps it's not possible to be a major Russian poet without having one's career end in catastrophe?[17]

As noted above, amid this melodrama Bednyi attempted to avoid blame for the fiasco by noting that his work had received the approval of party hierarchs such as Molotov and Iaroslavskii. He also invoked Lenin's authority, recounting that when he had inadvertently made a political mistake in the early 1920s, Lenin had forgiven him and allowed him to correct the error.[18] Lapsing back into hyperbole toward the conclusion of the letter, Bednyi begged not to be blacklisted. He even quoted a passage from the Bible in his final request for deliverance, prefacing the line "O my Father, if it be possible, let this cup pass from me" with a hesitant apology, and then ending the letter with the rest of this prayer of supplication: "Nevertheless, let it be not as I, but as thou wilt."[19]

Sent to Stalin on 8 December 1930, Bednyi's letter angered Stalin enough for him to personally respond to the poet just four days later. Eventually published in the general secretary's *Works*, this letter appeared in print only after the removal of a significant portion of the introduction, which chastised Bednyi for a variety of errors and misdeeds. According to the archival originals, Stalin's rebuke was expressed in the harshest of terms:

> You set C[omrade] Iaroslavskii against me ... Further on, you set C[omrade] Molotov against me, with assurances that he *did not find anything erroneous* in your "Get Down Off the Hearth" column. ... What's the point of setting C[omrade] Molotov against me?[20] There can be only one point: to suggest that the Central Committee Secretariat's decision is in fact not really that body's decision, but the personal opinion of Stalin, who is apparently giving out his own opinions as if they were the decisions of the Central Committee Secretariat. This is too much, C[omrade] Dem'ian. This is simply dirty trickery [*nechistoplotno*] ... I remember now how several months ago you told me by telephone that "it seems like there is some disagreement between Stalin and Molotov, Molotov is undercutting Stalin's position," etc. You ought to remember that I rudely interrupted you at that time and asked you not to indulge in gossip. I interpreted this "joke" of yours at the time as an unpleasant episode. Now I see that it was a gamble of yours, designed to play on our apparent differences and squeeze out some sort of profit. Try to play more fairly [*pobol'she chistoplotnosti*], C[omrade] Dem'ian.[21]

Having assailed the poet for his attempt to deflect blame for the affair, Stalin then turned to Bednyi's provocative use of the word *policy* in expressing his fears about being blacklisted. Ridiculing the poet's panic with a strong dose of sarcasm, Stalin pointed out to him the essence of his political error:

> So there exists, it seems, some sort of special policy "in relation to Dem'ian Bednyi." What is this policy—what does it consist of? This policy, it turns out, consists of measures to force "major Russian poets" "to end their careers in catastrophe". ... So this is the level of your faith in the Central Committee. I did not think that you were capable, even in a hysterical condition, of voicing such anti-party rot. ...
>
> You have developed a precise and effective critique of the deficiencies of everyday life and existence in the USSR, criticism that is mandatory and necessary, but you have become obsessed with it. This obsession has begun to transform your works into slander against the USSR. ... The revolutionary workers of all countries unanimously hail the Soviet working class and, most of all, the *Russian* working class, which is in the avant garde of the Soviet workers. ... The leaders of the revolutionary workers of the world thirst to study the instructive history of the Russian working class, its past and the

Russian past, knowing that besides the reactionary Russia, there was a revolutionary Russia as well. . . . All of this sows in the hearts of the Russian workers a feeling of revolutionary national pride (and how could it not!) that is capable of moving mountains and performing miracles.[22]

In other words, Stalin equated the history of the USSR with the history of Russia and indicated that disrespect in regard to the latter was no longer to be permitted. Bednyi's transgression was that he had "announced to the whole world that in the past, Russia had served as a vessel of rottenness and neglect."[23]

Stalin's letter to Bednyi reveals that as early as 1930, he had already lost interest in characterizing the old regime as backward and chauvinist. To underscore the importance of this turnabout in the party line, Stalin quoted to Bednyi an extended passage from Lenin's little-known 1913 article "On the National Pride of the Great Russians" in order to emphasize that Russian national interests were not only vital but also coincided with proletarian interests, both Russian and non-Russian. Declaring that "this means that you must turn back to the old, Leninist path, *no matter what*," he then ended the letter rather roughly. "There is no other way. . . . Is that clear? You demanded a clarification from me. I trust that I have given you an adequately clear answer."[24]

Attempting to save a desperate situation, Bednyi tried to correct his error in the same way that he had in the early 1920s—by writing a poetic apology to his readers. Devoted to the twenty-fifth anniversary of the 1905 uprising in Moscow, the poem was entitled "On the Heroic:"

Друзьями мне было резонно замечено,	My friends have resolutely observed,
что много мною добра искалечено,—	That what I've spoiled ought to be preserved—
что я с манерой самой беззастенчивою	It's the Motherland's history that I defame
Родную старину развенчиваю . . .	And all this without a hint of shame . . .
—Россия гнила на корню—	—Russia's rotten on the vine!—
И давай, и давай разносить ее хульно.	Let's leave her to her sorry fate.
Ошибка не в том, что я ее черню	My mistake wasn't just my critical line
А в том, что черню—всю, огульно.	But that I didn't try to discriminate.

Ведь Расея нам все-таки мать,	After all, isn't Old Russia still our mother?
Нас, детей, надо как понимать?	What about us, her children, my brother?
От хульного, мол, семени	Is it, as they say, that from a bad seed
Не жди доброго племени?	It's hopeless to expect a decent breed?
Откуда ж тогда	From where—pray tell—then
от какой мамаши	From which mother hen
Пролетарии наши . . . ?	Do we get our proletarian . . . ?

Such was Bednyi's attempt to embrace the line articulated in the general secretary's letter. Also evident in this new work was a series of images designed to ward off further accusations of political deviancy. For instance:

Я в прошлое вспомню—в глазах чернота!	When I remember the past, before me it grows dark!
И ругань моя неумеренна!	And my abuse is without compare!
Но это не значит, что глаз острота	But this doesn't meant that my once sharp
Мною утеряна.	Eyes are now beyond repair.
Зто значит: в них есть кривизна,	Instead, there must be a distortion.
Вот та, что в стеклах увеличительных,	One that in the magnifying glass,
Не правизна,	Is not rightism,
Не левизна,	Nor leftism,
А художественная кривизна	But an artistic distortion
(Она доходит до размеров значительных).	(Which sometimes assumes considerable proportions).

Wary of the risk he was taking with "On the Heroic," Bednyi reminded his readers of other famous cultural figures who had been punished for unintentional political errors:

Через глаз художника проходят явления	Through the eyes of an artist, all action
С каким-то углом преломления.	Comes at a certain angle of refraction.
(У сатириков угол "уродства," "изъяна")	(The satirists' angle is "ugliness" and "flaw.")

Так было во все времена—	It's always been like this, as if by
От Аристофана	law—²⁵
И Лукиана	First Aristophanes, then
До Гоголя и Щедрина,	Lukian
От Щедрина—до меня, до Демьяна.	then Gogol' and Shchedrin,
У Щедрина ведь картина былого	And then from Shchedrin on to me,
Не верна слово в слово,	Bednyi.
Но—с учетом уклона—верна.	Perhaps Shchedrin's view of the past,
	Isn't great from first page to last,
	But it's correct if you look past his artistry.

Although the archival evidence indicates that the party hierarchy seriously considered allowing this mea culpa to be published in *Pravda*, lingering doubts apparently stymied its appearance at the last moment.²⁶

Bednyi appears to have become something of a social pariah after this series of scandals and found himself virtually excluded from the party press. But as luck would have it, this enforced silence would last less than six months: as the Cultural Revolution in the arts climaxed and then began to wane, the radicalized atmosphere of 1930 gave way to greater artistic toleration. May 1931 marked Bednyi's twentieth year of service to the Bolshevik cause, and *Pravda* decided to mark the anniversary with an article about the poet. Alongside this fairly routine piece, Bednyi was allowed to append a new composition entitled "Let's Straighten It Out!!" Another attempt to apologize for his previous mistakes, this piece displayed none of Bednyi's earlier efforts to excuse his apparent lack of patriotism. Instead, it focused exclusively on the celebration of the Russian national past, indicating that Bednyi had finally grasped the nature of the authorities' objections to his recent work:

Что в былом есть и то, чем мы вправе гордиться:	If there is anything from the past that ought to have worth:
Не убог он, тот край, где могла народиться	It's that our land is fertile and able to give birth
Вот такая, как ныне ведущая нас	To those who now lead us—that is,
Революционная партия масс,—	The revolutionary party of the masses,—
Не бездарный народ дал—не только отечеству,	These are talented people who've now defined

А всему человечеству—
Славный ряд образцов,
Беззаветных борцов
За свободу, за творчество
    социализма,—
Беззаветных борцов
Против банков, против дворцов,
Против гнета царизма
Против хищно-разгульного
    капитализма . . .
	Not just for our fatherland, but for all
	    of mankind—
	An array of role models, all glory and
	    light—
	Selflessly committed to the fight
	In the name of freedom and the
	    creativity of socialism—
	Selflessly committed to the fight
	Against the banks and mansions of
	    the Right,
	Against the oppression of tsarism
	Against predatory capitalism.

In this contrite composition, Bednyi attempted to set certain key citations from Lenin's article on Russian national pride into poetic form, specifically his pronouncement that "the Great Russian nation . . . has shown itself capable of giving mankind great role models to follow in the struggle for freedom and socialism." Explaining his past mistakes, Bednyi confessed:

Я—злой.
Я крестьянски ушиблен Россией
    былой.
Когда я выхожу против старой
    кувалды,
То порою держать меня надо за
    фалды,
Чтобы я, разойдясь, не хватил
    сгоряча
Мимо слов Ильича . . .
	I'm fuming mad.
	Old Russia hurt my peasant soul bad.
	But when I sally forth against the
	    hammer and nails,
	Be sure to grab me by the coattails,
	So that in my passion, I do not
	    overreach
	And neglect the words of Il'ich . . .[27]

Thus Bednyi finally acknowledged that he had misjudged the party line and had failed to grasp the true meaning of Lenin's words. Humbled by this experience, he announced that in the future, he would rely on his readership to help keep him true "to the Leninist path." More than just an allusion to Stalin's letter, these lines indicate that Bednyi had lost confidence in his ability to judge the direction in which Bolshevik ideology was headed. Subsequent events would confirm these misgivings.

Three years passed. During this time period, the party hierarchy made a number of policy decisions that may be seen in retrospect as signaling the imminent rehabilitation of a patriotic, etatist understanding of Russian history. Efforts were made to improve the teaching of history in the public schools and promote the creation of a single, standardized history textbook.[28] Official support was also afforded to literary figures like Aleksei Tolstoi who were embracing this new focus in their creative endeavors. Aside from this, however, neither historians nor writers received any concrete directives on how to go about rehabilitating Russian historical themes. Substantial questions remained about how Russian history was to be approached and who was to be valorized as its heroes.[29] Such circumstances guaranteed that ideological mistakes and misunderstandings would continue to mar the emerging party line. Among the first to err in this regard was none other than Dem'ian Bednyi.

In approximately the middle of 1934, the director of Moscow's Kamernyi Theater, A. Ia. Tairov, turned to Bednyi with a proposal to revive *The Epic Heroes*, a comic opera that had been composed by A. P. Borodin in the mid-nineteenth century. At some point in 1867, this opera had been staged in the Bolshoi Theater and then promptly forgotten, to be recovered only after the Revolution.[30] Tairov, however, was sold on the brilliance of the production's musical accompaniment (with elements from A. Serov, Zh. Offenbakh, D. Rossini, and others), as well as the genius and talent of Borodin himself. As Bednyi would later explain to the secretary of the Soviet Writers' Union, V. P. Stavskii, after *The Epic Heroes* exploded into scandal, it was Tairov who had approached *him* with the idea of reviving the opera.[31]

"Efim Alekseevich," Tairov said to Bednyi, according to the latter's account, "it's a world-class event—some epic music has been found and it absolutely must be brought to realization. Who, besides you, could provide us with a text[?]'" To be sure, Tairov did not actually ask Bednyi to write a new libretto, so much as he asked the poet to update what had originally been written in the nineteenth century by the St. Petersburg litterateur V. A. Krylov.[32] As A. Koonen would later recall, Tairov "was obsessed with the notion of bringing this forgotten opera into the light.... *The Epic Heroes* was an amusing, silly tale about four foolish, lazy, and cowardly *faux*-epic heroes—Avos'ka, Nebos'ka, Chudilo, and Kupilo—who masqueraded as genuine epic heroes." In her memoirs, Koonen notes one other very important aspect of the affair. Tairov had commissioned Bednyi to rewrite the libretto at the request of P. M. Kerzhentsev, the chair of Sovnarkom's All-Union Committee for Artistic Affairs.[33]

This, of course, was not the first time that pre-revolutionary historical themes had been the subject of satire on the Soviet stage. During the waning days of the Cultural Revolution in 1932, the Theater of Satire and Comedy in Leningrad had staged *The Baptism of Rus'*, a burlesque of Kievan Prince Vladimir's selection of a state religion in the year 988. The piece focused on the prince's difficulty in choosing between Eastern Orthodoxy, Roman Catholicism, Islam, and Judaism. According to the reviews, *The Baptism of Rus'* was "musical buffoonery" that wasn't actually very satirical at all, being "predicated on the grotesque" instead. Critics wrote approvingly, however, about its

> array of bold projections into contemporary times, which raise the political relevance of the play. Epic heroes of yore are cast in the role of the tsarist gendarme Okhranka, [while] Nightingale-the-Brigand[34] becomes the personification of the landed merchantry and Byzantium acts as a stand-in for the fascist West. Prince Vladimir himself is cast as a general representative of the autocracy and not surprisingly assumed the features of the second-to-last tsar-gendarme[35] toward the end of the show. Mikula Selianinovich, the personification of "Orthodox Rus'," is portrayed as if physically weak and "downtrodden," as well as completely intoxicated, pronouncing mixed-up, incomprehensible words.

According to its critics, this dark play's only major shortcoming was its "insufficient social and anti-religious content."[36] It is possible that it was with thoughts of this earlier show that Kerzhentsev decided that the libretto of *The Epic Heroes* might benefit from the aid of a veteran atheist agitator like Bednyi.

At first, Bednyi seems not to have been interested in the project. As he would later recount to Stavskii, the opera was weak and clichéd:

> [T]he text was hopeless. There was some sort of theme about epic heroes, juxtaposed against a peasant named Foma. This simpleton was a foolish half-wit, the sort of simpleton you find in fairy tales, and—as in the fables—even though he does foolish things, they [always] seem to work out. This simpleton even walks around with a fly-swatter and when he hits the epic heroes with it, they all fall over. In a word, it was nonsense. I said to Tairov: "I can't freshen up this text—it's rubbish," and I refused to take part in it. A few months passed. He was calling me constantly, but I stubbornly refused. Finally, he summoned me to his office in the theater and Litovskii[37] was there and he began to tell me that it was a work of genius and that it was necessary to take it to the people. Again I refused. Well, I decided to think about it. I

invited the critic Braude over and asked him whether it would be possible to do something new with the subject. He answered no, it wouldn't.[38]

Whether Bednyi really refused to participate as stubbornly as he indicated to Stavskii, or whether—as one of the most prominent scholars of Bednyi's work has written—he "eagerly signed on to the affair,"[39] is somewhat hard to say. In any case, according to Bednyi himself, he eventually agreed to work with Tairov on the show:

> I thought about it a little bit more.... I thought to myself, perhaps I'll take up Prince Vladimir's drunken debauch following his baptism.[40] There they were, indulging themselves, as it were, after the baptism and then they became frightened. I wanted the farce to be farcical, but at the same time [I also wanted] it to resemble history. I therefore read the-devil-only-knows how many books in order to master fairy tale exposition! Then it seemed to me that I had found a brilliant way out: they weren't [really] epic heroes, but degenerate epic heroes. Back to the chronicles—I based [my interpretation] on the chronicles. And it seemed to me like this was the way it was in folktales, too. Again, I looked over all the folktales. In the folktales, Prince Vladimir crawls on all fours, Nightingale-the-Brigand whistles, and everyone falls over. Thus from my point of view at that time, it had to be highlighted that these were not epic heroes, but nonsense—"Kupilos" and "Chudilos," not epic heroes. But it was also necessary to have an element of heroism. I looked to folklore for that. There I got mixed up in folktales and brigands' songs. I thought that this is where I'd insert the heroism [into the opera]. It seemed to me that heroism was everywhere—in all the folktales, in Russian literature, and in the theater, brigands were always marked by an artistic, heroic presentation.[41]

So with his interpretation now revolving around the brigands, Bednyi returned to Tairov and got to work in earnest. "After we came to an agreement, I spun about and wrote and wrote and then gave it to Tairov. I told him that this thing was still a work-in-progress and that it should be left to sit for a while. But he hurried it into production as fast as possible. They snuck it over to Litovskii. Litovskii sanctioned it and called me to tell me what a marvelous thing I had created."[42]

Koonen remembered things somewhat differently: "Dem'ian Bednyi inserted an array of innovations into the plot that did not all appeal to Aleksandr Iakovlevich [Tairov]. He thought that they vulgarized the play, removing the fairy tale atmosphere that he had liked so much. But it was too late to redo anything."⁴³ Perhaps Tairov reconciled himself to the antireligious, agitational note that Bednyi had interpolated into the Krylov-Borodin creation by assuming that this was what Kerzhentsev had wanted in the first place.

Unaware of Tairov's misgivings, the poet cautiously circulated the text of the libretto among a number of authoritative people. He would later claim that everyone had seen the manuscript and had signed-off on it: "it [even] made it to Litovskii, Kerzhentsev, and Boiarskii.⁴⁴ In general, the wretched creature crawled all over the place. And the only thing that I ever overheard was that Kerzhentsev had said that it was 'frightfully boring and vulgar.' I fixed the text along those lines while working with the actors. I took into account Kerzhentsev's comment, although I was furious. 'How is it possible that I could have written something boring[?]' And I thought about how I could make it more amusing."⁴⁵

On 24 October 1936, Bednyi published an article in the press entitled "*The Epic Heroes* (On its Première in the Kamernyi Theater)."⁴⁶ As he revealed later to Stavskii, "I was so sure that the play was flawless and had no potential problems of any sort that I wrote an article and printed it in *Pravda*. I went and explained the whole concept of the play."⁴⁷ The article was intended to draw attention to the upcoming première and went on at considerable length about the intentions that underlay the work:

> The subject develops along three lines: the heroic, the lyric and the comic. The heroic line is expressed by the "honest brigands and epic heroes of the forest." The lyrical expression is supplied by the epic hero, Nightingale Budimirovich, who leads a successful struggle with brigandage, but loses the fight because of his affairs of the heart—the brigands are able to catch him in the confusion of his wedding banquet. The comic line is fulfilled by the well-known but cowardly Prince Vladimir and his group of "epic heroes," who are brave enough while drinking around a table or at banquets, but are seized with panic when danger appears.
>
> All the action of this opera is concentrated around two interconnected issues. First, the brigand Ugar, if it is the last thing he ever does, has to get his comrades away from "Nightingale-the-Epic-Hero," who has captured them. Second, Prince Vladimir has to deal with the inescapable fact that "the Russians have a great love of drink."⁴⁸ In connection with the baptism of Rus', the prince throws such a party that this solemn event takes on the appearance of a "drunken debauch"—the prince and the drunken epic heroes throw

themselves in the waters [of the Dniepr], drown many people in the river and even try to drown Perun. Sobering up and frightened by the wrath of Perun, Vladimir makes a sacrifice in order to determine whether Perun is still a god or not. And then there are the Greeks as well, who foist upon the prince a questionable Greek princess with an entourage of questionable maidens.

Bednyi concluded the article with the optimistic statement that "if this staging will in any way make even a minor step toward the creation and confirmation of a popular comic opera [tradition] here [in the USSR], it will be the sort of cultural success that all the participants of this extremely difficult affair have aimed for."[49]

Yet in the last days before the première, all was not as routine and by the book as this article suggests. As Bednyi later told Stavskii:

The next day, they received the play at Glaviskusstvo.[50] I took a look at it too. Something about it seemed boring to me. I thought about what I might do with it, as it was somewhat boring. They told me: "Don't you see that in the theatrical production, what you've written will change a bit in form and a somewhat different contour will become apparent[?] For instance, the epic heroes are so caricatured that it is almost excessive. But the brigands—they are just brigands, nothing more. They ought to be made somewhat more noble." Right there, in the theater, I wrote fifteen lines, as it was necessary to emphasize that one should feel sorry for the honest brigands and that these epic heroes weren't the famous ones. I then added a line as an apotheosis: ". . . Where are they, the epic heroes? Can these fellows really be *the* epic heroes? No, we must cultivate our epic heroes from among the people."[51]

Aside from such nuances, Bednyi remained confident in *The Epic Heroes* and expected the Soviet public to respond to it with great enthusiasm. Success was important because it would signal an end to the creative slump in which the poet had found himself since the early 1930s.

Something else, however, lay in store for the poet. According to Tairov, Molotov came to the première but stormed out after only one act, cursing: "Utter nonsense! The epic heroes were extraordinary people, after all!"[52] As Bednyi narrated it:

When Molotov came and watched the play and then boiled over, only then did I realize: "Good gracious! [*Mat' chestnaia!*] We've valorized a bunch of brigands!" . . .[I]n relation to the baptism, I didn't think that anything was amiss. Looking at the epic heroes as a farcical caricature, I also portrayed the baptism as a farce—I didn't see that it couldn't be approached as a farce. First of all, this was the old spirit of an anti-religious agitator inside of me talking, and then it was also true that my interpretation was backed up by some serious knowledge, as I had been guided by none other than the work of Professor Golubinskii. He writes of the baptism and the choice of faiths with aspersion: "I can't help but conclude that it is just a legend. Such legends about the acceptance and choosing of faiths are found in other countries."[53] Thus I approached it as if it were just a legend. . . . In a word, I only now realize that the baptism slipped past me.[54]

The play was banned within days. On 13 November 1936, Sovnarkom's All-Union Committee for Artistic Affairs drafted a resolution entitled "On the Play *The Epic Heroes*, by Dem'ian Bednyi," which was confirmed by the Politburo on the following day. These resolutions indicted Bednyi for casting brigands as "positive revolutionary elements;" for wantonly blackening an epic whose characters "are, in the popular mind, the incarnation of the Russian people's heroic qualities;" and for producing "an anti-historical and insulting treatment of the baptism of Rus', which was a genuinely positive stage in the history of the Russian people." *The Epic Heroes* was summarily purged from official repertoire lists as a work "alien to Soviet art."[55]

One day later, *Pravda* published an article by Kerzhentsev entitled "The Falsification of the People's Past (On *The Epic Heroes*, by Dem'ian Bednyi)." Lashing out viciously at the poet—and at his own deputy, Litovskii—Kerzhentsev essentially paraphrased the devastating terms of the above-mentioned resolutions. The fact that Kerzhentsev had been on vacation in Paris and London while the opera was being readied for the stage and had been sorely embarrassed by the scandal went unmentioned.[56]

These two resolutions, complemented by the broadside in *Pravda*, marked the start of a major ideological campaign during November 1936 that resonated until late 1938.[57] Bednyi's "brigand-like theory of Russian history" and his deprecation of the people's past were savaged both in print and at public gatherings, ranging from an expanded session of the Theater Workers' Committee at the All-Union Committee for Artistic Affairs to a meeting of the Central Committee of the Artistic Workers' Union. Bednyi's name even came up at a session of the Supreme Soviet, where A. A. Zhdanov accused him of behaving like a double-dealer and "insulting the history of the Russian people."[58]

Then came the Soviet Writers' Union, a body in which Bednyi had played a prominent role since its founding in 1934. Clearly, this institution had to react to the incident involving its ideologically wayward member. Speaking at a 21 November 1938 meeting of the Poets' Section, A. A. Surkov announced that "Bednyi's play is infused throughout with a vulgar relationship toward historical issues. Fascist literature says that Russia has neither nationhood nor statehood. In connection with such a reading, Dem'ian Bednyi's entire conceptualization takes on a politically harmful direction, essentializing and vulgarizing the entire Russian historical process."[59] Surkov did not mention the questionable taste or the biting humor with which Bednyi had infused his libretto, nor the forced nature of the subject, its primitiveness, or the inexpressiveness of the language in which it was written. Such issues were no longer important. The question had become purely ideological.

Aftershocks continued to be felt for years. Even after Bednyi's subsequent expulsion from the party, A. A. Fadeev felt further measures were necessary and declared at a meeting of the presidium of the Soviet Writers' Union that Bednyi "had either intentionally or unintentionally followed the fascists' ideology by attempting to sully the people's heroes of the past and by [painting] an untrue picture of Russian history."[60] It was at this meeting that Bednyi received the ultimate coup de grâce: formal expulsion from the Soviet Writers' Union.

Surveying the campaign against *The Epic Heroes* in the press and in transcripts like those quoted above, it seems necessary to credit the "engineers of men's souls," the masters of the creative word, with the most serious attacks against Bednyi. That said, the campaign itself was precipitated from above. Stalin and the party hierarchy had decided that it was necessary to promote a newly patriotic, etatist version of the official line—an ideological position that derived its legitimacy and authority from the imperial Russian past. They made an example of Bednyi because his literary work had lagged dangerously behind the times, remaining heavily influenced by the radicalism of the 1920s.

Excluded from the party, the Soviet Writers' Union, the press, and the public school curriculum after 1938, Bednyi lapsed into obscurity. Attempts on his part to at least partially restore his reputation came to naught, and in 1945 he died.[61] The poet's ideological error had, in other words, proven to be fatal, and his farce had turned into a tragedy. Bednyi, a participant in no few ideological campaigns, had now become the victim of one himself, and the hounding that he was forced to endure after 1936 justified with great irony the literary pseudonym he had adopted decades earlier: poor fellow.

Notes

For an earlier version of this chapter, see my "Kak Dem'ian Bednyi ideologicheskuiu oshibku sovershil," in *Otechestvennaia kul'tura i istoricheskaia nauka XVIII–XX vekov* (Briansk: BGPU, 1996), 143–51.

1. On V. I. Lenin's use of the Oblomov reference, see his *Polnoe sobranie sochinenii*, 55 vols. (Moscow: Gos. izd-vo polit. lit-ry, 1958–1970), 43:228; 44:365, 398; 45:3–4, 13. Oblomov is the archetype of a passive and vacillating nineteenth-century landowner created by I. A. Goncharov.

2. While not explicitly an examination of Soviet subjectivity per se, this article is informed by studies including Jochen Hellbeck, "Fashioning the Stalinist Soul: The Diary of Stepan Podlubnyi," *Jahrbücher für Geschichte Osteuropas* 44, no. 4 (1996): 233–73; Golfo Alexopoulos, "Portrait of a Con Artist as a Soviet Man," *Slavic Review* 57, no. 4 (1998): 774–90.

3. V. I. Lenin, "V redaktsiiu gazety 'Pravda' [1913]," 48:182; G. Lelevich, "Dem'ian Bednyi," in *Bol'shaia sovetskaia entsiklopediia*, 65 vols. (Moscow: Sovetskaia entsiklopediia, 1926–1947), 5:171–74.

4. See D. Bednyi, *Polnoe sobranie sochinenii*, ed. L. S. Sosnovskii (Moscow: Gos. izd-vo, 1930).

5. Russian peasant huts were typically dominated by a massive fireplace and chimney that during the long winters provided warmth and a comfortable place to sleep.

6. D. Bednyi, "Slezai s pechki," *Pravda*, 7 September 1930, 5. For the draft sent to Stalin, see RGASPI, f. 558, op. 11, d. 701, ll. 52–71.

7. D. Bednyi, "Pererva," *Pravda*, 11 September 1930, 4. For the draft sent to Stalin, see RGASPI, f. 558, op. 11, d. 701, ll. 74–88. "Mold" here means false or fake.

8. V. M. Molotov, politburo member and chair of Sovnarkom, the All-Union Council of People's Commissars.

9. D. Bednyi, *Slezai s pechki: Pamiatka udarniku* (Moscow and Leningrad: GIZ, 1930).

10. RGASPI, f. 558, op. 11, d. 702, l. 5, published in *Schast'e literatury: Gosudarstvo i pisateli, 1925–1938—dokumenty* (Moscow: Rosspen, 1997), 86.

11. Em. Iaroslavskii, senior editor at *Pravda*.

12. L. Z. Mekhlis, editor-in-chief, and M. A. Savel'ev, senior editor, at *Pravda*.

13. RGASPI, f. 558, op. 11, d. 702, ll. 5–50b, published in *Schast'e literatury*, 86. The editorial board at *Pravda*, it should be noted, disputed Bednyi's version of events. See ll. 37–370b.

14. D. Bednyi, "Bez poshchady," *Pravda*, 5 December 1930, 3–4. Patriotism was considered a negative, bourgeois emotion between the 1920s and early 1930s—a

form of false consciousness that distracted workers from class-based loyalties. See P. Stuchka, "Patriotizm," in *Entsiklopediia gosudarstva i prava*, 3 vols. (Moscow: Kommunisticheskaia akademiia, 1927), 3:252–54; M. Vol'fson, "Patriotizm," in *Malaia Sovetskaia entsiklopediia*, 10 vols. (Moscow: Sovetskaia entsiklopediia, 1931), 6:355–56.

15. An oblique allusion to Lenin's famous thesis from his 1913 article "On the National Pride of the Great Russians." See "O natsional'noi gordosti velikorossov," in *Polnoe sobranie sochinenii*, 26:106–10.

16. RGASPI, f. 17, op. 114, d. 201, 1. 13, published in *Schast'e literatury*, 85. See the draft resolution at f. 558, op. 11, d. 702, 11. 1–4. Stalin frequently credited the Russian people with the October 1917 Revolution in private and at closed party meetings during the 1920s and early 1930s, but the fact that these statements did not appear in the press until the late 1940s testifies to their "unofficial" nature.

17. A reference to A. S. Pushkin and M. Iu. Lermontov.

18. "There was a time, after all, when Il'ich himself corrected me and allowed me to respond in *Pravda* with the poem 'How Poets Ought to Be Read.' (see the seventh volume of my works, pg. 22, if you are interested)."

19. RGASPI, f. 558, op. 11, d. 702, 1. 50b, published in *Schast'e literatury*, 87. The New Testament references are to Matthew 26:39, Luke 22:41–42, and Mark 14:36.

20. Being set against Stalin enraged Molotov, who wrote a reproachful letter to Bednyi on 12 December 1930 and was still fuming about the incident fifty years later—see RGASPI, f. 558, op. 11, d. 702, 11. 35; *Sto sorok besed s Molotovym: Iz dnevnika F. Chueva* (Moscow: Terra, 1991), 269.

21. RGASPI, d. 558, op. 11, d. 207, 11. 7–8. The entire letter is reprinted in *Schast'e literatury*, 89–90.

22. See note 15.

23. RGASPI, f. 558, op. 11, d. 702, 11. 8–10, reprinted in *Schast'e literatury*, 89–93.

24. Ibid., 11. 11–12. These last lines were completely rewritten before publication—see "Tov. Dem'ianu Bednomu (vyderzhki iz pis'ma)," in I. V. Stalin, *Sochineniia*, 13 vols. (Moscow: Gos. izd-vo polit. lit-ry, 1947–1952), 13:23–27.

25. Stalin penciled onto the page proofs sent to him "Such modesty—ha-hah" [*Skromno—kha-kha*] next to this line. See RGASPI, f. 558, op. 11, d. 702, 1. 39.

26. RGASPI, f. 558, op. 1, d. 2939, 11. 12–17; also op. 11, d. 702, 11. 34–40. Although the party hierarchs authorized *Pravda* to print the piece, they demanded corrections that Stalin had proposed in a note written to Molotov on the poem's page proofs: "the issue is not only about Russia's *past*. There is nothing here about Russia's *present* (he dodged the issue). Why isn't there anything? Did Dem'ian take this angle to dodge us? It won't work! And in terms of Russia's past, Dem'ian is repeating again here what he's said before, that is, he's kept the style in which he made the mistakes. This isn't going to work." Bednyi apparently found such fundamental criticism impossible to accommodate and abandoned the piece instead. See f. 558, op. 1, d. 2939, 11. 11–12; op. 11, d. 702, 1. 44a.

27. D. Bednyi, "Vytianem!!" *Pravda*, 20 May 1931, 3.

28. See my "A. A. Zhdanov v rabote nad shkol'nym uchebnikom istorii," in *Otechestvennaia kul'tura i istoricheskaia nauka XVIII–XX vekov: Sbornik statei*

(Briansk: BGPU, 1996), 128–43; A. M. Dubrovsky, "'Veskii uchebnik' i arkhivnye materialy," in *Arkheograficheskii ezhegodnik za 1996* (Moscow: Izd-vo Akad. Nauk, 1998), 181–95; A. N. Artizov, "V ugodu vzgliadam vozhdia [konkurs 1936 g. na uchebnik po istorii SSSR]," *Kentavr [Voprosy istorii KPSS]* 1 (1991): 125–135. For the resolutions, see "O prepodavanii grazhdanskoi istorii v shkolakh SSSR," *Pravda*, 16 May 1934, 1; "O vvedenii v nachal'noi i nepolnoi srednei shkole elementarnogo kursa vseobshchei istorii i istorii SSSR," in *Spravochnik partiinogo rabotnika*, 9th issue (Moscow: Partizdat, 1935), 137.

29. See D. L. Brandenberger and A. M. Dubrovsky, "'The People Need a Tsar': The Emergence of National Bolshevism as Stalinist Ideology, 1931–1941," *Europe-Asia Studies* 50, no. 5 (1998): 876–78.

30. RGALI, f. 1038, op. 1, d. 3607, l. 28.

31. RGASPI, f. 17, op. 120, d. 257, l. 25.

32. RGASPI, f. 17, op. 120, d. 257, l. 25.

33. A. Koonen, *Stranitsy zhizni* (Moscow: Iskusstvo, 1985), 364–65. Koonen was A. Ia. Tairov's wife and a leading actress at the Kamernyi Theater.

34. Nightingale-the-Brigand (*Solovei-razboinik*) is a traditional Russian fairy tale character.

35. The expression is "*tsar'-derzhimorda*," a reference to a gendarme in N. Gogol's *Inspector General*, used here to refer to Alexander III.

36. V. Vidre, N. Doniko, and N. Magnitskaia, "Kreshchenie Rusi," *Rabochii i teatr* 1 (1932): 14.

37. O. S. Litovskii, chief of the theatrical division of the artistic censor, Glavrepertkom, and one of Kerzhenstev's deputies at the All-Union Committee for Artistic Affairs.

38. RGASPI, f. 17, op. 120, d. 257, l. 25.

39. I. S. Eventov, *Dem'ian Bednyi—Zhizn', poeziia, sud'ba* (Moscow: Khudozh. lit-ra, 1983), 177.

40. Reference to Prince Vladimir's choice of faith (ca. 988), when the prince supposedly interviewed emissaries from the German Latinists, the Khazar Jews, and the Bulgar Muslims before endorsing the Byzantine Christian rite.

41. RGASPI, f. 17, op. 120, d. 257, l. 26.

42. RGASPI, f. 17, op. 120, d. 257, l. 28.

43. Koonen, *Stranitsy zhizni*, 365–66.

44. Ia. I. Boiarskii, one of Kerzhentsev's deputies at the All-Union Committee for Artistic Affairs.

45. RGASPI, f. 17, op. 120, d. 257, l. 29.

46. D. Bednyi, "Bogatyri (k prem'ere v Kamernom teatre)," *Pravda*, 24 October 1936, 4.

47. RGASPI, f. 17, op. 120, d. 257, l. 29.

48. "The Russians have a great love for drink" (*Rusi est' veselie piti*,) a famous line from the Primary Chronicle.

49. Bednyi, "Bogatyri (k prem'ere v Kamernom teatre)," 4.

50. Main Directorate for Literary and Artistic Affairs, the artistic censor.

51. RGASPI, f. 17, op. 120, d. 257, ll. 29–30.

52. Iu. Elagin, *Ukroshchenie iskusstv* (New York: Izd-vo im. Chekhova, 1952), 199.

53. E. E. Golubinskii's *Istoriia russkoi tserkvi*, 2 vols. (Moscow: Imp. Ob-vo istorii i drevnostei rossiiskikh, 1901–1911), 1:105–43. Golubinskii's thesis that this tale was common to a number of national traditions in eastern Europe finds support in modern scholarship, e.g. Petro Tolochko, "Volodimer Sviatoslavich's Choice of Religion: Fact or Fiction?" *Harvard Ukrainian Studies* 12–13 (1988–1989): 818–19.

54. RGASPI, f. 17, op. 120, d. 257, l. 41.

55. RGASPI, f. 18, op. 3, d. 202, l. 80. The All-Union Committee for Artistic Affairs resolution was published as "O p'ese 'Bogatyri' Dem'iana Bednogo," *Pravda*, 14 November 1936, 3.

56. P. Kerzhentsev, "Fal'sifikatsiia narodnogo proshlogo (o 'Bogatyriakh' Dem'iana Bednogo)," *Pravda*, 15 November 1936, 3; L. Maksimenkov, *Sumbur vmesto muzyki: Stalinskaia kul'turnaia revoliutsiia, 1936–1938* (Moscow: Iuridicheskaia kniga, 1997), 216–17.

57. The public denunciation of Bednyi was dramatic enough to receive mention in the diary of Bulgakov's wife—see her entry from 14 November 1936 in *Dnevnik Eleny Bulgakovoi*, ed. V. Losev and L. Ianovskaia (Moscow: Knizhnaia palata, 1990), 124.

58. See, for instance, "Soveshchanie teatral'nykh deiatelei i rabotnikov iskusstv: Otkliki na postanovlenie o p'ese 'Bogatyri' Dem'iana Bednogo," *Pravda*, 17 November 1936, 3; "Liniia oshibok (O Kamernom teatre)," *Pravda*, 20 November 1936, 3; "Za pravdivoe, realisticheskoe iskusstvo (na soveshchanii teatral'nykh deiatelei i akterov po voprosu o p'ese 'Bogatyri,'" *Pravda*, 24 November 1936, 6; "Rech' deputata A. A. Zhdanova," *Izvestiia*, 18 January 1938, 3. For an interesting indication of how party hierarchs like Mekhlis stoked the fires of this scandal by manipulating its coverage in the press, compare "Kollektiv Kamernogo teatra zagovoril—A. Ia. Tairov smazyvaet oshibki," *Pravda*, 23 November 1936, 6, with its draft, excerpted in Maksimenkov, *Sumbur vmesto muzyki*, 222. For a description of a Moscow theater troupe's obligatory "discussion" of the resolution, see Elagin, *Ukroshchenie iskusstv*, 199–200.

59. RGALI, f. 631, op. 7, d. 7, l. 5. Accusations of "vulgarizing" history tied Bednyi to the indicted Pokrovskii "school"—see chapter 3 in this volume.

60. RGALI, f. 631, op. 15, d. 271, l. 19.

61. See, for instance, RGASPI, f. 558, op. 11, d. 702, ll. 142–420b, 145.

6
The Reaction of Writers and Artists to the Banning of D. Bednyi's Comic Opera

Public opinion was of considerable concern to the Stalinist regime, and both party and secret police officials were tasked with assessing what prominent social groups (e.g., the creative intelligentsia) thought about specific issues. Typically, informers would either eavesdrop on indiscrete conversations or directly engage people in provocative exchanges. Excerpts from these discussions were then compiled into summary reports called *svodki* that circulated within the party and secret police hierarchy.

In November 1936, concern about how members of the Soviet artistic elite were reacting to the fall of Dem'ian Bednyi led the secret police to compile a major report on public opinion within the Moscow theatrical world. Published in Russian in 1999, this report is remarkable for the variety of views that it encompasses regarding the scandal.[1] Only a fraction of those quoted seem to have realized that the affair revolved around the regime's newfound historical priorities; others seem to have assumed—with sympathy or schadenfreude, depending on their professional affiliations—that it was personal, and that Bednyi and Tairov had merely fallen out of favor. Only with time would the cultural elite realize that *The Epic Heroes* had been banned for its disrespectful treatment of the Russian national past.

We publish this piece here in full in order to capture the entire breadth of the NKVD's survey, insofar as it reveals much about the creative intelligentsia during these years. Acutely aware of the politically sensitive nature of their work, artists and writers spent a considerable amount of time attempting to gauge the evolution of official priorities. Unsatisfied with what was published in the party press, they routinely swapped gossip and rumors, reading between the lines of official communiqués in a desperate effort to avoid subjects and themes that threatened to contradict the party line. The NKVD's snapshot of public opinion among the Soviet elite reveals the surprising significance of information passed via "informal relationships"—professional alliances and intimate friendships—and the extent to which the Soviet state attempted to monitor this gossip and rumor-mongering.

Informational Report of the Secret Political Department of the NKVD Main Directorate on State Security: "On the Reactions of Writers and Artists to the Banning of D. Bednyi's Play *The Epic Heroes*"

A. Tairov[2] has been shaken by the [All-Union Committee for Artistic Affairs] resolution banning *The Epic Heroes*[3] and says that he is now suffering from heart problems. Members of the art world have come to visit him in order to express their sympathy. According to A. Koonen [his wife], many have come as if he were on his deathbed:

"I made a major mistake. I will take responsibility for it, despite the fact that even the Committee for Artistic Affairs, which reviewed the show, gave its approval. As an artist, I should have foreseen all eventualities—that is the essence of my error.

It pains me that this mistake is being treated in the press as an intentional provocation.[4]

This mistake came about because I placed great trust in Dem'ian Bednyi as an old communist. How could I have even imagined that Bednyi's text represented a dangerous deviation? How could I have acted as Bednyi's commissar?[5] I didn't make such a mistake with *Optimistic Tragedy* and *Motherland* because the authors were less authoritative and because I was able to subject their plays to the critique of experienced professionals.[6]

I'll go to the Central Committee and I hope they will receive me. I'll suggest to them that new shows should be reviewed not just by the Committee for Artistic Affairs, but by the Central Committee as well.

This is the only way to be certain.

But what really scares me is whether I'll be allowed to continue to work. It upsets me that some people want to make me out to be a heretic. This is so horrible that I can't even think about it calmly."

∽

A. Koonen [Tairov's wife], actress at the Kamernyi Theater:
"This is a lesson for Tairov. You can't rely just on yourself. If he hadn't, it wouldn't have cost us so dearly."

Tsenin, Distinguished Artist at the Kamernyi Theater:
"The theater will be haunted by political failures until it ceases to be a monarchy, until Tairov stops making all decisions unilaterally without consulting with the theater's leading lights."

Gersht, director at the Kamernyi Theater:
"In its essence, the resolution is correct. We are to stage *Evgenyi Onegin* and I expect to have precisely the same experience with this show as with *The Epic Heroes*."

Dem'ian Bednyi: The Committee for Artistic Affairs' resolution has left Dem'ian Bednyi completely in shock. For three days, he didn't leave his apartment and didn't see anyone; he summoned Stavskii,[7] the secretary of the Soviet Writers' Union, for a private conversation only yesterday. It has become clear that Dem'ian Bednyi has decided not to appeal directly to the secretaries of the Central Committee and wants to use Stavskii to convey his explanations and justifications. Finding Dem'ian Bednyi in a state of absolute crisis, Stavskii had a stenographer join him so that there would be a documentary account of the meeting.[8]

The general point of Dem'ian Bednyi's explanations concerning *The Epic Heroes*, as recorded in the stenogram, is as follows. The farsical tone and the interpretation of *The Epic Heroes* stem from the nature of the music—[Borodin had] the epic heroes sing arias from popular operettas, for instance. The farsical presentation of the Christening of Rus' and the incorrect interpretation of it stem from Dem'ian Bednyi's tendency toward anti-religious propaganda in his work. In addition, Bednyi was misled by historical works in his possession that are far from Marxist in character.

Admitting that he has made an enormous mistake, Dem'ian Bednyi explained that it came about because of his poor understanding of the material and his general foolishness. However, in the discussion, he returned again and again to the role of the [theater's] controlling organs. He noted that from the very start of work on *The Epic Heroes* a year and a half ago, he had been dissatisfied with the first draft, which had seemed simpleminded and silly. But Tairov and Litovskii[9] encouraged him to continue, assuring him that the text would work out brilliantly as a theatrical piece.

Not long before the piece was staged, a fairly polished version of the text was given to the Committee for Artistic Affairs, where Kerzhentsev, Boiarskii, and Orlovskii[10] familiarized themselves with it. When it was returned to Bednyi, it was accompanied by the single comment that Kerzhentsev thought that it was boring and a bit vulgar. Therefore, subsequent corrections of the text focused on condensing and revising individual phrases.

Dem'ian Bednyi also notes that his conceptualization of *The Epic Heroes* was laid out in an article that he published in *Pravda*, which at the time elicited no criticism whatsoever.[11] As a result, he considered the text of *The Epic Heroes* to have received complete approval.

Having said all of this, Dem'ian Bednyi added that "I have an artist's noggin, not a leader's."

Dem'ian noted that his diabetes has worsened. He said that he doesn't want to die as an enemy of the party and hopes that after this, if he is no longer to be allowed to publish, perhaps he'll at least be put to good use as a literary specialist—at the Knizhnaia Palata,[12] for instance.

Later on, after asking that it not be entered into the stenogram, Dem'ian said that it was his library that was his real enemy. This had been pointed out to him, but he hadn't understood it before. He announced that he was going to burn his library. Then he emphasized that he was most afraid that he would be condemned as an enemy of the party, working for foes of communism abroad, in spite of his earlier professional activities. He announced that he was afraid that if such a view of him became common, he'd be exiled from Moscow.

Dem'ian Bednyi remained in a deeply demoralized state even after his meeting with Stavskii, which apparently hadn't helped to calm him down at all.

∽

Stanislavskii,[13] People's Artist of the USSR:

"The Bolsheviks are geniuses. Nothing that the Kamernyi Theater does is art. It's formalism. It's theater-for-profit. It's Koonen's theater."

∽

Leonidov,[14] People's Artist of the USSR:

"After I read the committee's resolution, I lay down on a couch and kicked my legs up into the air. I jumped for joy: they've given Litovskii, Tairov and Dem'ian Bednyi a good slap. This is scarier than [what happened at] the Second Moscow Art Theater."[15]

∽

Iashin, Distinguished Artist of the Moscow Art Theater:

"The play was very bad. I am quite satisfied with the resolution. Nothing so ineffective should be allowed to continue for so long. Now the total inadequacy of Tairov's useless system has been exposed. The faster they close the theater, the better. If it was necessary to close the Second Moscow Art Theater, then this one should have been closed a long time ago."

Khmelev,[16] Distinguished Artist of the Moscow Art Theater:

"The decision is entirely correct. The leadership sees where the real art is and where there is only profanity. This decision should be followed by the liquidation of the entire theater. There's nothing left for the theater to do."

Kedrov,[17] Distinguished Artist of the Moscow Art Theater:

"If they close the Kamernyi Theater, then there'll just be one less bad theater."

Stanitsyn,[18] Distinguished Artist of the Moscow Art Theater:

"This is a theater in which they act badly, sing badly and dance badly. It should be closed."

Markov,[19] director of the literary section of the Moscow Art Theater:

"They made a rotten gamble on Borodin's and Palekh's good names.[20] A disgustingly awful show. The resolution is entirely justified."

Izrailevskii, director of the music section of the Moscow Art Theater, Distinguished Artist:

"The Kamernyi Theater's shows are formalism, through and through. There's nowhere else for such individuals to apply their talents. Throughout its entire existence, this theater has never given any satisfaction."

Samosud,[21] artistic director of the Bolshoi Theater:

"The resolution is absolutely correct. The Kamernyi is not a theater. Tairov is a trickster. The idea behind the production of *The Epic Heroes* was corrupt. Dem'ian Bednyi proposed this piece to me back when I was at the Mikhailovskii Theater and I turned it down."

Meyerhold,[22] People's Artist of the Republic:

"Finally, Tairov has been given the sort of slap he deserves. I keep a list of Tairov's plays that have been banned and *The Epic Heroes* is a real gem. Dem'ian got what he deserved, too. But most important is that the committee, and Boiarskii in particular, are all to blame. He persecutes me. The arts will not develop as long as the committee has such leadership."

∽

Natal'ia Sats,[23] Distinguished Artist of the Republic, artistic director of the Central Children's Theater:

"Tairov made a mistake. He used an incomplete musical score by Borodin. He shouldn't have depended on Dem'ian Bednyi, since he's a bad playwright. Inviting the Palekh masters was a gamble on form without the content to justify it. The theater is unable to say anything to its viewers."

∽

Sadovskii,[24] People's Artist of the RSFSR, at the Malyi Theater:

"The resolution makes sense. It was correct to rap Tairov and Bednyi across the knuckles. It's not acceptable to distort the history of the great Russian people."

∽

Trenev,[25] playwright, author of *Spring Love:*

"I am very pleased with the resolution. As a Russian person, it makes me proud. It's not acceptable to spit in our faces. I wasn't able to go to the show myself, but I sent my wife and daughter. They couldn't sit through it and got up and left, spitting as they went. The impression it produces is that revolting."

∽

Grigorii Sannikov,[26] poet:

"Well, I welcome the resolution and Kerzhentsev's article. It's helpful, not only for Dem'ian, but for all of us in our general approach to Russian history. For a long time, the Central Committee didn't have time for such things. But now, they've taken a serious look at the situation and have corrected it. We should have put an end to the vulgarization of history a long time ago."

∽

P. Romanov,[27] writer:

"It's good that they were given a hard kick. Dem'ian has been resting on his laurels, his connections and his vulgarity. This time he didn't get away with it. Not only that, but it is very good that they interceded on behalf of Russian folklore and the Russian epic heroes. We ought to be looking for Russian heroes."

∽

Gorodetskii,[28] poet:

"I cannot sympathize with any sort of suppression, but I am glad that they're not punishing those who make use of folklore—just those who ridicule it. It's not acceptable to relate to the people's history in that way; that the blow has been against Tairov is even more pleasant, since he's a swindler."

∽

Vsev[olod] Vishnevskii,[29] playwright:

"It serves Dem'ian right—he shouldn't be such an amateur. Let this be a history lesson: 'Don't mess with us.' History will come in handy yet, all too soon. The opera *Minin and Pozharskii—Salvation from the Interventionists* is already in preparation."[30]

∽

V. Lugovskoi,[31] poet:

"The resolution is correct in general, but what lies behind it is especially valuable. It will put a stop to the philistines who dare to mock the Russian people and their history. Until now, it has been considered good form to be ashamed of our history."

∽

I. Trauberg,[32] director of the film *Counterplan:*

"The Soviet government is becoming more and more national and even nationalistic. In this connection, the most unlikely things are being supported by the party leadership. It is becoming more difficult to work, especially when so many of those supervising things—both the theatrical censors and those in the Committee for Artistic Affairs—cannot correctly assess the plays, which then end up being banned after they've received official approval."

∽

S. Klychkov, writer:

"But then again, perhaps anything is possible. The great Russian people are one-hundred million strong and in terms of art they have the right, of course, to something more than pictures on tins of powder and kiosks *a la russe.* Perhaps some day the people will even dare to call me a Russian writer. Russian art should not be made to suffer out of deference to some sort of Vogul'[33] epic.

So who has been allowed to abuse the Russian epic? The kike Tairov and the wimp Bednyi. What else do you expect besides satire from Bednyi, who's basically a *feuilletoniste.* But some smart person, some discerning person, will grab them by the ass and shake out all of their stinking excesses.

Dem'ian Bednyi got himself into trouble again and has gotten what he deserves. This resolution rehabilitates Russian history, so they'll stop calling everything of ours shit. And it's about time. Now the progressive meaning that lies behind many things will be recognized; people will understand, if you please, that even a little bird [lit., a snipe] can be useful. Furthermore, the resolution also seems to rehabilitate Christianity; perhaps they'll finally understand that even now, believers won't steal and shouldn't be considered scoundrels.

I hope that it will become easier for writers to write the truth, and that critics will admit to their errors."

∽

Vs. Ivanov,[34] writer:

"I haven't fully grasped this affair yet. I think that there are some internal matters at work here, which are, of course, not mentioned in Kerzhentsev's article."

∽

Iu. Olesha,[35] writer:

"The major role here wasn't performed by the play. Dem'ian got too capricious and was punched right in the mouth. Today it's him, but tomorrow it'll be someone else. One can't be especially pleased about this. Dem'ian is paying for his sins."

∽

Ol'ga Forsh,[36] [writer]:

"Can a writer really be of two opinions? It's wonderful—marvelous that Dem'ian has been taught a lesson. Only now, perhaps, it will be more difficult for the rest of us who are currently writing plays. Litovskii, they say, has utterly lost his head and isn't certain about anything. Even without all of this, the theatrical censors have been making me cut down and revise my play about Kamo."[37]

∽

P. Antokol'skii,[38] poet:

"The fellows from the Kamernyi Theater are unlucky and I feel sorry for Bednyi. He could do a lot for the theater. In general, work in the theater is becoming more difficult, as there are desperate cowards all around. That is why all Moscow theaters without exception are so notable for their bureaucratism [*kazenshchina*] and total lack of ideas. They only stage what is commanded from above, like we did, for instance, with that mediocre play by Kirshon[39] at the Vakhtangovskii Theater."

∽

Lebedev-Kumach,[40] writer, satirist:

"If conclusions are drawn from this affair, then very good. It is necessary to rid the stage and poetry of the obscenity that Dem'ian has been cultivating and making into the official language of Soviet poetry. But now, having applied the stick to him, they'll probably give him the carrot, and pounce on someone else instead. You can't go about beating up your friends, after all."

Kozlovskii,[41] vocalist at the Bolshoi Theater:

"There's no doubt that the play was read earlier by the leadership, so why didn't they ban it before it was staged? Tairov is a major talent and this resolution won't be the death of him."

Kaverin, director at the Theater of the Russian Youth:

"The resolution is correct and everyone knows it; if many people refrain from harshly criticizing Tairov, it is only because every theater, if you please, has its own 'little epic heroes.'"

Eisenstein,[42] Distinguished Figure in the Arts, film director:

"I did not see the show, but am tremendously satisfied that at last they have finally given Dem'ian a good what-for. He had it coming—he's too full of himself. It's also good that that sycophant Litovskii got his for trumpeting out that celebratory article.[43] In all of this, I just wonder where they were before, when they let a counter-revolutionary play onto the stage?"

Leonid Sobolev,[44] author of *Capital Renovation:*

"I was just over at Tairov's. People have been going over since this morning. Just as I was arriving at Tairov's, Vs. Vishnevskii was leaving. Alisa [Koonen] is frightfully upset and depressed and says that everyone is coming to pay their respects like it's a funeral. I feel sorry for Tairov, although I consider the resolution to be correct. After all, when a book is published that distorts history, reality and so on, we don't release it to the reader— and the theater plays an educational role for thousands of audience members. It's odd—where was Kerzhentsev earlier? If the play was rehearsed and then staged for the audience as a finished show, that means that the Committee for Artistic Affairs had already sanctioned the play and given its approval. Even in the press, both the play and its staging were praised. They say that Molotov and Voroshilov saw *The Epic Heroes*. It's clear that they were the ones to expose the distortions in the play."

Barnet,[45] film director:

"Unfortunately, I didn't go to see the show in time. All I know is that it's high time they shut down rotten theaters like the Kamernyi."

Berenshtein, head of the theatrical department of the newspaper *Vecherniaia Moskva:*

"Litovskii was completely compromised by that article. It's clear that they'll remove him, but the Kamernyi Theater won't be closed. First, it is famous abroad, and besides, they've already closed ten theaters. This is an awful loss. When I was asked to write a column about premières this season, I couldn't find any theaters in Moscow, since literally all of them have been closed down."

Isidor Kleiner, theater critic:

"The affair with the staging of *The Epic Heroes* is instructive and useful for dramaturgy and the theatrical arts. True, Tairov had gotten written approval from the theatrical censor to stage the play. Everything was 'in order.' So Litovskii is no less responsible than Tairov. Today, there was an emergency meeting at Angarov's office in connection with this affair. Another 'battle of Kerzhentsev' [*secha pri Kerzhentseve*][46] took place.

The fate of the Kamernyi Theater is not clear. Perhaps they will be dispatched to the provinces, if you please, to be 'reforged.' That would be helpful. After all, Zavadskii[47] is flourishing in Rostov. His audience is good and, more importantly, fashionable: the Don Cossacks.[48]

As for Dem'ian, if you please, he's now truly poor.[49] He had already calculated that he'd receive 250 rubles a performance, and there were only 7–8 performances in all."

G. Bravin,[50] vocalist at the Operetta:

"I really like this tough line. There's no favoritism. Dem'ian got what he deserved—he's uncommonly cynical. He had everything—talent and a library, and he threw it all away."

Svobodin, vocalist at the Operetta:

"The decision of the committee is correct. Tairov's theater is hanging by a thread. It would have been shut down ages ago, if it weren't for Litvinov's[51] patronage."

Simonov,[52] Distinguished Artist of the Vakhtangov Theater:

"In our theater, we are very satisfied with the resolution. Tairov is not much loved for his eclectic theater, nor is Bednyi for being a 'vulgar' author.

The resolution is spectacular. If the decision regarding the Second Moscow Art Theater was quite unclear (why was it that they closed that theater?), this document is remarkably smart and clear."

∾

Gorchakov,[53] director, Distinguished Artist at the Moscow Art Theater:

"The play was just a bunch of words. Nothing interesting. The resolution is correct."

∾

Dzerzhinskii,[54] composer of the opera *And Quiet Flows the Don*:

"I am preparing to write an opera called *Pugachev*. After the committee's resolution, I am not sure what to do. I would like to speak to someone from among the leading comrades. It's now going to be necessary to approach historical themes with a maximum of caution."

∾

Okhlopkov,[55] artistic director of the Realist Theater:

"Now you have to be on guard. This is a sign. You ought to have your play read by the collective. It is necessary to relate with care to the repertoire. This was a big lesson for everyone."

∾

Pol',[56] actor at the Satire Theater:

"I am very glad that they've dealt a blow to Dem'ian: he was so full of himself that he wouldn't shake your hand properly. I pity Tairov, though. True, he also ought to have watched out, but while he was in Dem'ian's shadow, he let his guard down."

∾

Orbeli,[57] academician and director of the Hermitage (after a meeting in the Committee for the Arts [sic, Artistic Affairs]):

"What sort of conclusions have I drawn? The resolution is wonderful. It's less necessary to punish Tairov than it is to punish Dem'ian Bednyi. There's no need to finish off Tairov. Meyerhold annoyed me with his hooliganistic speech. It's grandstanding."[58]

∾

Roshal',[59] Distinguished Figure in the Arts, film director:

"I don't understand a thing. I don't know what to work on now. It turns out now that it is not acceptable in general to stage any satire at all."

∾

Ptushko,[60] Distinguished Figure in the Arts, film director:
"In general, [this affair] has made me very upset. They tried to have fun with the Christening of Rus' and that turned out to be unacceptable. It's terrifying to work and my hands have gone limp."

∽

Lenin, actor, Distinguished Artist at the Malyi Theater:
"The show has been banned. Good job. Under Tsar Nicholas, there was a single censor, who was able to make all the decisions unilaterally, but now our censors were intimidated by Dem'ian Bednyi and let the play slip past."

∽

Iaron,[61] vocalist at the Operetta:
"I am in despair. I feel defenseless again. If Kerzhentsev can write such an article now, having seen *The Epic Heroes*, having sanctioned it, and even having given it his approval, that means that if someone from above doesn't like our show, it can be banned and harshly criticized for what was considered praiseworthy only yesterday.

This hopeless double-dealing and cowardice is very demoralizing."

∽

D. N. Morozov, playwright:
"Tairov wanted to earn political capital by means of D. Bednyi's play and has 'come up short.' Incidentally, could you really expect a high-quality artistic production from D. Bednyi? Composing propaganda posters is far from genuine dramaturgy. As for the fact that the play was banned, here Kerzhentsev is also to blame. The play was banned, of course, by order of the boss. And that's correct. It's about time we talked about culture without whispering."

∽

V. A. Aver'ianov, playwright:
"This sleight of hand is striking. The artistic authorities, specifically Kerzhentsev, sanctioned the staging of *The Epic Heroes*. I don't believe that Kerzhentsev didn't know about Dem'ian's play and didn't give it a political evaluation. After all, the Kamernyi Theater isn't some sort of third-rate amateur theater. Tairov's theater is one of the leading Moscow theaters and Kerzhentsev, who is responsible for theatrical policy, could not have not known what was going on. But now—and you have to see it to believe it—this same Kerzhentsev is punishing Dem'ian and Tairov and, incidentally, his own toady Litovskii, as well. How many people can you fool by such a sleight of hand?"

Mikhail Romm,[62] film director:
"In essence, the article is of course correct, and everyone got what they deserved. But where was the Committee for the Arts [sic] earlier? It is clear that one of the higher ups in the government saw the play and suggested to Kerzhentsev that he engage in some self-flagellation."

Arkadin, Distinguished Artist at the Kamernyi Theater:
"The Committee for Artistic Affairs is to blame for *The Epic Heroes* affair. After all, the committee could have refused to allow the play to be staged, as they had read the play and, in the end, they even saw the dress rehearsal. The committee, in this case, intended to embarrass the theater."

Golubov,[63] theater critic for *Izvestiia* and *Vecherniaia Moskva*:
"People who are far removed from the committee believe that this resolution is a victory for the committee; people who are closer to the events consider it to be a major blow to the committee."

Litovskii, chair of the Main Repertory Committee:
"I will say nothing at the [upcoming] nonparty meeting. At the party meeting, I will say that we shouldn't blame Litovskii alone for all of this, but the committee too: Kerzhentsev, Boiarskii, and also Gorodinskii, who sanctioned the show."

M. Bulgakov,[64] author of *The Days of the Turbins*:
"Given his personality, it's a rare day when Dem'ian cannot gloat; this time, he himself is the victim and will not be snickering at others. Let him see how it feels."

[Signed: G.] *Molchanov*, Commissar of State Security, 2nd Class, Head of the Secret Political Department of the NKVD Main Directorate on State Security

Notes

1. "Spravka Sekretno-politicheskogo otdela GUGB NKVD SSSR 'Ob otklikakh literatorov i rabotnikov iskusstv na sniatie s repertuara p'esy D. Bednogo 'Bogatyri,'" TsA FSB, f. 3, op. 3, d. 121, ll. 98–107, published in *Vlast' i khudozhestvennaia intelligentsiia: Dokumenty TsK RKP(b)-VKP(b), ChK-OGPU-NKVD o kul'turnoi*

politike, 1917–1953 gg., ed. A. N. Iakovlev, A. Artizov, and O. Naumov (Moscow: Demokratiia, 1999), 333–41. For a similar survey of public opinion within the intelligentsia regarding the banning of D. D. Shostakovich's *Lady Macbeth of Mtsensk District*, see 290–95, 302–4.

2. A. Ia. Tairov (1850–1950), long-time director of the Kamernyi Theater.

3. For the text of the resolution, see "O p'ese 'Bogatyri' Dem'iana Bednogo," *Pravda*, 14 November 1936, 3.

4. See, for instance, P. M. Kerzhentsev, "Fal'sifikatsiia narodnogo proshlogo (o 'Bogatyriakh' Dem'iana Bednogo), *Pravda*, 15 November 1936, 3.

5. A reference to the Red Army practice of having a commanding officer serve in tandem with a political commissar in order to ensure that battlefield decisions were both tactically and ideologically correct.

6. Vs. Vishnevskii's *Optimistic Tragedy* was staged in 1933; B. Levin's *Motherland* was staged in 1936.

7. V. P. Stavskii (Kirpichnikov, 1900–1943).

8. This stenogram serves as the basis for portions of chapter 5 in this volume.

9. O. S. Litovskii, chair of the Main Repertory Committee and editor of *Sovetskoe iskusstvo*.

10. P. M. Kerzhentsev (Lebedev, 1881–1940), chair of the All-Union Committee for Artistic Affairs; Ia. I. Boiarskii, deputy chief of All-Union Committee for Artistic Affairs; Orlovskii, deputy chief of Glavisskustvo's theatrical division.

11. D. Bednyi, "Bogatyri (k prem'ere v Kamernom teatre)," *Pravda*, 24 October 1936, 4.

12. The Knizhnaia Palata was an institution that monitored aspects of state publishing.

13. K. S. Stanislavskii (Alekseev, 1863–1938), the founder and director of the Moscow Art Theater and originator of the influential Stanislavskii acting method. At the time of this document, he was the director of the Opera Studio of the Bolshoi Theater, which he founded and which was subsequently known as the Stanislavskii Musical Theater.

14. L. M. Leonidov (1873–1941), classical actor at the Moscow Art Theater.

15. I. N. Bersenev's Second Moscow Art Theater was disbanded by official decree in late February 1936, ostensibly because of the weakness of its repertoire. This occurred in the wake of the denunciation of D. D. Shostakovich's *Lady Macbeth of Mtsensk District* and anticipated the banning of M. A. Bulgakov's *Molière*. See "O Vtorom Moskovskom khudozhestvennom teatre," *Pravda*, 28 February 1936, 2.

16. N. P. Khmelev (1901–1945), starred in M. A. Bulgakov's *The Days of the Turbins*.

17. M. N. Kedrov (1894–1972).

18. V. Ia. Stanitsyn (1897–1976).

19. P. A. Markov (1897–1970).

20. The set design for *The Epic Heroes* was modeled on folk designs made famous by the Palekh artisan commune's black lacquer boxes.

21. S. A. Samosud (1884–1964).

22. V. E. Meyerhold (Meierkhol'd, 1874–1940), avant-garde director, arrested in 1939.
23. N. I. Sats (b. 1903).
24. P. M. Sadovskii (1874–1947), acted in K. A. Trenev's *Spring Love*.
25. K. A. Trenev (1876–1945), author of historical plays such as *The Pugachevshchina* (1924) and *On the Banks of the Neva* (1937). *Spring Love* (1926) focuses on heroism during the Civil War.
26. G. A. Sannikov (1899–1969).
27. P. S. Romanov (1884–1938), best known for *Rus'* (1922–1936).
28. S. M. Gorodetskii (1884–1967), known for his folkloric *Iar'* (1907). He adapted M. I. Glinka's *Life for the Tsar* for the Soviet stage—see chapter 17 in this volume.
29. Vs. Vishnevskii (1900–1950), wrote *The First Cavalry Army* (1929) and *We Are from Kronshtadt* (1933). He was known for his Russian nativist sentiments.
30. The NKVD informant added after the quotation the barb that "This judgment did not prevent Vishnevskii from going to Tairov to express his sympathy."
31. V. A. Lugovskoi (1901–1957), wrote romantic works about the Civil War.
32. I. Z. Trauberg (b. 1902), director of the cinematic *Maksim* trilogy (1935–1939).
33. Vogul' is an archaic term for the Mansi ethnic group.
34. Vs. V. Ivanov (1895–1963), author of *Partisans* (1921) and *Armored Train 14–69* (1923).
35. Iu. K. Olesha (1899–1960), author of *Envy* (1927).
36. O. D. Forsh (1873–1961), author of historical novels like *Radishchev* (1932–1939).
37. Kamo was a revolutionary-era hero from the Caucasus.
38. P. G. Antokol'skii (1896–1978), poet often occupied with historical themes.
39. V. M. Kirshon (1902–1938), playwright, executed during the terror.
40. V. I. Lebedev-Kumach (1898–1949), prominent poet and lyricist, remembered for his lyrics to Grigorii Aleksandrov's musical comedies *The Jolly Fellows* (1934), *Circus* (1936), and *Volga Volga* (1938) and for his wartime anti-fascist hymns "Song of the Motherland" and "Holy War."
41. I. S. Kozlovskii (b. 1900), classical tenor.
42. S. M. Eisenstein (1898–1948), directed *Aleksandr Nevskii* (1938), *Ivan the Terrible*, pts. 1–2 (1944–1945). See chapters 10 and 15 in this volume.
43. O. S. Litovskii, "Bogatyri: novaia postanovka Kamernogo teatra," *Sovetskoe iskusstvo*, 29 October 1936.
44. L. S. Sobolev (1898–1971). His *Capital Renovation* (1932–1962) concerned the pre-revolutionary Russian fleet.
45. B. V. Barnet (1902–1965).
46. Pun styling the scandal as an epic battle from the medieval chronicles.
47. Iu. A. Zavadskii (b. 1894), prominent actor and director associated during the mid-1930s with the Central Red Army Theater. Banished to Rostov-on-Don in 1936, he returned to Moscow in 1940 to a leading role at the Mossovet Theater.
48. After more than a decade of stigma in the wake of the Russian civil war, the Cossacks returned to official favor during the mid- to late 1930s.

49. Pun on Bednyi's last name (lit. "the poor one").

50. N. M. Bravin (N. M. Vasiatkin, 1883–1956).

51. M. M. Litvinov (M. Vallakh, 1871–1951), Old Bolshevik, commissar for foreign affairs.

52. R. N. Simonov (1899–1968).

53. N. M. Gorchakov (1898–1958), artistic director of the Satire Theater who attempted to stage M. A. Bulgakov's *Ivan Vasil'evich* in early 1936—see chapter 9 in this volume.

54. I. I. Dzerzhinskii (1909–1978). His opera *And Quiet Flows the Don* debuted in 1935.

55. N. P. Okhlopkov (1900–1967), an associate of Meyerhold's theater and an actor in films including *Lenin in October* (1937) and *Aleksandr Nevskii* (1938).

56. P. N. Pol', actor who was to play in Bulgakov's *Ivan Vasil'evich*—see chapter 9 in this volume.

57. I. A. Orbeli (1887–1961), prominent orientalist.

58. Orbeli makes reference to comments Meyerhold apparently made at a meeting of the All-Union Committee for Artistic Affairs. Meyerhold had been scapegoated for the Soviet theater's incomplete break with the avant-garde since January 1936 and seems to have attempted to place some of the blame on his rival, Tairov.

59. G. L. Roshal' (1899–1983), director of films including the anti-fascist *Oppenheim Family* (1939).

60. A. L. Ptushko (1900–1973), specialist in animation, folkloric themes.

61. G. M. Iaron (1893–1963).

62. M. I. Romm (1901–1971), director of *Lenin in October* (1937) and *Lenin in 1918* (1939).

63. Possibly S. N. Golubov (1894–1962), author of the historical novels *From the Sparks of the Flame* (1940) and *Bagration* (1943).

64. M. A. Bulgakov (1891–1940)—see chapter 9 in this volume.

Nikolai Leskov

7
The Adventures of a Leskov Story in Soviet Russia, or the Socialist Realist Opera That Wasn't

༄ Andrew B. Wachtel

The broad question to be considered in this essay is how authors, works, or even whole traditions of one period are assimilated into the culture of another, particularly after moments of cataclysmic change. I am concerned here with the reception of nineteenth-century Russian literature in early Soviet culture, but the general problem is by no means confined to Russia in the twentieth century.[1] To adduce only one example, in fourth-century Rome after conversion to Christianity a generation that had been educated according to the best principles of pagan rhetoric and literature had to reconceive their previous cultural canon in a new ideological context. One method they chose was the cento, a patchwork literary genre that, in its most celebrated exemplar, used nothing but whole poetic lines taken out of context from the works of Virgil in order to retell the stories of the Old and New Testaments.[2]

By the late 1920s members of the Soviet creative intelligentsia found themselves in an analogous position. They were heirs to a vigorous literary tradition, one they knew practically by heart and could not easily jettison, yet the ideological changes introduced in the wake of the October Revolution ensured that the nineteenth-century canon could not be folded unproblematically into the new culture. To be sure, some urged the wholesale abandonment of pre-revolutionary Russian culture, but the advocates of a complete purge of the "steamship of modernity" were in the minority and eventually lost out. Instead, in tandem with the development of Soviet culture, a slow process of assimilation and, necessarily, reinterpretation of the classics began. In the case of some authors, the process went fairly smoothly, either because, like N. G. Chernyshevskii, they had been on the right side (or, more accurately, the left) in the tsarist days, or because, like L. N. Tolstoi, they had received the stamp of approval from on high. On the other end of the spectrum were writers like K. N. Leont'ev, whose religious and aesthetic views were simply incompatible with those of the Soviet state and who could not be assimilated at all. For most nineteenth-century writers, however, the situation was not clear cut. Active mediation was needed, either by critics who could contextualize the work of an author in terms needed for acceptance, or by writers and artists who could revise, borrow from, adapt, or otherwise integrate a given work for the new cultural scene.

Nikolai Leskov was one of those nineteenth-century figures who did not easily fit into the new interpretive schema. For one thing, his political qualifications were decidedly questionable: he had written novels vilifying the left (*No Way Out*, 1864, and *At Daggers Drawn*, 1870–1871). And although in later years he had mostly avoided politics, his extravagant writing style and fondness for folk religiosity did not endear him to those who would soon come to see writers as "engineers of men's souls." The problematic nature of Leskov for Soviet culture is reflected in post-revolutionary publishing history and criticism. According to Hugh McLean's authoritative study, the first collected edition of Leskov in the Soviet period did not appear until 1956–1958, and "apart from a few scattered articles, no new full-length study of Leskov was published until 1945."[3] But if the Soviet publishing industry and the critics were uninterested in packaging Leskov for the new culture (with the exception of a few innocent tales like "Lefty"), the same cannot be said of Soviet artists. Their efforts to Sovietize Leskov are the focus of my discussion here. In particular, I concentrate on the adventures of a single Leskov story, "Lady Macbeth of the Mtsensk District," in the artistic maelstrom of the first decades of Soviet culture.[4]

"Lady Macbeth" is by no means a typical Leskov story. It describes how the wife of a provincial merchant (Katerina L'vovna Izmailova) murders her father-in-law, her husband, and her nephew in concert with her lover (Sergei). The murders are discovered, however, and she and Sergei are sentenced to Siberian exile. On the way there, enraged by Sergei's unfaithfulness, Katerina hurls his new lover and herself to their deaths by drowning. This tale does not employ *skaz*, the colloquial narrative style present in most of Leskov's more famous works, nor at first glance does it foreground the peasant, folkloric aspects of Russian culture.[5] On the other hand, it makes a fine candidate for transposition into other genres, adaptation, or stylization, because it is itself a transposition, a Russification of

Shakespeare's tragedy. As such it is by no means unique in Russian nineteenth-century realism, joining Turgenev's "Hamlet of Shchigrov District" and "King Lear of the Steppes," among others.⁶

Remaking Leskov's story into a work that would be acceptable within the artistic canons of incipient Socialist Realism was the intent of the twenty-three-year-old composer Dmitrii Shostakovich when he began work on his opera *Lady Macbeth of Mtsensk District* in 1930.⁷ This becomes apparent as soon as we read the statements he made concerning the piece in the early 1930s. For example, in the program book that accompanied the first production, Shostakovich claimed that "no work of Russian literature ... more vividly or expressively characterizes the position of women in the old pre-revolutionary times than Leskov's." But, he continued, "Leskov, as a brilliant representative of pre-revolutionary literature, could not correctly interpret the events that unfold in his story."⁸ Statements of this kind were standard fare in the rehabilitation of classic Russian writers. As the message of the story in question could not be approved, it was imperative to attribute that message to the ideological constraints of the author's time, constraints against which he was seen to have been struggling. This method could be called Soviet deconstructionist criticism, and its initiator was the great deconstructor himself—Lenin—in his influential articles on Tolstoi.⁹

Shostakovich, however, felt it necessary to do more than explicate those moments of Leskov's story that could be seen as "politically correct" in 1930. In order to be elevated from the merely acceptable into the pantheon of classics, Leskov's story needed further interpretation. It had to be understood as a harbinger of the most progressive trends; it had to contain positive elements, as opposed to being merely an implicit criticism of its own time. Shostakovich found these positive elements through a clever reinterpretation, or more accurately, revision of the main character Katerina L'vovna Izmailova. According to the composer: "N. Leskov depicts the main heroine of his story ... as a demonic figure. He finds no reasons either for a moral or even a psychological justification of her.... I interpreted Katerina L'vovna as an energetic, talented, beautiful woman, who is destroyed by the gloomy, cruel family surroundings of serf-holding-merchant Russia." Katerina is thus transformed from a voluptuously lustful and crazed murderess into a victim of nineteenth-century society, while her lover Sergei is dubbed "a future kulak." Leskov's story is lauded as "a depiction of one of the gloomiest epochs of pre-revolutionary Russia," a hymn to the "suffering people of that epoch—an epoch built on the humiliation of the exploited by the exploiters."¹⁰ The loaded words Shostakovich employs to describe the world depicted by Leskov betray the kind of anachronistic and revisionist thinking about history that was typical among the Soviet creative intelligentsia.

It is the revision of Katerina, however, that reveals Shostakovich's basic sympathy for the thrust of early Socialist Realist art, particularly its obsession with the creation of a positive hero.[11] As Shostakovich put it: "My task was to justify Katerina L'vovna in every way possible, so that that the listener and viewer would be left with the impression that she is a positive character." This was, as the composer was aware, a tall order. As he noted immediately: "it is not very easy to elicit sympathy: Katerina L'vovna commits a series of acts which are not in accord with morals or ethics—two murders."[12] Here, of course, anyone who has read Leskov's story recognizes that one way in which the composer tries to rehabilitate Katerina is by eliminating the third, most disturbing murder in the story—that of her young nephew and co-heir Fedor Liamkin—a murder that cannot be explained away by reference to the cruel domination of patriarchal Russia.

Shostakovich's attempt to rehabilitate Katerina was not confined to omitting uncomfortable material. He used the full range of resources available to an operatic composer. Indeed, as Richard Taruskin observes, the effort to raise Katerina to the level of heroine is even more pronounced in the music than in the libretto: "Evoking a wealth of familiar musical genres and invoking a bewilderingly eclectic range of styles, the composer makes sure that only one character is perceived by the audience as a human being. From the very first pages of the score, Katerina's music is rhapsodic, soaring, and—most telling of all—endowed with the lyric intonations of the Russian folk song. . . . In total contrast, every other member of the cast is portrayed as sub-human."[13] Katerina's lyrical laments, distinguished from the more dissonant vocal lines of the other characters, draw a sharp boundary between positive and negative figures.

Furthermore, there is evidence that had Shostakovich's plans not been interrupted, Katerina would have come to be seen as still more heroic through her association with a trio of further operas devoted to the "position of women in Russia." In a 1934 interview Shostakovich said: "I want to write a Soviet *Ring of the Nibelungen*. This will be an operatic tetralogy in which *Lady Macbeth* will be a kind of *Rheingold*. The main image of the following opera will be a heroine of the 'People's Will' Movement. Then a woman of our century. And finally, I will describe our Soviet heroine who combines in herself the qualities of the women of today and tomorrow, from Larissa Reisner to the best concrete pourer at Dneprostroi, Zhenia

Roman'ko."[14] Katerina would thus have become a progenitor of female heroism, and Shostakovich's operatic reinterpretation of Leskov would have placed both the twentieth-century composer and the nineteenth-century author firmly within the Socialist Realist canon.

Yet here the question arises: if Shostakovich composed an opera that was meant to be a politically correct statement and if he did so in keeping with what would be the main lines of Socialist Realist aesthetics, why did his opera fail (ideologically speaking, that is)? For fail it certainly did, and in the most spectacular of fashions. The story of the disaster has been told frequently. *Lady Macbeth* premièred almost simultaneously in Leningrad and Moscow in January 1934. It ran for almost two years, until Stalin went to a performance in early 1936. Unfortunately for Shostakovich, the Soviet leader and arbiter of good taste hated the work, which was banned almost immediately afterward. The new attitude toward *Lady Macbeth* was expressed in a notorious *Pravda* editorial entitled "Muddle Instead of Music."[15] "The music wheezes, hoots, puffs, and pants in order to depict love scenes with a maximum of naturalism," accused *Pravda*. "'Love' is smeared all over the entire opera in the most vulgar manner. The merchant's double bed takes center stage in the set. . . . The composer has merely tried to use all the means at his disposal in order to win public sympathy for the coarse and vulgar aspirations of the merchant woman Katerina Izmailova."[16]

The problem, as the above excerpt makes clear, was that Shostakovich failed to realize that overt eroticism was no longer acceptable in the Soviet arts. All his efforts at creating a model Soviet opera foundered on the explicit sexuality that was, first and foremost, a property of the music, although it was evident in the staging and the libretto as well. Interestingly enough, in this area, too, Shostakovich took considerable liberties with his source text, for Leskov's story, while built around Katerina's passion, is nowhere near as blatantly sexual as Shostakovich's transposition. Various theses have been advanced to account for the increased eroticism of Shostakovich's opera, but to appreciate fully the reasons behind his foregrounding of sexuality we need to know how Shostakovich became interested in the story. Furthermore, an excursus into the origins of Shostakovich's interest in the story may also help us to understand why the young composer chose Leskov to rehabilitate, for, given Leskov's absence from the Soviet pantheon, this was hardly inevitable. Shostakovich's opera was not, in fact, the first Soviet-era transposition of "Lady Macbeth." Indeed, it is my contention that the operatic transposition was made not directly from Leskov, but rather from

Figure 8. B. M. Kustodiev, *A Beauty* (*Krasavitsa*, 1915). Russian State Tret'iakov Gallery, Moscow.

an intermediary transposition dating from the early 1920s. This version comes from a surprising source: not literature or music but rather visual art. Moreover, the transposition in question introduced an entirely new cultural layer to Leskov's nineteenth-century realism: a layer of high modernist culture in its Russian incarnation.

In 1919–1920, the celebrated artist Boris Kustodiev painted a series of "Russian types."[17] When he contracted with the Akvilon publishing house to issue them in book form, they asked the young writer Evgenii Zamiatin to contribute an accompanying text. The result was the story *Rus'*, published together with the images in 1923.[18] This collaboration is unusual, particularly because it represents a rare example of a writer working in response to illustrations rather than the other way around. For our purposes, however, it is more important to note, on the one hand, the erotic nature of some of Kustodiev's images and, on the other, the links between Zamiatin's text and Leskov's "Lady Macbeth of Mtsensk District." The former is clearest in two of Kustodiev's pictures—the well-known *A Beauty*

Figure 9. B. M. Kustodiev, *Au Bain (Vénus russe)* (*V bane*, 1919–1920). In *Rus': Russkie tipy B. M. Kustodieva, slovo Evg. Zamiatina* (St. Petersburg, 1923).

(*Krasavitsa*, 1915) and a picture from *Rus'* entitled *Au Bain* (*Vénus russe*, 1919–1920)—both of which depict voluptuous nudes with the same face, a general feature of many of Kustodiev's paintings featuring merchant-class women (see Figures 8, 9).

Rus' is a minor masterpiece, a tour de force that incorporates most of the "types" depicted in Kustodiev's drawings into a narrative derived from Leskov's "Lady Macbeth." The story concerns a young, well-endowed (in all senses of the word) orphan, Marfa, who is encouraged by her aunt to choose a husband from among the rich merchants in her provincial town. She marries Vakhrameev, an older man who treats her well but who is clearly unable to satisfy her desires. The story hints that she takes a lover, probably from among her husband's employees. One day her husband dies: "after dinner he lay himself down to sleep—and he never got up. It seems that the cook had fed him some toadstools at dinner together with the morels, that's what did him in, supposedly. Others said something different—well, what don't people say."[19] Marfa then remarries (her young lover, evidently), but in contrast to Leskov's tale, this story ends happily.

A wealth of circumstantial evidence leads to the conclusion that the connection between Leskov's story and Zamiatin's is not, as at least one critic believes, merely coincidental.[20] First, it is well known that Zamiatin was a great admirer of Leskov. In particular, one might recall his wildly spectacular "people's theater" piece *The Flea* (1925), a loose adaptation of Leskov's story "Lefty." The sets and costumes for that work's Leningrad and Moscow productions were, by the way, executed by Kustodiev.[21] More important, in both of these stories folkloric material is used in the same way, not on the level of language, but rather as a structuring element in the narrative.[22] Further evidence that *Rus'* and "Lady Macbeth" were related, at least in Kustodiev's eyes, can be found by comparing his drawings of "Russian types" with the illustrations he produced in 1923 for an edition of "Lady Macbeth."[23] The latter drawings, like the previous set, are in many cases unabashedly erotic (see Figures 10–15). But the most compelling evidence is the drawing that accompanies the opening of chapter 1, which is nothing more than a revision of the first drawing in the book edition of *Rus'* (see Figures 16, 17).

But what does this sequence of visual artworks have to do with Shostakovich and his opera? After all, the Soviet Union of the mid-1930s was worlds apart culturally from that of the early 1920s. It turns out, however, that although Shostakovich should have been far too young to have been actively aware of the cultural climate of the immediate post-revolutionary

Figures 10–12. Title page and Kustodiev's illustrations from the 1930 edition of N. S. Leskov's *Lady Macbeth of Mtsensk District*.

Figures 13–15. Kustodiev's illustrations from the 1930 edition of N. S. Leskov's *Lady Macbeth of Mtsensk District.*

Figure 16. Katherine Izmailova, from Kustodiev's illustrations to the 1930 edition of N. S. Leskov's *Lady Macbeth of Mtsensk District*.

Figure 17. Kustodiev, untitled depiction of a merchant's wife. In *Rus': Russkie tipy B. M. Kustodieva, slovo Evg. Zamiatina* (St. Petersburg, 1923).

years (he was born in September, 1906), he had been a frequent visitor in the Kustodiev household as early as 1919, when as a child prodigy he had been asked by his schoolmate, Irina Kustodieva, to play for her wheelchair-bound father. Kustodiev took a liking to the young pianist and his family, who even spent part of the summer of 1923 at the painter's Crimean dacha. At the time Kustodiev was working to complete his illustrations for "Lady Macbeth."

In *Testimony*, Solomon Volkov recounts the following remarks of Shostakovich concerning Kustodiev:

> I was deeply impressed by Kustodiev's passion for voluptuous women. Kustodiev's painting is thoroughly erotic, something that is not discussed nowadays. Kustodiev made no secret of it. He did blatantly erotic illustrations for one of Zamyatin's books. If you dig deeper into my operas *The Nose* and *Lady Macbeth*, you can find the Kustodiev influence in that sense. Actually, I had never thought about it, but recently in conversation I remembered a few things. For instance, Leskov's story "Lady Macbeth of Mtsensk District" was illustrated by Kustodiev, and I looked through the drawings at the time I decided to write the opera.[24]

At this point it might be of interest to see, in turn, the origins of Kustodiev's voluptuous women, for this was his main legacy to the young Shostakovich. Although Kustodiev could hardly be called the most avant-garde of early-twentieth-century Russian artists, his Russian beauty had an excellent modernist pedigree. Her immediate predecessor can be found in two works from 1912 by Mikhail Larionov. The first, quite realistic for Larionov, depicts a voluptuous, although somewhat awkward and grotesque, woman lying on a bed in practically the same position as Kustodiev's *Beauty* (Figure 18). By her feet is a large red cat, a detail absent from Kustodiev's *Venus* painting but present in his illustrations for "Lady Macbeth." While Kustodiev's woman is clearly meant to tempt the prurient gaze, it is not clear whether the woman in Larionov's painting has any sexual allure to speak of. The other painting, more typical of Larionov's naif work of this period, has the word "Venera" (Venus) written boldly on the painting and depicts a highly stylized woman oriented in a similar fashion to Kustodiev's (Figure 19). The vase with a single flower echoes the floral wallpaper and painted bedframe in Kustodiev's work.

Tracing the origins of these works in turn, we can guess that the Larionov paintings are Russified versions of an original French work that itself

Figure 18. M. F. Larionov, *Katsap Venus* (1912). Nizhnii-Novgorod State Art Museum, Nizhnii-Novgorod.

Figure 19. M. F. Larionov, *Venus* (*Venera*, 1912). The Russian Museum, St. Petersburg.

Figure 20. Paul Gauguin, *The King's Wife* (*Te arii vahine*, 1896). The Pushkin Museum of Fine Arts, Moscow.

marked a melding of modern French art with a primitive and, to European eyes, highly erotic culture. I have in mind Paul Gauguin's 1896 canvas *The King's Wife* (Figure 20). This painting now hangs in Moscow's Pushkin Museum, which means that it was in Sergei Shchukin's private collection in Moscow and would have been known to Larionov. What we can deduce from this progression is that Larionov borrowed from Gauguin's work, simultaneously further primitivizing and rendering grotesque his exotic South Sea's beauty. Kustodiev domesticated Larionov's work, making his Venus incontestably Russian and undoubtedly sexually tempting.

With all of this information at our disposal, we can now trace the path that Leskov's story traveled on its way toward Shostakovich's opera. In our reconstruction, the initial impulse was provided by Zamiatin, who fashioned *Rus'* as an adaptation of Leskov's "Lady Macbeth." Kustodiev evidently recognized the underlying plot connection, and this probably inclined him to illustrate "Lady Macbeth" in 1923. In his mind, the temptress Katerina was connected to the archetype of the Russian beauty, the primitive

Venus as she had been portrayed by Larionov and before him by Gauguin. The young Shostakovich did not, then, come to Leskov by accident, but rather through the mediation of Kustodiev, who gets credit for the hypersexualization of Leskov's tale.[25] By the time Shostakovich started work on the opera he may well have forgotten the intermediate steps, but they remained present in the heightened eroticism of the opera, the very thing that got the composer in trouble despite all his conscious efforts at remaking Leskov's story for the Socialist Realist canon. Thus, although most critics have seen Shostakovich's work as a transposition of Leskov's story, it was in fact a double transposition. The intermediate layer, provided by high modernist culture, proved decisive for its ultimate failure as a Socialist Realist work despite the composer's intentions. By the mid-1930s, sex in public was unacceptable. So although it might have been possible to bring Leskov's story into the Soviet canon in the mid-1930s, it proved impossible to do so for a Lady Macbeth seen through the mediation of Kustodiev and Larionov.

The case of Shostakovich's opera forces us to recognize that in at least some instances, it is incorrect to assume that the connection between a classic work and a later reinterpretation/adaptation is direct. Rather, such rehabilitations tend to occur as an accumulative and semi-continuous process. A new interpretation is often mediated by and to some extent dependent on previous reinterpretations, and it may even be the case that an intermediate transposition can have a decisive impact on what a newer version looks like, sometimes despite the desires of an author. That was certainly the case with *Lady Macbeth*, as the mediation of Russian modernism interfered with Shostakovich's desire to recanonize a classic work.

From our contemporary standpoint, it is of little concern whether or not Leskov and his story succeeded in entering the Soviet canon in the 1930s. Rather, the fact that Shostakovich's opera has outlasted much of the rest of the cultural production of this period suggests that the most powerful art works created in the Soviet Union in the 1930s resulted from attempts to work within the system that failed—spectacularly. To Shostakovich's opera we can add Kazimir Malevich's faceless peasant paintings from 1928 to 1932 and Andrei Platonov's *Foundation Pit*.[26] In each of these cases, we find a productive tension when cultural paradigms typical of Russian high modernism collided with those of incipient Socialist Realism. Unlike the destructive collision of matter and anti-matter, however, this interaction of seemingly opposite forces was at times capable of generating genuine works of art.

Notes

This essay was inspired by Hugh McLean's article "The Adventures of an English Comedy in Eighteenth-Century Russia: Dodsley's *Toy Shop* and Lukin's *Scepetil'nik*," in *American Contributions to the Fifth International Congress of Slavists—Sofia, September 1963*, 2 vols. (The Hague: Mouton, 1963), 2:201–12. A shorter version appears in *O Rus! Studia litteraria slavica in honorem Hugh McLean*, ed. Simon Karlinsky, James Rice, and Barry Scherr (Berkeley, Calif.: Berkeley Slavic Specialties, 1995): 358–68.

1. In this essay early Soviet culture means Soviet culture starting in the late 1920s. The period from immediately after the Revolution until the late 1920s was one of artistic ferment and general tolerance (although many individuals and groups were, of course, highly intolerant). It was not until the late 1920s that a state-approved Soviet culture began clearly to emerge.

2. For an excellent discussion of this phenomenon, see Jeffrey Schnapp, "Reading Lessons: Augustine, Proba, and the Christian *Détournement* of Antiquity," *Stanford Literature Review* 9, no. 2 (1992): 99–124.

3. Hugh McLean, *Nikolai Leskov: The Man and His Art* (Cambridge, Mass.: Harvard University Press, 1977), 749.

4. For a general catalogue of versions of "Lady Macbeth" in Soviet culture of this period, see L. Anninskii, *Leskovskoe ozherel'e*, 2nd ed. (Moscow: Kniga, 1986), 70–108.

5. As Faith Wigzell puts it, "from the Formalists onwards Leskov's language, particularly in its contribution to an obviously stylized narrative texture, has undergone a reevaluation. Critical attention, as a consequence, has tended to be directed towards the works with the most colourful *skaz*, at the expense of those works which do not possess a so obviously stylized narrative texture, such as *Ledi Makbet Mtsenskogo uezda*." See her "Folk Stylization in Leskov's *Ledi Makbet Mtsenskogo uezda*," *Slavonic and East European Review* 67, no. 2 (1989): 169. Wigzell goes on to show quite convincingly that folkloric elements are present in the story, albeit on different and more subtle levels.

6. According to Hugh McLean: "The point of such titles is to juxtapose a Shakespearean archetype at a high level of psychological universalization with a specific, local, utterly Russian, and contemporary milieu. The effect on a Russian reader of that time was almost oxymoronic: how could there be a 'Lady Macbeth,' especially nowadays, in such a mudhole as Mtsensk?" (*Nikolai Leskov*, 146).

7. In discussing the transposition of a short story into an opera, we must be careful not to ascribe automatically all changes to genre: some have to do with medium, as Caryl Emerson notes. See her *Boris Godunov: Transpositions of a Russian Theme* (Bloomington: Indiana University Press, 1986), 4–8. In this case, however, we will see that the changes to Leskov's story were the result of generic/ideological choices rather than medium constraints.

Clearly, I reject Ian MacDonald's assertion that the opera "can reasonably be interpreted as a deliberate, if necessarily disguised, expression of antagonism to

Communism"—see his *The New Shostakovich* (Boston: Northeastern University Press, 1990), 93. This claim, which is based primarily on the most dubious sections of Solomon Volkov's *Testimony: The Memoirs of Dmitri Shostakovich*, flies in the face of everything Shostakovich said about his own opera and, even if one believes that he was consciously or unconsciously coerced into the statements I quote here, it is belied by the extent to which the work adheres to the basic patterns of incipient Socialist Realist art.

8. Quoted in Richard Taruskin, "The Unmaking of Lady Macbeth," *San Francisco Opera Program* (1988), 29.

9. See chapters 1 and 2 in this volume.

10. All quotations here are taken from the unpaginated introduction to D. D. Shostakovich, *Sobranie sochinenii v sorok dvukh tomakh*, 42 vols. (Moscow: Muzyka, 1979–1987), vol. 20.

11. For more on the search for a positive hero at this time, see Régine Robin, *Socialist Realism: An Impossible Aesthetic,* trans. Catherine Porter (Stanford, Calif.: Stanford University Press, 1992), 217–96.

12. Shostakovich, unpaginated introduction.

13. Taruskin, "The Unmaking of Lady Macbeth," 31.

14. Shostakovich, unpaginated introduction.

15. For a blow-by-blow account of the cultural situation in the Soviet Union surrounding the *Pravda* editorial, see L. Maksimenkov, *Sumbur vmesto muzyki: Stalinskaia kul'turnaia revoliutsiia, 1936–1938* (Moscow: Iuridicheskaia kniga, 1997), 72–112.

16. For a complete translation of this important editorial, see chapter 8 in this volume.

17. For reproductions of some of the watercolors, see *Boris Kustodiev,* ed., M. G. Etkind (Moscow: Sovetskii khudozhnik, 1982), 177, 179, 181, 183, 189.

18. *Rus': Russkie tipy B. M. Kustodieva, slovo Evg. Zamiatina* (St. Petersburg: Akvilon, 1923).

19. Ibid., 21.

20. Leonore Scheffler minimizes the possible connections between the two works in her *Evgenij Zamjatin: Sein Weltbild und seine literarische Thematik* (Köln: Böhlau, 1984), 238.

21. See *Boris Kustodiev,* 301, 302, 309, 310, 312–13 for reproductions of sketches for this production's sets and costumes.

22. For more on the folkloric element, see Wigzell, "Folk Stylization in Leskov's *Ledi Makbet Mtsenskogo uezda,*" and Thomas R. Beyer, "'Rus': A Modern Russian Folk Tale," *Russian Language Journal* 40, no. 135 (1986): 107–13.

23. For reasons I have not been able to discover, the edition of "Lady Macbeth" that contained these drawings was not published until 1930—see N. S. Leskov, *Ledi Makbet Mtsenskogo uezda,* with illustrations by B. Kustodiev (Leningrad: Izd. Pisatelei v Leningrade, 1930).

24. Solomon Volkov, *Testimony: The Memoirs of Dmitri Shostakovich,* trans. Antonina W. Bouis (New York: Harper & Row, 1979), 18–19. Serious questions have

been raised concerning the veracity of Volkov's book. See Laurel Fay, "Shostakovich versus Volkov: Whose *Testimony?*" *Russian Review* 39, no. 4 (1980): 484–93; *A Shostakovich Casebook*, ed. Malcolm Hamrick Brown (Bloomington: Indiana University Press, 2004). There is little doubt that *Testimony* is based on actual conversations between the two men—most questions have to do with Volkov's attempt to present Shostakovich as a dissident rather than in circumstances like the one detailed here. In any case, it is unlikely that Volkov could have invented this particular conversation, as it could have required knowledge about the composer's early years that would not have been available except from Shostakovich himself.

25. Alternatively, Zamiatin might have reminded Shostakovich of the "Lady Macbeth"—Kustodiev connection, for the two worked together on a scene for Shostakovich's previous opera, *The Nose*.

26. For a treatment of these other works, see Andrew Wachtel, "Meaningful Voids: Facelessness in Platonov and Malevich," in *Boundaries of the Spectacular: Russian Verbal, Visual and Performance Texts in the Age of Modernism*, ed. Catriona Kelly and Stephen Lovell (Cambridge: Cambridge University Press, 1999), 250–77.

8
The Official Denunciation of Shostakovich's *Lady Macbeth of Mtsensk District*

The unsigned editorial below appeared in *Pravda* on January 28, 1936, two days after Stalin attended a performance of D. D. Shostakovich's opera *Lady Macbeth of Mtsensk District*.[1] It is significant both as an illustration of the character and rhythm of Soviet cultural life and as an important episode in the biography of one of the most prominent composers in Soviet history. Readers at the time concluded that the article reflected Stalin's own appraisal of Shostakovich's work; recently, even the phrase "muddle instead of music" has been attributed to the general secretary.[2] Although performances of the opera in leading Soviet theaters had enjoyed critical success for some two years by January 1936, the publication of "Muddle Instead of Music" quickly purged *Lady Macbeth* from the official repertoire, where it was not to reappear until after Stalin's death.

The editorial epitomizes in many ways the relationship of the state to Soviet cultural life during the 1930s. In addition to the official bureaucratic mechanisms that exercised daily oversight over the arts, the party elite, including Stalin himself, hovered over the cultural scene as well, often intervening without warning according to an ill-defined set of norms and protocols. Bureaucrats and cultural agents treated these periodic emanations from above as a form of bellwether, dictating the general path that future artistic activity and cultural policy were to take. In this regard, "Muddle Instead of Music" may be seen as one of the first signs of an impending crackdown on works judged to deviate from the officially prescribed (but poorly defined) Socialist Realist mainstream. In the wake of this article and another, condemning Shostakovich's *The*

Bright Stream, virtually all remaining vestiges of the avant-garde élan of the early Soviet period were violently eliminated in a campaign that ran parallel to the infamous Great Terror.

"Muddle Instead of Music" is of profound importance to Shostakovich's individual biography as well. Hissing that the composer was playing "a game which can end very badly," the article hinted that there was more at stake in 1936 than just the composer's career. The director V. E. Meyerhold had just fallen from favor for his stubborn refusal to break with the avant-garde; Shostakovich could easily have shared that director's fate, insofar as he was also accused of "Meyerholdism" in "Muddle Instead of Music." That he avoided stigma and arrest during these years attests to the young composer's willingness to compromise with the powers that governed Soviet cultural life. Indeed, Shostakovich's next major work, his Fifth Symphony (1937), won instant and enduring acclaim for its melodic appeal and classical form—characteristics that were to form the core of the Socialist Realist canon. Echoes of the "Muddle Instead of Music" scandal continued to resonate in Shostakovich's professional life for the rest of his career, however. In much of his later work the composer observed a fine balance between accessibility and innovation—and never returned to the genre of opera again.

[P. M. Kerzhentsev], Muddle Instead of Music: Concerning the Opera *Lady Macbeth of Mtsensk District*

Pravda, 28 January 1936

Along with the overall rise in the cultural life of our country, demands for good music have also risen. Never before and in no other place have composers faced a more appreciative audience. The popular masses want good songs, but they also want good instrumental compositions and good operas.

A number of theaters have offered Shostakovich's opera *Lady Macbeth of Mtsensk District* to the culturally maturing Soviet public, presenting it as a novelty and as an artistic achievement. Overly deferential music critics have praised this opera to the skies, granting it extraordinary fame. Thus, in place of serious, professional criticism that could aid a young composer in his future work, he has heard nothing but compliments.

From the first minute of the opera, the listener is flabbergasted by an intentionally dissonant, confused stream of noise. Fragments of melody and the bare beginnings of musical phrases seem to submerge, then burst forth, then disappear again amidst crashes, scrapings and squeals. It is difficult to follow this "music" and impossible to commit it to memory.

And so it goes for practically the entire opera. Screaming takes the place of singing on stage. Whenever the composer happens to stumble upon a simple and comprehensible melody, he immediately—as if frightened by this unfortunate turn of events—plunges back into the debris of his musical muddle, which turns into a simple cacophony in places. The expressiveness demanded by listeners been replaced by a maniacal rhythm. Musical noise is called upon to represent passion.

Yet this is not a result of the composer's lack of talent or of his inability to express simple, strong feelings in music. This is music that has been composed in an intentionally "inside-out" manner in order to have no resemblance to classical operatic music or symphonic tonality—the simple, commonly accessible language of music. This is music that has been composed in order to negate opera, just as "leftist" art in the theater generally negates simplicity, realism, the intelligibility of images and the natural intonations of words themselves. It transplants into opera and music the most flawed features of "Meyerholdism" in an exaggerated form.[3] This is a leftist muddle in place of natural, human music. The ability of good music to captivate the masses has been sacrificed to petty bourgeois, formalist[4] etudes in a vain attempt to achieve originality by means of cheap novelty. This is simply a nonsensical game—a game that can end very badly.[5]

The danger of such a movement in Soviet music is clear. Leftist ugliness in music springs from the same source as leftist ugliness in painting, poetry, pedagogy and science. Petty bourgeois "innovation" leads to a break with genuine art, genuine science and genuine literature.

The composer of *Lady Macbeth of Mtsensk District* even turned to jazz for nervous, convulsive, epileptic music in order to endow his protagonists with "passion."[6]

At a time when our critics, music critics included, are hailing Socialist Realism, the stage has presented us with the most vulgar naturalism via Shostakovich's opera.[7] Everyone, both the merchants and the people, is presented in the same animalistic mode. A predatory merchant woman who has murderously clawed her way to wealth and power is presented as some kind of "victim" of bourgeois society. New meaning, which is absent from Leskov's tale of daily life, has been foisted upon the story.

And it's all just coarse, primitive and vulgar. The music wheezes, hoots, puffs and pants in order to depict love scenes with a maximum of naturalism. "Love" is smeared over the entire opera in the most vulgar manner.

The merchant's double bed takes center stage in the set. It is here where all "problems" are resolved. Death from poisoning and whipping are shown in this same coarsely naturalistic style on stage—virtually in front of our very eyes.

Apparently, the composer did not take the trouble to consider what the Soviet audience is looking for and expecting in music. It's as if he intentionally encoded his music and confused all of its resonances, in order to appeal to only those aesthete formalists who have lost a healthy sense of taste. He has overlooked the demands of Soviet culture that have expunged barbarity from all aspects of Soviet life. Certain critics have called this tribute to merchant lasciviousness a satire. But there can be no serious discussion of satire here. The composer merely tried to use all the means at his disposal in order to win public sympathy for the coarse and vulgar aspirations of the merchant woman Katerina Izmailova.

Lady Macbeth enjoys success among the bourgeois public abroad. Could it be that the bourgeois public praises this opera precisely because it is so confused and absolutely apolitical? Could it be that it tickles the bourgeois audience's perverted tastes with its convulsive, clamorous, neurasthenic music?

Our theaters have expended no small effort in order to stage Shostakovich's opera. The actors have exhibited significant talent in overcoming the noise, clamor and squealing of the orchestra. They have attempted to compensate for the opera's melodic poverty. Unfortunately, this has rendered the coarsely naturalistic features of the work even more apparent. Their talented acting deserves our recognition, yet their wasted efforts deserve only our pity.

Notes

1. "Sumbur vmesto muzyki: Ob opere 'Ledi Makbet Mtsenskogo uezda,'" *Pravda*, 28 January 1936, 3.

2. L. Maksimenkov, *Sumbur vmesto muzyki: Stalinskaia kul'turnaia revoliutsiia, 1936–1938* (Moscow: Iuridicheskaia kniga, 1997), 97–98. Maksimenkov persuasively attributes the article to P. M. Kerzhentsev, while Ian Macdonald points to Stalin, Solomon Volkov to Stalin and David Zaslavskii, Elizabeth Wilson exclusively to Zaslavskii, Sheila Fitzpatrick to A. A. Zhdanov, and Frans Lemaire to Kerzhentsev and V. Gorodinskii. See Ian McDonald, *The New Shostakovich* (Boston: Northeastern University Press, 1990), 103–4; *Testimony: The Memoirs of Dmitri Shostakovich*, ed. Solomon Volkov, trans. Antonina W. Bouis (New York: Harper & Row, 1979),

113–14; idem, *Istoriia kul'tury Sankt-Peterburga: S osnovaniia do nashikh dnei* (Moscow: Nezavisimaia gazeta, 2001), 386; Elizabeth Wilson, *Shostakovich—A Life Remembered* (Princeton: Princeton University Press, 1994), 109; Sheila Fitzpatrick, "The Lady Macbeth Affair: Shostakovich and the Soviet Puritans," in *The Cultural Front: Power and Culture in Revolutionary Russia* (Ithaca, N.Y.: Cornell University Press, 1992), 187; Frans Lemaire, *La musique du XXe siecle en Russie et dans les anciennes Republiques sovietiques* (Paris: Fayard, 1994), 85.

3. The word used in the original is *meierkhol'dovshchina*.

4. "Formalism" was the derogatory label applied in the cultural politics of the early 1930s to much of the avant-garde movement in art.

5. "Nonsense" in the original Russian is *zaumnye veshchi*. This refers to the term *zaum*, sometimes translated as "trans-sense," coined by certain Futurists of the 1910s–1920s to describe their version of a utopian, futuristic poetry.

6. Jazz was described in Soviet critical discourse as a degenerate form of bourgeois music.

7. "Naturalism" here describes the opera's indulgent focus on vulgarity and the erotic, contrasted against the propriety and modesty of Socialist Realism.

Ivan the Terrible

9
The Terrible Tsar as Comic Hero
Mikhail Bulgakov's *Ivan Vasil'evich*

∾ Maureen Perrie

The "idealization" of Ivan IV in the Soviet Union was primarily a phenomenon of the 1940s. That decade saw the appearance of V. I. Kostylev's three-part novel, *Ivan the Terrible*, A. N. Tolstoi's two-part play of the same title, I. L. Sel'vinskii's play, *The Livonian War*, and V. A. Solov'ev's play, *The Great Sovereign*, as well as Sergei Eisenstein's famous film. In historical scholarship, the "rehabilitation" of Ivan reached its apogee with the wartime publication of popular biographies by S. V. Bakhrushin, R. Iu. Vipper, and I. I. Smirnov. Artistic representations of the tsar, however, turned out to be problematic. The best known case involved the criticism and withdrawal of part 2 of Eisenstein's film in 1946. A. N. Tolstoi also encountered difficulties when his first play about Ivan was proscribed in 1942.[1] But the earliest controversy involving the depiction of Ivan Groznyi on the Soviet stage took place some ten years before the Eisenstein scandal and involved M. A. Bulgakov's comedy *Ivan Vasil'evich*, which was banned in May 1936.

Various commentators have discussed Bulgakov's play. Some have suggested that it was a harmless lightweight piece that became an accidental victim of the campaign against formalism; others have argued that it was intended by its author as a subversive allegory that compared the despotism of sixteenth-century Muscovy with that of Stalin's Russia.[2] In this chapter I propose to reexamine the context within which the banning of *Ivan Vasil'evich* took place. I consider the possibility that it was thought to draw an unflattering parallel between Groznyi and Stalin, and I explore the way in which Bulgakov presents the figure of Ivan the Terrible in his play. But I go on to argue that the episode should properly be viewed not only in the narrow context of Soviet representations of Ivan IV, but also in the broader context of the overall rehabilitation of tsarist history that was under way at the time that Bulgakov's play came under official fire. An examination of the circumstances surrounding the play may thus cast some light on the development of official Soviet attitudes toward the prerevolutionary Russian past in the mid-1930s.

The most generally accepted explanation for the banning of *Ivan Vasil'evich* places it in the context of the attack on Bulgakov's play *Molière*, which fell victim to the campaign against formalism that was unleashed in early 1936. This is indeed the most obvious reason for the ban, and I therefore begin by reviewing the events that culminated in the prohibition of the play.

Bulgakov's works were regarded as controversial throughout the 1920s, and by the summer of 1929 all of his plays had been banned. In 1929 he had been working on *The Cabal of Hypocrites* (*Kabala sviatosh*), a play about Molière. The prohibition of this new play by Glavrepertkom[3] provoked the author to write a letter "To the Government of the USSR" on 28 March 1930. This elicited Stalin's intervention, and after a telephone call from the general secretary in April 1930, Bulgakov was allowed to work as a director at the Moscow Art Theater (MKhAT). Nevertheless, his plays were still not performed.[4] A year later, however, however, his fortunes improved: *The Cabal of Hypocrites* was approved by Glavrepertkom on 3 October 1931, under the title of *Molière*, and soon afterward MKhAT agreed to stage it.[5] In early 1932, as a result of Stalin's personal intervention, *The Days of the Turbins*, which had been banned along with Bulgakov's other works in 1929, was allowed to return to the stage at MKhAT.[6] But the Molière project encountered further difficulties. A biography of Molière that Bulgakov had written in 1932–1933 for the series "Lives of Remarkable People" was rejected in April 1933, apparently because it was thought to contain Aesopian commentary about contemporary Soviet reality.[7] The same fate was subsequently to befall the Molière play, as well as another play about Pushkin (*The Last Days*). Indeed, both were banned for similar reasons: Bulgakov's depiction of famous writers' troubled relationships with rulers who sought to control them provided too close an analogy to the Soviet situation.[8] In connection with *Molière*, P. M. Kerzhentsev, the chairman of the All-Union Committee for Artistic Affairs, complained to Stalin that Bulgakov "wants to evoke for the spectator an analogy between the position of the writer under the dictatorship of the proletariat and under the 'arbitrary tyranny' of Louis XIV."[9]

In 1933–1934 Bulgakov wrote a science fiction play entitled *Bliss* (*Blazhenstvo*), which dealt with the theme of time travel. When the play was completed, however, the scenes set in the future were considered unsuccessful and even dangerous (for obvious reasons, anti-Utopian visions of the future were unwelcome during the Stalinist 1930s). That said, it was felt that the episodes set in the past, in the reign of Ivan the Terrible, were not only quite harmless but also held considerable promise as the seed of a comedy for the Satire Theater.[10] "They've all . . . fallen in love with Ivan Groznyi," Bulgakov noted wryly.[11] The play, now entitled *Ivan Vasil'evich*, was completed by October 1935, and when Bulgakov read it to colleagues, the theme provoked great merriment.[12]

The hero of *Ivan Vasil'evich* is an inventor, Timofeev, who is found at the beginning of the first act working in his apartment on a powerful new radio receiver. The communal radio loudspeaker in the hallway suddenly breaks into crackly life with the strains of Rimskii-Korsakov's opera *The Maid of Pskov*, which is set in the reign of Ivan the Terrible. Unable to concentrate ("I'm fed up with Ioann and his bells!"), Timofeev falls asleep. The rest of the play subsequently turns out to be a dream sequence.[13]

As a result of a mishap with a time machine designed by Timofeev in his dream, Ivan the Terrible arrives in the inventor's apartment, while two figures from the present day are transported to Ivan IV's palace. One of these Soviet time travelers is Ivan Vasil'evich Bunsha, the manager of Timofeev's apartment block and a self-important minor official whose name and patronymic are, of course, identical with those of the Terrible Tsar; the other is Zhorzh Miloslavskii, a clever thief who has broken into the apartment of Timofeev's next-door neighbor, Shpak. The plot subsequently develops as a comedy of imposture and mistaken identity. Bunsha plays the part of the tsar—very badly at first, the situation being saved thanks only to Miloslavskii's quick wits. But Bunsha soon grows into his royal role, shouting at the tsar's secretary and flirting outrageously with the tsaritsa.[14] Back in the twentieth century, Timofeev's actress wife, Zinaida, initially mistakes the real tsar for an actor in costume, but after realizing her mistake she persuades Ivan to change out of his royal attire into a modern suit. This leaves him looking uncommonly like Bunsha, for whom he is subsequently mistaken by the residents of the apartment block.[15]

Glavrepertkom was worried about possible subversion in Bulgakov's play but reported to the Satire Theater's management that their five-person commission had been unable to find anything suspicious in it. Minor suggestions—"would it be possible for Ivan Groznyi to say that things are better now than they were then?"—belied less tangible misgivings about the play and playwright.[16] Glavrepertkom remained unhappy. Bulgakov's wife,

Elena Sergeevna, noted sardonically that one member of the committee, V. M. Mlechin, had been unable to decide whether to approve the work: "At first he had looked for a harmful idea in the play. Having failed to find one, he was disturbed by the thought that it had no ideas in it at all."[17] In spite of continuing reservations on the part of the authorities, *Ivan Vasil'evich* was judged to require only minor amendments, and it went into rehearsal in November 1935.[18]

At the beginning of 1936, however, an official attack on formalism was launched with an onslaught against Shostakovich's opera *Lady Macbeth of Mtsensk District* on 28 January and his ballet *The Bright Stream* on 6 February.[19] Soon it was Bulgakov's turn, with *Pravda*'s denunciation of *Molière* on 9 March.[20] "When he read it," Elena Sergeevna noted in her diary, "M[ikhail] A[fanas'evich] said, 'That's the end of *Molière*, and the end of *Ivan Vasil'evich.*'"[21] Surprisingly, though, while *Molière* was removed from the MKhAT repertoire that very day, rehearsals of *Ivan Vasil'evich* continued. True, the Satire Theater suggested some new amendments to the play, with the director, N. M. Gorchakov, even proposing the introduction of a Young Pioneer into the cast. But Bulgakov "categorically refused," Elena noted indignantly; "how could he take such a cheap step!"[22] A dress rehearsal was held on May 11, but Bulgakova was dissatisfied with the production: "Gorchakov for some reason was afraid that the role of Miloslavskii (a brilliant thief, as [Bulgakov] had conceived him) was too attractive, and had asked [the actor P. N.] Pol' to be made up as a kind of pink piglet with funny ears . . . Yes, Gorchakov is weak, a weak director. And a coward into the bargain."[23] Two days later, the main dress rehearsal was held. Elena Sergeevna recorded that apart from immediate members of the Bulgakov family, the only people present were Ia. I. Boiarskii, the deputy director of the Committee for Artistic Affairs, and A. I. Angarov, the deputy head of the culture and enlightenment section of the party's Central Committee:

> at the end of the play, Furer came into the auditorium, still in his overcoat and holding his cap and briefcase—it seems he's from the Moscow Party Committee.
>
> Immediately after the performance the play was banned. Gorchakov reported that Furer had said straight away, "I don't advise you to put it on."[24]

Elena Bulgakova's account of the fate of *Bliss/Ivan Vasil'evich* in 1934–1936 suggests that the suppression of the play was a by-product of the developing campaign against formalism, as well as a renewed campaign against "bourgeois" intellectuals. She also indicates, however, that the censors suspected it of subversive intent. In the following section, I examine the view that the play drew an unflattering parallel between Ivan IV and Stalin and consider the possibility that this may have been the focus of the censors' suspicions.

Bulgakov's *Ivan Vasil'evich* is a fairly light-hearted piece,[25] which primarily satirizes aspects of contemporary Soviet life. Nevertheless, its depiction of Ivan the Terrible may have provided grounds for official concern. In light of Kerzhentsev's suspicion that *Molière* was intended as a political allegory, it is likely that the authorities feared that *Ivan Vasil'evich* involved a subversive analogy between Ivan IV and Stalin. Derogatory parallels between Stalin and historical figures represented on the stage were already a perennial concern of the censor. A. N. Tolstoi's "insufficiently heroic" depiction of Peter the Great in his *On the Rack* had aroused suspicion in 1929,[26] and at the end of 1936 Dem'ian Bednyi's comic opera *The Epic Heroes* (*Bogatyri*) was to be seen by some to contain disrespectful allusions to the party secretary and his entourage.[27] Certainly Bulgakov's *Ivan Vasil'evich* has been interpreted as a political parable. Peter Doyle has argued that it is "a skilful political satire on dictatorial rulers in general, and, by implication, on Stalin in particular;"[28] and a Russian writer has recently referred to "the equals-sign placed by M. A. Bulgakov between the 'house-managers' of Russia in the sixteenth and twentieth centuries."[29] The medievalist Ia. S. Lur'e also found elements of allegory in the play, observing that its depiction of the *oprichnina* terror "could have evoked very unpleasant associations."[30] To illustrate his point, Lur'e cites an episode in which Miloslavskii introduces himself to Ivan's secretary as "Prince Miloslavskii" and is told that he had been hanged three days earlier, on the tsar's orders. The quick-witted thief explains that he is a cousin of the executed man, a fellow from whom he had in any case dissociated himself (*otmezhevalsia*). This was a provocative use of vocabulary employed by relatives of "socially alien elements," such as kulaks and priests, in the early 1930s, as they attempted to escape social stigma.[31] Ivan the Terrible's tyranny "also affected officials of the diplomatic service," Lur'e comments, quoting a scene in which Miloslavskii learns that the only German interpreter at court had been boiled alive in a cauldron.[32] Although Lur'e is unwilling to attribute the play's ban to this seemingly Aesopian use of allegory, he asserts that if the play had appeared with the references to these victims of the *oprichnina* terror, "it would probably have brought the author no less unpleasantness than *The Days of the Turbins* and *Molière*."[33]

It would not be surprising if the censor had suspected that Bulgakov's Ivan was intended as a surrogate for the Soviet leader. There is evidence that some of Stalin's critics compared him to Ivan the Terrible in the 1930s. According to Isaac Deutscher, oppositionists referred to Stalin "as the Genghiz Khan of the Politbureau, the Asiatic, the new Ivan the Terrible."[34] Sarah Davies cites a letter to Zhdanov from workers of the Kirov plant in Leningrad in 1935, which criticized the Bolsheviks as "oppressors of everyone except their *oprichniki* [the tsar's fierce bodyguard]."[35] And the writer Iu. I. Iurkin is known to have denounced Stalin as a new Ivan the Terrible in 1937.[36]

The critical significance of these analogies derived, of course, from the persistence of a negative perception of the tsar as a tyrant and of the *oprichnina* as an arbitrary instrument of state terror. Such an evaluation of Ivan and his *oprichniki* had been common in pre-revolutionary historical, literary, and artistic works. But Ivan had also found a number of nineteenth-century defenders, such as K. D. Kavelin and S. M. Solov'ev; and two highly positive assessments of the tsar—by R. Iu. Vipper and S. F. Platonov—were published in the early 1920s.[37] At the time when Bulgakov began to write *Ivan Vasil'evich*, however, the dominant voice in Soviet historiography was still that of the Marxist historian M. N. Pokrovskii. Although he had downplayed the influence of the tsar's personality in line with his "materialist" ideological stance, which attributed minimal significance to the role of the individual in history, Pokrovskii had nevertheless described Ivan as a "hysterical blockhead" and egomaniac.[38] Hostile assessments of Ivan persisted well into the 1930s,[39] and in the article on the tsar that was published in the *Great Soviet Encyclopedia* in 1933, Pokrovskii's pupil M. V. Nechkina criticized the favorable view of Ivan IV provided by Vipper and Platonov as counter-revolutionary monarchist apologetics.[40] The official "rehabilitation" of Ivan began only in the later 1930s, with the publication of new textbooks on Russian history for secondary schools and higher educational establishments; as I have argued elsewhere, it may have been their concern to avoid suspicion of subversive analogies between Ivan's *oprichnina* and Stalin's Great Terror of 1937–1938 that led historians to provide justifications for the tsar.[41]

Bulgakov's image of the Terrible Tsar in *Ivan Vasil'evich* is in many respects consistent with the negative depiction of the tsar that had predominated in the pre-revolutionary period, although the author tailors it to the comedic genre of his play by describing some of Ivan IV's cruelly humorous methods of execution. For example, Ivan tells Timofeev that he had once punished the inventor of a set of wings by sitting him on a barrel of gunpowder, "to make him fly."[42] Sixteenth-century Russia turns out to be a harsh environment (the tsar predicts, to Timofeev's horror, that Bunsha and Miloslavskii will be beheaded there),[43] and Bulgakov derives black humor from his twentieth-century characters' expressions of indignation on hearing about its cruel practices. ("That is a typical excess," Miloslavskii exclaims, when told that thieves are hanged by the rib in Muscovy.)[44] But the writer does not depict the full horror of the *oprichnina*, and the *oprichniki* appear only briefly in the play, when Miloslavskii sends them off to fight the Crimean khan.[45]

In fact Bulgakov—like some nineteenth-century writers—depicts Ivan not as a stereotypical tyrant, but as a complex and contradictory character. On the one hand, he is hot-tempered and willing to resort to harsh and violent punishments: he threatens to impale Zinaida's lover, the film director Iakin, for cuckolding Timofeev and beats Iakin up when the director tries to hire him for a production. But the tsar is also shown to be impulsively generous: he offers to compensate Shpak for being robbed and eventually grants Iakin an estate when he agrees to marry Zinaida.[46] Thus Bulgakov's depiction of Ivan contains elements of the broadly positive folklore image of the tsar to which Maksim Gor'kii had drawn attention at the First Congress of the Soviet Writers' Union in 1934.[47] Lur'e notes that, "In accordance with the folksongs about Ivan IV, the tsar in Bulgakov's play is not only terrible (*groznyi*) but also at times benevolent (*milostiv*)." And Lur'e hints that the writer may have seen an analogy between Groznyi and Stalin in this respect: Ivan rewards Iakin, just as Stalin had acted as Bulgakov's benefactor in 1930 and 1932. Even after 1936 Bulgakov continued to hope for further favors from Stalin, as Lur'e points out, but his hopes turned out to be illusory. In using the term *illusion* in relation to Bulgakov's expectations of Stalin's benevolence,[48] Lur'e is—no doubt consciously—evoking a favorite cliché of Soviet scholars about the "naïve monarchist illusions" cherished by the peasants in relation to the "good tsar." Ironically, in the Soviet period it was the creative intelligentsia, rather than the peasants, who believed in Stalin's benevolence.[49] Thus if Bulgakov did intend to suggest a parallel between Ivan and Stalin, the analogy was a complex and subtle one. It was apparently undetected by the censor in 1935, when the authorities were unable to find anything in the play to justify its prohibition.

Nor is there any evidence that the censors were concerned that Bulgakov's depiction of Ivan Groznyi was too negative. As we have already noted, the rehabilitation of the tsar did not get under way until the publication of the new history textbooks in the later 1930s. But the *Ivan Vasil'evich* episode coincided not only with the onslaught against formalism in the arts but also with a new stage in the campaign for the reform of history teaching in Soviet schools.[50] In the final section of this chapter, I examine this campaign and its significance for the fate of Bulgakov's play.

In May 1934 the approach to history associated with Pokrovskii was publicly criticized for its "abstract, schematic character," and new school textbooks were commissioned that were to stress dates and facts and to present pupils with information about important historical events and individuals.[51] At the beginning of 1936, criticism of the draft textbooks on USSR history focused on their negative depiction of the Russian past: articles in the central press stressed the "positive" and "progressive" character of many aspects of tsarist history, such as the formation of the centralized Russian state, Minin and Pozharskii's liberation of Moscow from the Poles, and the reforms of Peter the Great.[52]

The adoption of this revised approach to history was connected with a new stress on "Soviet patriotism" in the mid-1930s. Emerging in the context of the threatening international situation created by Hitler's advent to power, the patriotism campaign linked love for the Soviet present with knowledge of the tsarist past and pride in its achievements.[53] A related concern was the refutation of "fascist falsifiers" of Russian history who, like the "Pokrovskyites," presented a distortedly negative picture of the Russian past that threatened to undermine popular morale.[54] Although stress continued to be placed on class struggle and on the role of the ordinary people as the makers of history, the need for heroic exemplars in the field of national defense was soon to involve the glorification of grand princes, tsars, and generals who had served as the leaders of successful military campaigns (the "mobilization" of Aleksandr Nevskii in 1937–1938 was an early and strikingly effective example of this policy). These priorities militated against the depiction of major "progressive" figures and events of the Russian past in a comedic mode. Although this was to famously precipitate the banning of Dem'ian Bednyi's farcical opera *The Epic Heroes* in November 1936, Bulgakov's *Ivan Vasil'evich* is best seen as the first casualty of this campaign.[55]

Bulgakov's Ivan is depicted in a distinctly unheroic mode. He is terrified by the unexpected appearance in his palace of the time travelers, whom he identifies as demons.[56] He gratefully accepts a shot of vodka that Timofeev offers him to calm his panic at finding himself in the twentieth century.[57] Left alone in Timofeev's apartment, he first is fascinated by the gramophone and the telephone,[58] and then is scolded for his drunkenness by Bunsha's nagging wife and Shpak, both of whom mistake him for the house manager.[59] Ivan's court is also presented in an unflattering light. The *oprichniki* are easily fooled by Miloslavskii into accepting Bunsha as the tsar, while the secretary—a fawning, kowtowing lackey—fails to prevent Miloslavskii from ceding Russian territory to the Swedes. The situation at court rapidly degenerates into farce when Bunsha and Miloslavskii dance a rumba with the tsaritsa and the secretary.[60] Such a disrespectful depiction of the Russian past was clearly out of line with the stridently patriotic sensibilities of the emerging new official approach to history.

Although attempts were subsequently made to resurrect Bulgakov's plays about Molière and Pushkin, *Ivan Vasil'evich* was permanently abandoned.[61] The reason for this probably lies in its fundamental approach to its historical theme, and in its comedic genre in particular. Bulgakov seems to have drawn the appropriate conclusion from the episode. He continued to work on themes from early Russian history but played it safe by focusing on figures who had already been rehabilitated and by dealing with them in conventionally heroic artistic modes. He even considered entering a competition to author a new primary school textbook on Russian history. On reading the press announcement of the competition in March 1936,[62] he underlined the words "prize" and "100,000 roubles" as well as the adjectives "clear, interesting, artistic," which were used to describe the desired stylistic qualities of the textbook. He began work on it the very next day and produced several chapters, including one on Pugachev, before eventually abandoning the project.[63]

Later, when working at the Bolshoi Theater, Bulgakov proposed an opera on Pugachev.[64] Still later, while secretly devoting himself to *The Master and Margarita*, Bulgakov was to work on the librettos of operas about patriotic figures from early-modern Russian history: Peter the Great, and Minin and Pozharskii.[65] But the Petrine project ran into difficulties, and *Minin and Pozharskii* was scrapped when the Bolshoi decided to put on S. M. Gorodetskii's version of Glinka's *A Life for the Tsar*.[66] That said, Bulgakov played an important (and unacknowledged) role assisting Gorodetskii in the reworking of the libretto of Glinka's opera while working on more recent historical topics.[67] In 1936–1937 he returned to the period of the Civil War that had inspired his *Days of the Turbins*, with an opera libretto entitled *The Black Sea*; and in 1938–1939 he wrote *Batum*, a play about the young Stalin's role as a revolutionary leader in the Caucasus.

This chapter has suggested several possible reasons for the banning of

Bulgakov's *Ivan Vasil'evich*. Long described as an accidental victim of the prohibition of *Molière*, in the context of the anti-formalism campaign of early 1936, it seems likely that two other factors have been overlooked that may have played a substantial role in the play's demise. First, with its discussions of cruelty and "excesses," *Ivan Vasil'evich* may have been read by the censor as an allegorical criticism of the brutality of the Stalin era. Second, the play's comedic mode may have been judged inappropriate for the depiction of the architect of the "expansion of the Russian state" at a time of patriotic mobilization, when so many figures and events of pre-revolutionary Russian history were being recognized as "progressive."

But although either of these considerations could have contributed to the prohibition of the play, the latter is the more plausible of the two. The fact that attempts were subsequently made to resurrect Bulgakov's plays about Molière and Pushkin, but not *Ivan Vasil'evich*, suggests that the problem lay in its fundamental approach, rather than in its allegorical potential (which could, after all, have been eliminated by relatively minor editing). Such reasoning certainly explains the banning of Bednyi's *The Epic Heroes*. This at least seems to be the conclusion that Bulgakov drew: as visible from his subsequent work on themes from early Russian history, Bulgakov focused after 1936 on figures who had already been "rehabilitated," dealing with them in only conventional, "realistic" artistic modes. Whatever the specific reasons for the banning of *Ivan Vasil'evich* in March 1936, there was no possibility, after Bednyi's fiasco later that year, that Bulgakov's comedic representation of sixteenth-century Muscovy would ever be allowed to appear on the Stalinist stage.

Notes

1. On the complex course of the rehabilitation of Ivan the Terrible see, for example, Bernd Uhlenbruch, "The Annexation of History: Eisenstein and the Ivan Grozny Cult of the 1940s," in *The Culture of the Stalin Period*, ed. Hans Günther (London: Macmillan, 1990), 266–87; Maureen Perrie, "The Tsar, the Emperor, the Leader: Ivan the Terrible, Peter the Great and Anatolii Rybakov's Stalin," in *Stalinism: Its Nature and Aftermath—Essays in Honour of Moshe Lewin*, ed. Nick Lampert and Gábor Rittersporn (London: Macmillan, 1992), 77–100; Maureen Perrie, "Nationalism and History: The Cult of Ivan the Terrible in Stalin's Russia," in *Russian Nationalism, Past and Present*, ed. Geoffrey Hosking and Robert Service (London: Macmillan, 1998), 107–27; and Kevin M. F. Platt and David Brandenberger, "Terribly Romantic, Terribly Progressive, or Terribly Tragic: Rehabilitating Ivan IV under

I.V. Stalin," *Russian Review* 58, no. 4 (1999): 635–54. The process is discussed in detail in Maureen Perrie, *The Cult of Ivan the Terrible in Stalin's Russia* (London: Palgrave, 2001).

2. For an assessment of these two positions, see Peter Doyle, "Bulgakov's *Ivan Vasil'evich*: Light-Hearted Comedy or Serious Satire?" *Journal of Russian Studies* 43 (1982): 33–42.

3. Main Repertory Committee, the theatrical censor.

4. *Dnevnik Eleny Bulgakovoi*, ed. V. Losev and L. Ianovskaia (Moscow: Knizhnaia palata, 1990), 19–21; J. A. E. Curtis, *Manuscripts Don't Burn: Mikhail Bulgakov—A Life in Letters and Diaries* (London: Bloomsbury, 1991), 72–73, 103–14; Vitaly Shentalinsky, *The KGB's Literary Archive* (London: Harvill, 1995), 81–94.

5. *Dnevnik Eleny Bulgakovoi*, 23.

6. Ibid., 23–24. *The Days of the Turbins* was based on Bulgakov's novel *The White Guard*, which is set in Kiev during the Civil War.

7. Curtis, *Manuscripts Don't Burn*, 147–48, 158–59. See also *Dnevnik Eleny Bulgakovoi*, 337.

8. Spencer E. Roberts, *Soviet Historical Drama* (The Hague: Martinus Nijhoff, 1965), 130–31; Curtis, *Manuscripts Don't Burn*, 72, 230; *Dnevnik Eleny Bulgakovoi*, 116–18, 367–68; L. Maksimenkov, *Sumbur vmesto muzyki: Stalinskaia kul'turnaia revoliutsiia, 1936–1938* (Moscow: Iuridicheskaia kniga, 1997), 182–96.

9. Maksimenkov, *Sumbur vmesto muzyki*, 191.

10. *Dnevnik Eleny Bulgakovoi*, 56, 71–72, 345; Curtis, *Manuscripts Don't Burn*, 150.

11. See his letter to P. A. Popov dated 28 April 1934 in M. A. Bulgakov, *Pis'ma: Zhizneopisanie v dokumentakh*, ed. V. I. Losev and V. V. Petelin (Moscow: Sovremennik, 1989), 287.

12. *Dnevnik Eleny Bulgakovoi*, 104–5.

13. M. A. Bulgakov, *Ivan Vasil'evich; Mertvye dushi* (Munich: Tovarishchestvo zarubezhnykh pisatelei, 1964), 9–10.

14. Ibid., 54, 62–63.

15. Ibid., 34–47.

16. *Dnevnik Eleny Bulgakovoi*, 106.

17. Ibid., 107.

18. Ibid., 108–9.

19. On this campaign, see Sheila Fitzpatrick, *The Cultural Front: Power and Culture in Revolutionary Russia* (Ithaca, N.Y.: Cornell University Press, 1992), 183–215; Maksimenkov, *Sumbur vmesto muzyki*, 72–181.

20. "Vneshnii blesk i fal'shivoe soderzhanie," *Pravda*, 9 March 1936, 3. On the banning of *Molière*, see Roberts, *Soviet Historical Drama*, 130–31; Maksimenkov, *Sumbur vmesto muzyki*, 187–91.

21. *Dnevnik Eleny Bulgakovoi*, 116.

22. Ibid., 118.

23. Ibid., 120.

24. Ibid. The text of the play was first published in 1964 in Munich and in the USSR in 1965. It served as the basis for the 1971 film *Ivan Vasil'evich Changes*

Professions. Furer is linked to the All-Union Central Committee in Mikhail Bulgakov, *Dnevnik, pis'ma, 1914–1940*, ed. V. I. Losev (Moscow: Sovremennik, 1997), 407.

25. In June 1940 the critic Iu. Iuzovskii, recommending its inclusion in a proposed posthumous publication of Bulgakov's plays, described it as a "cheerful, witty joke." K. N. Kirilenko, "Teatral'noe nasledie M. A. Bulgakova v TsGALI SSSR," in *Problemy teatral'nogo naslediia M. A. Bulgakova: Sbornik nauchnykh trudov* (Leningrad: LGITMiK, 1987), 135, 146.

26. Roberts, *Soviet Historical Drama*, 103–4.

27. I. S. Eventov, *Davnie vstrechi—vospominaniia i ocherki* (Leningrad: Sovetskii pisatel', 1991), 268–75. On this episode see Roberts, *Soviet Historical Drama*, 130–37; Maksimenkov, *Sumbur vmesto muzyki*, 212–22; Perrie, *Cult of Ivan the Terrible*, 31–33; and chapter 5 in this volume.

28. Doyle, "Bulgakov's *Ivan Vasil'evich*," 34.

29. A. L Nikitin, "O pol'ze al'ternativnykh vzgliadov v istoricheskoi nauke," in *Kogo boialsia Ivan Groznyi? K voprosu o proiskhozhdenii oprichniny*, ed. G. L. Grigor'ev (Moscow: IGS, 1998), 3.

30. Ia. S. Lur'e, "Ivan Groznyi i drevnerusskaia literatura v tvorchestve M. Bulgakova," in *Trudy Otdela drevnerusskoi literatury*, vol. 45 (St. Petersburg: Nauka, 1992), 320.

31. Bulgakov, *Ivan Vasil'evich*, 52–53. On the renunciation of former identities, see Sheila Fitzpatrick, *Everyday Stalinism: Ordinary Life in Extraordinary Times—Soviet Russia in the 1930s* (New York: Oxford University Press, 1999), 127–28.

32. Lur'e, "Ivan Groznyi," 320; cf. Bulgakov, *Ivan Vasil'evich*, 56. The state treasurer N. A. Funikov was boiled alive in an execution on Red Square in July 1570—see I. Taube and E. Kruze, "Velikogo kniazia Moskovskogo neslykhannaia tiraniia," *Russkii istoricheskii zhurnal* 8 (1922): 51. This punishment appears to have made an impact on the popular imagination, as it is featured in historical folklore about Ivan—see Maureen Perrie, *The Image of Ivan the Terrible in Russian Folklore* (Cambridge: Cambridge University Press, 1987), 60, 210, 218.

33. Lur'e, "Ivan Groznyi," 321. V. Kaverin had earlier drawn attention to these two episodes in his introduction to the first edition of Bulgakov's plays to include *Ivan Vasil'evich*—see M. A. Bulgakov, *Dramy i komedii* (Moscow: Iskusstvo, 1965), 14.

34. Deutscher adds: "The grumblings and epithets were immediately reported to Stalin, who had his ears everywhere." See Isaac Deutscher, *Stalin: A Political Biography*, rev. ed. (Harmondsworth, UK: Penguin Books, 1990), 349–50.

35. Sarah Davies, *Popular Opinion in Stalin's Russia: Terror, Propaganda and Dissent, 1934–1941* (Cambridge: Cambridge University Press, 1997), 135.

36. Eduard Sheiderman, "Benedikt Livshits: Arest, sledstvie, rasstrel," *Zvezda* 1 (1996): 84.

37. R. Iu. Vipper, *Ivan Groznyi* (Moscow: Del'fin, 1922); S. F. Platonov, *Ivan Groznyi (1530–1584)* (St. Petersburg: Brokgauz-Efron, 1923).

38. M. N. Pokrovskii, *Izbrannye proizvedeniia v chetyrekh knigakh*, 4 vols. (Moscow: Mysl', 1966), 1:256, 3:57.

39. Platt and Brandenberger, "Terribly Romantic," 637–38.
40. M. Nechkina, "Ivan IV," in *Bol'shaia sovetskaia entsiklopediia*, 65 vols. (Moscow: Sovetskaia entsiklopediia, 1933), 27:329.
41. Perrie, *Cult of Ivan the Terrible*, 78–84.
42. Bulgakov, *Ivan Vasil'evich*, 30. This is a creative adaptation of the circumstances surrounding Ivan's execution of the landowner Nikita Kazarinov, as recounted by Andrei Kurbskii. When Kazarinov sought to escape the *oprichniki* by becoming a monk ("he accepted the great angelic habit"), the tsar ordered him to be placed atop several barrels of gunpowder with a lit fuse ("He is an angel: he ought to fly up to heaven!"). See *Prince A. M. Kurbsky's History of Ivan IV*, ed. J. L. I. Fennell (Cambridge: Cambridge University Press, 1965), 228–31. On Ivan's grimly humorous punishments, some of which—like boiling alive—are reflected in folklore, see Perrie, *Image of Ivan the Terrible*, 96–101. On Bulgakov's use of Old Russian literary sources, including Kurbskii's *History*, in *Ivan Vasil'evich*, see also Lur'e, "Ivan Groznyi," 318.
43. Bulgakov, *Ivan Vasil'evich*, 29.
44. Ibid., 60.
45. Ibid., 53–54.
46. Ibid., 30, 35, 37, 40.
47. M. Gor'kii, *Sobranie sochinenii v tridtsati tomakh*, 30 vols. (Moscow: Nauka, 1953), 27:312.
48. Lur'e, "Ivan Groznyi," 321.
49. On Bulgakov's faith in Stalin, fueled by their April 1930 phone conversation, see Curtis, *Manuscripts Don't Burn*, 111–13. On the creative intelligentsia as obedient clients of highly placed party patrons, see Fitzpatrick, *Everyday Stalinism*, 110–11.
50. "Prepodavanie istorii v nashei shkole," *Pravda*, 27 January 1936, 1; "V Sovnarkome Soiuza SSR i TsK VKP(b)," *Pravda*, 27 January 1936, 2.
51. "Za vysokoe kachestvo sovetskoi shkoly," *Pravda*, 16 May 1934, 1; "O prepodavanii grazhdanskoi istorii v shkolakh SSSR," *Pravda*, 16 May 1934, 1.
52. N. Bukharin, "Nuzhna li nam marksistskaia istoricheskaia nauka?" *Izvestiia*, 27 January 1936, 3–4; V. Bystrianskii, "Kriticheskie zamechaniia ob uchebnikakh po istorii SSSR," *Pravda*, 1 February 1936, 2–3; P. Drozdov, "Reshenie partii i pravitel'stva ob uchebnikakh po istorii i zadachakh sovetskikh istorikov," *Istorik-Marksist* 1 (53) (1936): 9–22.
53. "Znat' i liubit' istoriiu svoei rodiny," *Pravda*, 7 March 1936, 1; "Liubit' svoiu rodinu, znat' ee istoriiu," *Pravda*, 22 May 1936, 1.
54. See, for example, Bystrianskii, "Kriticheskie zamechaniia," 2.
55. On Dem'ian Bednyi's farce, see chapter 5 in this volume.
56. Bulgakov, *Ivan Vasil'evich*, 25–27, 28.
57. Ibid., 29.
58. Ibid., 42.
59. Ibid., 43–45.
60. Ibid., 64.
61. On resurrecting Bulgakov's plays, see Curtis, *Manuscripts Don't Burn*, 223,

235, 238. Intriguingly, in Bulgakov's unfinished last novel, *Black Snow*, the character representing K. S. Stanislavskii, the co-director of the Moscow Art Theater whom Bulgakov largely blamed for the failure of *Molière*, was named Ivan Vasil'evich. See Michael Glenny's introduction to Mikhail Bulgakov, *Black Snow: A Theatrical Novel* (London: Fontana, 1986), 5–11.

62. "Ob organizatsii konkursa na luchshii uchebnik dlia nachal'noi shkoly po elementarnomu kursu istorii SSSR s kratkimi svedeniiami po vseobshchei istorii," *Pravda*, 4 March 1936, 1.

63. *Dnevnik Eleny Bulgakovoi*, 116, 366–67. An editorial in *Pravda* a few days later specifically encouraged literary figures to enter the competition, citing Dickens, H. G. Wells, Pushkin, and L. N. Tolstoi as examples of belletrists who had successfully written historical works—see "Znat' i liubit' istoriiu svoei rodiny," *Pravda*, 7 March 1936, 1. Extracts from Bulgakov's draft textbook, including the Pugachev chapter, have been published: see M. A. Bulgakov, "'Kurs istorii SSSR' (vypiski iz chernovika)," ed. A. K. Rait, *Novyi zhurnal* 143 (1981): 54–88; and Ia. S. Lur'e and V. M. Paneiakh, "Rabota M. A. Bulgakova nad kursom istorii SSSR," *Russkaia literatura* 3 (1988): 183–93. The draft does not appear to have dealt with Ivan the Terrible in any detail.

64. *Dnevnik Eleny Bulgakovoi*, 154.

65. On Peter the Great, see ibid., 154–55, 167, 373–75. On Minin and Pozharskii, see 120, 121, 125, 138, 144, 157, 171, 178, 372–73; Bulgakov, *Pis'ma*, 392–418. The progressive and positive character of the activities of Peter, and of Minin and Pozharskii, had been praised in the press comment on the draft history textbooks in 1936.

66. On Kerzhentsev's criticisms of the libretto about Peter, see *Dnevnik Eleny Bulgakovoi*, 374–75. On the proposed opera about Minin and Pozharskii, see Perrie, *Cult of Ivan the Terrible*, 62–64.

67. *Dnevnik Eleny Bulgakovoi*, 373–74.

10
Terribly Pragmatic
Rewriting the History of Ivan IV's Reign, 1937–1956

◆ DAVID BRANDENBERGER AND KEVIN M. F. PLATT

The idiosyncratic valorization of Ivan the Terrible in Stalinist public life has long intrigued scholars concerned with Soviet historical mythology. Their work has illustrated how the first Russian tsar and his Muscovite domain were represented as glorious antecedents to Stalin and Soviet society.[1] Indeed, this historical parallel is emphasized so frequently that ascribing to Stalin some sort of perverse fascination with the sixteenth-century tsar has become something of a sine qua non for commentary on Soviet high politics.[2]

Perhaps because of the audacity of Ivan IV's rehabilitation, its contextualization within the ideological currents of the time has often been neglected.[3] Disputing the facile reduction of Ivan the Terrible's rehabilitation to a mere symptom of Stalin's cult of personality,[4] this chapter examines the campaign from the perspective of the period's russocentric etatist ideological line. In so doing, our investigation into the agenda behind the campaign uncovers the pragmatic rationale behind Stalin's rehabilitation of the Terrible Tsar.

◆

If the notoriety surrounding Ivan IV made him a problematic hero at best for Russian historians before 1917, he—like most other tsarist-era political figures—was thoroughly marginalized by early Soviet materialist historians who were committed to a conception of the historical process in which individual actors had limited significance.[5] As this understanding of history gave way to a broad rehabilitation of the role of the state, individual, and the Russian people as a whole during the early to mid-1930s, official views on prominent pre-revolutionary personalities began to change markedly.

In line with the party hierarchy's emerging preoccupation with state-building and legitimacy, a number of figures previously denigrated as representatives of the old regime were even popularized as models of decisive leadership. Along with Peter the Great and Aleksandr Nevskii, Ivan IV was discussed as a possible candidate for rehabilitation in light of his status as one of the most recognizable figures within the USSR's potential Muscovite political lineage. M. Gor'kii speculated in 1934 at the First Conference of the Soviet Writers' Union that folkloric investigations of Ivan the Terrible might temper tsarist historiography's disdainful treatment of the leader.[6] In the following year, A. N. Tolstoi considered a reappraisal of the sixteenth-century tsar as an outgrowth of his work on Peter.[7] In 1936, historians participating in the editing of new elementary school history texts voiced a variety of views on Ivan, some of which assessed his policies and historical legacy quite positively.[8] Yet official statements during the early stages of the Stalinist rehabilitation of the tsarist past indicate that the line concerning Ivan's historical legacy remained primarily negative.[9]

Although the cancellation of Bulgakov's sixteenth-century satire *Ivan Vasil'evich* may have hinted at a change of policy in regard to Ivan, the initiative necessary for a profound revision of the official interpretation appears to have arisen somewhat later under rather peculiar circumstances. While leafing through a manuscript of A. V. Shestakov's *Short Course on the History of the USSR* in early 1937, Stalin struck out a reproduction of I. E. Repin's classic painting *Ivan the Terrible and His Son Ivan,* apparently believing it to be prejudicial.[10] Following Stalin's cue, another passage was quickly cut from the draft textbook:

> As a child, Ivan grew up among despotic boyars, who insulted him and fostered all his character flaws. ~~As a youth, Ivan would ride through Moscow on horseback, scaring and running down peaceful residents for amusement; he sentenced one of his closest boyars, Andrei Shuiskii, to be torn apart by dogs.~~
>
> In 1547, at the age of seventeen, Ivan proclaimed himself "tsar-autocrat." He was the first of all Muscovite rulers to do so. From this time on he began to rule the state by himself, not consulting with the boyars.[11]

Shortly thereafter, A. A. Zhdanov picked up his red pencil and rewrote other portions of the same textbook in an explicit endorsement of Ivan IV. Zhdanov made the following cuts in an intermediate copy of the textbook's page proofs concerning the 1552 siege of Kazan':

But [then] Kazan's defenders became exhausted. Ivan IV's troops—some 150,000 of them—overwhelmed the Tatars. Kazan' was sacked and burned ~~; on his orders, they killed all the residents of Kazan'~~.[12]

Commentary on the *oprichnina* was also revised:

> For the battle [with the boyars], Ivan IV formed a special detachment of several thousand men from the landowners and called them "*oprichniki.*"
> The *oprichniki* had their own special uniform. ~~The oprichnik, clad in black from head to toe, rode on a black horse with a black harness.~~ On the *oprichnik*'s saddle was affixed a dog's head and broom. These were symbols of his duties: to sniff out and track down the enemies of the tsar and sweep out the traitorous boyars.[13]

In addition to the removal of unflattering details concerning Ivan's sacking of Kazan' and his *oprichnina* guard, Zhdanov also interpolated a new conclusion into the text that defined in no uncertain terms the tsar's chief accomplishment: "With this, [Ivan IV] essentially completed the gathering of the various principalities into a single strong state that had been initiated by Kalita."[14] This casting of Ivan as the quintessential Muscovite state-builder was reflected soon thereafter in the *Great Soviet Encyclopedia* and other textbooks.[15] Following the lead of these authoritative texts, in the late 1930s the history curricula for public schools and party study circles characterized the tsar as a skilled politician, diplomat, and military strategist who employed every means at his disposal, including political terror, to centralize a disorganized cluster of fiefdoms into a powerful state.[16] Already at this early stage of the rehabilitation campaign, it is evident that the Stalinist establishment viewed Ivan as part of its historical lineage and as a positive model for political practice.

Yet despite the flurry of activity, the rehabilitation of Ivan the Terrible was still by no means a fait accompli, especially when it came to detailed descriptions of his reign. The rehabilitation of figures associated with the tsarist regime was a delicate matter under any circumstances, and the spin control necessary to popularize someone as unsympathetic as Ivan was extremely complicated. S. V. Bakhrushin skirted the issue of the tsar's bloody reputation in a 1939 article in *Propagandist* by focusing instead on the socio-economic history of Ivan's reign. K. V. Bazilevich adopted a similar approach to analysis of Ivan shortly thereafter.[17] B. G. Verkhoven' proved more ambitious with the publication later that year of his popularized pamphlet

Russia during the Reign of Ivan the Terrible. While he praised Ivan's consolidation of state power and his "completely necessary and correct" use of terror to punish treason, Verkhoven' also diagnosed the tsar as a "psychologically unbalanced person." Presenting the *oprichnina* in a similarly nuanced manner, Verkhoven' characterized it as a generally progressive institution, yet one which was also responsible for "ravaging" the peasantry.[18] Tellingly, Verkhoven's work elicited a decidedly negative reaction at the hands of the academic establishment.[19] While the party elites had already signaled a new course on Ivan in the late 1930s, it appears that historians—with the exception of Verkhoven'—hesitated to comment directly on the ruler's personality or his personal contributions to Muscovite history.[20]

Such unusual reticence on the part of the Stalinist historians was not to last for long, however. At some point in 1940 or 1941, the Central Committee pronounced the accomplishments of the rehabilitation campaign unsatisfactory and issued specific instructions on future representations of Ivan IV. It seems likely that this intervention resulted in part from the perceived failure of Verkhoven's book, which had been too equivocal.[21] Maureen Perrie adds that official interest in Ivan may have related to the tsar's territorial claims to "historic Russian patrimony" in the Baltics, as the signing of the Molotov-Ribbentrop pact in the fall of 1939 had just facilitated the Soviet annexation of the Lithuania, Latvia, and Estonia.[22]

While the actual wording and circumstances surrounding the instructions remain elusive, their later paraphrasing by Central Committee ideology chief A. S. Shcherbakov in a 1942 memorandum can be used to reconstruct the Stalinist party hierarchy's "official" position on Ivan the Terrible. (This memo, criticizing A. N. Tolstoi's drama concerning Ivan IV, is published for the first time in this volume.) According to Shcherbakov, the Central Committee had had to intervene in the rehabilitation campaign between 1940 and 1941 because "the image of Ivan IV in historical science and artistic literature has been seriously distorted both by reactionary gentry and bourgeois historiography and related publicistic and artistic literature."[23] Noting that "a historically-sound understanding of Ivan IV in the history of the Russian state has enormous significance for our times," Shcherbakov then proceeded to summarize the prevailing view of Ivan the Terrible within the party hierarchy. In his account, the sixteenth-century tsar was "an outstanding political figure" who "completed the establishment of a centralized Russian state, a progressive endeavor initiated by Ivan III." This last phrase, which appears repeatedly in the memorandum, clearly indicates that the party hierarchy's primary interest in Ivan IV's historical legacy was his role as a state-builder.

Turning to the details of Shcherbakov's assessment, one is struck by its unapologetically positive valence. Among the accomplishments of the tsar, Shcherbakov listed Ivan IV's efforts to reform the Muscovite court, the central administration, finance, the military, and the rural church. Moreover, the tsar had been a "champion of the broad dissemination of knowledge," insofar as Muscovy's first printing press was established during his reign. Ivan's military accomplishments received a similarly eulogistic treatment, the tsar having "personally led the conquests of Kazan' and Astrakhan.'" With regard to the ultimately inconclusive Livonian War, this Stalinist insider's evaluation focused on Ivan's "stunning diplomatic skills." Finally, after elevating Ivan IV to the status of one of Russia's greatest statesmen, Shcherbakov condemned the tsar's political opponents as "hardened patrimonial landowners," whose "tenacious insistence on the preservation of the feudal order" had forced Ivan to "resort to harsh measures." Little more was said about the excesses of the era. Shcherbakov's memorandum serves as clear evidence that by 1940–1941, the party hierarchy viewed Ivan the Terrible as one of the chief architects of the Russian state and as a ruler whose ambitions anticipated the state-building designs of the Soviet era.[24] Stalin confirmed this emphasis two years later in the fall of 1944 while editing a document Zhdanov was drafting on the party's historical line. Repeatedly urging Zhdanov to emphasize the *oprichnina*'s positive dimensions, he altered the wording of a critical passage in order to reiterate Ivan's state-building priorities:

> the Terrible Tsar was an undoubtedly progressive and enlightened man of his time who was able to find support among the petty gentry against the feudal lords, and with the gentry's help he was able to strengthen his *the state's* absolute power [ukrepit' svoiu absolutnuiu *gosudarstvennuiu* vlast'].[25]

Such changes clearly indicate that Ivan's rehabilitation was designed to focus on his service to the state rather than the personal aspects of his notorious rule.

The party's intervention in the rehabilitation campaign was not, however, just limited to questions of historical interpretation. Expanding the rehabilitation of Ivan beyond the scholarly realm, attempts were made to introduce the subject into truly mass-appeal forums ranging from drama and literature to film and even opera. Between 1940 and early 1941 Tolstoi and S. M. Eisenstein were recruited to produce major works on the sixteenth-century tsar.[26] Shortly thereafter, Shcherbakov approached T. M. Khrennikov—the future chair of the Soviet Composers' Union—with a proposal for a full-scale historical opera about Ivan. As Khrennikov recounts in his memoirs, Shcherbakov turned to him one evening during an intermission at the Stanislavskii Theater with the following proposition:

> You know, Comrade Khrennikov, you ought to write an opera entitled *Ivan the Terrible*. I've just been at Iosif Vissarionovich's. We were talking about the Terrible Tsar. Comrade Stalin attributes a lot of significance to this theme. He sees it differently than it has been seen to up until now: despite the fact that Ivan was considered terrible [and despite the fact] that this reputation has been strengthened since [his reign], Comrade Stalin believes that he wasn't terrible enough. This was because if on one hand he got even with his opponents, on the other, he then would then repent and beg for forgiveness from God. And while he was repenting, his opponents would again gather their forces against him and attack all over again. The Terrible Tsar had to do battle with them, etc. In other words, one has to wage an unceasing and merciless battle against one's enemies to eliminate them if they are interfering with the development of the state. That is Stalin's position.[27]

The scope and direction of the new campaign was signaled by an article in *Izvestiia* in March 1941 by V. I. Kostylev, an author of rather modest talent who had been researching Ivan the Terrible's life and times since the success of his popularized novel about Minin and Pozharskii two years earlier.[28]

Although Khrennikov managed to demur on the proposed opera (as did D. D. Shostakovich shortly thereafter[29]), the list of authors, playwrights, and directors recruited to develop Ivan as a symbol of contemporary Soviet state-building is nevertheless impressive. Of particular note are the projects by Kostylev, Tolstoi, and Eisenstein, who aspired to provide a definitive vision of Ivan IV on the printed page, stage, and screen, respectively. Kostylev serialized the first novel of an eventual trilogy in the literary journal *Oktiabr'* in 1942, publishing it as a separate edition in 1943. The two remaining volumes were released in 1945 and 1947, with the entire trilogy being republished in two separate mass editions in 1948 and 1949.[30] Tolstoi published a segment of the first of his two plays about Ivan in *Literatura i iskusstvo* in 1942 as well.[31] This pair of plays—or, as the author called it, a "dramatic novella in two parts"—was published in its entirety in the

Figure 21. M. O. Dlugach's 1945 poster advertising Eisenstein's *Ivan the Terrible* (part 1). Courtesy of the Russian State Library, Moscow.

November–December 1943 issue of *Oktiabr'* and republished in a revised edition in 1945 and 1950. The first play debuted in the Moscow Malyi Theater in the fall of 1944 and was immediately reworked for restaging during the following spring. The second premièred in the Moscow Art Theater in 1946. Eisenstein's participation in the campaign is even more complex. After writing preliminary articles for *Izvestiia* in April 1941 and *Literatura i iskusstvo* in August 1942, Eisenstein published his initial screenplay in the journal *Novyi mir* in late 1943, after first winning Stalin's sanction, expressed in the following note to the head of the State Film Committee that September:

> Comrade Bol'shakov: The screenplay hasn't turned out badly. C[omrade] Eisenstein has coped well with the task. Ivan the Terrible as the progressive force of his time and the *oprichnina* as his expedient instrument haven't turned out badly. The screen play ought to be sent into production.[32]

The first part of what quickly evolved into a cinematic trilogy hit the screens after much delay only in January 1945. This same year also saw the appearance of other lesser-known works about the first Russian tsar. V. A. Solov'ev published his verse tragedy *The Great Sovereign*, which was staged during that same year in Moscow, Leningrad, and Tbilisi. I. L. Sel'vinskii's play *The Livonian War* rolled off the presses and onto the stage in 1945 as well.

If the Central Committee's intervention had shifted the initiative for the Ivan rehabilitation from historians to the creative intelligentsia, work on the "historical front" resumed with renewed fervor following the German invasion of June 22, 1941. Tsarist-era heroes—including Ivan the Terrible—were mobilized to demonstrate age-old Russian martial prowess and to offset widespread fears of German invincibility.[33] The most prominent contribution to the historiography on Ivan was the 1942 publication of a revised edition of a little-known apologetic biography first published in 1922 by R. Iu. Vipper. Bakhrushin released a fresh account shortly thereafter that

Figure 22. N. K. Cherkasov as Ivan the Terrible, from the Pushkin State Academic Drama Theater's 1945 production of V. A. Solov'ev's *The Great Sovereign*. In *Ocherki istorii russkogo sovetskogo dramaticheskogo teatra* (Moscow, 1960).

was only slightly more materialist in its approach.³⁴ At about the same time, a conference was convened in Tashkent concerning Ivan, which brought together the most prominent Soviet scholars in Central Asian evacuation to hear addresses by Tolstoi, Vipper, and others.³⁵ At this event, a new volume of scholarly articles on Ivan was discussed that would further refine the dominant line.³⁶ While little came of this scholarly project, a steady flow of popularized treatments concerning the sixteenth-century tsar continued to appear regularly in the press for the duration of the war, with 1944 seeing the publication of a third original historical biography.³⁷

Visible between the lines of all of these works is an implicit symmetry between Ivan's epoch and the Stalin era. Vipper makes this connection most transparently when he proclaims in the conclusion to the 1944 edition of his monograph that Heinrich Staden's plan for the conquest of Russia, presented to Habsburg emperor Rudolph II in 1578, was no less than a "prophecy and a plan for the future" that would later inspire Nazi Germany to conquer and enslave the Slavs.³⁸ Bakhrushin's 1943 article on the era of Ivan IV in *Bol'shevik* employed anachronistic rhetoric to suggest a similar parallel between past and present. For instance, Muscovy at the start of Ivan IV's reign is described as "pressed upon from all sides, as if in a vice, by states hostile to her"—an image reminiscent of the "encirclement" of the Soviet Union by hostile capitalist powers following the 1917 Revolution. This conflation of ancient conflicts with the 1918–1921 Civil War was reinforced by descriptions of the Baltic Teutonic Order's "blockade" of the region during the thirteenth century and the Poles' "intervention" during the seventeenth-century Time of Troubles. Echoes of the political rhetoric of the 1930s are also present in Bakhrushin's choice of words when he describes Ivan's "construction [*stroitel'stvo*] of a national state." Other examples include Bakhrushin's reference to Ivan's favorite servants and fighting men as his "cadres" and his description of Ivan's opponents as the "holdovers" [*perezhitki*] of the appanage estate system.³⁹

Yet beyond these oblique equations of the tsarist past and the Soviet present, more direct comparisons seem to have been avoided. While the ideological climate of the late 1930s and 1940s encouraged the allegorical linking of the present with the past, it did not tolerate more explicit associations. This awkwardness stemmed from a massive contradiction embedded in Stalin-era historical propaganda that required committed Marxists to traffic in tsarist heroes and imagery. A pragmatic, instrumentalist affair, this style of agitation was designed to harness the most emotionally charged political iconography available. That said, there could be no question of a more thoroughgoing rehabilitation of the tsarist political experience and cultural values, much less any attempt to emulate the sensibilities of the old regime.[40] Indeed, it is one of the great ironies of Soviet history that at the same time that the party's propaganda machine was engaged in the rehabilitation of the tsarist past, most of the living representatives of tsarist cultural and political traditions—"fellow travelers," "bourgeois specialists," and so forth—were fading from the scene, their attrition accelerated by the purges and the advancement of promotees (*vydvizhentsy*) trained to replace them. Soviet historians and cultural agents were thus faced with the difficult task of foregrounding certain mythical (if not mystical) Russian antecedents to contemporary Soviet heroism, while somehow sidestepping any blurring of the distinction between the evils of the ancien régime and the wonders of the post-revolutionary epoch.[41] The Central Committee's 1940–1941 contextualization of the Ivan rehabilitation indicates that the campaign was to be limited to a rousing narrative concerning the trials and tribulations of a Muscovite state-builder who could epitomize the region's long history of charismatic, decisive leaders. Ivan was repeatedly described as "progressive for his time" in order to emphasize the differences between the sixteenth and twentieth centuries. The direction of the campaign makes it clear that a more apologetic stance (i.e., using Ivan's bloody rule as a legitimating precedent for the Stalin era's excesses) was not to be part of the officially sanctioned line.

But despite the campaign's official endorsement—or perhaps because of it—the implications of Ivan's reign for Soviet political culture complicated the completion of the commissioned works. Those trying to dramatize the subject were placed in a particularly awkward position: as David Bordwell has noted, "drama thrives on imperfections in character," which could not be acceptably ascribed to such epic figures."[42] According to M. Iu. Bleiman, cultural agents like Eisenstein searched and searched for palatable themes that would not require an imperfect dramatis personae before settling on the motif of "the tragedy of power and retribution,"[43] only to realize later that such an interpretation caused as many problems as it resolved. Eisenstein was forced to distance himself from his *Novyi mir* screenplay after it drew fire for historical inaccuracies that stemmed from such thematic compromises.[44] Although the first part of his cinematic trilogy would ultimately be considered a success, it provoked considerable disagreement during its pre-release screening on account of its excessively sober and bleak cinematography.[45] Tolstoi's plays were subjected to an even more withering assault by Shcherbakov and others for their inadequately

Terribly Pragmatic 167

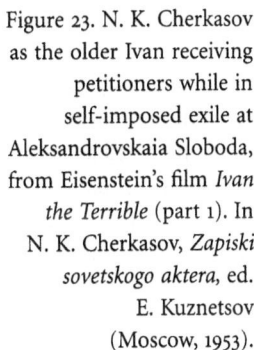

Figure 23. N. K. Cherkasov as the older Ivan receiving petitioners while in self-imposed exile at Aleksandrovskaia Sloboda, from Eisenstein's film *Ivan the Terrible* (part 1). In N. K. Cherkasov, *Zapiski sovetskogo aktera*, ed. E. Kuznetsov (Moscow, 1953).

triumphalist tone.[46] The playwright managed to deflect this assault only by means of massive rewrites and repeated appeals to Stalin.[47] Kostylev, too, was forced to defend his work again and again.[48] Discouraged from emplotting their work with dramatic complexity and tension, all three ended up producing material that was both uneven and highly eccentric.

The struggle over the rehabilitation campaign reached a crescendo in early 1946, when only weeks after awarding Stalin prizes to Tolstoi, Eisenstein, and Solov'ev for their works on Ivan,[49] the party hierarchy banned the release of the second part of Eisenstein's film trilogy.[50] In essence, a single complaint united much of the controversy: the party hierarchy had commissioned rousing patriotic treatments concerning the history of sixteenth-century Muscovy and found their eventual dramatization as psychological tragedies inappropriate.[51] Tellingly, in the Central Committee's September 4, 1946 resolution "Concerning the Film 'The Great Life,'" Eisenstein was accused of:

> ignorance in his depiction of historical facts, presenting Ivan the Terrible's *oprichniki* as a band of degenerates along the lines of the American

Ku-Klux-Klan, and Ivan the Terrible, a man of strong will and character, as weak and irresolute, like some sort of a Hamlet.[52]

The phrasing of the resolution follows almost word for word comments that Stalin had made a month earlier to a select audience at his dacha. Eisenstein's confidant Vs. Vishnevskii, who was present at this informal discussion, later shared his notes with the director. Apparently, Stalin declared that:

> [Eisenstein] got distracted from the history and inserted something "of his own." He depicted not a progressive *oprichnina*, but something else entirely—degenerates. He didn't understand.... He didn't understand the Terrible Tsar's repressions either [—] Russia had been plundered and wanted to unite together.... She was justified in punishing her enemies.... Ivan the Terrible, as we know, was a willful man, a difficult man.... But that's not what's been given here.... He's a Hamlet or something like that.[53]

Stalin's repeated references to Hamlet confirm the party hierarchy's objections to any sort of tragic interpretation of Ivan the Terrible.

Stunned by the rejection of his portrayal of Ivan, Eisenstein petitioned for an audience with Stalin in order to clarify the nature of the official line. Somewhat later, on 25 February 1947, the director was summoned to the Kremlin with N. K. Cherkasov, the actor who had played the film's title role. There, in the presence of Molotov and Zhdanov, Stalin gave the most articulate explanation of his view of Ivan's life and times:

STALIN: Have you studied history?

EISENSTEIN: More or less.

STALIN: More or less? I also know a bit of history. You have depicted the *oprichnina* incorrectly. The *oprichnina* was the soldiery of the crown [*korolevskoe voisko*]. In contrast to the feudal army, which could roll up its banners and withdraw from battle at any time, a regular army was formed, a progressive army. You have depicted the *oprichnina* as the Ku Klux Klan....

Your tsar has turned out as an indecisive character, resembling Hamlet. Everyone tells him what to do and he is unable to make a decision himself.

Tsar Ivan was a great and wise ruler, and if one compares him to Louis XI (you have read about Louis XI, who set the stage for Louis XIV's absolutism), then Ivan is seventh heaven [*na desiatom nebe*].... Ivan the

Terrible was very cruel. It is fine to show that he was cruel. But it is necessary to show why he was cruel.[54]

As these statements make clear, Stalin saw Ivan as the quintessential medieval etatist, the founder of a powerful kingdom described obediently by Vipper as "the prototype of the great multinational state of the USSR."[55] Heroic rather than tragic and Hamlet-like, Ivan was nevertheless not to be understood as a transcendent figure, insofar as his cruelty was patently medieval in nature. That said, Stalin made it clear that such excesses had to be viewed as exigencies of the time that did not negate the progressiveness of Ivan's reign.

By late 1946 the Ivan campaign was in crisis. Its most prominent artistic statements had proven to be fatally flawed. Moreover, the question of further work on the project by the two titans of Soviet propaganda "on the historical front" had been rendered moot by Tolstoi's death in 1945 and by Eisenstein's mistakes and failing health. At least as frustrated with the line on Ivan in the early postwar years as it had been in 1940, the party hierarchy withdrew the initiative for the rehabilitation campaign from the creative intelligentsia[56] and returned a much-diminished mandate to the court historians. While existing works in the Stalinist canon on Ivan would be republished, restaged, and rescreened during the late 1940s and early 1950s, the only new works to make it into print after 1946 were pieces of exceedingly conservative historical scholarship.[57] The line on Ivan would lie dormant until several years after Stalin's death, when in 1956 it would be denounced—ironically enough—for its alleged links to Stalin's personality cult rather than for its inappropriateness as a model for Soviet state-building.[58]

~

In the introduction to this volume, we argue that during the early to mid-1930s, the Soviet party hierarchy decided to create a historical "myth of origins." This was done in order to generate popular support and historical legitimacy for the regime and involved the interpolation of traditional Russian heroes, myths, and symbols into the Marxist narrative of revolutionary history that had until then held sway. The details surrounding the attempt to rehabilitate Ivan IV indicate that the cooptation of such figures to serve as Stalinist propaganda forced Soviet historians, authors, and playwrights into uncharted ideological waters that required them to plot a cautious course between tsarist apologetics and outdated Soviet materialism. Although some commentators have concluded that the pervasive tension "on the historical front" stemmed from Stalin's manic need for self-aggrandizement and his ostensibly nationalist sympathies, there is little direct evidence to support this interpretation. In our view, the tension was instead symptomatic of the fundamental irreconcilability of efforts to advance the cause of Soviet state-building through positive references to the tsarist past.

To be sure, the problematic nature of the party hierarchy's decision to delve into tsarist history for mythical predecessors may not have been clear at the time. Stalin, Shcherbakov, and many others considered Ivan to be the perfect vehicle to express their vision of a glorious state led by a vigorous, powerful ruler. To loyal members of the Stalinist establishment, it was clear that societies were best led by strong personalities who possessed the vision and determination necessary to defend their interests. In this vein, they contended that Ivan had been systematically misunderstood by tsarist historians, who had overlooked his services to the Russian state in their determination to criticize his cruel excesses. Indeed, in Stalin's mind, Ivan actually hadn't been "terrible enough"[59] in his suppression of Russia's enemies.

Yet the architects of the rehabilitation campaign proved overconfident in their attempt to co-opt Ivan. Although the textbooks, histories, plays, novels, and films that they commissioned were not supposed to examine the tsar's psychological complexities, this side of Ivan ultimately proved to be inseparable from his overall legacy. In a sense, the equivocal nature of Ivan's notorious personality and his potential for tragic melodrama "bled through" the triumphalist fabric of the propaganda campaign, despite one of the most active cases of political "management" of culture ever attempted. The resulting political infighting and confusion brought the campaign to a standstill in 1946.

Although the party hierarchs do not seem to have recognized the contradiction at the heart of their campaign, a statement penned by Zhdanov in 1944 reveals that he was at least aware that something was amiss. This document, with its curious insistence that the Ivan story was, in essence, a simple and didactic one, provides a suitable conclusion to our analysis. Attempting to explain how propagandists were to navigate the perilous waters between old-regime apologia and radical, imprudent rejections of the lessons of Russian history, Zhdanov counseled:

> It is imperative to note the concrete historical conditions of Ivan the Terrible's reign. Demands for economic growth, on one hand, and defense of the

Russian state from its numerous enemies, on the other, required the strengthening of centralized state power. Feudal fragmentation was a source of state weakness. The feudal grandee did not want to give up any of his privileges in the interests of the state. The Terrible Tsar's attempts to restrain the feudal grandees met with sharp resistance and treachery on the part of the boyars that threatened the state with destruction. In such conditions, the Terrible Tsar—who was for his time without doubt an advanced and educated person—was able to find support in the minor service gentry against the major feudal notables and with the help of the gentry managed to strengthen his absolute power.

. . . However appalling the Terrible Tsar's methods and means and his numerous excesses and executions may seem to us and our contemporaries, Ivan's role was progressive, as he administered a blow to feudal reaction, facilitated the acceleration of the historical process, and transformed Russia into a powerful, centralized 'Great Power.'

. . . Some of our historians apparently do not understand that there is a principle difference between recognizing the progressiveness of one or another historical phenomenon and endorsing it, as such.[60]

For Zhdanov, Stalin, and the other members of the Stalinist party hierarchy, then, Ivan's consolidation of state power justified the exigencies of his reign. Viewing Ivan as "the progressive force of his time and the *oprichnina* as his expedient instrument," Stalin had authored a vision of the sixteenth-century tsar that was noble and triumphalist, but also overdetermined and rather one-dimensional. Indeed, it was probably the sterility and pragmatism of this vision that ultimately doomed Ivan's rehabilitation to failure.

Notes

This chapter has benefited from advice from A. M. Dubrovsky, Maureen Perrie, Joan Neuberger, and Katia Dianina.

1. Konstantin Shteppa, *Russian Historians and the Soviet State* (New Brunswick, N.J.: Rutgers University Press, 1962), 126, 168, 172, 186, 271, etc.; Alexander Werth, *Russia at War, 1941–1945* (New York: Dutton, 1964), 249, 739; Lowell Tillett, *The Great Friendship: Soviet Historians on the Non-Russian Nationalities* (Chapel Hill: University of North Carolina Press, 1969), 46, 54; Marie Seton, *Sergei M. Eisenstein*, rev. ed. (London: Dobson, 1978), 413, 421–25, 431; Rosalind Marsh, *Images of Dictatorship: Portraits of Stalin in Literature*, 2nd ed. (London: Macmillan, 1989), 33; Bernd Uhlenbruch, "The Annexation of History: Eisenstein and the Ivan Groznyi

Cult of the 1940s," in *The Culture of the Stalin Period*, ed. Hans Günther (New York: St. Martin's, 1990), 266–87; Maureen Perrie, "The Tsar, the Emperor, the Leader: Ivan the Terrible, Peter the Great and Anatolii Rybakov's Stalin," in *Stalinism: Its Nature and Aftermath—Essays in Honor of Moshe Lewin*, ed. Nick Lampert and Gábor Rittersporn (London: Macmillan, 1992), 77–100; Maureen Perrie, "Nationalism and History: The Cult of Ivan the Terrible in Stalin's Russia," in *Russian Nationalism Past and Present*, ed. G. Hosking and R. Service (New York: St. Martin's, 1998), 107–28; Leonid Kozlov, "The Artist and the Shadow of Ivan," in *Stalinism and Soviet Cinema*, ed. Richard Taylor and Derek Spring (London: Routledge 1993), 109–30; Herman Ermolaev, *Censorship in Soviet Literature, 1917–1991* (Lanham, Md.: Rowman & Littlefield, 1997), 88.

2. Iu. Osokin, "Stalinizatsiia istorii," *Sotsialisticheskii vestnik*, 14 October 1937, 7–8. See also "Ivan the Terrible [review]," *Time*, 14 April 1947, 102; Klaus Mehnert, *Stalin versus Marx: The Stalinist Historical Doctrine* (London: G. Allen & Unwin, 1953), 76, 84–86; Frederick Barghoorn, *Soviet Russian Nationalism* (New York: Oxford University Press, 1956), 156; John Dunlop, *The Faces of Contemporary Russian Nationalism* (Princeton, N.J.: Princeton University Press, 1983), 18, 21; Moshe Lewin, *The Making of the Soviet System: Essays in the Social History of Inter-War Russia* (London: Meuthen, 1985), 309; Adam Ulam, *Stalin: The Man and His Era*, expanded ed. (Boston: Beacon, 1989), 52, 320–21; A. Siniavskii, "Stalin—geroi i khudozhnik stalinskoi epokhi," in *Osmyslit' kul't lichnosti*, ed. L. Anninskii (Moscow: Progress, 1989), 119; Robert Tucker, *Stalin in Power: The Revolution from Above, 1928–1941* (New York: Norton, 1990), 7, 52, 319–22, 481–86, 557; Gerhard Simon, *Nationalism and Policy toward the Nationalities in the Soviet Union: From Totalitarian Dictatorship to Post-Stalinist Society*, trans. Karen and Osward Forster (Boulder, Colo.: Westview, 1991), 181; Yuri Glazov, "Stalin's Legacy: Populism in Literature," in *The Search for Self-Definition in Russian Literature*, ed. Ewa Thompson (Houston: Rice University Press, 1991), 93, 98; Peter Kenez, *Cinema and Soviet Society, 1917–1953* (New York: Cambridge University Press, 1992), 201, 219; Gennadii Kostyrchenko, *V plenu u krasnogo faraona: Politicheskie presledovaniia evreev v SSSR v poslednee stalinskoe desiatiletie—dokumental'noe issledovanie* (Moscow: Mezhdunarodnye otnosheniia, 1994), 87; D. M. Volkogonov, *Sem' vozhdei: Galereia liderov SSSR* (Moscow: Novosti, 1995), 254, 312; E. A. Rees, "Stalin and Russian Nationalism," in *Russian Nationalism Past and Present*, 86; R. G. Pikhoia, *Sovetskii soiuz: Istoriia vlasti, 1945–1991* (Moscow: RAGSPRF, 1998), 71; Jeffrey Brooks, *"Thank You Comrade Stalin": Soviet Public Culture from Revolution to Cold War* (Princeton, N.J.: Princeton University Press, 1999), 118.

3. Exceptions include Maureen Perrie's *Cult of Ivan the Terrible in Stalin's Russia;* our "Terribly Romantic, Terribly Progressive or Terribly Tragic: Rehabilitating Ivan IV under I. V. Stalin, 1937–1953," *Russian Review* 58, no. 4 (1999): 635–54; Joan Neuberger, *Ivan the Terrible* (New York: I. B. Taubris, 2003); and Kevin M. F. Platt, "Toward a New Sergei Eisenstein" (review essay), *Slavic and East European Journal* 48, no. 2 (2004): 287–93.

4. See, for example, Kozlov, "The Artist and the Shadow of Ivan," and Richard

Taylor, "Red Stars, Positive Heroes and Personality Cults," in *Stalinism and Soviet Cinema*, 109–30, 88–89.

5. For overviews of historiographic traditions concerning Ivan IV, see I. U. Budovnits, "Ivan Groznyi v russkoi istoricheskoi literature," *Istoricheskie zapiski* 21 (1947): 271–330; Leo Yaresh, "Ivan the Terrible and the Oprichnina," in *Rewriting Russian History: Soviet Interpretations of the Russian Past*, ed. C. E. Black (New York: Praeger, 1956), 78–106; Richard Hellie, "In Search of Ivan the Terrible," foreword to S. F. Platonov, *Ivan the Terrible*, ed. and trans. Joseph L. Wieczynski (Gulf Breeze, Fla.: Academic International, 1974), ix–xxiv; Kevin M. F. Platt, "Antichrist Enthroned: Demonic Visions of Russian Rulers," in *Demonism in Russian Literature*, ed. Pamela Davidson (Oxford: Berghahn Books, 2000), 87–124. On Pokrovskyian historiography of the 1920s, see the introduction and chapter 3 in this volume.

6. The commonplace that representations of Ivan IV in Russian folk epics were more positive than contemporary and historiographic assessments dates to Karamzin. M. Gor'kii revived this observation at the First Congress of the Soviet Writers' Union, over which he presided alongside A. S. Shcherbakov. See N. M. Karamzin, *Istoriia gosudarstva rossiiskogo*, 5th ed., 3 vols. (St. Petersburg: Eduard Prats, 1842–1845; Moscow: Kniga, 1988–1989), 3:278–80; *Pervyi vsesoiuznyi s"ezd sovetskikh pisatelei, 1934—Stenograficheskii otchet* (Moscow: Khudozhestvennaia literatura, 1934), 10.

7. V. D. Bonch-Bruevich wrote to M. Gor'kii in January 1935 that Tolstoi "is devoting much time to the history of Ivan the Terrible, collecting material and portrayals. He says that in his opinion Peter has his source in Ivan the Terrible and that Ivan the Terrible is even more interesting than Peter—more colorful and varied. He wants to write about him." See V. R. Shcherbina, *A. N. Tolstoi: Tvorcheskii put'* (Moscow: Sovetskii pisatel', 1956), 471.

8. RGASPI, f. 77, op. 1, dd. 332–33.

9. M. V. Nechkina, "Moskovskoe gosudarstvo" in *Malaia sovetskaia entsiklopediia*, 10 vols. (Moscow: Sovetskaia entsiklopediia, 1930–1931), 5:420; idem, "Ivan IV Vasil'evich, Groznyi," 3:352; idem, "Oprichnina," 4:105–6; idem, "Ivan IV," *Bol'shaia sovetskaia entsiklopediia*, 65 vols. (Moscow: Sovetskaia entsiklopediia, 1926–1947), 27:326–29. See also the publication announcement for *Novye izvestiia o Rossii vremeni Ivana Groznogo* in "Novye knigi," *Pravda*, 13 July 1934, 4.

10. On the exclusion of Repin's painting from the textbook, see Stalin's page proofs for *Elementarnyi kurs istorii SSSR* dating from early 1937, RGASPI, f. 558, op. 3, d. 374, ll. 108–9.

11. Compare p. 39 of the early 1937 page proofs for *Elementarnyi kurs istorii SSSR* (RGASPI, f. 558, op. 3, d. 374) with p. 37 of the late July 1937 page proofs for *Kratkii kurs istorii SSSR* (f. 77, op. 1, d. 854).

12. Compare p. 38 of the late July 1937 page proofs for *Kratkii kurs istorii SSSR* (RGASPI, f. 77, op. 1, d. 854) with *Kratkii kurs istorii SSSR*, ed. A. V. Shestakov (Moscow: Gos. uchebno-pedadog. izd-vo, 1937), 38.

13. Compare p. 40 of the page proofs for *Kratkii kurs istorii SSSR* (RGASPI, f. 77, op. 1, d. 854) with *Kratkii kurs istorii SSSR*, 40.

14. Zhdanov's revision is on p. 40 of the page proofs for *Kratkii kurs istorii SSSR* (RGASPI, f. 77, op. 1, d. 854) and appears in *Kratkii kurs istorii SSSR*, 41.

15. S. V. Bakhrushin, "Moskovskoe gosudarstvo," in *Bol'shaia sovetskaia entsiklopediia*, 40: 458–67; [M. V. Nechkina,] "Oprichnina," 43: 226–28; *Istoriia SSSR*, ed. A. M. Pankratova, 3 vols. (Moscow: Uchpedgiz, 1940), 1: chap. 8; *Istoriia SSSR*, ed. V. I. Lebedev, B. D. Grekov, and S. V. Bakhrushin, vol. 1 (Moscow: Goz. izd-vo polit. lit-ry, 1939), 389–90; etc. N. Rubinshtein demonstrated awareness of the new interpretation in his "Kliuchevskii i ego Kurs russkoi istorii [review]," *Pravda*, 15 August 1937, 4.

16. *Programmy nachal'noi shkoly* (Moscow: Narkompros RSFSR, 1938), 42–43; *Kratkii kurs istorii SSSR*, chap. 5; A. N. Khmelev, "Oprichnina (stenograficheskaia zapis' uroka)," in *Opyt prepodavaniia istorii SSSR v nachal'noi shkole* (Moscow: Narkompros RSFSR, 1938), 20–27; *V pomoshch' grupovodu politzaniatii: Materialy k teme "Rasshirenie russkogo natsional'nogo gosudarstva,"* ed. A. V. Shestakov (Leningrad: Politicheskoe upravlenie KBF, 1938).

17. S. V. Bakhrushin, "Rasshirenie russkogo gosudarstva pri Ivane IV," *Propagandist* 1 (1939): 15–22; K. V. Bazilevich, "'Torgovyi kapitalizm' i genezis moskovskogo samoderzhaviia v rabotakh M. N. Pokrovskogo," in *Protiv istoricheskoi kontseptsii M. N. Pokrovskogo: Sbornik statei*, ed. B. D. Grekov et al., 2 vols. (Moscow: Izd-vo Akademii nauk, 1939), 1:147–59. Bakhrushin's piece was authoritative enough to be included the following year in Pankratova's influential *Istoriia SSSR* textbook.

18. B. Verkhoven', *Rossiia v tsarstvovanie Ivana Groznogo* (Moscow: Gospolitizdat, 1939), 43, 45. This publication was based on a 1938 pamphlet, *Rasshirenie russkogo gosudarstva*.

19. Interestingly, one prominent reviewer avoided contesting Verkhoven's characterization of Ivan IV directly—see Iu. V. Got'e, "Plokhaia kniga," *Kniga i proletarskaia revoliutsiia* 11 (1939): 92–95. For a different reading of Verkhoven', see Perrie, *Cult of Ivan the Terrible*, 81–82.

20. A. M. Dubrovskii, *S. V. Bakhrushin i ego vremia* (Moscow: Izd-vo Rossiiskogo universiteta druzhby narodov, 1992), 121–22.

21. Verkhoven's book was virtually the only post-1937 work on Ivan not to be republished, indicating its poor reputation within the party hierarchy.

22. Perrie, "Nationalism and History," 112. Uhlenbruch made the point first in his "The Annexation of History," 269.

23. RGASPI, f. 17, op. 125, d. 123, ll. 161–69, published in this volume for the first time.

24. Ibid.

25. RGASPI, f. 558, op. 11, d. 731, ll. 112, 69. This document was kept at Stalin's dacha until his death, suggesting that he had continued to think about these issues in the late 1940s and early 1950s.

26. Shcherbakov's memorandum refers to the Committee for Artistic Affairs as having commissioned Tolstoi and Eisenstein to develop a portrayal of Ivan IV for the stage and screen. While Tolstoi had already been considering the subject for

several years, Eisenstein had been exploring other projects on the Fergana Canal and the pre-revolutionary Beillis affair—subjects that were fading from fashion on the eve of war. The party hierarchy's sentiments on this account were expressed none too subtly: as Eisenstein's Soviet biographer writes, Zhdanov "sat Eisenstein down next to him and addressed him as author—which is to say that the issue was settled. He offered every assistance. Consultations?—but, of course: Vipper, Bakhrushin, Grekov, Nechkina—they will be asked." See RGASPI, f. 17, op. 125, d. 123, l. 165; d. 297, l. 134; R. Iurenev, *Sergei Eizenshtein: Zamysly, fil'my, metod*, 2 vols. (Moscow: Iskusstvo, 1985–1988), 2:210. More generally, see Shcherbina, *A. N. Tolstoi*, 471; Iurenev, *Sergei Eizenshtein*, 2:192–93, 210, 223, 234–35; G. Mar'iamov, *Kremlevskii tsenzor: Stalin smotrit kino* (Moscow: Kinotsentr, 1992), 69–71; Kozlov, "The Artist and the Shadow of Ivan," 109–11; Rostislav Iurenev, "Tragediia Sergeia Eizenshteina," *Rodina* 11 (1993): 104–5. Letters in Eisenstein's personal archive characterize aspects of the assignment: RGALI), f. 1923, op. 1, d. 561, l. 1; d. 657, ll. 3–4. Elena Bulgakova noted earlier operatic projects involving Tolstoi and Shostakovich that apparently came to nothing in a 7 April 1939 diary entry—see *Dnevnik Eleny Bulgakovoi*, ed. V. Losev and L. Ianovskaia (Moscow: Knizhnaia palata, 1990), 252.

27. To Khrennikov's relief, the war distracted Shcherbakov from following up on the proposition. Despite the clear indication that the Ivan saga was an allegory on Soviet state-building, Khrennikov contends simplistically that: "Stalin looked back into history for examples to imitate and ... deployed references of these historical figures in order to justify his own actions." Tikhon Khrennikov, *Tak eto bylo: Tikhon Khrennikov o vremeni i o sebe*, ed. V. Rubtsova (Moscow: Muzyka, 1994), 110.

28. V. I. Kostylev, "Literaturnye zametki," *Izvestiia*, 19 March 1941, 5. Many consider this article to mark the start of rehabilitation campaign—see *Perepiska Ivana Groznogo s Andreem Kurbskim*, ed. Ia. S. Lur'e and Iu. D. Rykov (Leningrad: Nauka, 1979), 216–17; Uhlenbruch, " Annexation of History," 269–70; Kozlov, "Artist and the Shadow of Ivan," 112; Perrie, "Nationalism and History," 112–13. Boris Pasternak shared this impression at the time—see his 4 February 1941 letter to Ol'ga Freidenberg, published in *Novyi mir* 6 (1988): 218.

29. S. Khentova, *Shostakovich: Zhizn' i tvorchestvo*, 2 vols. (Leningrad: Sovetskii kompozitor, 1985), 1:519.

30. The trilogy was republished in 1955 and 1986.

31. Aleksei Tolstoi, "'Ivan Groznyi,'" *Literatura i iskusstvo*, 21 March 1942, 3. Eisenstein, who had initially hoped to co-author his Ivan screenplay with Tolstoi, reportedly felt threatened by this article's mention of Tolstoi's competing project. See Iurenev, *Sergei Eizenshtein*, 2:213, 224.

32. S. M. Eizenshtein, "Ivan Groznyi, kino-stsenarii," *Novyi mir* 10–11 (1943): 61–108; Mar'iamov, *Kremlevskii tsensor*, 70; Iurenev, *Sergei Eizenshtein*, 2:223, 231–35. Kozlov asserts that Stalin's patriotic reading of the screenplay threw Eisenstein into a tailspin that caused him to shoot the subversive sequel, a conclusion that is based on circumstantial evidence and post-Stalin memoirs that tendentiously cast the director as a dissident and martyr. See Kozlov, "Artist and the Shadow of Ivan," 121–30.

33. See, for instance, A. Tolstoi, "Rodina," *Pravda*, 7 November 1941, 1.

34. R. Iu. Vipper, *Ivan Groznyi* (Moscow: Del'fin, 1922; 2nd ed: Tashkent: Gos. izd-vo polit. lit-ry, 1942); S. V. Bakhrushin, *Ivan Groznyi* (Moscow: Gos. izd-vo polit. lit-ry, 1942; 2nd ed., 1945). Vipper's book went into a third edition in 1944 and a number of foreign language editions in the early postwar years. For a discussion of Bakhrushin's book, see Brandenberger and Platt, "Terribly Romantic, Terribly Progressive or Terribly Tragic," 645–47.

35. For the historians' low opinions of Tolstoi's presentation, see N. A. Gorskaia, *Boris Dmitrievich Grekov* (Moscow: Rossiiskaia akademiia nauk, 1999), 166 n. 20; Platt and Brandenberger, "Terribly Romantic, Terribly Progressive or Terribly Tragic," 650.

36. G. D. Burdei, *Istorik i voina, 1941–1945* (Saratov: Izd-vo Saratovskogo un-ta, 1991), 188. Discussion about such a collection dates to 1941—see Gorskaia, *Boris Dmitrievich Grekov*, 123–24.

37. A. M. Pankratova, "Sovetskaia istoricheskaia nauka za 25 let i zadachi istorikov v usloviiakh Velikoi Otechestvennoi Voiny," in *Dvadtsat' piat' let istoricheskoi nauki v SSSR*, ed. V. P. Volgin, E. V. Tarle, et al. (Moscow and Leningrad: Izd-vo Akademii nauk, 1942), 30; *Stenogramma publichnoi lektsii akademika Vipper R. Iu., prochitannoi 17 sentiabria 1943 goda v Kolonnom zale Doma soiuzov v Moskve* (Moscow: Lektsionnoe biuro, 1943); "Ivan Groznyi," *Pravda*, 19 September 1943, 2; S. V. Bakhrushin, "Ivan Groznyi," *Bol'shevik* 13 (1943): 48–61; I. I. Smirnov, *Ivan Groznyi* (Leningrad: Gospolitizdat, 1944). See also R. Iu. Vipper, "Ivan Groznyi," *Prepodavanie istorii v shkole* 1 (1946): 29. Kozlov mistakenly contends that the campaign waned in 1942 before being revived in 1943—see his "Artist and the Shadow of Ivan," 120–21.

38. R. Iu. Vipper, *Ivan Groznyi*, 3rd ed. (Moscow: Gos. izd-vo polit. lit-ry, 1944), 159. The same claim appears in Vipper's 1946 article in *Prepodavanie istorii v shkole*.

39. Bakhrushin here avoids common historical terms associated with such discussions like "centralization of power," "the gathering of lands," etc. See his "Ivan Groznyi," 48–61.

40. On Stalin's views on historical parallels, see the introduction to this volume.

41. Tolstoi's caveat during a 1937 discussion of the Soviet mythical past—"we do not want to down-play the significance of the personality towering above our own epoch"—illustrates his unwillingness to explicitly equate Stalin with representatives of the old regime. See "Petr I i kino," *Literaturnaia gazeta*, 30 March 1937, 6.

42. David Bordwell, *The Cinema of Eisenstein* (Cambridge, Mass.: Harvard University Press, 1993), 224.

43. M. Iu. Bleiman, *O kino—svidetel'skie pokazaniia* (Moscow: Iskusstvo, 1973), 424–25.

44. Iurenev, *Sergei Eizenshtein*, 2:236; Kozlov, "Artist and the Shadow of Ivan," 117. A. M. Pankratova and N. M. Rubinshtein, among others, criticized Eisenstein's attribution of populist tendencies to Ivan—see RGASPI, f. 17, op. 125, d. 224, ll. 60ob—70; f. 77, op. 2, d. 971, ll. 7–8; Burdei, *Istorik i voina*, 152, 156–57, 188;

"Stenogramma soveshchaniia po voprosam istorii SSSR v TsK VKP(b) v 1944 godu," *Voprosy istorii* 3 (1996): 96.

45. For the behind-the-scenes debates concerning Eisenstein's first and second films, see RGALI, f. 2456, op. 1, dd. 956, 957, 1277, 1278, partially published in E. Levin, "Istoricheskaia tragediia kak zhanr i kak sud'ba: po stranitsam dvukh stenogramm 1944 i 1946 godov," *Iskusstvo kino* 9 (1991): 83–92.

46. Aside from Shcherbakov's memorandum to Stalin, see his report on the first staging of Tolstoi's play in the Malyi Theater, which includes a negative review by the editor of *Izvestiia*, L. F. Il'ichev: RGASPI, f. 17, op. 125, d. 297, ll. 109–16. See also M. Zh[ivov], "Na chtenii p'esy A. Tolstogo 'Ivan Groznyi,'" *Literatura i iskusstvo*, 14 March 1942, 4; S. O. Shmidt, "Otzyv S. B. Veselovskogo o dramaticheskoi povesti 'Ivan Groznyi' A. N. Tolstogo," in *Arkheograficheskii ezhegodnik za 1988 god*, ed. S. O. Shmidt (Moscow: Izd-vo Akademii nauk, 1989), 296–313; Burdei, *Istorik i voina*, 188; RGASPI, f. 17, op. 125, d. 297, l. 140; d. 297, l. 140; d. 367, ll. 18–20; M. Khrapchenko, "Sovremennaia sovetskaia dramaturgiia," *Literatura i iskusstvo*, 30 May 1942, 3.

47. Tolstoi's letters, held in the Presidential Archive (APRF), are published in Iu. Murin, "Istoriia—oruzhie bor'by," *Glasnost'*, 28 November 1991, 7. K. I. Chukovskii describes Tolstoi's anxiety while waiting for the party hierarchy's decision on the fate of his play in his *Dnevnik, 1930–1969*, 2 vols. (Moscow: Sovetskii pisatel', 1994), 2:164. Ultimately, Stalin called Tolstoi by telephone to tell him of the play's approval—according to Andrei Siniavskii, the author's now-closed collection of papers contains "a transcript of a telephone conversation with Stalin. Stalin personally phoned Tolstoi, approved his piece, and noted in relation to Ivan that there had been one shortcoming to his personality. For some reason between his executions of the boyars, he suffered pangs of conscience and repented for his cruelty." See Siniavskii, "Stalin—geroi i khudozhnik stalinskoi epokhi," 119.

48. Sergei Borodin, "'Ivan Groznyi'—roman V. Kostyleva," *Literatura i iskusstvo*, 15 May 1943, 3; V. I. Kostylev, "Pis'mo v redaktsiiu," *Oktiabr'* 8–9 (1943): 261–63; see also A. Iakovlev, "Kniga ob Ivane Groznom," *Literatura i iskusstvo*, 4 March 1944, 3.

49. The Stalin Prizes for 1943–44 were publicly announced on 27 January 1946. Eisenstein's first film earned first prizes for him as director, as well as for the film's leading actor, N. K. Cherkasov, its composer, S. S. Prokof'ev, and its cinematographers, A. N. Moskvin and E. K. Tisse. A first prize also went to Tolstoi, posthumously. The prizes for 1945 were announced 29 June 1946: Solov'ev won a second prize for his play, while its production at Tbilisi's Rustaveli Theater earned first prizes for its director, A. A. Khorava, and the actors, A. A. Vasadze and G. M. Davitashvili. Kostylev and Sel'vinskii were also nominated but did not win prizes—see RGASPI, f. 17, op. 125, d. 399, ll. 1–11.

50. RGASPI, f. 17, op. 116, d. 249; Zhdanov's undated handwritten draft is at f. 77, op. 3, d. 179, ll. 73–75; Central Committee resolution of 4 September 1946, "O kinofil'me 'Bol'shaia zhizn','" *Kul'tura i zhizn'*, 10 September 1946, reprinted in *O partiinoi i sovetskoi pechati: Sbornik dokumentov* (Moscow: Pravda, 1954), 575–76. I. G. Bol'shakov's reminiscences of the film's screening for Stalin are reproduced in Kozlov, "Artist and the Shadow of Ivan," 127.

51. Konstantin Simonov adds perceptively that the second part of the film was less relevant to Soviet propaganda needs after the war, as victory in 1945 reduced the need for heroic templates from the tsarist past. See K. Simonov, *Glazami cheloveka moego pokoleniia* (Moscow: Novosti, 1989), 186–87. See our treatment of the conflicting expectations for the Ivan saga's emplotment in "Terribly Romantic, Terribly Progressive or Terribly Tragic."

52. "O kinofil'me 'Bol'shaia zhizn'," 575–76.

53. According to Vishnevskii's notes, the meeting took place on 9 August 1946. See RGALI, f. 1923, op. 1, d. 1712, l. 38, cited in Iurenev, "Tragediia Sergeia Eizenshteina," 111.

54. "Stalin, Molotov i Zhdanov o 2-i serii fil'ma 'Ivan Groznyi': Zapis' Sergeia Eizenshteina i Nikolaia Cherkasova," *Moskovskie novosti*, 7 August 1988, 8. Eisenstein was quite aware of this interpretation, putting the same thoughts to paper in 1945—see his "Ivan Groznyi," in *Izbrannye proizvedeniia*, 6 vols. (Moscow: Iskusstvo, 1964), 1:193.

55. *Stenogramma publichnoi lektsii akademika Vipper R. Iu.*, 8–19.

56. Kozlov asserts without evidence that I. A. Pyr'ev received a commission in 1952 to begin shooting another film about Ivan. In fact, Pyr'ev had briefly considered the idea of screening Sel'vinskii's play in 1946 but had abandoned the idea after grasping the complexity of the task. See Kozlov, "Artist and the Shadow of Ivan," 130; Mar'iamov, *Kremlevskii tsenzor*, 94.

57. See, for instance, S. V. Bakhrushin, "Moskva Ivana Groznogo," *Vestnik Moskovskogo universiteta* 9 (1947): 61–73; I. A. Korotkov, *Ivan Groznyi: Voennaia deiatel'nost'* (Moscow: Voennoe izd-vo, 1952); "Ivan Groznyi," in *Bol'shaia sovetskaia entsiklopediia*, 17:266–69; etc.

58. Interestingly, it was *Voprosy istorii*'s editor Pankratova who helped undermine the Stalinist mythology surrounding Ivan IV. The best account is "Iz dnevnikov Sergeia Sergeevicha Dmitrieva," *Otechestvennaia istoriia* 1 (2000): 164–71. Generally, see L. A. Sidorova, "Anna Mikhailovna Pankratova," *Istoricheskaia nauka Rossii v XX veke* (Moscow: Skriptorii, 1997), 429–33; and the epilogue to Perrie, *Cult of Ivan the Terrible*, esp. 179–86.

59. Khrennikov, *Tak eto bylo*, 110. See also N. K. Cherkasov, *Zapiski sovetskogo aktera* (Moscow: Iskusstvo, 1953), 135–39. A possibly apocryphal story reports Stalin musing: "Was the English [Queen] Elizabeth less cruel when she was fighting to strengthen absolutism in England[?] . . . How many heads rolled during her rule? She didn't even have pity on her cousin Mary Stuart. But the English people are not foolish—they respect her and call her 'Great.'" Mar'iamov, *Kremlevskii tsenzor*, 92.

60. RGASPI, f. 17, op. 125, d. 222, ll. 39–40, 44.

11
Internal Debate within the Party Hierarchy about the Rehabilitation of Ivan the Terrible

The following is a draft of the only known official record testifying to the direct involvement of the party hierarchy in the campaign to rehabilitate Ivan the Terrible. This internal memorandum, written by A. S. Shcherbakov, the party's ideology chief, assails A. N. Tolstoi's play about the sixteenth-century tsar, which had been commissioned by the All-Union Committee for Artistic Affairs in late 1940 or early 1941. Its criticism of the play's dramatic dimensions and failure to focus on Ivan's qualities as a strong leader and state-builder clarify the priorities underlying the campaign.[1] Shcherbakov's memorandum exists in three drafts: a concise, signed version, dating to 28 April 1942, which is stored at the Archive of the President of the Russian Federation;[2] a somewhat longer, unsigned version, located in the former Central Party Archive;[3] and the longest, most detailed redaction, also from the Central Party Archive, which is presented here in print for the first time.[4]

Only a month after the first draft of the memorandum was completed, the head of the Committee for Artistic Affairs, M. B. Khrapchenko, published an article in the newspaper *Literatura i isskustvo* lambasting Tolstoi's play in almost precisely the same terms used in Shcherbakov's memorandum, indicating a broad unanimity of views regarding the play within the party hierarchy.[5] Later versions of the document attest to Shcherbakov's continued opposition to Tolstoi's plays. Shcherbakov's intermediate draft was submitted to the Central Committee archive on 3 December 1942. The final draft was filed at the same archive on 24 May 1945, although it is clear from the language of this version that it too was written in 1942 or early in 1943. Indeed, Tolstoi seems to have referred to it in 1943 as he rewrote the play to accommodate some of Shcherbakov's objections. Premièring later that year, the play ultimately won Stalin prizes for dramaturgy and performance after the war.[6] The delay in consigning the memorandum to the archive speaks to the continuing controversy that surrounded the play throughout its composition and various performances.

A. S. Shcherbakov, "Memorandum to Stalin concerning A. N. Tolstoi's Play *Ivan the Terrible*"

1941–1943

A. N. Tolstoi's play "Ivan the Terrible" was nominated by the Stalin Prize Committee for a prize for the year 1941.

Yet upon analysis of the play, it was decided not to act on the nomination, both out of formal considerations (the play had not been printed or staged in a single theater, it was unknown to the Soviet public, the critical establishment had not expressed any opinions concerning it, etc.), and out of material considerations, as the play distorts the historical image of one of the greatest representatives of the Russian state—Ivan IV (1530–1584).

Yet it is hardly sufficient to simply withdraw A. N. Tolstoi's *Ivan the Terrible* from consideration for a Stalin Prize.

The fact of the matter is that this play was written by a special order of the [All-Union] Committee for Artistic Affairs, following the decision of the Central Committee of the All-Union Communist Party (Bolsheviks) establishing the necessity of rehabilitating the authentic image of Ivan IV in Russian history—an image that has been distorted by aristocratic and bourgeois historiography.

Ivan IV was an outstanding political figure of sixteenth-century Russia. He completed the establishment of a centralized Russian state, a progressive endeavor initiated by Ivan III. Ivan IV fundamentally eliminated the country's feudal fragmentation, successfully crushing the resistance of representatives of the feudal order. There is literally not a single aspect of domestic policy, beginning with finance and ending with the army, that did not undergo revision or reorganization during this period (court reforms, rural church reforms, the restructuring of the central administration, the creation of a new army, the introduction of new forms of weaponry, etc.). Ivan IV himself was one of the most educated men of the day and a champion of the broad dissemination of knowledge. He passionately supported such progressive endeavors as the introduction of the printing press in Russia. All of these reforms met with vigorous resistance on the part of representatives of the feudal order—entrenched patrimonial estate-holders, tenaciously insisting on the preservation of the feudal order. Ivan the Terrible was forced to resort to harsh measures in order to strike at the feudal, patrimonial privileges of the boyars.

Ivan was the bearer of the most progressive ideas on governance of his time. He saw Russia's salvation in the formation of a mighty centralized Russian state.

Ivan IV was an outstanding military leader. He personally led the conquests of Kazan' and Astrakhan'. In foreign policy he demonstrated his brilliant diplomatic skills. Only his mighty will and outstanding political abilities allowed him to overcome the great difficulties of the almost quarter-century-long Livonian War. Despite the resistance and treason of representatives of the feudal order and an enormous expenditure of resources, the Russian state came to occupy a prominent place among the mightiest European powers under the leadership of Ivan the Terrible.

Figure 24. Picture of N. K. Cherkasov as Ivan the Terrible that the actor gave to A. A. Zhdanov in May 1944. The dedication quotes the final line of the unfinished third part of Eisenstein's film, referring to Ivan's conquest of the Baltic region in the Livonian war: "We are standing on the edge of the sea and will continue to stand here." RGASPI, f. 77, op. 2, d. 105.

It must be said, with regard to historical consequences, that the actions of Ivan IV helped Russia to overcome the dangers of the Time of Troubles[7] and to withstand the mad attack of the Polish interventionists. Furthermore, it is quite possible that if Ivan IV had been able to fully implement his reforms, there would have been no Time of Troubles at all.

Aristocratic and bourgeois historians have been unable to grasp in a historically correct manner the energetic and multifaceted activity of Ivan the Terrible in the creation and strengthening of the centralized Russian state, in overcoming the antiquated past and in raising the international prestige of Russia. Moreover, aristocratic and bourgeois historians have diligently avoided mention of the progressive deeds of Ivan IV in their works. In their characterizations of Ivan IV, a significant number of historians have unfairly emphasized only the cruelty and severity of his measures against the boyars.

As unbelievable as it sounds, the polemical letters of Ivan IV's enemy Kurbskii,[8] a traitor to the fatherland, have exerted a strong influence on the subsequent development of bourgeois and aristocratic historiography (everyone from Karamzin to Vipper).[9] Karamzin, an ideologist of the conservative aristocracy, divides the history of Ivan the Terrible's reign into such periods as "the epoch of executions;" "the epoch of murders;" "the epoch of the most terrible torments" and the final era—the "epoch of slaughter." In his final analysis, Karamzin equates the reign of Ivan IV with the Tatar Yoke.[10]

Ilovaiskii,[11] characterizing Tsar Ivan as a short-sighted and hapless politician, concludes that Ivan's deeds precipitated the Time of Troubles and, in this way, brought the state to the brink of annihilation.

Kliuchevskii[12] and Solov'ev[13] offer little new insight into the deeds of the Terrible Tsar when compared to Karamzin. In his *Course on Russian History* Kliuchevskii analyzes in great detail Ivan's political, diplomatic and military accomplishments. He compares Ivan to "the blind knight in the Old Testament who collapses a building on top of himself in order to destroy the enemies who are sitting on the roof."[14] Kliuchevskii seeks out all the shortcomings of Ivan's biography in order to diminish the significance of his accomplishments in the history of the Russian state.

In his historical works, Plekhanov describes the significance of the Terrible Tsar's accomplishments as the final phase of the transformation of "the Muscovite state ... into an Oriental despotism."[15]

A similar sort of distortion of the image of Ivan the Terrible has been expressed in Russian literature. A. K. Tolstoi's broadly disseminated early historical novel, *Prince Serebrianyi*, and the same author's play, *The Death of Ivan the Terrible*, can serve as salient examples.[16]

It seems that every possible insult has been hurled against Ivan IV by historians and authors—despot, bloody tyrant, madman, coward, deserter, "marauder," murderer, etc.—in a repetition of the slander that was first concocted by the most nefarious of Ivan's internal enemies and, second, by foreign enemies who feared the strengthening of the Russian state under Tsar Ivan's leadership.

Only epic folktales, the *byliny*,[17] offer a more colorful and historically accurate evaluation of Ivan the Terrible, especially concerning his reprisals against the "long-bearded" boyars. In the folk epics, Ivan the Terrible is represented as the champion of truth and a fair judge.

> O, you mountains, steep mountains!
> O, you golden spires of Orthodox churches!
> O, you shuttered windows of the Tsar's palace!
> It's as if the Orthodox Tsar lives in seclusion.
> The Orthodox Tsar Ivan Vasil'evich:
> He is terrible, O father, terrible and merciful,
> He rewards the truth, but for falsehood he grants only death.[18]

Thus the task of reestablishing the historical truth about Ivan IV and rehabilitating him as a political figure has long been a priority and remains so to the present day. It is for this reason that the Committee for Artistic Affairs, on the basis of specific instructions, issued an official order for the creation of plays and a film script about Ivan the Terrible.

Yet despite the fact that nearly a year has passed since writers and historians took up the task of the historical rehabilitation of the Terrible Tsar, the results of their work remain unsatisfactory thus far. A. N. Tolstoi's play *Ivan the Terrible* exemplifies this situation, for it not only fails to represent Ivan the Terrible correctly, but it actually distorts his image.

The main flaw of A. N. Tolstoi's play about the Terrible Tsar is that Ivan is not shown as a major, talented political actor, the gatherer of the Russian state,[19] and an implacable foe of the feudal fragmentation of Rus' and the reactionary boyars. The play portrays the struggle between Ivan and the boyars as an internal conflict at court. Ivan's disagreement with the boyars appears to be primarily personal in nature, and his repression of the boyars seems to have been provoked by their personal offenses against him. In actual fact, Ivan's struggle with the boyars was a conflict between the two fundamental tendencies of the day: the progressive determination of Tsar Ivan to create a unified Russian state, and the reactionary drive of the boyars, who insisted on their patrimonial *mestnichestvo*[20] interests and the feudal order.

The Terrible Tsar's intense, energetic governmental service is expressed in the play only rhetorically. Over the course of the entire play no transformative, progressive activity is visible. One may assess the political ideas of the tsar only on the basis of his statements in intimate discussions with the Tsaritsa Mariia Temriukovna (in acts three and five). In this A. N. Tolstoi directly follows bourgeois historians who have sought by any and all means to diminish Ivan IV's role and significance. Thus, Kliuchevskii writes: "the positive significance of Tsar Ivan in the history of our state is not nearly as great as one might have thought, were one to judge by his plans and undertakings or by the noise that his activity produced. The Terrible Tsar planned more than he accomplished, and had a greater effect on his contemporaries' imagination and nerves than on the contemporary state order."[21]

The Terrible Tsars's measures against the boyars, which were necessary in order to break the boyars' stubborn resistance against Ivan's governmental reforms, are not shown in the play. If one were to judge Ivan the Terrible by A. N. Tolstoi's play, then one might think that these measures were limited to verbal threats against the boyars. In conversation with Princess Efrosin'ia Staritskaia (act five) Ivan says: "Just wait—you will all experience a much greater dishonor. You will vanish like cabbage worms." Or: "Soon, soon I will grant the people's will in Moscow. Then you will scream for real." Or: "Why have I visited my retribution upon them? I have not yet visited true retribution upon them—but I will. May children be frightened by the mere mention of my name!" Ivan tells Maliuta (in act seven): "Don't you dare smirk when I write letters to my enemies . . . I have a passion for the literary arts . . ." "I write letters to my enemies when what is needed is the axe and the scaffold."

The relationship between the people and the Terrible Tsar is shown in a simplified and primitive manner in Tolstoi's play. The people are represented by the figure of the holy fool, Vasilii the Blessed, who gives the tsar a "coin" in the name of the people to support his war against Livonia, and who sacrifices his own life by shielding Ivan the Terrible from a traitorous boyar arrow.

A. N. Tolstoi attempts to show that Ivan IV is engaged in a struggle with a powerful and numerous caste—the boyars. Ivan must defeat them. But why? The answer is not clear from what the play has to offer, as Ivan the Terrible is shown acting alone, without the support of any other force that potentially might be more powerful than the boyars.

Ivan tells Maria: "I have no friends. Andrei Kurbskii was a friend, but he no longer will look me in the eye. There are to be no friends for me. Whatever friends I might have become frightened and are left behind." It is precisely at this point that the *oprichnina* should have been shown as a serious force for Ivan to rely upon. Tolstoi, however, sidestepped the whole question.

Ivan the Terrible's wars for control of Kazan' and Astrakhan', which played a significant and positive role in the development of trade contacts and the strengthening of the Russian state, are not shown in the play at all. And Ivan's war with Livonia is depicted in a historically inaccurate manner. There is not a single word in the play about the the Russian troops' rout of the Livonians. The war ends with Kurbskii's treason and the Russian forces' retreat. In this way, the play distorts historical events.

The conclusion of the play is entirely unacceptable. Instead of a portrayal of triumphant victory over the Livonians and the realization of Ivan's plans for the creation of a unified Russian state, the play ends with a scene at the grave of the tsaritsa, murdered by the boyars, and Ivan's ambiguous command: "*Oprichniki, we march on Moscow!*"

The following is also worthy of note: events in Tolstoi's play that took place many years apart are rearranged to appear as if they occurred at the same time. Here is a chronology of specific events shown in the play:

1. Conquest of Kazan' — 1552
2. Conquest of Astrakhan' — 1556
3. Ivan IV's illness — 1553
4. Start of the Livonian War — 1558
5. Death of Ivan's first wife Anastasiia — 1560
6. Sil'vestr's fall from favor — 1560
7. Marriage to Maria Temriukovna — 1561
8. Kurbskii's flight — 1564
9. Ivan's departure for Aleksandrovskaia Sloboda — 1565
10. Elevation of Filipp Kolychev to Metropolitan — 1566
11. Death of Filipp and execution of Ivan's cousin Vladimir Andreevich — 1569
12. Death of Maria Temriukovna — 1569
13. Simeon Bekbulatovich crowned as "Lord" of Moscow by Ivan etc., etc. — 1575[22]

A. N. Tolstoi has many of these events coincide with the illness of Ivan IV in 1553 [when contemporaries thought the tsar lay on his deathbed]. The Boyar Repin exclaims, for instance: "Wash his body, and put it in its coffin. But they have forgotten to make the coffin! Oh, mortal glory! He conquered Kazan' and conquered Astrakhan', but in his hour of death there is no one to make a coffin for him." Ivan fell ill in 1553, but the conquest of Astrakhan', to which Repin refers, did not take place until 1556.

Further, Ivan was married to Maria Temriukovna in 1561, but in the play this event is dated to 1553.

Filipp Kolychev was made Metropolitan in 1566, but in the play it appears that Ivan appointed him to this post in 1553, shortly after he recovered from his illness.

Tsar Ivan's dispatch of Hans Schlichte to bring scholars, armorers and architects from Western Europe occurred in 1547. Schlichte's second attempt to bring specialists to Moscow took place in 1549. Both attempts ended in failure, as a result of intrigues on the part of the Magistrate of the Livonian Order. These events, which took place in 1547 and 1549, are referred to in the play as the immediate cause of the Livonian War, which began in 1558.

Incidentally, the Livonian War, which began in 1558, is also described as following immediately after the events of 1553 in the play.

Ivan's departure for Aleksandrovskaia Sloboda took place in 1565, and Ivan crowned Simeon Bekbulatovich as the "Lord" of Moscow in 1575, but these events are, once again, depicted as following just after 1553. And so on . . .

To a certain extent, one must recognize the playwright's right to depart from the strict chronology of events and to unite or separate them in time if this does not distort historical and political tendencies, and if instead it serves to emphasize the most important and essential historical issues. But A. N. Tolstoi's numerous historical inaccuracies do not emphasize the most important and essential issue in the play: the progressive deeds of Ivan IV. On the contrary, they distort the political and historical tendencies of the period. I am referring, first and foremost, to A. N. Tolstoi's depiction of the Shuiskiis. As is well known, the Shuiskiis played an extremely negative and despicable role in Ivan's life and the history of the Russian state at that time.

Ivan IV, recalling his childhood, wrote with indignation that: "I would be playing as a boy, and Prince I. V. Shuiskii would be sitting nearby, leaning on his elbow, with his leg resting on my father's bed, not even bowing to me!" The Shuiskiis were brazen enough not to fear insulting Ivan, breaking into his residence at night to settle scores with people close to Ivan. In subsequent years the Shuiskiis betrayed him and participated in many conspiracies against Ivan. At the time of Ivan's serious illness, when he demanded that the boyars swear an oath of fealty to his minor son, a significant portion of the boyars, led by Ivan Mikhailovich Shuiskii, refused to swear fealty to the tsarevich and selected their own obedient little tsar in the person of Ivan's cousin Vladimir Andreevich Staritskii.

Later, the pathologically traitorous, fair-weather friend and classic double-dealer Vasilii Shuiskii emerged from the Shuiskii clan.[23] Such was the nature of the Shuiskiis and such was their role. And if one must discuss Tsar Ivan's mistakes and miscalculations, then one such mistake was his failure to eliminate the Shuiskiis.

Nevertheless, A. N. Tolstoi eulogizes the Shuiskiis in his play. He depicts Petr Ivanovich Shuiskii as devoted to Tsar Ivan, and relies on an unproven hypothesis (perhaps devised by A. N. Tolstoi himself) that this Petr Ivanovich Shuiskii swore fealty to Ivan's son, while completely ignoring the historical fact that Ivan Mikhailovich Shuiskii was the ringleader of those who refused to swear the oath of fealty.

For all the aforementioned reasons, A. N. Tolstoi's confused play about Ivan the Terrible cannot be considered acceptable for performance or publication by virtue of its failure to rehabilitate the image of Ivan IV. The Soviet public would mistake the performance or publication of this play as an acceptable response to the demand that Soviet literature and historical science reestablish the authentic image of this great Russian political figure. The performance or publication of this play would also deepen the confusion that historians and writers are finding themselves in concerning sixteenth-century Russian history and Ivan IV.

In conclusion, it is necessary to ban the performance of A. N. Tolstoi's play *Ivan the Terrible* in Soviet theaters and also to prohibit the publication of the play in the press.

Notes

1. A. N. Tolstoi had been considering taking up Ivan the Terrible since the late 1930s—see chapter 10 in this volume.
2. Part of this draft was published along with several of Tolstoi's letters to Stalin in Iu. Murin, "Istoriia—oruzhie bor'by," *Glasnost'*, 28 November 1991, 7.
3. RGASPI, f. 17, op. 125, d. 123, ll. 161–69.
4. RGASPI, f. 17, op. 125, d. 297, ll. 130–40.

5. M. B. Khrapchenko, "Sovremennaia sovetskaia dramaturgiia," *Literatura i isskustvo*, 30 May 1942, 3.

6. This last draft of the memorandum is unsigned, but it is located in a Committee for Artistic Affairs folder in close proximity to another memorandum from Shcherbakov to Stalin. In this latter memorandum, dated 25 October 1944, Shcherbakov passed on to the general secretary an article critiquing the 1944 Malyi Theater production of the play, which was ultimately shut down. It seems likely that Shcherbakov recirculated his 1942 memorandum lambasting the play in connection with his objection to its subsequent performance.

7. The term "Time of Troubles" refers to civil and political disorders during Muscovy's early-seventeenth-century interregnum.

8. A. M. Kurbskii (1528–1583) was a prominent member of Ivan IV's court who defected to the Polish-Lithuanian Commonwealth in 1564, from which he supposedly conducted a famous polemical correspondence with Ivan IV. Significant doubt has been cast on the attribution of these documents—see Edward Keenan, *The Kurbskii-Groznyi Apocrypha: The Seventeenth-Century Genesis of the "Correspondence" Attributed to Prince A. M. Kurbskii and Tsar Ivan IV* (Cambridge, Mass.: Harvard University Press, 1971); idem, "Putting Kurbskii in His Place, or: Observations and Suggestions Concerning the Place of the *History of the Grand Prince of Muscovy* in the History of Muscovite Literary Culture," *Forshungen zur osteuropaischen Geschichte* 24 (1978): 132–61.

9. N. M. Karamzin (1766–1826), Russia's first official historiographer and author of the *History of the Russian State* (1818–1826). R. Iu. Vipper (1859–1954), a specialist in the history of antiquity and Christianity, authored the apologetic monograph *Ivan the Terrible* (1922; 2nd ed., 1942; 3rd ed., 1944), which served as one of the key texts in the Stalinist rehabilitation of Ivan IV.

10. The "Tatar Yoke" refers to the period of Mongol-Tatar domination over Muscovy from the thirteenth to the fifteenth centuries.

11. D. I. Ilovaiskii (1832–1920), monarchist historian and author of popular conservative textbooks on Russian history.

12. V. O. Kliuchevskii (1841–1911), historian of the late imperial period and author of the most famous pre-revolutionary history of Russia.

13. S. M. Solov'ev (1820–1879), prominent historian and public figure of the mid-nineteenth century and author of a standard multivolume history of Russia. Despite Shcherbakov's remarks, Solov'ev championed a fundamentally new interpretation of Ivan IV and his reign.

14. The reference is to the story of Samson's repentance, faith, and death, from book 3, chapter 20 of the Old Testament. See V. O. Kliuchevskii, *Kurs russkoi istorii*, 5 vols. (Moscow: Gosudarstvennoe sotsial'no-ekonomicheskoe izdatel'stvo, 1937), 2:212.

15. G. V. Plekhanov (1856–1918), founder and leading theorist of Russian Marxism. See G. V. Plekhanov, *Istoriia russkoi obshchestvennoi mysli*, ed. D. Riazanov (Moscow: Gosudarstvennoe izdatel'stvo, 1925), 193.

16. A. K. Tolstoi (1817–1875), conservative author, remembered for his lyric poetry,

his novel *Prince Serebrianyi* (1862), and his trilogy of historical plays, the first of which is *The Death of Ivan the Terrible* (1866).

17. On the Soviet revival of epic folklore, see chapter 10 in this volume.

18. *Moskovskaia politicheskaia literatura XVI veka: izbornik*, ed. M. N. Kovalenskii (St. Petersburg: Energiia, 1914), 129.

19. Shcherbakov's phrase "the gatherer of the Russian state" is related to the traditional formulation "the gathering of the Russian lands," commonly applied to Muscovite expansionism during the fourteenth through the sixteenth centuries, reflecting his fascination with Ivan's role as a state-builder.

20. *Mestnichestvo* refers to the customary hierarchy of prominent families in Muscovy, derived from genealogical rankings.

21. Kliuchevskii, *Kurs russkoi istorii*, 2:211.

22. An undated draft of this chronology is found in one of Shcherbakov's private notebooks—see RGASPI, f. 88, op. 1, d. 928, ll. 17–18.

23. Vasilii Ivanovich Shuiskii (1552–1612), boyar and tsar (1606–1610) during the Time of Troubles.

Aleksandr Pushkin

12
The 1937 Pushkin Jubilee as Epic Trauma

༄ STEPHANIE SANDLER

One of the more bizarre proposals to commemorate the 1999 bicentennial of Pushkin's birth was to replace the obelisk at Chernaia Rechka, the site of his fatal duel, with a chapel. A letter signed by the head of the Union of Russian Writers, V. Ganichev, repeated an old Petersburg rumor that the obelisk placed at Chernaia Rechka in 1937 had been illicitly taken from someone else's grave.[1] Few moments in the commemoration so perfectly represented contemporary views about the hidden reality of 1937: as this urban legend has it, the monumental essence of that awful jubilee required that a ritual marker of death be disturbed. In order that Pushkin be mourned, someone else had to be forgotten, their memory defaced. This false tale of substitution and concealment preserves the essential components of public discourse from the 1937 commemoration. I, too, focus on death, concealment, substitution, and trauma as I consider several literary works of 1937. Mikhail Zoshchenko, Mikhail Bulgakov, and Daniil Kharms were masters in mixing horror with hilarity, and their rereadings of the Pushkin story encode the strange 1937 amalgamation of death with celebration, of feast in a time of plague. They draw out the symptomatic features of the official commemoration discourse but in an exaggerated manner, something akin to what the Formalists called "baring the device" (*obnazhenie priema*). I begin by commenting on the nature of the jubilee itself and on what the public events of January 1937 signify about emerging Soviet culture.

More than other rituals celebrating the consolidation of Soviet power, several of them well studied by Karen Petrone,[2] the 1937 jubilee was significant for its forceful recuperation of an episode from the imperial past.

The revisionism that is the broader subject of the present volume was clearly at work in the Pushkin jubilee: the national poet was seen anew, transformed into a hero to be admired and emulated. David Brandenberger has rightly noted that the impulse behind the grand commemoration of the 1930s was the realization that "Pushkin was more useful alive than dead"; and a poet who had seemed an aristocrat with European sensibilities in the aftermath of the Revolution now provided the first test for a new style of "mobilizational politics."[3] As another scholar, Arlen Blium, has put it, "the regime needed a certain legitimization, and the great ghosts of the past were perfectly suited to this task."[4] A "mythologized, heroic view of the past" was created, and the 1937 anniversary provided the perfect occasion to elevate Pushkin, his "'shining image'... singled out as a model for 'the new Soviet man.'"[5] Pushkin's ability to see himself as Russian above all, and to envision a different future for his nation, was crucial.[6] He was well-suited to this new role, despite his elite background, which was always described in such a way as to show that his love for Russia's language and people (*narod*) overcame the inherently weak interests of the aristocratic class.[7] And his writings were consonant with the spirit of vitality, energy, and optimism required of the new Soviet hero.[8] In particular, they were praised for their simplicity and clarity.[9] The new slogan of realism was stretched to fit the emerging canon of Pushkin's writings. Censors and party officials kept a tight watch on references to Pushkin's political writings, ensuring that short quotations could not be misread as anti-revolutionary and that inferences about Pushkin's changing political views could not be easily drawn.[10] More easily available and readily cited in academic and journalistic publications were his historical writings and lyrics with social content, such as "My ruddy-faced critic" ("Rumianyi kritik moi," 1830), with its understated description of rural poverty.[11]

Yet it was not a grim Pushkin whom the Soviets emphasized, far from it. Among his most widely reprinted poems was "Bacchic Song" ("Vakkhicheskaia pesnia," 1825), with its rousing last line, "Long live the sun; let darkness be hidden!" ("Da zdravstvuet solntse, da skroetsia t'ma!").[12] Such praise for the light of reason as against the darkness of excessive emotion accorded with official discourse in the mid-1930s; eliding references to women and wine in the opening lines, many journalists and critics used the last lines of this enthusiastic lyric poem to express the urgent gaiety that filled public life. For a glimpse of celebration in a time of hidden terror, one has to look no farther than the newsreels of the 1930s: a revealing set became newly available in 1999 in Pavel Gromov's *Three Songs of Pushkin*

(*Tri pesni o Pushkine*), which relied on documentary footage much like its model, the Dziga Vertov film *Three Songs of Lenin* (*Tri pesni o Lenine*, 1934). *Three Songs of Pushkin* is didactic in the extreme, as was Vertov's film. Gromov adds relentless voice-over to hammer home its message of the excesses and evils of Stalin's regime. Its first "song," about the Stalin period, bears a Pushkinian title, *Feast in a Time of Plague* (*Pir vo vremia chumy*, 1830), and interprets the 1937 jubilee as a false celebration in a desperate time. Pushkin may indeed remain, as one observer put it in 1999, a writer who could withstand any jubilee,[13] but the celebrations of 1937 put him to a strenuous test. Pushkin's good humor, his spirited identification with the Russian people, and the appealing clarity and simplicity of his writing (all much praised) made Pushkin's life a model for Soviet citizenship. More important, his persecution by tsarist officials could be invoked for a completely different purpose—to point to the oppression of the new Soviet state. For some, then, Pushkin stood as an example of how to withstand the pressures of a new but no less diminishing idea of citizenship.

A historical experience of collective trauma lay just beneath the public performance of happiness and achievement required by the Pushkin jubilee in February 1937. The Pushkin jubilee provided a blanket cover of optimism beneath which individual citizens suffered terrifying injustices. The cover, however, painfully repeated patterns observed in the hidden traumas of millions. The grim humor that could link overt happiness to private pain produced some remarkable jokes from the late 1930s, one of which has Stalin observing that if Pushkin had lived in the twentieth century he still would have died in a year ending in "37."[14] Repetition is the key to this joke, 1837 turning into 1937, the tragedy of the poet's death in a duel re-imagined as an execution at the hands of the Soviet state.

The only rhetorical trope more prominent than repetition in 1937 was hyperbole, perhaps because the experience of loss was as heightened as the rhetoric designed to cover it. The grand, puffed-up rhetoric of the celebration is not lost in translation: 10 February 1937 was one hundred years "after the day of death of the great Russian poet, creator of the Russian literary language, and founder of the new Russian literature—Aleksandr Sergeevich Pushkin, who enriched humankind with his immortal creations in artistic language," announced the party's Central Committee in 1935.[15] The word *great* (*velikii*) resounded constantly: it described Pushkin, elevating him to heroic status,[16] but also the new Soviet state, the jubilee, and Stalin himself. Lest anyone miss the association of greatness between the political leader and the literary hero, any number of public places and ceremonies provided reminders: in the vestibule of the restored Moika 12 apartment in Leningrad, for example, busts of Stalin and Pushkin were placed alongside one another.[17]

The commemoration also emphasized unity. Unity of perception—claims that everywhere in the Soviet Union everyone would turn their attention to Pushkin—suggested that all of culture could be signified by a single symbol, Pushkin.[18] Unity was realized as ideological conformity; the Central Committee of the Soviet Writers' Union forbade organizations to use Pushkin material without its permission.[19] This emphasis on unity was not entirely new, but no commemoration had attempted to unify so many events across such a span of time.[20] It is difficult to grasp the extent and scope of events leading up to February 10, 1937. An editorial in *Pravda* could proclaim that Pushkin had never been so loved as he was in 1937 because there had never been so many literate people in Russian-speaking society.[21] A staggering number of people were involved in the vast preparations. During the four months *before* February 1937, there were 1,495 paid lectures and 1,737 presentations by artists in Leningrad alone, heard by some 700,000 people.[22] Similar preparations occurred in thousands of cities, towns, farm villages, schools, factories, and political institutions across the vast territory of the Soviet Union.[23] Pushkin's writings were republished in huge print runs. One émigré newspaper reported that every fifth book in Soviet libraries was by Pushkin.[24] The total volume of jubilee Pushkin editions was set at 13.4 million copies.[25] In 1937, every major journal and newspaper and every minor publication, no matter what its official subject matter (agriculture, statistics, film, or steel working), covered the jubilee with enthusiasm and even abandon, especially in January and February.[26] The first issues of literary journals in 1937 were given over entirely to Pushkin. Articles on Lenin's love for Pushkin were common, and the emerging canon of Russian literature typically placed Pushkin alongside Tolstoi, Maiakovskii, and Gor'kii. On 10 February 1937, official gatherings were held in the Bolshoi Theater in Moscow, in the recently renamed Kirov Theater in Leningrad, and in similarly prestigious forums in every major city across the Soviet Union. The Central Committee ordered theaters throughout the USSR to organize concerts or dramatic spectacles based on Pushkinian themes.[27] The official Bolshoi commemoration was recorded for radio transmission across the country.[28] Commemorative speeches were reprinted in newspapers, as were relevant decrees of the Central Committee.

The experience of rereading these newspapers decades later is a revelation, not just because the context for commemorative events changed over

Figure 25. L. G. Brodata's cover for *Krokodil* 3 (1937), the "Special Prophylactic Pushkin Issue." Soviet critics and readers are seen restoring A. M. Opekushin's famous 1880 monument to Pushkin, which had been vandalized with graffiti reading "liberal landlord," "petty landowner," "*déclassé* feudal lord," "bourgeois nobleman," etc.

the years 1934–1937 in ways that we can now track, but also because in the very dailiness and repetitiveness of newspaper rhythms one begins to sense how large Pushkin must have loomed in daily life by 1937.[29] You didn't just read about him on the front page of every paper, you went to Pushkin reading groups in your place of work, you organized Pushkin plays in your apartment building, you criticized new Pushkin-related art in your regional party gatherings. In a brilliant series of feuilletons published in *Krokodil* in 1937, Mikhail Zoshchenko recorded the confusion and hilarity of poorly educated Soviet men trying to speak at Pushkin gatherings.[30] Two speeches are attributed to the fictional M. M. Konopliannikov-Zuev, a minor official who boasts that a 6 ruble 50 kopeck volume of Pushkin has been purchased for all his apartment building dwellers to share; a bust of the poet now adorns the building supervisor's office; a portrait graces the building's exterior. These objects are meant by the speaker to evidence the building's superior participation in the Pushkin festivities, although Zoshchenko undercuts his sense of achievement by making each acquisition seem shabby. In this and another speech on the same topic, Konopliannikov-Zuev then descends into an unfortunate mix of misquotation and misguided commentary about those who live in the building with him, and suffers the interruptions and corrections of an audience impatient with his digressions. The audience members who prod him to return to the subject at hand, that is, to speak *about Pushkin,* themselves repeat the command of the culture. Konopliannikov-Zuev wanders from the topic, speaks of himself and his neighbors as much as of Pushkin, confuses Pushkin with Lermontov and *Eugene Onegin* with "The Queen of Spades," all the while reflecting the confusion of a public on whom the requirement to speak about Pushkin had been imposed. Zoshchenko, always quick to note speech patterns and narrative devices that reveal hidden anxieties, here presents the performance of adulation for Pushkin at its most theatrical.[31] Weariness and ignorance about Pushkin show through, as does a wish to use any public gathering to air petty grievances against one's neighbors (the satirist misses no opportunity to record what people were allowed to squabble about in those troubled times).

When the jubilee finally took place, it was less a culmination than a significant event in an apparently endless series. Most journals continued their special coverage through the year. The name *Pushkin* multiplied before the eyes, appearing in new and unlikely spaces: seven sites were renamed by the Central Committee during the jubilee, including Moscow's old Bol'shaia Dmitrovka Street, the town of Detskoe Selo (formerly Tsarskoe Selo), and the Leningrad Academic Theater.[32] Dramatic and musical spectacles that premièred during the "Pushkin Days" continued in repertoire during the year (except those that were closed for ideological reasons), and exhibits in various museums extended well into 1937.[33]

The jubilee seemed to have no end, and the beginning was difficult to pinpoint.[34] In this sense it lived up to its epic proportions in temporal as well as spatial terms. Preparations were extensive, lengthy, and public. The public quality of these preparations (and the critical reactions to planned events) allowed for greater self-consciousness than in earlier commemorations in 1880, 1899, or 1924, and the long lead time meant that the experience of the commemoration itself was prolonged. Discussion of the jubilee was to be found in nearly every issue of the literary newspapers in 1936, and not infrequently in 1935. Some references were mere reports of planned events or publications, and some were pro forma criticisms of inadequate preparation.[35] Other initiatives were more tangible. Responding to general pressures surrounding industrialization and intensified economic production, the Pushkin jubilee put more books in schools in order to help teachers, fight illiteracy, and spread an ideological message.[36] That is, some preparations used Pushkin as motivation for needed social change. The Pushkin theme filled large spaces in the domains of culture, education, politics, and ideological struggle. Many scholars, writers, and poets published Pushkin-related work in advance of the actual jubilee, and commemorative events had plenty of "rehearsals": a June 1936 gathering in Mikhailovskoe, for example, was huge (officially, 13,500 people, but an eyewitness put the crowd closer to 30,000).[37] By the time February 1937 rolled around, speakers were recycling their best ideas, and anyone who had read a newspaper or listened to a radio would have heard it all before.

No less mind-numbing, but much more fraught with danger for Soviet citizens, were the ever-increasing reports of arrest and sabotage. Newspapers in January and February 1937 featured two stories that received equally intense coverage: the trial, sentencing, and execution of Karl Radek, Iurii Piatakov, and fifteen others; and the Pushkin celebration. Side-by-side front-page treatment was common.[38] Blium cites an example of this parallelism at its most paradoxical, from *Literaturnaia gazeta:* a quotation from Pushkin's famous monument poem that says he will be remembered for having urged mercy toward the fallen appears across from a banner headline insisting that "Trotskyite traitors and murderers be wiped from the face of the earth."[39] The purges invoked Pushkin's legacy to justify cultural and political reforms, including purges within literary organizations. As a report from the Soviet Writers' Union Plenum put it:

> Particularly in light of the political events during the last year, an orientation toward the Pushkinian heritage helped the plenum define more precisely the watershed dividing the basic core of Soviet literature [. . .] from the small number of little groups and individuals who are trying to separate themselves from the basic questions of reality with their nonsensical, mumbling lies or to hide their confusion and ruin beneath a mask of false innovation (which in fact is nothing more than concealed formalism).[40]

We note here all the hallmarks of the pejorative labeling used against writers who did not share the state's view of "the basic questions of reality" or who dared to value "innovation," false or otherwise. Purges within organizations, including the Writers' Union and the newspapers and journals covering the purges, meant that accounts of the Pushkin commemorations were repeatedly contextualized by criticism, self-criticism, and news of the replacement of writers, journalists, and theater workers. The social processes of a cultural commemoration and a society undergoing violent transformation were inevitably fused. As the celebration began, demands for critical vigilance did not subside, and virtually no speech, publication, film, play, exhibit, ballet, or musical performance, even when positively reviewed, escaped critical commentary.

Despite this watchfulness, the 1937 commemoration was surprisingly varied.[41] This unevenly textured intellectual life during the terror was well described by Lydia Ginzburg:

> People wrongly imagine the disastrous epochs of the past as occupied only with their disasters. These periods consisted of a great deal else—chiefly, that which generally makes up life itself, although against a certain, unmistakable background. The thirties were not just labor and fear, but also many talented people with a will to realize their talents.[42]

Ginzburg's comments invite us to imagine educated Soviet men and women seeking to go about their business in the 1930s. She herself exemplified this behavior, as we can tell from her lively notes from this period and from her published contribution to the Pushkin celebrations—a fine discussion of Pushkin's lyrics under the innocuous title "Pushkin's Path to Realism," in which she lucidly showed that his poems moved away from "poetical" epithets toward ordinary, prosaic words.[43]

Yet it would be false to imagine that the version of Pushkin's life and legacy produced in 1937 was entirely immune to the pressures that made up daily life during the Terror. The discourse of death and punishment, deviously renamed in the show trials, was transferred onto the narrative of Pushkin's death as a form of martyrdom. Trotskii's "hirelings" (*naimity*), who deserve death for their treason, are little different from the foreign "hireling" (D'Anthès) who murdered Russia's national poet. Xenophobia linked the two stories as much as did the choice of words, and both told tales of death. Many texts from the 1937 jubilee, in fact, retell Pushkin's death, often in ways that refer indirectly to the tragic fate of ordinary Soviet citizens that year.

Mikhail Bulgakov's controversial play *The Last Days* (*Poslednie dni*) well exemplifies the fascination with Pushkin's death. Written in 1934–1935 and intended for performance in 1937 in Moscow's Vakhtangov Theater, the production was halted and the play was not seen until 1943, several years after Bulgakov's death. The delay attests to the jubilee's atmosphere of nervousness and unpredictability. The stakes were especially high in the theater, and calls for successful dramatic work on Pushkinian themes were shrill, frequent, and apparently futile. Bulgakov does not interpret Pushkin's death much differently from most writers at the time, in part because all were influenced by Pavel Shchegolev's 1927 book *Pushkin's Duel and Death* (*Duel' i smert' Pushkina*), even though the playwright had engaged in his own research and had the collaboration, at least for a time, of V. V. Veresaev, who had researched Pushkin's life. Like others, Bulgakov presents Pushkin's death as a near-conspiracy among his enemies, the secret police, and to some extent even his ineffectual friends (Bulgakov especially derides the poet Vasilii Zhukovskii, who had long protected Pushkin). The death is a tragedy, although contemporary critics found Bulgakov's play insufficiently tragic.[44]

It is an open question whether *The Last Days* succeeds as drama. Critics are divided, some extolling its subtle and precise re-creation of Pushkin's era, others finding a number of historical inaccuracies.[45] As one scholar rightly notes, the play is structured by citations from Pushkin's poetry rather than by his biography;[46] the result risks obscurity. Even admirers have seemed uncomfortable with the play's virtual exclusion of Pushkin from the action (he fleetingly appears twice and is mentioned often, but he does not figure actively in the unfolding drama of his death). Bulgakov apparently believed that including Pushkin would be vulgar; thus the poet's energy is sensed in the play by the effect he has on others.[47] Such transference means that attention shifts away from Pushkin, who becomes the passive victim of others' intrigues. This reading of Pushkin, while continuing a tradition of emphasizing the poet's passivity (for example, in Aleksandr Blok's 1921 speech),[48] is made paradoxical by the fact that this play was intended to be staged during the 1937 jubilee, and by Bulgakov's preferred name for the drama, *Aleksandr Pushkin*.

There is a different explanation for Bulgakov's wish to keep Pushkin off the stage in *The Last Days*, however. Bulgakov, I believe, excluded Pushkin as if he were trying to keep him out of the picture, by which I mean the picture of 1937. His play becomes a mirror held up to his own historical era, which shows an image that he cannot bear for Pushkin to see. Whereas others tried to suppress their horror at what their culture was doing to the image of Pushkin, Bulgakov turns that sense of revulsion around. His play displays an acute sense of shame in regard to the world within which it was to be performed; the allegory of that world that his play presents yearns for a possible alternative in which Pushkin, at least, would not have to know the nightmare of Stalin's Terror. This is a large and perhaps largely intuitive claim, but let me buttress it by showing how the Terror finds its way into the play.

The violence and fear of the 1930s, in my view, permeate the play at all levels of its action—its combinations of players, its language, its atmosphere of heightened anxiety and impending doom. It begins in Pushkin's apartment, where his sister-in-law Aleksandra Nikolaevna Goncharova contends with money lenders. We see social settings, like a salon and a ballroom, then a dark government office and the apartment that Baron Louis Heeckeren shared with D'Anthès, with whom Pushkin dueled. The scenes rush forward to the site of the duel, Pushkin's apartment, and eventually a station master's house on the road to Sviatogorsk Monastery, where Pushkin was buried. The action is furiously paced, as if it cannot move fast enough toward the terrible, inevitable ending. Aleksandra Nikolaevna says to Zhukovskii that she feels as if she is standing over an abyss; Pushkin's dark poem "Winter Evening" ("Zimnii vecher," 1825) is a leitmotif in the play, echoed in several references to winter storms.[49]

Nature's violence seems almost calm, however, in comparison to the suggestions of human force. An example occurs in the most bizarre scene in the play, one that seems an almost incomprehensible aside. In his salon, Sergei Saltykov tells two disturbing tales, one familiar from Pushkin lore (that Pushkin was whipped by the gendarmes), the other utterly idiosyncratic (that Saltykov had shot a horse rather than sell it to the tsar). Both are told with uncanny calm. Saltykov speaks to two writers, Nestor Kukol'nik and Vladimir Benediktov, in the company of others, telling them that a fellow writer, Pushkin, was recently flogged in the Third Section. Saltykova, his wife, finds this outrageous:

> SALTYKOV: Please, my friends, keep eating. (*to Saltykova*) A pity that you react to this so indifferently, you too could be flogged.
> DOLGORUKOV: Well, they say it's true. I heard the same thing, although long ago.
> SALTYKOV: No, I have just heard it. I was riding past the Chain Bridge and I heard someone yelling. I asked what was going on? Oh, my Lord, that's Pushkin being thrashed.
> BOGOMAZOV: Oh, Sergei Vasil'evich, this is Petersburg folklore!
> SALTYKOV: Why folklore? Once I, too, was very nearly flogged. The Emperor Alexander wanted to buy my horse and offered a good price, 10,000 rubles.

But in order not to sell him the horse I shot it with a pistol. I put the pistol up to its ear and shot it.⁵⁰

Saltykov rides around the city and hears the cries of Pushkin being flogged; when the story is dismissed as an invention, he tops himself, now telling of a horse of his that he shot through the head. The passing rebuke to his wife that she, too, could be whipped, like the claim that he was almost thrashed over the horse incident, makes this strange violence pervasive and unpredictable.⁵¹

The moment of overhearing the cries of a man being beaten betrays a fascination with what goes on behind the walls of official institutions. Moreover, the play is obsessed with the workings of the secret police: their conversations and decisions occupy one long scene, and individual agents appear in Pushkin's apartment several times. We watch a spy, Bitkov, at work (impersonating a clockmaker, insinuating himself into Pushkin's household, observing at an alarmingly intimate proximity the sufferings, death, and removal of the dead poet). We see others confer and make decisions about how much to reward one spy versus another and about whether to intervene to stop Pushkin's duel. The investigation of those who control the fates of others reveals an ugly sense of their self-importance (from the tsar and Aleksandr Benkendorf down to Leontii Dubel't and the invented Bitkov). In a play written during a time of tyranny, we watch a tsar lash out at a courtier who speaks with insufficient deference about the tsarina; we hear Dubel't effectively cut off any argument about the police's presence in Pushkin's apartment by making Zhukovskii's protestations sound unpatriotic. We watch a policeman penetrate Pushkin's apartment while he is alive, then others swarm in once he has died. The sense that the state can invade a family's scene of grief has a special sting in a play written in 1934–1935 (when, for example, Bulgakov had learned of Mandel'shtam's exile in 1934 and had just survived a period of immense fear of going out in public himself).⁵²

The play is also strangely fascinated by the character of D'Anthès, but with flat results.⁵³ With Pushkin absent from the action, our attention turns inevitably to the perpetrator of the crime, but the fascination is also a sign of Bulgakov's general interest in evil.⁵⁴ He was working intensely on *The Master and Margarita* at this time, and *The Last Days* shares some concerns with Bulgakov's great novel: who is to be held responsible for the demise of a truly heroic individual, one who will not act in his own behalf? Can one apprehend the inner qualities of someone who has committed a great sin, a sin not just against an individual, but against an entire culture? Unlike the novel, Bulgakov's play does not try to answer the latter question. He does not explore D'Anthès's affections, leaving viewers uncertain whether he loves Natal'ia Nikolaevna, whether his loyalty to Heeckeren is genuine and perhaps based on an erotic bond, or whether he cares only for his own career. The longest speech D'Anthès gives is about Petersburg's dismal weather. Bulgakov shows a banal side of evil, a man who commits an act he cannot comprehend nor, as a result, much intend.

This portrayal is complemented by the police spies in *The Last Days* since they, too, commit acts of evil—indeed, their responsibility in the tragedy is greater. Bitkov, Dubel't, and Benkendorf have privileged knowledge (it is their business to collect information), including prior warning about the duel. When they talk of stopping it but do not, they become the real murderers. Bulgakov spreads responsibility for Pushkin's demise far beyond D'Anthès, then, and in doing so he follows the script first set forth by Mikhail Lermontov in "The Poet's Death" ("Smert' poeta," 1837).[55] Bulgakov has Lermontov's poem recited outside the Moika apartment where Pushkin has died, in a scene of utter pandemonium. The poem was standard fare in the 1937 jubilee; it was among the most reprinted texts about Pushkin, and its moral outrage resonated successfully with the angry rhetoric of 1937. Bulgakov turns the poem in a different direction, however, not by diminishing the anger, but by using its recitation to reveal a popular response to Pushkin's death and to the state's control of its citizens. The lines of the poem transfix the policemen who are supposed to arrest the student who recites it. An officer rises above the crowd and shouts, "My fellow citizens! What we have heard just now is all too true. Pushkin was killed deliberately, intentionally. And our entire people is insulted by this loathsome murder. [. . .] A great citizen has perished because unlimited power has been given over to the unworthy. They treat the people as prisoners [*nevol'niki*]."[56] These words, while they safely repeat Soviet views of the tsarist autocracy as responsible for Pushkin's death and as indifferent to the fate of its people, also more dangerously suggest a contemporary world in which citizens are prisoners and where the state's power is unlimited.

It may seem as if I am suggesting that Bulgakov's play was a completely rational allegory for the insane world of the Terror. His world was obsessed with evil, crowded with police spies, and built upon forms of violence that were unmentionable but horribly pervasive. But, in his decision to exclude Pushkin from the play's action, I believe that Bulgakov also goes beyond such a rational or allegorical model of drama. On February 11, 1937, the

New York Times wrote that "All Moscow was Pushkin-mad today on the hundredth anniversary of the poet's death."[57] It is the "Pushkin madness" that Bulgakov's play manages to reproduce. For in addition to conveying the insane conditions of daily life in the 1930s, Bulgakov reveals a lunatic reality about the jubilee itself. Like his play, it is a performance from which Pushkin was virtually absent. The events whirled around other interests and different obsessions.

The jubilee required a hardening of soul and spirit to its violence, distortions, and genuine dishonesties. One cannot overestimate the irony that a commemoration (which is after all a public experience that has the potential to *heal* trauma, to be a positive moment of national self-definition) became an occasion for further injury and pain.[58] But traumatic it was, a seemingly endless experience that defied absorption, thinking, reaction, and action. The automatized behaviors and benumbed survival strategies of the Stalin period were institutionalized in events like this commemoration, and the remaining Pushkin commemorations of the twentieth century, even those that occurred after the Stalin period, have had the burden of overcoming this trauma. Put another way, no later commemoration could fully put the nation in touch with the loss of Pushkin himself, so powerfully did this trauma stand in its way. It did not help matters that the next Pushkin commemoration came in 1949, still a period of recovery from World War II, which gave a nationalist tone to all celebrations. The late 1940s was a time of great Russian chauvinism, and new purges were gearing up a campaign against "cosmopolitanism."

These commemorations of Pushkin were also divisive, even as they preached unity. They did an enormous amount of nation-building work in the middle of the twentieth century, but at the expense of building a sense of citizenship and national identity among the Soviet people. They showed the now consolidated Soviet state how to re-create the heroes of the nineteenth century for twentieth-century purposes, and they gave the populace opportunities to fashion themselves as interested citizens in this new era, but they did this within a Russian-dominated framework. There were many ways to express this sense of belonging, and even at the height of Stalin's purges, grim humor was a response of some, as the Zoshchenko feuilleton well demonstrates. It also showed that self-fashioning could occur by resisting the command to celebrate Pushkin. To conclude, I look at one other such example, by Daniil Kharms.

The short anecdotes about Pushkin included by Kharms in his "Incidents" ("Sluchai," 1939) recall Zoshchenko in their mix of humor with strangely revealing truths. Rather than the jubilee's grand claims about Pushkin's greatness, Kharms's deflated rhetoric creates the opening for wry witticisms such as "Pushkin was a poet and he was always writing something." Kharms offers not a Pushkin of heroic exploits, but one with deficiencies (he cannot grow a beard). His Pushkin sleeps, throws stones, and breaks his legs. He doesn't thrill to the culture of simple peasants and signals to them that they smell foul. Rejecting the long-winded discourse of anniversary commemorations, Kharms created Pushkin stories of a single paragraph or a few sentences with sparse dialogue. His minimalist recreations satirize the project of commemorating Pushkin, rather than attacking Pushkin himself. The last of his seven stories tells of Pushkin's four sons, all of them idiots falling off their chairs, one after another. Perhaps here Kharms allows himself not just his usual absurd non sequiturs but also a bit of allegory, where it is the generations that came after Pushkin who are fallen.[59]

Kharms implicitly asks what it meant to listen to Pushkin. He gave a tentative answer to this question in a Pushkin story he did not finish, one that takes up the scene in which Pushkin read his verse to Gavriil Derzhavin at the Tsarskoe Selo Lyceum.

> Words flew into Derzhavin's ears, into his eyes and his nostrils. One word even flew by the scruff of his neck and hit hard against the old man's back. Derzhavin put his hand under his shirt and caught the word and tried to smash it with his nails against the table. But the word tore out of Derzhavin's old fingers and skipped away. Derzhavin listened. His eyes filled with tears. Every word seemed wonderful.[60]

Anthony Anemone is right in emphasizing that, for Kharms, signifier could wander very far from signified (and thus, when we read of Pushkin's four idiot sons, the name *Pushkin* points well beyond the biography of a poet who had two entirely sane sons).[61] In the Lyceum reading scene with Derzhavin, names and details recall Pushkin's written version of the recitation of "Remembrances in Tsarskoe Selo" ("Vospominaniia v Tsarskom sele," 1813), including his observation that an errant word "skipped away" (in Pushkin's record of the reading, it is the poet who slips away at the end).[62] But the attack of words on the listener is pure fantasy, a Kharmsian delight in showing us the futile attempts of any listener or reader to capture a poet's words, to make of them what he or she will. When the word escapes,

Derzhavin listens. And then his eyes fill with tears, and he listens on with pleasure. The pleasure intensifies precisely because the words cannot be captured, because the meanings cannot be grabbed and held.

This unfinished text, not destined for publication and found only when scholars ferreted it out of the archives some fifty years later, would seem the very opposite of the traumatic artistic texts that, I have argued, best convey the lived experience of a jubilee observed in a time of Terror. Kharms offers instead the scene of one poet listening to another, with pleasure. We might read that opposition as fantasy, as Kharms's escape from the grimmer realities of Soviet life in the late 1930s, as a retreat to an other world in which the critical audience for an artistic work would be someone of the stature of Gavriil Derzhavin, and one in which assaults on the body were performed by words, not blows. One has only to read Kharms's diary for the late 1930s to see how dreadfully he suffered the deprivations and constraints of Soviet life (21 January 1937: "I am dying. I am dying as matter, and I am dying as a creative artist"),[63] and thus how strong might have been the desire to imagine some magical alternative. But even fantasies of escape are marked by the world they flee. We might also read this tale, like the other "Incidents," as a bit of narrative that has been fractured by trauma.[64] Coherent, meaningful, sequential narratives can no longer hold (or, if they can, they are flattened into self-parody, as in Kharms's children's tale "Pushkin," to which the Derzhavin scene has a connection). The bits of story fly off, like the words Derzhavin tries to capture, and there is no holding them together. And where there is no story, there is also no narrating subject. As Mikhail Iampol'skii has put it, referring to "Incidents," "the disappearance of the word is a sign of the disappearance of subjectivity."[65] Kharms substitutes the disappearance of the word for Pushkin's tale of the poet's flight from the word ("they looked for me, but I was nowhere to be found"), but the result is to make the tale of disappearance all the more compelling. Nothing holds against such centrifugal force. Soviet officials may have succeeded in their wish to rehabilitate Pushkin for modern use by means of public commemoration, but Kharms shows how futile was the aim to construct a new Soviet subjectivity in this process. Rather than a new hero with whom to identify, Pushkin as sign and symbol is nearly overwhelmed by repetition and hyperbole. His idiot sons fall down, we might foresee, only to rise up with every new Pushkin anniversary and announce that the rites of celebration have not completely covered over the pain and disaffection of the seemingly joyous public.

Notes

Portions of this chapter are revised and adapted from Stephanie Sandler, *Commemorating Pushkin: Russia's Myth of a National Poet* (Stanford, Calif.: Stanford University Press, 2004), and appear here with the permission of Stanford University Press.

1. Mikhail Kuraev, "Ganichev i drugie na fone Pushkina," *Literaturnaia gazeta*, 17 February 1999, 9. The design and execution of the monument for 1937 is fairly well documented. For a short history of the site, see V. K. Zazhurilo, L. I. Kuz'mina, and G. I. Nazarova, *Pushkinskie mesta Leningrada* (Leningrad: Lenizdat, 1974), 203–12, slightly updated in the 1989 edition, retitled *Liubliu tebia, Petra tvoren'e* (222–30).

2. Karen Petrone, *Life Has Become More Joyous, Comrades: Celebrations in the Time of Stalin* (Bloomington: Indiana University Press, 2000), 113–48. A fuller discussion of Soviet ritual celebrations (through Brezhnev's rule) appears in Christel Lane, *The Rites of Rulers: Ritual in Industrial Society—The Soviet Case* (Cambridge: Cambridge University Press, 1981).

3. David Brandenberger, "Russocentric Populism during the USSR's Official 1937 Pushkin Commemoration," *Russian History* 26, no. 1 (1999): 72–73. For a post-Soviet revisionist view of the 1937 Pushkin jubilee, see Iu. A. Molok, *Pushkin v 1937 g.: Materialy i issledovaniia po ikonografii* (Moscow: NLO, 2000).

4. A. V. Blium, "'Sniat' kontrrevoliutsionnuiu shapku . . . ': Pushkin i leningradskaia tsenzura 1937 g.," *Zvezda* 2 (1997): 209.

5. Quotations from Marcus Levitt, *Russian Literary Politics and the Pushkin Celebration of 1880* (Ithaca, N.Y.: Cornell University Press, 1989), 165.

6. See, for example, B. Meilakh, "Nasledie Pushkina i sotsialisticheskaia kul'tura," *Krasnaia nov'* 1 (1937): 111–27, especially 125–26.

7. Nikolai Tikhonov, speaking at the Bolshoi Theater, was among those who performed this sleight of hand: "Rech' poeta N. Tikhonova," *Literaturnaia ucheba* 3 (1937): 16.

8. For an interesting discussion of the contradictions inherent in the preference for a triumphant narrative in Stalinist art, with particular reference to film, see Mikhail Iampol'skii, "Censorship as the Triumph of Life," *Socialist Realism without Shores*, ed. Thomas Lahusen and Evgeny Dobrenko (Durham, N.C.: Duke University Press, 1997), 165–77.

9. Among many examples, see N. Svirin, "Sozdatel' russkogo literaturnogo iazyka," *Leningradskaia pravda*, 8 February 1937. Article citations given without page numbers were read as clippings in the Pushkiniana collection of Pushkinskii kabinet, Pushkinskii dom in St. Petersburg. I take the occasion to thank the staff in the Pushkin room, particularly Valentina Zaitseva and Liubov' Timofeeva, for their help.

10. A. V. Blium, *Sovetskaia tsenzura v epokhu total'nogo terrora, 1929–1939* (St. Petersburg: Akademicheskii proekt, 2000), 170–72. An especially interesting example cited here is the objection to memoir accounts of Pushkin having composed his ode on liberty ("Vol'nost'. Oda," 1817) in an impromptu salon setting. Blium takes

his material from the censorship records in the party archives in St. Petersburg. In this case it was a historical document, not a contemporary account, that required editing. The incidents described in this book are largely recounted as well in Blium, "'Sniat' kontrrevoliutsionnuiu shapku.'"

11. To cite three examples from a vast literature: N. Stepanov, "Put' Pushkina k realizmu: Stat'ia tret'ia, Realizm Pushkina," *Literaturnyi Leningrad*, 11 February 1937, 2–3; N. Svirin, "Pushkin i nasha sovremennost'," *Literaturnyi Leningrad*, 11 February 1937, 1; L. Ginzburg, "Put' Pushkina k realizmu," *Literaturnyi Leningrad*, 6 June 1936, 2.

12. A. S. Pushkin, *Polnoe sobranie sochinenii*, 4th ed., 10 vols. (Leningrad: Nauka, 1975–1979), 2:240.

13. Petr Zaichenko, "'Russkii bunt': 1998 god," *Iskusstvo kino* 6 (1999): 5. Zaichenko, an actor, attributes this observation to the writer Andrei Bitov. The same sentiment was behind a headline in *Literaturnaia gazeta*, "On sterpel nashe vse," 9 June 1999, 9.

14. As reported in *Constructing Russian Culture in the Age of Revolution: 1881–1940*, ed. Catriona Kelly and David Shepherd (Oxford: Oxford University Press, 1998), 314.

15. Such statements were quoted repeatedly. I take these words from the flyleaf of the Leningrad journal *Zvezda* 1 (1937).

16. See Lane, *Rites of Rulers*, 204–20, on the proliferation of heroes in the Soviet period (the examples given are chiefly political, with an extended analysis of the cult of Lenin).

17. As noted in E. N. Mastenitsa, "Iz istorii muzeinoi pushkiniany, 1937 g.," *Peterburgskaia pushkiniana* (St. Petersburg: SpbGUKI, 2000), 116.

18. My favorite example of this unity of attention to Pushkin is a report that a provincial library organized Pushkin readings on the anniversary day aboard trains running between Rtishevo and Bekovo. See "Passazhiry poezda slushaiut stikhi Pushkina," *Kommunist*, 11 February 1937.

19. As reported in "V Sovnarkome Soiuza SSR," *Literaturnyi Leningrad*, 5 January 1937, 1.

20. The 1899 centennial festivities also tried to push the celebration outward across the country, to synchronize multiple sites for commemoration, and to imprint *Pushkin* on objects of everyday life, from lamps and perfume to postcards and toys. See Marcus Levitt, "Pushkin in 1899," in *Cultural Mythologies of Russian Modernism*, ed. Boris Gasparov, Robert P. Hughes, and Irina Paperno (Berkeley: University of California Press, 1992), 183–201. Such commercialization occurred in 1937, too (rugs, tea service, faience vases, cookies, stamps, etc). See articles in *Kommunist*, 9 February 1937; *Trud*, 11 February 1937; *Vecherniaia Moskva*, 14 February 1937; *Khar'kovskii rabochii*, 4 February 1937.

21. "Slava russkogo naroda," *Pravda*, 10 February 1937, 1—see also chapter 13 in this volume.

22. "700 tysiach slushatelei na lektsiiakh o Pushkine," *Literaturnyi Leningrad*, 11 February 1937, 4.

23. For a vivid description of the participation of factories, school groups, and labor organizations (couched as criticism of the Soviet Writers' Union for not providing leadership for these amateurs), see "Bez pomoshchi i rukovodstva: Na soveshchanii litkritikov v Dome pisatelia," *Literaturnyi Leningrad*, 20 January 1937, 4. In its next issue, the same newspaper criticized the amateurish nature of such evenings: R. Villemson, "Ptichka bozhiia ne znaet," *Literaturnyi Leningrad*, 5 February 1937, 4.

24. Iv. Tkhorzhevskii, "Cherez sto let," *Vozrozhdenie*, 6 February 1937, 9.

25. "V Sovnarkome Soiuza SSR," 1.

26. The entire first page was given to Pushkin-related material on 4 February in *Pravda*, *Izvestiia*, and *Leningradskaia pravda*; *Trud* followed two days later, while *Krasnaia zvezda*'s Pushkin issue appeared on 3 February. On 10 February, articles on Pushkin's poetry and his status as Russia's "national poet" even appeared in *Sovetskaia torgovlia* (*Soviet Trade*) and the newspaper of the Soviet food industry.

27. "O poriadke provedeniia pushkinskikh iubileinykh dnei," *Literaturnaia gazeta*, 5 February 1937, 1.

28. "Strana gotovitsia k pushkinskim dniam," *Literaturnaia gazeta*, 1 February 1937, 4.

29. One cannot underestimate the repetitiveness in newspaper publications during this period—anything printed in *Literaturnaia gazeta* or *Izvestiia* was reprinted many times in less central newspapers.

30. M. M. Konopliannikov-Zuev, "Chto mne khotelos' by skazat' o pokoinom poete," *Krokodil* 3 (1937): 4–5; idem, "Na Maloi Perinnoi, 7 (Rech', proiznesennaia na sobranii v zhakte po Maloi Perinnoi ulitse, no. 7, v dni pushkinskogo iubileia)," *Krokodil* 5 (1937): 8–9—see chapter 14 in this volume.

31. On nervousness in Zoshchenko, see A. K. Zholkovskii, *Mikhail Zoshchenko: Poetika nedoveriia* (Moscow: Shkola "Iazyki russkoi kul'tury," 1999).

32. For the full listing of name changes, see "Postanovlenie Tsentral'nogo Ispolnitel'nogo Komiteta SSSR," *Literaturnyi Leningrad*, 11 February 1937, 4. Except for the town of Pushkin, where the poet had been a Lyceum student and spent the first months of his marriage, none of these places had the slightest thing to do with Pushkin.

33. One such exhibit was described as the first public showing of Pushkin's original manuscripts: "Vystavka v Ermitazhe," *Literaturnaia gazeta*, 5 February 1937, 1.

34. The original idea for the commemoration was rumored to be L. B. Kamenev's, long before 1935. See K. I. Chukovskii, *Dnevnik, 1930–1969* (Moscow: Sovetskii pisatel', 1994), 116.

35. In December 1936, complaints in provincial newspapers escalated, perhaps as anxiety about the impending jubilee intensified, as did the pressure from Moscow. Among many examples, see "Nakanune pushkinskikh dnei: Usilit' tempy podgotovki," *Rabochii*, 21 December 1936; "'Ochered' eshche ne doshla,'" *Novyi put'*, 20 December 1936.

36. For a striking example, see the report on a conference for representatives from all "Pushkin villages" (collective farms in places where Pushkin himself once

lived). The representatives discussed increased flax production, electrification, mass literacy campaigns, a lack of books and pictures of Pushkin, and the absence of leadership from Pushkin scholars. See "Konferentsiia pushkinskikh sel," *Krest'ianskaia pravda*, 6 January 1937.

37. M. V. Stroganov, "'Nachalos' s mertvykh petel'' ili kak prazdnovali Pushkina v 1936 godu," *Novoe literaturnoe obozrenie* 37, no. 3 (1999): 176. The eyewitness is N. V. Zhuravlev (1901–1957).

38. The lead article in the journal *Literaturnaia ucheba* (a publication of the Soviet Writers' Union) combined both themes: it raised larger ideological questions, re-narrated the history of the Soviet Union since Lenin's death, praised the strength of a nation able "to eradicate from the face of the earth the spies, murderers, diversionary tacticians, and servants of Fascism" now threatening it, and then placed the importance of the forthcoming Pushkin celebrations into this context. See "Pod znamenem Lenina," *Literaturnaia ucheba* 1 (1937): i–iii.

39. Blium, *Sovetskaia tsenzura v epokhu total'nogo terrora*, 169.

40. "Literaturnoe zaveshchanie Pushkina," *Literaturnaia ucheba* 4 (1937): 5.

41. As one historian of Pushkin literary museums noted, despite all the vigilance and centralization, there were also numerous examples of innovation and creativity in museum expositions. See Mastenitsa, "Iz istorii muzeinoi pushkiniany," 119.

42. L. Ia. Ginzburg, "'I zaodno s pravoporiadkom . . . ,'" *Tynianovskii sbornik: Tret'i tynianovskie chteniia* (Riga: Zinatne, 1988), 219.

43. Ginzburg, "Put' Pushkina k realizmu." For her notes from the 1930s, see idem, "Zapisi 1920–1930-kh godov," *Chelovek za pis'mennym stolom* (Leningrad: Sovetskii pisatel', 1989), 91–166.

44. See A. Colin Wright, *Mikhail Bulgakov: Life and Interpretations* (Toronto: University of Toronto Press, 1978), 213; "Stenogramma zasedaniia Khudozhestvennogo soveta pri Direktsii MKhAT 24.X.1939," published in *Russian Literature Triquarterly* 15 (1978): 324.

45. For well-argued praise, see Ia. L. Levkovich, "Pushkin v sovetskoi khudozhestvennoi proze i dramaturgii," *Pushkin: Issledovaniia i materialy* 5 (1967): 177–79. More measured but still positive is A. Gozenpud, "'Poslednie dni' ('Pushkin') (Iz tvorcheskoi istorii p'esy)," in *M. A. Bulgakov—dramaturg i khudozhestvennaia kul'tura ego vremeni* (Moscow: Soiuz teatral'nykh deiatelei RSFSR, 1988), 154–67. Least enthusiastic is Wright, *Mikhail Bulgakov*, 210–22, who finds "considerable craftsmanship," but no mastery.

46. Susan Larsen, "'I'm an Actor, Not a Writer'—Acting and Authorship in Bulgakov's Works," *Theater* 22, no. 2 (1991): 46.

47. On Bulgakov's perception of vulgarity as reported in E. S. Bulgakova's diaries, see J. A. E. Curtis, *Manuscripts Don't Burn: Mikhail Bulgakov, a Life in Letters and Diaries* (Woodstock, N.Y.: Overlook, 1992), 185. See also Wright, *Mikhail Bulgakov*, 215–16.

48. "O naznachenii poeta," in Aleksandr Blok, *Sobranie sochinenii*, 6 vols. (Leningrad: Khudozhestvennaia literatura, 1980–1983), 4:413–20.

49. The poem begins: "Buria mgloiu nebo kroet, / Vikhri snezhnye krutia; / To, kak zver', ona zavoet, / To zaplachet, kak ditia," ("A storm covers the sky in darkness, / spiraling whirlwinds of snow; / It will howl like a wild beast, / Then start to cry, like a small child, "). See Pushkin, *Polnoe sobranie sochinenii*, 2:258.

50. Mikhail Bulgakov, *P'esy* (Moscow: Sovetskii pisatel', 1986), 251.

51. The aside to Saltykova is suggestive in two other directions. Her name and patronymic, Aleksandra Sergeevna, are used repeatedly as a form of address in this scene (this was also noticed by O. Esipova, in "Pushkin v p'ese M. Bulgakova," *Boldinskie chteniia* (1985): 185), giving her the role of a double for Aleksandr Sergeevich Pushkin (there are other doubles in the play, like the "Blackamoor" who stands guard in the fountain scene or the kamer-junker who approaches the tsar with a message). Saltykova also bears the brunt of her husband's misogynistic comments, which find many echoes in the play, as when Vorontsova's defense of Pushkin is dismissed as the chatter of a society woman; when Natal'ia Nikolaevna is called "the Blackamoor's wife"; and when Heeckeren says that he hates women.

52. See Curtis, *Manuscripts Don't Burn*, 186.

53. As noticed by A. Gozenpud, "'Poslednie dni,'" 163.

54. Gozenpud sees the concern for evil as typical of the age in which Bulgakov lived.

55. For an excellent discussion of Lermontov's poem in terms of the self-image it created for the poet who would mourn Pushkin, see David Powelstock, "Living into Language: Mikhail Lermontov and the Manufacturing of Intimacy," *Russian Subjects: Empire, Nation and the Culture of the Golden Age*, ed. Monika Greenleaf and Stephen Moeller-Sally (Evanston, Ill.: Northwestern University Press, 1998), 303–13.

56. Bulgakov, *P'esy*, 284–85.

57. "Vast Pushkin Fete Is Held in Soviet," *New York Times*, 11 February 1937.

58. Illuminating studies of trauma and nation include *Tense Past: Cultural Essays in Trauma and Memory*, ed. Paul Antze and Michael Lambek (New York: Routledge, 1996); Shoshana Felman and Dori Laub, *Testimony: Crises of Witnessing in Literature, Psychoanalysis, and History* (New York: Routledge, 1992); and Cathy Caruth, *Unclaimed Experience: Trauma, Narrative, and History* (Baltimore: Johns Hopkins University Press, 1996).

59. For a discussion of the motif of falling more generally in the "Sluchai," without reference to the Pushkin tales, see Robin Aizlewood, "Towards an Interpretation of Kharms's *Sluchai*," in *Daniil Kharms and the Poetics of the Absurd: Essays and Materials*, ed. Neil Cornwell (New York: St. Martin's, 1991), 109–11. Falling is also the subject of one chapter of Mikhail Iampol'skii, *Bespamiatstvo kak istok* (Moscow: NLO, 1998), 74–105; the psychoanalytic and post-modern approach to Kharms taken here has shaped my thinking.

60. Daniil Kharms, *Polet v nebesa* (Leningrad: Sovetskii pisatel', 1988), 531. The volume's editors note that this citation comes from archival materials held at the Institute of Russian Literature and the Arts (IRLI) but they do not provide other details as to provenance. I assume, though, after comparing the two extant versions

of Kharms's 1936 children's tale "Pushkin," that this is a trial run or a discarded passage from that text. See Kharms, *Polnoe sobranie sochinenii*, 3 vols. (St. Petersburg: Akademicheskii proekt, 1999), 3:190–95, 305–8.

61. Anthony Anemone, "The Anti-World of Daniil Kharms," in *Daniil Kharms and the Poetics of the Absurd*, 79.

62. Pushkin, "Derzhavin," *Polnoe sobranie sochinenii*, 8:48.

63. Daniil Kharms, "Gorlo bredit britvoiu," *Glagol* 4 (1991): 128.

64. Anemone suggests the possibility of such a reading when he persuasively sets out the terms for a moral and ethical interpretation of Kharms's later work: "Kharms gradually becomes aware that his role, as an artist, was one of complicity in the creation of a monstrous social order." See Anemone, "Anti-World of Daniil Kharms," 81.

65. Iampol'skii, *Bespamiatstvo kak istok*, 89.

13
Editorial Eulogy of A. S. Pushkin

Lead editorials in *Pravda* traditionally signaled the nature and dimensions of the "general line" and were therefore closely read by everyone in Soviet society from rank-and-file officials to members of the creative intelligentsia. This piece, published at the height of the 1937 Pushkin commemoration, outlines the official Stalinist interpretation of Pushkin's legacy, explaining the Golden Age poet's relevance to Soviet modernity in unmistakably clear terms.[1]

According to *Pravda*, Pushkin was a "people's poet," a populist who despised elite society and dreamed of a future in which the entire country might be able to enjoy the fruits of Russian high culture. Sympathizing with the Decembrists' Revolt in 1825, Pushkin apparently yearned for full-fledged social revolution, believing that it would take only a "single, frightening blow" to overturn the existing political order. These sentiments, according to Pushkin's Stalinist "publicists," led both to his murder at the hands of a foreign agent in 1837 and also to his posthumous character assassination during the Soviet period at the hands of Trotskyites and restorationists abroad. According to *Pravda*, Pushkin's exposure of the oppression, ignorance, and arbitrariness of Nicholas I's reign provoked these attacks, since the poet had not only indicted the tsarist system but established a convenient benchmark for assessing the accomplishments of Soviet power as well. Of course, the invocation of the poet's name in such contexts was rather opportunistic, as the USSR's achievements in 1937 would have seemed considerably more modest if evaluated according to more contemporary standards.

The editorial's strident emphasis on Pushkin's ethnic Russian identity was, if anything, an even more opportunistic manipulation of the poet's legacy. A new development in Soviet public life during the mid-to-late 1930s, this rhetoric described Pushkin and the October Revolution as the Russian people's "gifts" to the world. Within the USSR, Pushkin was also styled as a role model for the non-Russian peoples to admire and emulate, his influence facilitating the spread of literacy and the development of modern literary traditions. Pronouncements like these supported claims that the Russian people were "the first among equals" and the "elder brother" within the USSR's family of peoples, signaling the emergence of an ethnic hierarchy within Soviet society while undermining nearly twenty years of agitation against Russian ethnocentrism.

"The Glory of the Russian People"

Pravda, 10 February 1937

A hundred years have passed since the greatest of all Russian poets, Aleksandr Sergeevich Pushkin, was killed by the hand of a foreign aristocratic scoundrel and tsarist hireling.

But Pushkin belongs entirely to us and to our times; he is still alive and will live on in future generations. Pushkin, the glory and pride of the great Russian people, will never die.

Pushkin's influence on the development of our country's culture is boundless. His immortal creations have become the basis of our literacy. Hundreds of millions of people have been given a voice for the first time through Pushkin's great utterances. Pushkin elevated our language, which is by nature rich and flexible, to unheard of heights, making it the most expressive language in the world.

Pushkin has never been as popular and beloved as he is now. This is due first of all to the simple fact that there have never been so many literate, reading people in our country. But that is not the only reason. Now, for the first time, readers have become acquainted with the real Pushkin, without the selfish meddling of countless distorters, without the reactionary censor, and without the petty, small-minded commentators who have tried to brush and neatly part this unruly Pushkin with their bourgeois combs. Pushkin has been revealed to the people in his true form as a poet and a citizen. And the people have come to love him as their best friend.

Pushkin foresaw this time. He was always thinking of the people and created his works in their name. In many of the poet's works, it is possible to see his appeal to future generations. Simply recall, for instance, the striking poem "Monument." Pushkin also addresses the reader of the future in the second chapter of *Eugene Onegin*, where he imagines with a touch of irony, but also with profound feeling, how the future reader might gaze

> Upon my much-regaled portrait,
> and think: he was a Poet.[2]

To such a reader he sends his "gratitude." And the poet's words have certainly found their mark. His voice rings out like a powerful rallying cry for creativity and struggle. Reading the famous line "Young and unknown tribe, I greet you!"[3] the Soviet reader can rightfully reply: "Greetings, my dear Pushkin!"

Pushkin is entirely ours, entirely Soviet, insofar as it is Soviet power that has inherited all of the best in our people and that is, itself, the realization of the people's best hopes. Now, on the hundredth anniversary of the poet's death, there is no more pressing subject than Pushkin and modernity. Pushkin's creativity has, in the final analysis, merged with the October Socialist Revolution as a river empties into the ocean.

In the poem "The Countryside" (1819), Pushkin wrote:

> Oh, if only my voice were able to stir people's hearts!
> Why does this fire burn without issue in my breast
> When fate has not granted me the terrible gift of Poesy?
> Will I live to see, my friends, a people freed from oppression
> And an end to slavery, by the will of the tsar;
> And, above the fatherland of enlightened freedom,
> Will a magnificent dawn come at last?[4]

At that time, Pushkin still pinned his hopes on the appearance of an "enlightened monarch." But only two years later, musing over the fate and history of his motherland, Pushkin cried out: "Only a single frightening blow can eliminate the entrenched slavery in Russia."[5] And we know that this was not just a dream of his. Pushkin himself yearned for a rebellion and was very disappointed that he was not able to take part in planning it [with the Decembrists].

In our country, the exploiting classes have now been liquidated. This is a fact that can undoubtedly be counted among the greatest accomplishments in the history of humanity. This fact has given rise to a great deal of anxiety, cursing and slander in our enemies' camp! The despicable crimes of the Trotskyite bandits are, of course, the counter-revolutionary bourgeoisie's direct response to our liquidation of the exploiters in this country. But across the span of a century, Pushkin offers us a friendly hand in a sign of solidarity. Vivid testimony of Pushkin's attitude toward exploiters has come down to us in the diary of one of Pushkin's contemporaries, Prince P. Dolgorukov:

> Smirnov eagerly challenged him (Pushkin) to an argument, and the more he refuted him, the more Pushkin became incensed, enraged, and failed to control his temper. Ultimately, curses were hurled at all the estates in society. State bureaucrats are scoundrels and thieves; generals are, for the most part, beasts. Only those who work the land are worthy of respect. Pushkin particularly attacked the Russian landed gentry. They should all be hanged, and if that ever were to come to pass, he said he would string them up himself with pleasure.[6]

Of course, all this was said in the heat of an argument, but Pushkin's temperament is immediately recognizable. He would have applauded the downfall of the exploitative classes with great joy. His comment that Prince Dolgorukov found so offensive—"Only those who work the land are worthy of respect"—indicates how Pushkin regarded the oppressed peasantry and the people. Pushkin considered the emancipation of the peasantry to be the main condition for the continued development of his beloved motherland.

Pushkin was a member of the gentry. This has given foolish vulgarizers the excuse to label all of his work as characteristic of the gentry.[7] What vile slander! Pushkin was fundamentally a man of the people in both his works and his political views. M. Gor'kii expressed this well: Pushkin said that "'My form of thinking does not depend in any way upon my ancestry.' These are the words of a man," adds Gor'kii:

> who sensed that for him, the interests of the nation [*natsiia*] as a whole were more important than the interests of the gentry alone. He said this because his personal experience was broader and more profound than that of the gentry as a class.[8]

Pushkin's revolutionary views do not require exaggeration. His greatness is evident in his immortal works that will never be surpassed. But Pushkin would not have been a poet of genius if he had not been a great citizen and if he had not expressed in one way or another the revolutionary hopes of his people. He understood this himself. Summing up his creative work a few months before his fateful duel, Pushkin saw as his main achievement that "in my cruel age I hailed freedom." Precisely for this reason, the poet wrote: "Rumor of my fame will sweep across great Rus' / And my name will resound in every language that they speak."[9]

And his dreams have been realized! No longer are there ethnic groups in our vast country that do not have a written language. And with literacy, this multitude of peoples has come to know Pushkin's brilliant poetry. Pushkin is equally dear to the hearts of the Russian and the Ukrainian, the Georgian and the Kalmyk; he is dear to the hearts of all the ethnicities of the Soviet Union.

United in their national diversity, the Soviet people solemnly consider Pushkin to be a major milestone in their history, having enormous significance in the present day.

Pushkin long ago outgrew the borders of this country. Nowadays, progressive, cultured humanity as a whole bows down before his genius. Pushkin was profoundly connected with his nation [*natsionalen*]. For this reason, he has also become an international poet. All the peoples of the world find in the treasure house of his poetry an inexhaustible source of profound thought and noble feelings.[10]

The threatening clouds of Armageddon are now gathering over the world. This war is being prepared by fascist heretics and barbarians who would run roughshod over all the cultural values of humanity. The fascists are oppressing reason, science, and culture. The warmongers look to the darkness of the Middle Ages and the cannibalism of antediluvian times, finding there their "ideas" and morality. The works of the great humanist Pushkin serve as an indictment of these outcasts who would strangle freedom. All of those who have an interest in resisting the fascists repeat with us Pushkin's words, so full of optimism and humanity: "Long live the muse! Long live reason! / . . . Long live the sun; let the darkness be hidden!"[11]

The Russian people have given the world the genius of Pushkin. Under the leadership of the great party of Lenin and Stalin, the Russian people brought about the Socialist Revolution and will follow it through to its conclusion. The Russian people have a right to take pride in their role in history as well as their writers and poets.[12]

Pushkin is the glory of our people, and, with their actions, the people multiply this glory.

Notes

1. "Slava russkogo naroda," *Pravda*, 10 February 1937, 1.
2. "Na moi proslavlennyi portret, / I molvit: to-to byl Poet." See *Evgenii Onegin* (1823–1831), chap. 2.
3. "Zdravstvui, plemia mladoe, neznakomoe!" See "... Vnov' ia posetil ..." (1835).
4. "O esli b golos moi umel serdtsa trevozhit'! / Pochto v grudi moei gorit besplodnyi zhar / I ne dan mne v udel vitiistva groznyi dar? / Uvizhu l', o druz'ia, narod neugnetennyi / I rabstvo, padshee po maniiu tsaria, / I nad otechestvom svobody prosveshchennoi / Vzoidet li nakonets prekrasnaia zaria?" See "Derevnia" (1819).
5. "Tol'ko odno strashnoe potriasenie moglo by unichtozhit' v Rossii zakoreneloe rabstvo." See "O russkoi istorii XVIII veka" (1822).
6. Diary entry from 20 July 1822, in P. I. Dolgorukov, "35-i god moei zhizni, ili dva dni vedra na 363 nenast'ia," in *A. S. Pushkin v vospominaniiakh sovremennikov*, ed. V. V. Grigorenko et al., 2 vols. (Moscow: Khudozhestvennaia literatura, 1974), 2:361.
7. Reference to "vulgar sociological" literary criticism, which was defined after 1936 as "a system of views stemming from a one-sided interpretation of the Marxist position regarding the class determination of ideology and leading to a simplification and schematization of the historico-literary process." V. V. Kozhinov, "Vul'garnyi sotsiologizm," in *Kratkaia literaturnaia entsiklopediia*, ed. A. A. Surkov, 9 vols. (Moscow: Sovetskaia entsiklopediia, 1962–1978), 1:1062–63.
8. M. Gor'kii, ["A. S. Pushkin"], in *Sobranie sochinenii v tridtsati tomakh*, 30 vols. (Moscow: Gos. Izd-vo khudozhestvennoi literatury, 1949–1955), 24:98.
9. "Chto v moi zhestokii vek vosslavil ia svobodu"; "Slukh obo mne proidet po vsei Rusi velikoi / I nazovet menia vsiak sushchii v nei iazyk." See "Ia pamiatnik sebe vozdvig nerukotvornyi" (1836).
10. This messianic conception of Pushkin's significance for all humanity was first propounded by F. M. Dostoevskii in his famous 1880 Pushkin speech.
11. "Da zdravstvuiut muzy, da zdravstvuet razum! / ... Da zdravstvuet solntse, da skroetsia t'ma!" See "Vakkhicheskaia pesnia" (1825).
12. Although Stalin was known to credit the Russian people with the October Revolution in private as early as the 1920s, it was not until the mid-1930s that this connection began to appear in the press. See G. Vasil'kovskii, "Vysshii zakon zhizni," *Pravda*, 28 May 1934, 4; "RSFSR," *Pravda*, 1 February 1936, 1; "Velikii russkii narod," *Pravda*, 15 January 1937, 1; "Konstitutsiia geroicheskogo naroda," *Pravda*, 16 January 1937, 1; M. N. Kalinin, "O proekte konstitutsii RSFSR: Nasha prekrasnaia rodina," *Pravda*, 16 January 1937, 2.

14
The Pushkin Jubilee as Farce

There is probably no better illustration of popular ambivalence regarding the Pushkin commemoration of 1937 than the two pieces by Mikhail Zoshchenko that we offer below. A satirist specializing in short stories, Zoshchenko was by some reports the second most widely read author in the Soviet Union during the 1920s.[1] Most of his works are written in a style known as *skaz*—a highly stylized deadpan imitating oral speech patterns that can be traced back to nineteenth-century authors such as Gogol' and Leskov.[2] Equally characteristic of Zoshchenko's stories was the fact that they tended to be narrated by ignorant laymen, bumbling scholars, amateur wordsmiths, semi-literate correspondents, and folksy, poorly educated essayists. Hugh McLean explains that these oddball storytellers were the secret to Zoshchenko's "ruse," since they tended to be

> sharply distinguished in some way—origin, status, education or sex—from the author himself. The author then ostensibly figures merely as a transmitting agent and presumably cannot be held responsible for the narrator's statements. If the narrator expresses heretical ideas or reprehensible attitudes, they cannot be charged to the author; indeed, if the narrator is presented in a negative or satirical manner, the author may well maintain that his own position is diametrically opposed.[3]

It is perhaps on account of this distancing of author from narrator that Zoshchenko was able to comment in often bitingly ironic and irreverent terms about the marginal results of the Soviet "experiment" during the 1920s and 1930s without provoking the ire of the state censor.[4]

Zoshchenko associated during these years with a group of writers known as the Serapion Brotherhood, who, despite their pro-Soviet sympathies, believed that art should be independent of state and party ideology. Even after the relatively permissive 1920s gave way to the increasingly restrictive 1930s, Zoshchenko attempted to maintain an apolitical, ironic stance in much of his writing. Disgusted by the atmosphere surrounding the Pushkin commemoration, he poked fun at the pomp and circumstance by publishing two speeches in the humor magazine *Krokodil* attributed to one Matvei Mitrofanovich Konopliannikov-Zuev, chair of a housing cooperative. Rambling statements choked with glaring errors, non sequiturs, irrelevant aphorisms, and humorous references to the era's official Pushkin mythology, these speeches lampoon the banality of public discussions devoted to the great poet in 1937.[5]

M. M. Konopliannikov-Zuev, "What I Would Like to Say about the Late Poet"

Krokodil 3 (1937)

My dear comrades, I am, of course, not a literary historian. Thus I shall allow myself to approach this great date simply, as the saying goes, as a fellow human being.

Such a heartfelt approach, I think, will bring us even closer to the image of the great poet.

And so, a hundred years separate us from him! Time really does fly by!

The German war, as you all know, began 23 years ago. That is, when it began, Pushkin hadn't been gone a hundred years, but only 77.

And imagine—I was born in 1879. So it seems I am even closer to the great poet. Not close enough so as to have seen him, but, as the saying goes, only about forty years separated the two of us.

And here's an even more striking case: my grandmother was born in 1836. So Pushkin could have seen her and even picked her up in his arms. He could have rocked her, and she, God forbid, could have burst into tears, not realizing who it was who had picked her up.

Of course, it's doubtful that Pushkin ever rocked her, particularly since she was from Kaluga, and Pushkin doesn't seem to have spent any time there. But all the same, we can still allow for this exciting possibility, especially since he very well could have dropped by Kaluga to see friends.

Now my father was born in 1850. Sadly, Pushkin was already gone by then, or else he might have rocked my father too.

But he could definitely have taken my great-grandmother into his arms. Just imagine—she was born in 1763, so it is very possible that the great poet could have gone to her parents and demanded that they let him hold and rock her.... Although, incidentally, she was, if you please, sixty-some years old in 1837, so to tell you the truth, I don't know quite how things would have worked themselves out and how they would have managed it.... Perhaps it was she who would have rocked him.... But these matters, which are hidden from us by the mists of time, probably didn't trouble them at all, and they must have easily figured out who should be rocked and who should do the rocking. And if the old woman was really over sixty at the time, it's funny even to think that someone might have rocked her. She must have been the one doing the rocking.

Perhaps she awoke poetic emotions within him without even knowing it as she sang him little songs while she rocked him, and perhaps she, together with his famous nanny, Arina,[6] inspired him to write several of those poems of his.

As for Gogol' and Turgenev,[7] they could have been rocked by almost any of my relatives, since an even shorter time separated them from one another. I'd say in general that children are the light of our lives and a happy childhood is, as the saying goes, a matter of no small importance that has only been resolved in our present age. Creches, nursery schools, mothers' and children's rooms at train stations—they're all significant aspects of the same effort.... Hmm, where was I?

(VOICE FROM THE AUDIENCE: The subject of Pushkin ...)

Oh yes ... So I was saying, Pushkin. A hundred years have gone by. And look, soon other famous jubilees will come to pass—Turgenev, Lermontov, Tolstoi, Maikov,[8] and so on and so forth. They drag on and on.

In general, though, between you and me, I sometimes wonder why we have such an exceptional attitude toward poets. Singers, for example—I wouldn't say that we have a bad opinion of singers, but we don't carry on as much about them as we do about these other guys. Yet they, as the saying goes, are also talents. They tug at your heartstrings. And they stir up emotions. And many other things....

Of course, I won't question the fact the Pushkin is a great genius and that every one of his lines are of great interest to us. Some even respect Pushkin for his minor poems. I wouldn't go so far myself, however. Minor poems—they are, as the saying goes, minor and not really major works. Not to such an extent that just anybody could have composed them, but, as the saying goes, you look at them, and there's really nothing there that is all that original or artistic. For instance, take this collection of what I would say are simple and not-too-high-cultured words:

> A neighborhood boy is running ahead,
> Pulling his dog on a sledge. . . .
> Fooling around, his hands are frozen and red . . . [9]

(VOICE FROM THE AUDIENCE: That's *Eugene Onegin*. . . . That's not minor poetry.)

Really? When we were children, we learned it in school as a separate piece. Well, all the more then, that's fine with me. *Eugene Onegin* is a brilliant epic. . . . But of course every epic has its artistic shortcomings. In general, I would say this poet is very interesting for children. Indeed, in those days, they may have thought of him simply as a children's poet. But he has come down to us in a slightly different form, perhaps. All the more because our children have grown up so. Children's poetry is already so unsatisfying for them:

> Choo-choo-choo, steam engines sigh,
> Click-clack-click, the wheels reply.
> Hurrah for the state publisher!
> That's the author's bread and butter . . . [10]

I recall, you know, that once when I was a child, they gave my class a minor, worthless poem by Pushkin to memorize. Something about a little broom, or a bird—no, I think it was a branch. It was as if the branch was growing by itself, and the poet addresses it artistically: "Tell me, branch of Palestine . . ."[11]

(VOICE FROM THE AUDIENCE: That's from Lermontov.)

Really? You know, I often mix the two up. . . . Pushkin and Lermontov—for me, they're part of a greater whole. I don't differentiate between the two of them.

(NOISE IN THE HALL. A VOICE FROM THE AUDIENCE: Why don't you talk about Pushkin's creative works?)

I am getting to that, comrades. Pushkin's creative works evoke great wonder. Moreover, he was paid a *chervonets*[12] per line of poetry. And it was republished over and over. And in spite of that, he wrote and wrote and wrote. Just no restraint at all.

Of course, life at court seriously interfered with the composition of his poetry. There were balls, and other things as well. As the poet himself put it:

> Whence that noise, those wild cries?
> To whom are the tambourines and timpani calling . . .[13]

Of course, we won't dwell on the poet's biography here—everyone already knows it. On one hand, as the saying goes, there was his private life, his seven-room apartment, and his carriage, and on the other, the tsar himself, Nikolai Palkin,[14] court life, the Lyceum, D'Anthès, and so on. And, just between us, Tamara of course cheated on him . . .

(NOISE IN THE HALL. SOMEONE SHOUTS: Natal'ia, not Tamara.)

Really? Oh yes, Natal'ia. That's what I meant. Nikolai Palkin, of course, didn't write poetry himself. And against his will, he agonized over this and envied the poet . . .

(NOISE IN THE HALL. VOICES, SHOUTING. SEVERAL STAND UP AND CRY OUT: Enough! Remove the speaker!)

But I'm just concluding, comrades . . . Pushkin has had an enormous influence on us. He was an ingenious and great poet. Ultimately, we must regret that he is not alive to be here together with us today. We would carry the poet in our arms and arrange a fairy-tale life for him, if, of course, we knew that he would turn out to be Pushkin. Otherwise, it sometimes happens that some of our contemporaries look upon one of our own with high hopes and arrange a decent life for him, giving him cars and apartments, and then it turns out that he isn't all that great after all.[15] But then, as the saying goes, such is life [*vziatki gladki*] . . .

Well, to conclude my talk on this poetic genius, I would like to point out that after this portion of the ceremony, there will be an artistic concert.

(LOUD APPLAUSE)

M. M. Konopliannikov-Zuev, "A Speech Given during the Pushkin Days at a Meeting of the Tenants' Cooperative on Malaia Perinnaia, No. 7"

Krokodil 5 (1937)

It is with a feeling of pride that I would like to point out that our apartment building is not lagging behind recent events.

We have, for one, obtained a one-volume edition of Pushkin for general use for 6 r[ubles] and 50 k[opeks]. Second, a plaster-of-Paris bust of the great poet has been placed in the office of the tenants' cooperative where it will, in its own way, serve to remind irresponsible bill-payers about their delinquent rent payments.

Aside from that, we have hung an artistic portrait of Pushkin under the front gate, wreathed with pine branches.

And finally, this gathering speaks for itself.

Of course, perhaps this isn't all that much, but to tell you the truth, our tenants' cooperative never expected that there would be such goings-on. We thought that, as always, they'll point out in the press that he was an ingenious poet who lived in the cruel Nicholaevan epoch. And then there'll be all sorts of artistic readings at the theater or someone will sing something or other from *Eugene Onegin*.

But to tell you the truth, all the things going on at the present time have forced our tenants' cooperative to be a bit more cautious and to review our position on the *belle-lettres*, so that no one will be able to accuse us later on of undervaluing poetry, etc.

And you know what else? We're lucky that in terms of poets, our building has been, as the saying goes, spared by God's good graces. True, we do have one tenant, Tsaplin, who writes poems, but aside from the fact that he's really a bookkeeper and an ass to boot, I just don't know what I could say about him during these Pushkin Days. Just the day before yesterday, he comes into the cooperative office to threaten me. "You long-shanked devil," he yells, "I'll send you to your grave if you don't move my stove before the Pushkin Days." "It's burning me up," he says, "and 'cause of that, I can't write my poetry." "With all due respect to poets," I replied, "I can't move your stove at this time because our stove man has gone on a drinking binge." And so he just kept on yelling—he really went after me. The drunken runt!

Let's just be thankful that among our tenants we don't have other sorts of various—you know—literary cadres, and so on. Or else they'd definitely have gotten under my skin, like this Tsaplin.

And so what if he can write poetry! Pardon me, but then my seven-year-old boy Koliunka should also make demands at the cooperative office, because he also can write. He's got some little ditties that aren't half bad:

Us kids love it when a bird's properly in its cage.
And hate those who call the five-year plan an outrage.

The little guy is just seven years old, and look how boldly he writes. But that doesn't mean that I want to compare him to Pushkin. Pushkin is one thing, and a burnt-up tenant Tsaplin is quite another. What a slacker! The main thing is, my wife was coming up to me, and he just went after me. "I'll stick your head into my stove right now, you long-shanked scarecrow," he yells. Well, what sort of a thing is that? The Pushkin Days are going on right now, and he's left me so bothered that my hands are shaking.

Pushkin writes so that each of his lines is the height of perfection. If we had such a genius as a tenant, we'd have already offered to move his stove last fall. But to move Tsaplin's—that's too much.

A hundred years have passed, and Pushkin's verses still produce such wonder. Pardon me, but what will Tsaplin be in a hundred years? That ass! Or what if the same Tsaplin had lived a hundred years ago—I can only imagine what would have become of him and in what form he would have come down to us!

To tell you the truth, if I had been in D'Anthès's shoes, I would have shot Tsaplin full of holes right there myself. My second would have said, "Take a single shot," and I would have unloaded all five bullets into him, because I don't like such asses.

Great poetic geniuses always die before their time,[16] but this ass Tsaplin just hangs around and yanks on our chains.

(VOICE FROM THE AUDIENCE: Say something about Pushkin.)

I am talking about Pushkin. Did you think I was going on about Lermontov? As I was saying, Pushkin's poetry evokes such wonder. Every line is popular. Even those who haven't read anything know him. I personally like his lyrics from *Eugene Onegin* like "Hey, Lenskii, you don't dance?"[17] and this other heavenly verse:

> Let me perish, but first
> I will savor the magical poison of desire,
> I will delight in my unrealizable dream . . .[18]

When an actor sings this just right, tears just well up in your eyes. That's how brilliantly he writes.

(VOICE FROM THE AUDIENCE: But that's not Pushkin.)

What do you mean? How can *Eugene Onegin* not be Pushkin? Whose would you say it was, then? Lermontov's? The backwardness of this tenants' cooperative sometimes surprises me . . .

(VOICE FROM THE AUDIENCE—That's an aria from the opera and isn't in Pushkin's work.)

Really? And I thought they were singing Pushkin's lyrics. Well, isn't that something. You know, sometimes I've thought to myself that this or that aria vulgarizes reality. A tenor will sing "Where, where are you off to?"[19] and I've thought to myself that it was a bit weak. You know, it just doesn't sound like Pushkin.

(VOICE FROM THE AUDIENCE: Actually, that is Pushkin.)

Really? Well then, I guess that means it's the actor's fault. Naturally, he'll croak out something mediocre in his bad baritone and mislead the whole audience. What an ass! As far as *The Queen of Spades* is concerned, I don't know what to think anymore. Before, I thought that the words they were singing were Pushkin's. But now, I'm quickly paging through this one-volume collection of Pushkin, and I see that "The Queen of Spades" is prose! Isn't that something! To be honest, this is really too bad because what tugs at my heart strings the most from Pushkin is this quatrain:

> If only every good girl,
> Could, like a bird, fly and whirl....[20]

If this wasn't written by Pushkin, and if it was added to his *Queen of Spades* only later, then I don't know what to think about this jubilee.

True, Pushkin is known for more than just his poetry. I also appreciate his plot twists. Take, for example, the same *Queen of Spades*. There are lots of great moments that are valuable even without the lyrics. Like when Herman from *Queen of Spades* comes up to the old baroness with a pistol in his hands and sings: "Forgive me, heavenly creature, for disturbing your peace."[21] This of course upsets the old woman, and she tragically dies. The fact that Pushkin didn't write the lyrics doesn't change a thing. This brilliant work remains tip-top in terms of its scenes.

Pushkin was an ingenious poet, of course, but to be honest, each time I think about our Tsaplin, the holiday ceases to be a holiday. And I am not going to worry much about moving his stove. With all due respect to poetry, I must say that if Tsaplin is burned to a crisp, I won't shed a tear.

On that note, I'll allow myself to conclude this speech about the ingenious poet.

Notes

The editors would like to thank E. S. Dianina for research assistance in the preparation of these pieces.

1. Maksim Gor'kii was the most popular author. See the introduction to Mikhail Zoshchenko, *Nervous People and Other Satires*, ed. Hugh McLean (New York: Pantheon, 1963), ix.

2. On *skaz*, see Boris Eikhenbaum, "Illiuziia skaza," in *Skvoz' literaturu: Sbornik statei* (Leningrad: Academia, 1924), 152-57; V. V. Vinogradov, "Problema skaza v stilistike," in *Poetika: Vremennik slovesnogo otdela Gosudarstvennogo instituta istorii iskusstv* I (Leningrad: Academia, 1926), 24-40; Mikhail M. Bakhtin, *Problems of Dostoevsky's Poetics*, ed. and trans. Caryl Emerson (Minneapolis: University of Minnesota Press, 1984), 204-37.

3. Zoshchenko, *Nervous People and Other Satires*, xi.

4. Only in the context of harsh postwar conservatism would Zoshchenko be rebuked for his irreverent sense of humor. In 1946, Politburo ideology chief A. A. Zhdanov publicly assailed Zoshchenko for his lack of respect for Soviet accomplishments at the outset of the so-called *Zhdanovshchina*.

5. These pieces originally appeared as M. M. Konopliannikov-Zuev, "Chto mne khotelos' by skazat' o pokoinom poete," *Krokodil* 3 (1937): 4-5; idem, "Na Maloi Perinnoi, 7 (Rech', proiznesennaia na sobranii v zhakte po Maloi Perinnoi ulitse, no. 7, v dni pushkinskogo iubilei)," *Krokodil* 5 (1937): 8-9. They were reedited several times before inclusion in Zoshchenko's various collected works—see, for instance, "V pushkinskie dni," in M. A. Zoshchenko, *Sobranie sochinenii*, 2 vols. (Leningrad: Khudozhestvennaia literatura, 1986), 2:416-21. This translation is derived from the original *Krokodil* publication.

6. Arina Rodionovna, Pushkin's peasant nanny who is credited by the poet's Soviet biographers with introducing him to Russian folklore.

7. N. V. Gogol' (1809-1852), writer; I. S. Turgenev (1818-1883), realist writer.

8. Apparently an inappropriate reference to A. N. Maikov (1821-1897), a poet remembered for his refusal to mobilize art and aesthetics in service of society.

9. A misquotation of "Vot begaet dvorovoi mal'chik, / V salazki Zhuchku posadiv ... / sebia v konia preobraziv / Shalun uzh zamorozil palchik," from chap. 5, stanza 3, of *Evgenii Onegin*.

10. "Paravozik chuk-chuk-chuk, / Kolesiki tuk-tuk-tuk. / Gosizdatu gip-ura / Peti-meti avtora."

11. "Skazhi mne, vetka Palestiny," from M. Iu. Lermontov's "Vetka Palestiny" (1837).

12. A three-ruble coin, usually cast in gold.

13. A mistaken invocation of "Otkuda [chudesnyi] shum, neistovye kliki? / Kogo, kuda zovut i bubny i timpan," from Pushkin's "Torzhestvo Vakkha" (1818).

14. A popular reference to Nicholas I, from *palka*, or rod.

15. A reference to the growing inequalities of Soviet society in the 1930s, in which leading members of professions, Stakhanovite workers, popular authors, etc., gained material rewards far in excess of the norm. The phrase puns on the popular refrain from P. German and Iu. Khait's "Ever Higher" (1920): "We were born to make fairy tales come true."

16. Note Bednyi's invocation of this same cultural myth—see chapter 5 in this volume.

17. A misquotation of "Ty ne tantsuesh', Lenskii?" from the first scene of the second act of P. I. Tchaikovskii's 1879 opera *Evgenii Onegin*.

18. "Pushchai pogibnu ia, no prezhde / Vkushu volshebnyi iad zhelanii, / Up'ius' nesbytochnoi mechtoi," an aria from *Evgenii Onegin*.

19. A distortion of "Kuda, kuda, kuda vy udalilis'," from the second scene of the second act of *Evgenii Onegin*.

20. "Esli by milye devitsy / Vse by mogli letat' kak ptitsy," actually by G. R. Derzhavin.

21. "Prosti, nebesnoe sozdan'e, chto ia narushal tvoi pokoi," from *Evgenii Onegin*.

Aleksandr Nevskii

15
The Popular Reception of S. M. Eisenstein's *Aleksandr Nevskii*

◯ David Brandenberger

The authors of this volume argue that as Soviet ideology came to emphasize a more pragmatic, populist agenda in the mid- to late 1930s, seemingly innocent celebrations of Russian history and culture like the centennial of Pushkin's death in early 1937 quickly matured into more explicitly russocentric propaganda. That fall's publication of A. V. Shestakov's new textbook, *The Short Course on the History of the USSR*,[1] and the release of V. M. Petrov's cinematic blockbuster *Peter I* were quickly followed in 1938 by a well-advertized exhibition of Russian historical art in the Tret'iakov Gallery[2] and the première of S. M. Eisenstein's *Aleksandr Nevskii*. These ideologically charged events played an important role in developing a new vocabulary of imagery and iconography that would be used to mobilize Soviet citizens during the coming war.

But it would be incautious to automatically equate the *production* of ideology with its *consumption*.[3] Audiences, after all, rarely accept patently ideological pronouncements at face value. This chapter, therefore, examines the resonance that this turn-about elicited among Soviet citizens during the last years of the interwar period by focusing specifically on Eisenstein's *Aleksandr Nevskii*. Although much is known about the production of the film, its popular reception is much less well understood.[4] Taking advantage of an array of fragmentary accounts that provide glimpses of popular opinion under Stalin,[5] this piece examines how members of Soviet society responded to the film. Such an approach not only allows for a greater appreciation of the significance of Eisenstein's epic for its contemporary audiences, but it also illustrates in clear terms the distinction between the production of the official line and its mass reception during these years.

Aleksandr Nevskii's intellectual origins are properly situated in 1937 at the height of the Stalinist purges. The debacle surrounding the banning of Eisenstein's collectivization drama *Bezhin Meadow*, combined with rumors about incautious social contacts abroad during the shooting of *Viva Mexico*, forced the director to seek political rehabilitation at the same time that the party hierarchy was searching for a more successful way to rally social support. Eisenstein considered a number of different projects that could serve as vehicles for a simple patriotic message before ultimately settling on the idea of a medieval epic—a project that was suggested to him by his friend and confidante, the Stalinist insider Vs. Vishnevskii.[6]

The nature of Eisenstein's own interest in this project remains controversial to the present day. In print, the director referred to *Aleksandr Nevskii* as a film that would stimulate a sense of patriotic loyalty to the USSR while using historical allegory to graphically illustrate the nature of the contemporary Nazi threat.[7] More recently, commentators have drawn attention to Eisenstein's representation of Nevskii himself, arguing that the film played into Stalin's burgeoning cult of personality or functioned as a sort of a cinematographic exercise in character study.[8] Although a variety of motivations likely fueled the director's work on the epic film, Eisenstein certainly understood that his professional future depended on the creation of an inspiring tale of valor and heroism that was neither ambiguous nor equivocal. And he delivered precisely such a film.

Initially entitled *Rus'*, the narrative focused on one of the most famous events in the history of Old Russia: Prince Aleksandr Iaroslavich Nevskii's 1242 defeat of the Teutonic knights. At first glance, this was an odd subject to receive official sanction during the year of the October Revolution's twentieth anniversary, but Eisenstein knew that the party hierarchy was interested in themes that would lend a sense of legitimacy and pedigree to the Soviet state.[9] Apparently enjoying the confidence of Stalin, V. M. Molotov, and A. A. Zhdanov despite the *Bezhin Meadow* debacle, he joined forces with P. A. Pavlenko, a loyal Stalinist who had been working on similar subject matter for quite some time.[10]

Substantial public interest in the film was generated almost a year before its release by the publication of Eisenstein and Pavlenko's screenplay and related articles in late 1937 and early 1938.[11] Although some of this attention surely stemmed from the director's previous successes (*Battleship Potemkin, October*, etc.), the screenplay itself must have been equally intriguing, as this was one of the first Soviet propaganda films to promote a positive treatment of the tsarist past. In response to the pre-publicity surrounding the film, some were even moved to suggest to Eisenstein ways in which he might improve the script. A teacher in Khar'kov named A. T. Miakshin, for instance, wrote to the director to say that there wasn't enough action in the screenplay—a superior plot line would stretch from the prince's clash with the Swedes in 1240 to his descendant Dmitrii Donskoi's defeat of the Tatars on the Kulikovo Field in 1380.[12] A missive from a third grader in Krapivensk named Boris Novikov was even more prescriptive:

> My grandmother often used to tell me stories about the battle on Lake Chud'. In her account, I especially liked the description of the battle's last moments when, with his spear, Aleksandr Nevskii inflicts a wound *on the face of Birger*, the chief of the German knights who dared to attack the Russian lands. This facial wound was considered most shameful and the bastard-invader got what he deserved [*tak emu mertsavtsu-zakhvatchiku i nado*].
>
> If it is possible, please capture this brilliant moment in the film for the edification of Hitler and Co. Please, I beg of you—after all, it was in a history textbook and *Istoricheskii vestnik*.[13]

If many such suggestions ended up being simply filed away in Eisenstein's personal archive, a series of articles in the press demanded more serious attention, as they criticized the screenplay for its numerous historical inaccuracies and excessive artistic license.[14] More damning still was a communist idealist's public indictment of Eisenstein and Pavlenko for "*faux patriotism*" [*susal'nyi patriotizm*], a charge that betrayed the critic's misgivings about the film's non-Marxist populism.[15] Eisenstein also faced major challenges behind the scenes from several historians serving as consultants to the project who assailed the screenplay for its tendency to essentialize historical events and interpolate overtly anti-German and anti-Japanese imagery into the medieval tale.[16] Even Stalin himself intervened to make the ending more triumphant.[17] The intensity of this scrutiny took a heavy toll on Eisenstein. Vishnevskii wrote in his diary in mid-1938 that "Eisen[stein] is anxious and worried. Either [he] will again return to the fore or. . . ." Continuing, Vishnevskii noted suggestively that "the film is historical. Everything concerning this category is incredibly strict for us these days," a statement that reflects the difficulties that members of the creative intelligentsia experienced during the mid- to late 1930s as they attempted to navigate the era's shifting ideological currents with regard to the tsarist past.[18]

Further work on the screenplay—now retitled *Aleksandr Nevskii*—and success during its shooting later that summer dispelled the air of uncertainty that had dogged the project early on. Two months after Vishnevskii recounted Eisenstein's fear and nervousness, he described the director's renewed sense of confidence: "the film's style is legendary and a bit over-the-top.... It will be exot[ic]."[19] This was certainly true, especially by the standards of Soviet cinema. Emplotted in epic fashion with hyperbolic two-dimensional characters, a rousing musical score, and deliberately ungainly props and segues between scenes, the film opens with a panoramic view of an ancient battlefield littered with the corpses of warriors clad in stereotypically Russian armor. Intertitles inform the viewer that much of Old Russia had been defeated and subjugated by the Tatar-Mongol armies of Chingiz Khan. Already bowed under the burden of the Mongol Yoke, northwestern Rus' is then attacked from the direction of the Baltic sea by the opportunistic Teutonic knights, who sack the major city of Pskov. Senseless sadism during the city's capture illustrates in graphic terms the Teutonic knights' contempt for the local Slavic population. As word of atrocities spreads throughout the surrounding lands, the citizenry of nearby Novgorod assemble to discuss the new threat. Although the latter town's officials, merchant guilds, and Russian Orthodox clergy are prepared to capitulate in the face of the Teutonic Order, the simple Novgorodian citizenry recruits Prince Aleksandr Iaroslavich (known as "Nevskii" due to his 1240 victory over the Swedes on the River Neva) to repulse the invaders. After raising a peasant army and engaging in a series of inconclusive skirmishes, Nevskii's forces meet the Teutonic knights on the frozen surface of Lake Chud'. Outnumbered and lightly armed, Nevskii's forces are nevertheless able to deal the enemy a resounding defeat by making use of a pincer-like attack inspired by a bawdy campfire story. Reclaiming Pskov in the wake of the Battle on the Ice, Nevskii presides over the veneration of his fallen warriors and the punishment of the German prisoners and local collaborators, issuing the triumphant proclamation: "Whosoever comes to us with the sword shall perish by the sword. Such is the law of the Russian land and such shall it always be."[20]

In limited release in time for the twenty-first anniversary of the Revolution on November 7, 1938, *Aleksandr Nevskii* was hailed in the press as a cinematic tour de force.[21] Apparently resonating well with the Soviet public, *Nevskii* drew record audiences. V. S. Ivanov, the director of Moscow's Art Cinema, told a newspaper reporter that "not since the days of *Chapaev* has there been such an enormous flood of viewers."[22] Far away in the town of Shakhty, an amateur correspondent wrote that long lines were

The Popular Reception of *Aleksandr Nevskii*

Figure 26. A. P. Bel'skii's poster advertising Eisenstein and Pavlenko's *Aleksandr Nevskii*. The caption in the lower left-hand corner reads: "Dedicated to one of the most heroic events in Russian life: the defeat of the Teutonic knights on Lake Chud', 1242." Courtesy of the Russian State Library, Moscow.

forming every day outside the local movie theater's ticket office some two hours before the window would even open. Apparently, some twenty-one thousand people had seen the film during the first seven days of its run in this provincial town.[23] Elsewhere, people were reported to be queuing up to see the film two or even three times in order to relive the experience.[24] In Moscow, tickets remained virtually impossible to obtain for weeks after the film's première.[25]

Vecherniaia Moskva ran stories regarding the film almost daily in late November and early December of 1938. One such piece asked audience members what they had thought of the film. Among their responses were the following:

> The film touched me to the depths of my soul. It is a genuine masterpiece of Soviet cinematography. The unforgettable "Battle on the Ice" episode characterizes the patriotism of the Russian people, their unwavering bravery and their deep love for their motherland. [Comrade Shliakhov, Red Army officer]

A spectacular film has been created that tells in a simple and beautiful way of the power and heroism of the Russian people. This film fills [you] with a sense of pride for our great motherland. [V. Vagdasarov, schoolboy from School No. 26]

The greatness of the ideas and the grandiose nature of their staging make the film one of the best means of mobilizing our people in the struggle with those who in 1938 have forgotten about the "subtle" lessons of the year 1242. May the contemporary "mongrel knights"[26] remember the tragic and shameful role played by their forefathers, the "crusader-scum!" [P. Lunin, engineer]

"Whosoever comes to us with the sword shall perish by the sword." These words of Aleksandr Nevskii's, pronounced seven hundred years ago, are relevant even now. We will answer every blow of the enemy with a triple-blow. The Russian people have [always] beaten their enemies, are beating them [now] and will continue to beat them. [Comrade Galotov, metal worker in the Gorbunov factory][27]

The enduring impact of *Aleksandr Nevskii* can be gauged by the extent to which clichés from the film were assimilated into the *mentalité* of the era.[28] Particularly striking in these contemporary reactions is the blurring together of the Russian and Soviet past. In one case, after Leningrad school teacher E. E. Kozlova finished describing Nevskii's 1242 defeat of the Teutonic knights, children from her class announced with confidence that if any enemies "are brave enough to attack our Union, we'll give them a Battle on the Ice or even worse."[29] Similar sentiments were voiced by three students named Vasil'ev, Golant, and Gamynin outside of a Moscow movie theater: "*Aleksandr Nevskii* is an awesome [*groznoe*] warning to the fascist aggressors whose forefathers were so thoroughly beaten by the Russian people. If the enemy attacks, he'll be even more devastatingly rebuffed than the 'mongrel knights' were on the ice of Lake Chud'."[30] Maya Turovskaya probably only slightly overstates the case when she asserts that the film's "costumed fairy-tale heroes" Vas'ka Buslai and Gavrilo Oleksich even replaced Chapaev late in the decade at the center of children's playground games![31]

It would, of course, be problematic to rely on official sources to map popular opinion in Soviet society. Private letters drawn from Eisenstein's personal archive, however, echo the enthusiasm that resounded throughout the Soviet mass media. They also reflect the popular tendency to conflate the Russian and Soviet historical experiences. Fifth and six graders

V. Chulkova, Z. Kiseleva, P. Ladokhina, and P. Sokolinskaia, for instance, wrote to Eisenstein and the *Aleksandr Nevskii* cast that "the historical film *A. Nevskii* is playing right now in Morshansk. We like it so much. The Russians fought so hard for their independence 700 years ago."[32] An older correspondent waxed rhapsodic about characters like Vas'ka Buslai and noted in regard to the film's lead role that "You have depicted the image of Aleksandr Nevskii very well. It even anticipates what was to be 700 years later. It speaks to us in contemporary terms that 'Whosoever comes to us with the sword shall perish by the sword,' 'Where go the Russian lands,' etc."[33] Addressing Eisenstein with the ancient Slavic word for an epic folk hero—*bogatyr'*—a sailor named V. Bunits wrote: "I learned from *Pravda* about your victory over the 'mongrel knights.' I am very glad. I send you my congratulations and my Red Army man's greeting from the harsh shores of the Pacific Ocean. . . ."[34]

Figure 27. N. K. Cherkasov as the eponymous hero of Eisenstein and Pavlenko's *Aleksandr Nevskii* just before the Battle on the Ice. In N. K. Cherkasov, *Zapiski sovetskogo aktera*, ed. E. Kuznetsov (Moscow, 1953).

The director's archive also preserves amateur manuscript reviews of the film—perhaps written by worker or peasant correspondents—that were apparently forwarded to Eisenstein by newspaper editors. In one, Elena Shishko narrates the film's entire plot, emphasizing the "Russian" identity of the drama's principle figures. Her last paragraph declares defiantly: "If Rus' was able to defend herself in the XIII cent[ury], then in the XX century the great Soviet people in tight cooperation with the brotherly people[s] of the socialist republics should deliver a decisive and devastating blow to the enemy."[35] Another, by the sailor I. G. Shilov, is entitled "A Victory of Soviet Cinematography" and is slightly more sophisticated. Comparing *Aleksandr Nevskii* to the more orthodox *Lenin in October* and *Man with a Gun*, Shilov wrote that

> These motion pictures will go down in the history of Soviet art depicting the great strength of the Soviet Russian people. For millions of honest toilers in this Soviet country, these films will serve as a brilliant document in their study of the history of the peoples of the USSR and a historical document in the history of the All-Union Communist Party.
>
> *Aleksandr Nevskii* is one of the first successful films that has shown the Russian people's patriotism in the struggle for independence and freedom, heroically fighting on Lake Chud' with the German invaders.[36]

A long piece by the coal miner G. I. Dovbnia also found its way into Eisenstein's archive. Stating the obvious, Dovbnia notes that the depiction of the Tatars could be said to prefigure the "Eastern menace" [*vostochnaia opasnost'*] of imperial Japan and that the conduct of the Teutonic knights in Pskov presents a similar precedent for the anti-semitic pogroms in Germany in 1938. Deserving particular note, according to Dovbnia, was the film's depiction of "the working people of Novgorod who wished to give their lives for the motherland and peaceful labor." Returning to this theme several pages later, he applauded the film's treatment of how the "heroic Russian people ... repulsed the attack of the German invaders and cracked them 'over the head' [*na golovu*].... The image of the field, strewn with the dead and wounded, shows what the Russian people are capable of, loving their motherland and free labor."[37] Both Shilov's and Dovbnia's comments make it clear that the rehabilitation of the distant Russian past directly affected the way that they thought about their fellow Russians in the late 1930s.

Of course, it would be incorrect to conclude that the Soviet public's reaction to *Aleksandr Nevskii* was universally positive. Some disliked the film's emplotment, its clumsy special effects, and its deliberate playing down of popular religiosity among the medieval Novgorodians.[38] An editorialist for *Literaturnaia gazeta* complained that Nevskii's character was underdeveloped and rather two-dimensional.[39] Others objected to the film's deployment of Nevskii as a positive hero at all—chapter 21 in this collection focuses on the literary critic V. I. Blium, who denounced the film for precisely this reason at a January 1939 meeting of the All-Union Theatrical Society. But the film also seems to have confused people as often as it irritated them. The valorization of a medieval lord in Soviet mass culture was iconoclastic enough to prompt a number of uneasy audience members to ask one of the leading historians of the day, A. V. Shestakov, for his authoritative appraisal of the film.[40] Similar sentiments led others to address their questions directly to Eisenstein himself at public lectures. At one such talk, for instance, the following diplomatically worded question was scribbled onto a piece of paper and passed up to the podium:

> How did Com[rade] Eisenstein and the other creative members of the team arrive at the image of Aleksandr Nevskii and where did they get the historical material for the creation of the film?[41]

Others were more straightforward, asking Eisenstein bluntly: "who prompted you with the idea for the film?"[42] Underlying such queries was the unspoken question on many people's minds: Which of the party hierarchs had authorized Eisenstein to shoot such a positive portrayal of the old Russian nobility? Had the film won official party endorsement? Was it to be treated as an isolated case, or did it signal a larger transformation in the thematic focus of Soviet mass culture?

But if *Nevskii* was provocative, it was also quite memorable. Much of the admittedly fragmentary evidence characterizing the film's popular reception suggests widespread interest and enthusiasm. Many opinions resembled the sentiments expressed by V. Rogach, a middle school teacher from Kriukovsk. He observed that the image of "the Russian warriors' readiness to sacrifice themselves in the defense of their motherland evokes great love. One develops a burning hatred for the German occupiers who dared to [tread on] the Russian land." His conclusion? Rogach declared that "We need more films which will stimulate the viewer's patriotic sentiments!"[43] Seconding this view was a Russian worker from Central Asia named I. A. Sudnikov, whose semi-literate manuscript nevertheless deserves to be quoted at length:

There are lines at the ticket windows. . . . Many have gone to the movie several times in order to watch this notable cinematic page from the history of our motherland's distant past again and again.

This is not coincidental. Our country's best directors have created an unusually brilliant, truthful image of the Russian people, defending their right to independence against the middle ages' mongrel knight feudal lords, the relatives of today's fascists.

This profoundly well thought-out historical film opens up before us the pages of the history of what was and awakens within us a feeling of pride which strengthens [our resolve] to defend our independence forever.

. . . We need such films. I, for one, as an audience member, consider it impermissible to stop with *Aleksandr Nevskii*. It would not hurt to move toward the production of films on the subject of "The 1812 Invasion of Napoleon Boneparte," "The Sevastopol' Campaign of 1856," "The Battle of Kulikovo Field," "The Battle on the Kal'ka," "The Invasion of Batyi," "Tamerlane's March," etc.[44]

Sudnikov's wish list for Soviet cinema—a repertoire of subjects drawn exclusively from the Russian national past—serves to indicate the extent to which Eisenstein's film blurred the distinction between Russian and Soviet history in audience members' minds. Soviet cinematographers responded to such calls for pre-revolutionary, russocentric subjects in surprisingly short order. The year 1939 saw the release of *Ruslan and Liudmila* and *Minin and Pozharskii*, with *Bogdan Khmel'nitskii* and *Suvorov* following two years later. *Dmitrii Donskoi, Field Marshal Kutuzov, Ivan the Terrible* (pt. 1), *Nakhimov, Admiral Ushakov*, and many others would appear before the death of Stalin.[45] Apparently, the party hierarchy was not only aware of the effect that the film had on its viewers but found the upswell of interest in the Russian national past to be compatible with Soviet state interests as well. Although many commentators on interwar cinema have argued that films with everyday subject matter such as G. V. Aleksandrov's *Circus* and *Volga-Volga* eclipsed more explicitly propagandistic pieces in the mid-1930s,[46] the return of the Russian historical hero epitomized by *Aleksandr Nevskii* clearly gave new life to the Soviet political cinema after 1937.

But the film did not just contribute to the formation of a new genre of historical cinema. *Nevskii* also affected the way Soviet audiences viewed more contemporary subjects shot according to the aesthetics and conventions of Socialist Realism. Schoolboy Iurii Baranov's 1941 description of the film *Chkalov*, for instance, suggests that he responded to this film about a famous Soviet flyer because it reminded him of the Russian folkloric tropes popularized in *Aleksandr Nevskii*:

> From the first frame it was possible to sense a certain uniqueness to the film—finally it became clear: in the picture Chkalov was cast as an Old Russian epic folk hero [*bogatyr'*]. The picture was filled with that fairy-tale romanticism. There are a multitude of examples, but it was especially visible in the farewell scene with the "Little Father" [*Bat'ka*] after the crash ("The Comrades' Farewell"). The tone was convincing and the picture unforced. I liked it.[47]

Complementing other sorts of official propaganda already in circulation during the mid- to late 1930s, the *Nevskii* genre of patriotic historical cinema clearly captured the public's imagination.

A good index of the potency of *Aleksandr Nevskii*'s message is the fact that it acquired its reputation as one of the most memorable and influential films of the decade in under a year's time. Indeed, it was removed from circulation only ten months after its release when the August 1939 signing of the Molotov-Ribbentrop Treaty put a halt to the further screening of anti-German material. Re-released roughly a year and a half later in the wake of the 22 June 1941 Nazi invasion,[48] *Aleksandr Nevskii* quickly returned to the fore. Not only were military medals and partisan brigades named after the medieval prince,[49] but the film again proved relevant enough to people's lives to receive prominent mention in diaries and private correspondence. At the front with a detachment of troops a month after the outset of hostilities, Vishnevskii noted in his diary that music from the film's climatic Battle on the Ice scene had been played at a Baltic Fleet rally.[50] A week later, he contextualized the struggle to stem the German advance by noting that clashes were occurring at "the historic Lake Chud'."[51] Two lieutenants named Ovdin and Subochev similarly allowed the film to script their impressions of the war when they wrote home to Tambov somewhat later that:

> Seven hundred years ago, the great Russian military commander Aleksandr Nevskii said: "Whosoever comes to us with the sword shall perish by the sword. Such is the law of the Russian land and such shall it always be." The German fascist invaders came to us with the sword. And by the sword they shall perish. They shall be eliminated by fire and bayonet; they will be crushed and destroyed by tanks and planes built by the hands of the Soviet people.[52]

A collective letter written by a group of officers from a guards' regiment revealed a similar identification with Nevskii's famous rallying call, albeit without Ovdin's and Subochev's attempt to apply it to the Soviet people as a whole. According to the guards, Russians were "a people who have always beaten all of those who have raised the sword against the Russian state." Senior lieutenant A. M. Lukankin expressed similar russocentric sentiments, couched in humorous bravado: "The German dogs came to enslave our Russian people and capture our land. And we'll give each of them some land—six feet under [*na kazhdogo po tri arshina*]." Apparently in need of an authoritative citation to emphasize his point, Lukankin concluded with what was already almost a ritualized declaration: "He who comes to the Russian lands with the sword shall perish by the Russian sword."[53]

In the wake of Nevskii's official rehabilitation between 1937 and 1938, it should come as no surprise that Stalin included the medieval prince in his invocation of an array of great Russian military leaders from the distant past during his 7 November 1941 Red Square speech.[54] The power of Nevskii's name as a touchstone for popular patriotic sentiments is visible in the public reaction to the speech. Underscoring the success of prewar investments in historical agitation, a professor at Leningrad State University noted, "in his speech, Stalin was able to find precisely those words that awaken hope and stimulate a Russian's best feelings, his love for the Motherland, and, what is especially important, [the words that] connect us with Russia's past." Meanwhile, P. S. Barkov of the Moscow Svarz plant noted simply that "Com[rade] Stalin reminded us of the names of the great Russian military leaders. They sounded like a rallying call, a battle cry for the annihilation of the occupiers."[55]

Of course, *Nevskii*'s peculiar ability to inform the Soviet-German war was not limited to workers, soldiers, and intellectuals. Far away in Irkutsk, seventh-grader Volodia Fel'dman wrote in a school essay: "May the fascists know and remember the words of Aleksandr Nevskii: 'Whosoever comes to us with the sword shall perish by the sword.'"[56] Transcripts of an exchange between a teacher named I. A. Portsevskii and his student Rozhkova in a classroom outside Moscow indicate the enormous attention that the epic of 1242 commanded among Soviet school children during the war:

> TEACHER: The theme of the last lesson was "Novgorod's and Pskov's struggle with the Swedish and German feudal lords."
> [. . .]
> STUDENT: The Germans and Swedes long wished to seize the Finnish lands.

But no sooner had the Swedes landed at the mouth of the river Neva than Aleksandr, Prince of Novgorod, fell upon them. The Novgorodians fought bravely.... Aleksandr began to be known as "Nevskii" for this battle. But the prince didn't get along with the boyars. The boyars had extensive power and didn't want to share with anyone. Aleksandr wanted to concentrate it in his hands because the Swedes and Germans were threatening Russia. Soon, the Germans attacked Rus'. Novgorod summoned Aleksandr Nevskii. Then the battle on Lake Chud' took place. The Germans were forced to conclude a peace.

TEACHER: What does the Soviet government appreciate Aleksandr Nevskii for?
STUDENT: Because he defended Rus' from seizure by the Germans.
TEACHER: How are soldiers distinguished?
STUDENT: Soldiers and officers are distinguished by the Order of Aleksandr Nevskii.
TEACHER: And what do the German knights, who lived 700 years ago, have in common with today's fascists?
STUDENT: They too were engaged in the physical destruction of the Slavic population.
TEACHER: What great person referred to them as "mongrel-knights?"
STUDENT: Karl Marx called them the "mongrel-knights."

Intentionally connecting Nevskii with the Soviet war effort and even the authority of Karl Marx, Portsevskii's pedagogical approach was calculated to maximize the epic hero's propaganda value. Another excerpt from the same transcript helps to confirm this analysis. Portsevskii directed the following question to an unidentified female student:

TEACHER: What sort of preparation did Aleksandr conduct in order to achieve such success? His greatness consisted of the fact that he dismissed the personal insults which the boyars had inflicted upon him and returned [to Novgorod] to command the troops and defend his motherland. What else?
STUDENT: His army was well-armed. Aleksandr carried out a maneuver.
TEACHER: Aleksandr Nevskii greeted them with a trick [*piatakom*]. When the Germans came at them in their "pig" formation [*poshli 'svin'ei'*, a triangular wedge-like style of attack], he weakened the center of his lines but strengthened the flanks. Driving them inward, he destroyed them. Stalin's armies similarly surrounded and destroyed the German fascists at Stalingrad.[57]

As is visible from these examples, Nevskii was mobilized not only to bolster the legitimacy of the state, but to inform Stalin's personality cult as well.

Although the public invocation of Nevskii's name is quite instructive, perhaps most telling—and certainly most tragic—is a personal letter that Vasilii Romashin sent home from the front before being killed in combat late in the spring of 1942. Searching for the right words with which to reassure his father about the struggle with the Germans, the soldier wrote: "sooner or later, Hitler's band will be exterminated, as it is possible to force the Russian people back, but not to beat them: 'whosoever comes to us with the sword shall perish by the sword; such is the law of the Russian land and such shall it always be' (A. Nevskii)."[58] Better than anything else, Romashin's quotation of *Aleksandr Nevskii*'s concluding lines some four years after the film's release testifies to its enduring presence in the popular Soviet *mentalité* of the late 1930s and early 1940s.

∽

By triangulating letters from Eisenstein's personal archive with official accounts and selections from personal diaries, this chapter provides glimpses of the way in which Soviet citizens responded both to the film and to the party hierarchy's ideological about-face during the mid- to late 1930s. If Marxism-Leninism had been too arcane for this poorly educated society to grasp during the first twenty years of the Soviet "experiment," fundamental changes in the party hierarchy's patriotic sloganeering, epitomized by the grand historical vision of Eisenstein's *Aleksandr Nevskii*, had a more tangible effect on Soviet social *mentalité*. Rousing and inspirational, the film not only stimulated a sense of popular patriotism among its audiences, but also allegorically informed the increasingly strained relations between the USSR and its neighbors on the eve of the Second World War.

This chapter also speaks, however, to the importance of differentiating between the production and reception of ideological propaganda. If Eisenstein had intended to shoot a patriotic, anti-German film designed to bolster the authority of the Soviet state and its leaders,[59] ordinary Soviet citizens seem to have understood the film to be a statement about the primacy of the Russian people as well. Probably only dimly recognized by party ideologists, this misunderstanding did not affect the mobilizational potential of *Aleksandr Nevskii* in the near term. That said, this deployment of ethnic particularism tended to undermine the internationalist ethic of the Revolution's first twenty years and would encourage an ever greater reliance on nativist and populist sloganeering within the party hierarchy in the years to come.

Notes

This chapter benefited from communications with Joan Neuberger, Katia Dianina, Benjamin Schenk, and Barry Scherr.

1. *Kratkii kurs istorii SSSR*, ed. A. V. Shestakov (Moscow: Gos. uchebno-pedagog. izd-vo, 1937).
2. "Vystavka russkoi istoricheskoi zhivopisi," *Pravda*, 11 November 1938, 6; "Russkaia istoricheskaia zhivopis' v Gosudarstvennom muzee," *Vecherniaia Moskva*, 13 November 1938, 3; N. Morgunov, "Vystavka russkoi istoricheskoi zhivopisi," *Krasnaia zvezda*, 26 February 1939, 4.
3. These terms are drawn from Michel de Certeau, *The Practice of Everyday Life*, ed. Stephen F. Rendall (Berkeley: University of California Press, 1984), xii–xiii and chap. 3.
4. For instance, R. Iurenev included only two sentences on the reception of *Aleksandr Nevskii* in the 20,000-word section on the film in his authoritative biography on Eisenstein: "the film enjoyed enormous success with its audiences. Entire collectives went to see it together." See R. Iurenev, *Sergei Eizenshtein—zamysly, fil'my, metod*, 2 vols. (Moscow: Iskusstvo, 1985–1988), 2:172. See also N. Gromov, "Tvorcheskie prozreniia Eizenshteina . . . ," *Ogonek* 6 (1973): 9.
5. Although one commentator has recently quipped that "the plural of anecdote is not data," such standards are unrealistic for discussions of *mentalité* anywhere in the world before the era of systematic postwar public opinion research. In the absence of reliable statistical surveys, the analysis of admittedly impressionistic accounts remains the only feasible way of assessing popular reception during the Stalin era. On anecdote and data, see Robert Johnson, "'Stalin's Peasants: Resistance and Survival in the Russian Village after Collectivization,' by Sheila Fitzpatrick [review]," *Slavic Review* 55, no. 1 (1996): 187.
6. RGASPI, f. 17, op. 3, d. 987, l. 34, published in L. Maksimenkov, *Sumbur vmesto muzyki: Stalinskaia kul'turnaia revoliutsiia, 1936–1938* (Moscow: Iuridicheskaia kniga, 1997), 248–49; Iurenev, *Sergei Eizenshtein*, 2:131–32.
7. S. M. Eizenshtein, "Patriotizm—nasha tema," *Kino*, 11 November 1938, 3–4, republished as "My Subject Is Patriotism," *International Literature* 2 (1939): 90–93.
8. For Stalin's cult of personality, see Rosalind Marsh, *Images of Dictatorship: Portraits of Stalin in Literature* (London: Macmillan, 1989), 33. For an exercise in character study, see Barry Scherr, "Alexander Nevsky: A Film without a Hero," in *Eisenstein at 100: A Reconsideration*, ed. Al Lavalley and Barry Scherr (New Brunswick, N.J.: Rutgers University Press, 2001), 207–26. For a broader study of the uses of Aleksandr Nevskii, see Frithjof Benjamin Schenk, *Aleksandr Nevskij: Heiliger—Fürst—Nationalheld. Eine Erinnerungsfigur im russischen kulturellen Gedächtnis (1263–2000)* (Köln: Böhlau Verlag, 2004).
9. Eizenshtein, "Patriotizm—nasha tema," 3–4.
10. Maksimenkov, *Sumbur vmesto muzyki*, 248–49; Iurenev, *Sergei Eizenshtein*, 2:134.

11. P. Pavlenko and S. M. Eizenshtein, "Rus': Literaturnyi stsenarii," *Znamia* 12 (1937): 102–36; "Fil'm o ledovom poboishche," *Uchitel'skaia gazeta*, 27 February 1938, 1; I. Smirnov, "Ledovoe poboishche," *Leningradskaia pravda*, 11 April 1938, 3; S. M. Eizenshtein, "Zametki rezhissera," *Ogonek* 22 (1938): 20–21; "Aleksandr Nevskii i razgrom nemtsev," *Izvestiia*, 12 June 1938, 3; etc. Perhaps inspired by the latter article, N. G. Kuznetsov was moved to announce in a speech to the RSFSR Supreme Soviet seven days later: "700 years ago, the Russian people, defending their national independence, gave the "mongrel knights" a good lesson on the ice of Lake Chud'. The German rapists [*nasil'niki*] were destroyed. Let this be remembered by our enemies!" E. Sitkovskii, "O sovetskom patriotizme," *Pod znamenem marksizma* 9 (1938): 51.

12. RGALI, f. 1923, op. 1, d. 2289, 1. 39–40ob. The Battle of Kulikovo Field, which is fleetingly mentioned in the *Znamia* screenplay, played a major role in a subsequent draft. It is unclear whether the idea originated with Miakshin or whether Eisenstein arrived at it on his own.

13. Emphasis in original. RGALI, f. 1923, op. 1, d. 2289, 11.41–41ob. Novikov confuses the name of the leader of the Teutonic Order with that of the Swedish lord whom the prince had defeated in 1240.

14. P. Evstaf'ev, "O stsenarii 'Rus'": Blizhe k istoricheskoi pravde," *Literaturnaia gazeta*, 26 April 1938, 6; K. Malakhov, "Po protorennoi doroge Ilovaiskikh," *Pravda*, 7 June 1938, 4; M. N. Tikhomirov, "Izdevka nad istoriei (o stsenarii 'Rus')," *Istorik-marksist* 3 (1938): 93–96. Eisenstein responded publicly only to the first of these articles, although Iurenev contends that he took them all seriously—see "Otvet tov. P. Evstaf'evu," *Literaturnaia gazeta*, 26 April 1938, 6.

15. A. Akhutin, "Za khudozhestvennuiu pravdu," *Literaturnaia gazeta*, 30 May 1938, 3. Such criticism of projects that seemed to break with Soviet propaganda's focus in the revolution was not uncommon in the mid- to late 1930s; writers like S. Sergeev-Tsenskii, E. V. Tarle, A. N. Tolstoi, and A. E. Korneichuk all faced opposition until the party hierarchy intervened to overrule their critics. See B. S. Kaganovich, *Evgenii Viktorovich Tarle i peterburgskaia shkola istorikov* (St. Petersburg: Dmitrii Bulanin, 1995), 58–60; and chapters 3, 4, and 21 in this volume.

16. Iurenev, *Sergei Eizenshtein*, 2:144–45. On Eisenstein's work with historians, see Vishnevskii's diary entries from 26 June and 27 December 1938, RGALI, f. 1038, op. 1, d. 2075, 11. 36, 56.

17. Eisenstein had originally planned to end the film with Nevskii dying a martyr's death while returning from a diplomatic mission to the Mongol Khan. Stalin apparently protested that "such a good prince must not die," prompting the decision to end the film following the Battle on the Ice. S. Eizenshtein, "Avtobiograficheskie zametki," in *Izbrannye proizvedeniia v 6-i tomakh*, 6 vols. (Moscow: Iskusstvo, 1964–1971), 1:500.

18. Vishnevskii, diary entry from 26 June 1938 at RGALI, f. 1038, op. 1, d. 2075, 1. 36; ellipsis in original.

19. Vishnevskii, diary entry from 11 August 1938 at RGALI, f. 1038, op. 1, d. 2075, 1. 38. Vishnevskii's attention to the "exotic" may have referred to the sexual overtones

of the original screenplay. Eisenstein's cameraman E. Tisse complained to Vishnevskii late in December of that year that "Eisenstein is always brimming over with strange ideas: aesth[etic] slants, erot[ic] hints, details.... This was reflected in the development of *Al[eksandr] Nevskii* when, for instance, two boys, hermaphrodite types, were supposed to have been paired with Gavrilo Oleksich in the battle[.] Gavrilo fears for the fate of these beauties, and when he catches sight of one of them dying, he . . . leans over to kiss him[.] Tisse demanded that this be thrown out. Tisse understood that this was an issue of reputation and the restoration of their names [after *Bezhin Meadow*, etc.]." See diary entry from 12 December 1938 (ll. 55–6).

20. "Kto k nam s mechom pridet, tot ot mecha i pogibnet. Na tom stoit i stoiat' budet russkaia zemlia." For more traditional analyses of the film, see David Bordwell, *The Cinema of Eisenstein* (Cambridge, Mass.: Harvard University Press, 1993), 210–23; Richard Taylor, *Film Propaganda: Soviet Russia and Nazi Germany*, 2nd ed. (London: I. B. Tauris, 1998), 85–98.

21. M. Koltsov, "Narod-bogatyr'," *Pravda*, 7 November 1938, 2. See also I. Izhorskii, "'Aleksandr Nevskii': Novaia kartina proizvodstva kinostudii 'Mosfil'm'," *Krasnaia gazeta*, 28 November 1938, 3; S. Kara, "Aleksandr Nevskii," *Leningradskaia pravda*, 28 November 1938, 4; A. Levshin, "'Aleksandr Nevskii' (zvukovoi istoricheskii fil'm proizvodstva 'Mosfil'm')," *Uchitel'skaia gazeta*, 5 December 1938, 4.

22. L. V., "Zritel' o fil'me 'Aleksandr Nevskii,'" *Vecherniaia Moskva*, 4 December 1938, 3; Maya Turovskaya, "The Tastes of Soviet Moviegoers during the 1930s," in *Late Soviet Culture: From Perestroika to Novostroika*, ed. Thomas Lahusen with Gene Kuperman (Durham, N.C.: Duke University Press, 1993), 103. *Chapaev* (Sergei and Georgii Vasil'ev, 1934) was an ideologically orthodox Civil War epic.

23. RGALI, f. 1923, op. 1, d. 2289, ll. 27–29ob.

24. RGALI, f. 1923, op. 1, d. 2289, l. 32

25. "Uspekh fil'ma 'Aleksandr Nevskii,'" *Vecherniaia Moskva*, 2 December 1938, 3; N. Kruzhkov, "Aleksandr Nevskii," *Pravda*, 4 December 1938, 4.

26. The term "mongrel knights" [*psy-rytsari*] stems from Karl Marx's treatment of the Teutonic Order. See K. Marks, "Khronologicheskie vypiski," in *Arkhiv Marksa i Engel'sa*, 16 vols. (Moscow: Politizdat, 1932–1982), 5:344.

27. L. V., "Zritel' o fil'me 'Aleksandr Nevskii,'" 3. See similar comments by a captain in the Red Army named Dubrovskii, reported in L. V., "Na prosmotre fil'ma 'Aleksandr Nevskii,'" *Vecherniaia Moskva*, 29 November 1938, 3.

28. For persuasive analysis of the ability of artistic productions to shape popular memory, see Anton Kaes, *From Hitler to Heimat: The Return of History as Film* (Cambridge, Mass.: Harvard University Press, 1989), 196, 198. The author is grateful to Katia Dianina for this reference.

29. S. Dziubinskii, "Vospitatel'naia rabota na urokakh istorii SSSR," in *Vospitatel'naia rabota v nachal'noi shkole: Sbornik statei*, ed. S. N. Belousov (Moscow: Narkompros RSFSR, 1939), 102; see also 109–10. Equally telling was the seriousness with which authorities in the Leningrad Military District treated an incident in a political study circle when a certain private Erofeev was caught unable to make

the connection between Nevskii's defensive victory at Lake Chud' and the "contemporary international situation." See RGVA, f. 9, op. 36s, d. 3778, 1. 64.

30. L. V., "Zritel' o fil'me 'Aleksandr Nevskii,'" 3.

31. Turovskaya, "Tastes of Soviet Moviegoers," 103. Turovskaya may be obliquely referring to a statement of Viktor Shklovskii's in his memoiristic *Eizenshtein* (Moscow: Iskusstvo, 1973), 249. The author is grateful to Benjamin Schenk for this reference.

32. RGALI, f. 1923, op. 1, d. 2289, 1. 38. A different student from Voronezh, Sergushin, wrote an entire essay to Eisenstein about the film on the basis of an article Eisenstein published in *Izvestiia* on December 7, 1938. See ibid., 11. 43–45.

33. RGALI, f. 1923, op. 1, d. 2289, 11. 55–36, cite on 1. 36.

34. RGALI, f. 1923, op. 1, d. 2289, 1. 24.

35. Note Shishko's conflation of Russian and Soviet identity in her statement. RGALI, f. 1923, op. 1, d. 2289, 1. 68.

36. RGALI, f. 1923, op. 1, d. 2289, 11. 61–62. See *Lenin v Oktiabre* (M. Romm, 1937); *Chelovek s ruzh'em* (S. Utkevich, 1938).

37. RGALI, f. 1923, op. 1, d. 2289, 11. 27–29. Echoing the centennial commemoration of Pushkin's death celebrated two years earlier, Dovbnia noted that the film's opening shot—a desolate field littered with the bleached white bones of those who had fallen while resisting the Tatar-Mongol Yoke—could be read as a literary reference. After all, "here is the field with the remains of those who fell in the struggle with the Tatars. We recall [the lines of] Pushkin: 'O field, field, who has strewn you with dead bones?' This is the picture that Pushkin's reader had strained for so long to imagine."

38. Journalists like those of the Kuibyshev paper *Vodnyi transport* (P. Fal'kovskii, N. Appatov, and A. Kustov) complained of the film's schematic nature (RGALI, f. 1923, op. 1, d. 2289, 11. 47–48). G. Gerasimov, from Leningrad, was one of those who attacked the film on account of its plot, cast, and technical aspects (11. 51–53ob, 70–70ob, etc.). F. Voronkin, a Ukrainian journalist, wondered why the film skirted the issue of popular religiosity (11. 56–57). For other criticism, see 11. 70–105.

39. "Patrioticheskaia tema v iskusstve," *Literaturnaia gazeta*, 11 December 1938, 1.

40. A. V. Shestakov was the editor of the seminal 1937 *Short Course on the History of the USSR*. See notes passed to him at public lectures in 1939–1940 at Arkhiv RAN, f. 638, op. 3, d. 333, 11. 4, 6, 120, 123, 125, 130, 136.

41. RGALI, f. 1923, op. 1, d. 2289, 1. 86.

42. RGALI, f. 1923, op. 1, d. 2289, 1. 78. Many, however, didn't have to ask this question. Dovbnia, for instance, automatically assumed that it was a state-run project—see f. 1923, op. 1, d. 2289, 1. 27.

43. L. V., "Zritel' o fil'me 'Aleksandr Nevskii,'" 3.

44. RGALI, f. 1923, op. 1, d. 2289, 11. 32–32ob. Similar themes were suggested by Iu. V. Ivanov and other letter writers in early 1939—see 11. 65–66ob, 102, etc.

45. See *Ruslan i Liudmila* (I. Nikitchenko and V. Nevezhin, 1939), *Minin i Pozharskii* (Vs. Pudovkin, 1939), *Bogdan Khmel'nitskii* (I. Savchenko, 1941), *Suvorov* (Vs. Pudovkin and M. Doller, 1941), *Fel'dmarshal Kutuzov* (V. Petrov, 1944), *Ivan Groznyi*,

ch. 1 (Eisenstein, 1945), *Admiral Nakhimov* (Pudovkin, 1946); *Kreiser 'Variag'* (V. Eizymont, 1947), *Admiral Ushakov* (Romm, 1953), etc.

46. See, for instance, S. A. Shinkarchuk, *Obshchestvennoe mnenie v Sovetskoi Rossii v 30-e gody (po materialam Severo-zapada)* (St. Petersburg: Izd-vo Sankt-Peterburgskogo univ. ekonomiki i finansov, 1995), 123–24; Richard Taylor, "Ideology and Popular Culture in Soviet Cinema," in *The Red Screen: Politics, Society and Art in Soviet Cinema*, ed. Ann Lawton (London: Routledge, 1992), 61–62; Peter Kenez, *Cinema and Soviet Society, 1917–1953* (Cambridge: Cambridge University Press, 1992), 162.

47. Diary entry from April 1941. Iurii Baranov, *Goluboi razliv: Dnevniki, pis'ma, stikhotvoreniia, 1936–1942* (Iaroslavl': Verkhne-Volzhskoe knizhnoe izd-vo, 1988), 109.

48. Jay Leyda, *Kino: A History of the Russian and Soviet Film* (New York: Collier, 1960), 365–56. The symbolic value of this film was high due to its popularity between 1938 and 1939. A worker-diarist in Leningrad, for instance, noted during the first days of the war that "Cherkasov, who not long ago played the role of Aleksandr Nevskii in a film, called from the pages of a newspaper [for us] 'to beat the enemy like our forefathers did.'" Georgii Kulagin, *Dnevnik i pamiat'* (Leningrad: Lenizdat, 1978), 27.

49. The Order of Aleksandr Nevskii was instituted in 1942, the year of the 700th anniversary of the Battle on the Ice. For mention of a partisan brigade named after the prince, see *Soviet Partisans of World War II*, ed. John Armstrong (Madison: University of Wisconsin Press, 1964), 705.

50. See Vishnevskii, diary entry from 26 July 1941 at RGALI, f. 1038, op. 1, d. 2083, l. 24.

51. Vishnevskii, diary entry from 1 August 1941 (l. 33).

52. *Pis'ma s fronta* (Tambov: n. p., 1943), 11.

53. Ibid, 107, 42. Lukankin's comment about giving each German a plot of land six feet under seems to have been a fairly common quip—see another soldier's use of this expression on 112.

54. Declaring that "you must draw inspiration from the valiant example of our great ancestors," Stalin pointed to a number of exclusively Russian pre-revolutionary heroes who were to define patriotic conduct during the war: Aleksandr Nevskii, Dmitrii Donskoi, Kuz'ma Minin, Dmitrii Pozharskii, Aleksandr Suvorov, and Mikhail Kutuzov. See "Rech' Predsedatelia Gosudarstvennogo komiteta oborony i Narodogo komissara oborony tov. I. V. Stalina," *Pravda*, 8 November 1941, 1.

55. Arkhiv UFSBg.SPbLO, reprinted in *Mezhdunarodnoe polozhenie glazami leningradtsev, 1941–1945 (iz Arkhiva Upravleniia Federal'noi sluzhby bezopasnosti po g. Sankt-Peterburgu i Leningradskoi oblasti)* (St. Petersburg: Evropeiskii dom, 1996), 19–20; Nauchnyi Arkhiv IRI RAN, f. 2, razr. x, op. 1, d. 1, l. 54, reprinted in *Moskva voennaia, 1941–1945: Memuary i arkhivnye dokumenty* (Moscow: Mosgorarkhiv, 1995), 153.

56. GAIO, f. 1929, op. 1, d. 192, d. 64, cited in N. A. Trotsenko, "Patrioticheskoe vospitanie starshikh shkol'nikov obshcheobrazovatel'nykh shkol RSFSR v gody

Velikoi Otechestvennoi voiny, 1941–1945 gg. (Na materialakh vostochnoi Sibiri)" (Candidate's diss., MGU, 1973), 95.

57. TsAODM, f. 3, op. 82, d. 9, ll. 177–78.

58. "Poslednye pis'ma s fronta," *Voenno-istoricheskii zhurnal* 10 (1991): 92. N. S. Khrushchev used the same formula in his memoirs to talk about victory in 1945—see *Khrushchev Remembers*, ed. Edward Crankshaw, trans. Strobe Talbott (Boston: Little, Brown, 1970), 219.

59. Instructive in this regard is a possibly apocryphal account of Stalin's exclamation to Eisenstein after seeing the film: "So, Sergei Mikhailovich, you are a good Bolshevik after all!" See Marie Seton, *Sergei M. Eisenstein* (London: A. A. Wyn, 1952), 386.

16
Aleksander Nevskii as Russian Patriot

In the 1920s, Mikhail Kol'tsov was a leading film critic for *Pravda* with strong ties to members of the "Left Front" of the Russian avant-garde visual arts movement like Dziga Vertov. Kol'tsov's association with Eisenstein dates to his favorable review of the director's first feature film, *Strike*. Yet by the mid-1930s Kol'tsov was increasingly known as a newspaper correspondent covering ideologically complex, front-page issues like the Spanish Civil War. This background made him the ideal candidate to write a celebratory piece on Eisenstein's return to the forefront of ideologically correct film in 1938 after a decade of false starts and political errors.[1] In this review of Eisenstein's *Aleksandr Nevskii*, Kol'tsov offers a deceptively simple, enthusiastic discussion of the film, promoting it for mass audiences as a lesson from the past with direct bearing on the Soviet present.[2]

More than just a tale of a bygone age, *Aleksandr Nevskii* appears in Kol'tsov's account as a timeless narrative about state-building and national defense. The critic seamlessly segues from a discussion of medieval valor to a description of the growing standoff in Europe between the Soviet Union and fascist Germany, which culminates in a clear and unequivocal statement on the allegorical significance of the film. The past, as Kol'tsov puts it, is no "dusty museum," but a vital, engaging dimension of the contemporary world.

Worthy of note is the critic's rather awkward and unconvincing attempt to distance Soviet historical propaganda from the use of the same historical mythology under the old regime. Specifically, Kol'tsov asserts that the Soviet revival of heroes from Russian history for mobilizational purposes rings much more true than the tsarist elite's invocation of the same figures and myths because "only the people" can really love their motherland. This rather vacuous argument reveals a certain nervousness on the part of the Soviet propaganda establishment concerning the rehabilitation of semi-mythical figures like Nevskii. What if the people remembered that this rhetoric had been used before 1917 to sell the Great War? After all, for many Soviet men and women, the last decade of the Romanovs' reign was still within living memory. Ultimately, however, there was little need for concern: despite the glaring ironies of epic revisionist films like *Aleksandr Nevskii*, few voiced any objections.[3]

Mikhail Kol'tsov, "An Epic Hero-People"

Pravda, 7 November 1938

Just before the holiday,[4] we saw an impressive new work of Soviet art: the film *Aleksandr Nevskii*. This masterwork inspires a profound intellectual and emotional response.

A product of Sergei Eisenstein's superior talent, temperament and sense of culture—in collaboration with the writer Pavlenko,[5] the composer Prokof'ev,[6] the artist Cherkasov,[7] the cameraman Tisse,[8] the director Vasil'ev[9] and a large collective of inspired Soviet individuals—this picture depicts the struggle of the Russian people at the dawn of their history against German invaders, the Livonian Teutonic knights.

The outcome of their efforts is historically very accurate—as close to the real events as possible, given the documents and artifacts that survive from thirteenth-century Rus'.

That said, we are not sitting in some museum, nor are we contemplating documents that have yellowed with age, nor are we listening to a scholarly presentation. We are sitting in a moviehouse, watching actors—living people, our contemporaries—and we are listening to music composed this year, in 1938.

This is no chronicle, but rather a screen drama—it could almost be called a theatrical presentation, or even a play with a substantial operatic dimension. Yet it doesn't come across as deficient or staged; instead, this is lyrical operatic pageantry in the best of all possible senses. Before us is a play, a contemporary work of art, a labor of love on the part of the contemporary Soviet director Eisenstein and his colleagues. The role of "Saint" Aleksandr Nevskii is played engagingly by the actor Cherkasov, an atheist and a Bolshevik.

And in the moviehouse, the Soviet audience—Komsomol members, communists, workers and the intelligentsia—sits watching the victorious campaign of the Novgorodian forces in rapture.

These people watch and cheer for Aleksandr Nevskii, his militia and his followers—a family that is centuries removed from us and long since turned to dust: Vas'ka Buslai, Gavrilo Oleksich, and Amelfa Timofeevna. The audience applauds their valor, their depth, their brilliance and their devotion to the motherland.

Why is it that a picture portraying such a far-removed epoch is received with such enthusiasm and interest? Why is it that in 1938 audiences clap so loudly for thirteenth-century events?

It's because these events are not depicted on the screen through museum-like naturalism or with stylized conventions,[10] but instead through the Socialist Realist method—by communicating the fundamental, inner truth of the events. This truth has not grown old in over seven centuries. It remains fresh and new—as if it took shape only yesterday. It quivers and stirs with life.

This truth is the enormous sense of self-respect and patriotism that our people have been granted. Centuries old, this characteristic has been with us for our entire independent existence, and it gains a special intensity now, in Soviet times, in the wake of our victory in the Patriotic War[11] against foreign invaders and a plague of bourgeois White Guard landowners, as well as today, when we face a possible new war with fascist aggressors and invaders.

In capitalist Russia, the landowners, industrialists, priests and aristocrats attempted to monopolize the notion of patriotism as they did with all fine human emotions. Everywhere and in every way, they denigrated the child-like soul of the "god-bearing people." Yet only the people truly love the motherland, which they've built with their own hands, irrigated with their own sweat, and defended against enemies with their own blood.

When the Bolshevik party appealed to the people to put an end to rapacious imperialist conflict,[12] calling upon the working class and peasantry to transform it into a civil war, the bourgeoisie attempted to drown out the Bolsheviks with ersatz-patriotic hypocrisy.[13] And after the October Revolution, when the toilers became the country's masters, this same bourgeoisie moved to sell off or simply cede enormous swathes of the country's territory to foreign interventionists—to the Germans and Japanese in particular.

In this we see the nature and character of a dying class. They ceased to be patriotic defenders of their motherland. Instead, they become the motherland's greatest traitors—its worst enemies.

Before leaving Prague,[14] I had a conversation that at any other time would have seemed monstrous, unbelievable, and fantastic. In the wake of Czechoslovakia's punishment after the Munich accords,[15] however, it appears completely understandable and even the norm. A director said to me: "I am not sure what to do now. What sort of play should I put on? Perhaps Maeterlinck or Hauptmann?"[16]

"Why Maeterlinck or Hauptmann?" I replied. "Stage something Czech, something uplifting and patriotic. The people are demoralized by the German intervention, and you ought to boost their spirits. Do something from the Czech classics. What are the old patriotic classics?"

Waving his hands, the director replied: "What's wrong with you? How can we have patriotic plays? They'll take me for a communist! They'll close the theater! I could be put in prison!"

Of course, he was right. In crippled, haggard, frightened Europe, only the communists are working to lift the people's spirits and sense of national dignity (in those countries where it is still possible for communists to speak out loud), encouraging resistance to the fascist invaders and the defense of their native lands.

The bourgeoisie, in league with fascism, downplay their countries' capacity to defend themselves, spreading—in state decrees even—demoralization, panic, defeatism, disbelief and fear in the face of "all-powerful" fascism. They proclaim that resistance is futile and that capitulation is inevitable—even beneficial.

The film *Aleksandr Nevskii* is excellent in that it shows the enemy in all his frightening and demonic strength. While not downplaying the difficulties of the struggle, the film convincingly depicts the victorious potency of the people's organizational skills, persistence and bravery.

The mongrel knights'[17] bonfires and executions are as ominous as the bloody amusements of the fascists of the twentieth century. The struggle against them is not as simple and quick as the impatient might have it. In this regard, the scene of the Battle on the Ice is not at all drawn out, as some hasty critics may judge it to be. In this scene, there is a moment in which it seems as if victory is already assured. The fiercest are already singing joyously, and a relaxed Vasia Buslai takes a drink from a jug of mead. But the main column of knights still remains intact, bristling with spears. The Novgorodians are unable to break through this wall of blades. Once again, with new intensity, the battle heats up, to last for a considerable period until, as it is said in the chronicles, the ice reddens with blood.... Only then comes the true joy of victory.

Aleksandr Nevskii comes down to us in the history of the Russian people as a great military and political leader. He was not a usurer or a slave trader like the majority of the Novgorodian princes. He was a military strategist who defeated the Swedes and Germans. He strengthened our country's northwestern borders. His descendants understand and treasure this, and that is why in 1938, Komsomol members applaud with such gratitude.

What devilishly interesting times these are! Never before have our people stood before the whole world with such strength and calm as we do today, in the present. Our strength, self-confidence, ability and art have been magnified tenfold by the great Revolution, socialist construction, the Bolshevik party, and by Lenin and Stalin. The people's sense of sight and sound has grown more acute, and our consciousness has been raised. Crimson clouds hang low over every part of the world. New "mongrel knights" and other ordinary mongrels have broken free of their chains and threaten to tear humanity apart. But we as a people, armed but calm, standing firm at our full, gigantic height, look to the West and East without fear or doubt. Ours is an immortal, invincible, epic-hero people.

Notes

1. M. E. Kol'tsov's efforts on Eisenstein's behalf are significant, not least because he himself was consumed by the purges shortly after writing this piece. It remains unclear whether his fate was related to errors in his Spanish reportage or his ties to members of the leftist intelligentsia, the Red Army high command, and N. I. Ezhov. See B. Sopel'nik, "Pulia dlia Mikhaila Efimovicha," *Rodina* 6 (2004): 65–71.
2. Mikhail Kol'tsov, "Narod-bogatyr'," *Pravda*, 7 November 1938, 2.
3. Or at least few voiced objections openly—see chapter 21 in this volume.
4. 7 November 1938, the twenty-first anniversary of the revolution.
5. P. A. Pavlenko (1899–1951), trusted "court" playwright.
6. S. S. Prokof'ev (1891–1953), famous Soviet composer, pianist, and conductor.
7. N. K. Cherkasov (1903–1966), one of the best-known actors of the Soviet stage and screen specializing in historical epics. He played the role of Ivan IV in Eisenstein's scandalous wartime trilogy *Ivan the Terrible*. See his memoirs, *Zapiski sovetskogo aktera* (Moscow: Iskusstvo, 1953).
8. E. K. Tisse (1897–1961), Eisenstein's longstanding cinematographer.
9. D. M. Vasil'ev, little-known co-director of *Aleksandr Nevskii*.
10. Perhaps a veiled reference to Bednyi's *Epic Heroes*—see chapter 5 in this volume.

11. An unusual reference to the 1918–1921 Civil War using a term until then reserved for the War of 1812. In 1941, the term *Patriotic War* would be appropriated by Soviet propagandists to describe the struggle with Nazi Germany.

12. The First World War, 1914–1918.

13. On Russian "hurrah-patriotism" [*ura-patriotizm*] during the First World War, see Hubertus Jahn, *Patriotic Culture in Russia during World War I* (Ithaca, N.Y.: Cornell University Press, 1995), 172–75. See V. I. Blium's criticism of this style of agitation in chapter 21 in this volume.

14. Kol'tsov was returning from assignment in Europe covering the Spanish Civil war.

15. Appeasement at Munich in 1938 paved the way for the Nazi annexation of Czech territory in several stages between the fall of 1938 and the spring of 1939.

16. Morris Maeterlinck (1862–1949) and Gerhard Hauptmann (1862–1946), Dutch and German naturalist playwrights, respectively.

17. See chapter 15 in this volume, note 26.

Ivan Susanin

17
Reinventing the Enemy
The Villains of Glinka's Opera *Ivan Susanin* on the Soviet Stage

○∾ SUSAN BEAM EGGERS

In February 1939 the Bolshoi Theater in Moscow staged Mikhail Ivanovich Glinka's opera *Ivan Susanin* for the first time in the Soviet era. Contemporary critics lavishly praised the work, and during its first season the Bolshoi performed the opera no less than twenty-six times.[1] *Ivan Susanin* went on to enjoy widespread acclaim throughout the Soviet period and beyond. Yet such fame was not new: Russian music lovers had thrilled to the sounds and sights of the composition known as "the first Russian opera" for generations before 1917. Originally entitled *A Life for the Tsar*, the work premiered at St. Petersburg's Bolshoi Theater in November 1836 before an enthusiastic audience that included such notable cultural figures as A. S. Pushkin and N. V. Gogol' in addition to Tsar Nicholas I and the royal family. Henceforth, it became a mainstay of the repertoire of the Russian imperial theater, opening every season for the next eight decades until the revolutions of 1917 rendered it "ideologically obsolete."[2]

The opera's nineteenth-century librettist, a courtier of German descent named G. F. Rozen, colored the text of Glinka's masterpiece in undeniably monarchical tones.[3] As a result, *A Life for the Tsar* required substantial revision before its Soviet debut in 1939 as *Ivan Susanin*. While Glinka and his musical compositions have been the subject of numerous studies, the details of S. M. Gorodetskii's transformation of *A Life for the Tsar* have received scant attention. On occasions when Soviet musicologists discussed the rewriting of the libretto, they took great pains to justify the changes by attempting to prove that Rozen, influenced by imperial courtiers or the tsar himself, perverted Glinka's original intentions by forcing the composer to glorify the autocracy. While "disrespect for libretti and accusations against librettists have a long and respectable history,"⁴ this attack on Rozen assumed a particularly opportunistic character because it justified the Soviet rewriting of the libretto and the appropriation of Glinka's music, which before the Revolution had been regarded as a Russian national treasure.⁵ Indeed, it is ironic that Soviet musicologists attempted to defend the revisions to Glinka's opera by blaming the libretto's "shortcomings" on the political atmosphere of the 1830s even as they avoided mention of the social realities and political exigencies that gave shape to the Stalinist version of the opera. As a social-historical document, the text of the libretto can serve as an avenue for studying the political and cultural climate of the society that produced and received it.⁶ This chapter provides a new perspective on the study of Glinka's opera by examining a key feature of the revision, the depiction of the Polish villains, in light of these historical circumstances.

∼

While the creators of the Soviet version of Glinka's opera supplied the work with a heavily revised libretto, the basic contours of the legend remained intact. According to the story, which was first popularized in the late eighteenth and early nineteenth centuries, a Russian peasant named Ivan Susanin sacrificed his life during the winter of 1612–1613 in order to save the newly elected tsar, Mikhail Fedorovich Romanov.⁷ Taking advantage of the political confusion of the interregnum known as the Time of Troubles, Polish armies invade Muscovy, scheming to place a Polish prince on the Russian throne. At a village near Kostroma, the Poles look for a guide from among the local peasants who would help them capture Mikhail Fedorovich. Pressed into Polish service, Susanin feigns cooperation with the Poles, all the while secretly intending to lead them astray and send a warning to the young Romanov. Ultimately, Susanin guides the invaders deep into a dense, snowy forest. When the Poles realize that the faithful peasant has deceived them and has no intention of disclosing to them the whereabouts of the tsar, they torture him to death before they themselves perish from exposure.

In the years following the Bolshevik Revolution, *A Life for the Tsar* vanished from the stage due to its overtly monarchist character. In the mid- to late 1930s, however, a dramatic shift in party ideology linked to the development of more effective mobilizational propaganda led the Stalinist party hierarchy to selectively reinterpret aspects of the tsarist past.⁸ As other contributions to this volume detail, historical figures such as Peter the Great, Aleksandr Nevskii, and even Ivan the Terrible came to be seen in a more favorable light. But Mikhail Fedorovich Romanov was no Peter the Great.

Indeed, the founder of the Romanov dynasty has traditionally been depicted as a sickly, weak-willed puppet of the Muscovite boyars.[9] This could explain why Gorodetskii chose to retitle the opera after the peasant hero and to remove all mention of the tsar from the libretto: the Soviet text depicts Susanin's sacrifice as a heroic act made in the name of the motherland rather than the future Romanov tsar. In this new version of the opera, lines from the epilogue's well-known "Slav'sia" chorus, "Glory, glory to our Russian tsar! To our God-sent tsar and lord!" became "Glory, glory to you, my Russia! Glory to you, our Russian land!"[10]

As such changes indicate, once the most offensive elements had been purged from the tsarist libretto, Glinka's opera offered the Soviet state a marvelous opportunity to educate the public about the patriotic duty that citizens owe their motherland. Bolshevik ideologists had long recognized the arts as a powerful weapon of propaganda and believed that music, literature, and the visual representation could be used to promote the values and cultural mores of the "new Soviet person."[11] By rehabilitating Ivan Susanin, the Soviet leaders co-opted a model for self-sacrifice that resonated with the imperatives of the Soviet state in the 1930s and would be evoked frequently during the coming war. Susanin's ability to mobilize patriotic sentiment made Glinka's opera a mainstay of the Soviet stage, just as it had been during the imperial period.

∽

While the removal of the tsar from *A Life for the Tsar* may be the most obvious alteration in the making of *Ivan Susanin*, Soviet revisions went far beyond the mere elimination of Mikhail Fedorovich. One of the most extensive areas of revisionist attention was the depiction of the Poles, who pose the critical threat to Muscovy in the opera.[12] The original version of the second act of Glinka's opera, known as the Polish act, contains no glaringly objectionable material from a Soviet perspective—there are no references to the glory of the Russian tsar, nor even mention of his name. And yet the text was thoroughly rewritten, presenting a riddle that is well worth resolving: how did the revised representation of the Poles serve Soviet propaganda interests?

The Polish acts in *A Life for the Tsar* and *Ivan Susanin* share superficial similarities. In both libretti, Polish noblemen and women enjoy a glittering ball while hungrily anticipating their "inevitable" victory over Muscovy. The scene opens with a chorus of Polish nobles singing about their battle with the Russians. After the Polish noblewomen echo their kinsmen, the act turns to dancing. Glinka chose dances such as the krakowiak (cracovienne), the polonaise, and the mazurka, explaining in his memoirs that these traditional Polish dances were to draw a contrast between Russian and Polish music. Later critics proclaimed this to be one of the most successful aspects of his work.[13] After the festivities are interrupted by an announcement that the Muscovite forces have rallied, the Poles return to talk of future victories and resume their dancing.

The similarities between the two versions end there: the setting, the language, and even the main characters all differ in the revised text of the scene. In the nineteenth-century libretto, the action takes place in what the Poles describe as the "wastes of Muscovy," in the quarters of the Polish detachment's field commander. The Soviet version replaces the commander with King Sigismund III and sets the scene, not in Muscovy, but in his ancient castle in Poland. Yet although these changes are hardly minor, perhaps most striking of all is the difference in the overall tone of the act, for Gorodetskii recast Rozen's fairly generic Polish adversaries as bloodthirsty aggressors, intoxicated by greed, wine, and a desire to exploit the Russian people.

One of the most remarkable features of the transformed libretto is Gorodetskii's preoccupation with the socioeconomic differences between the Polish nobles and the Russian peasants. This theme does not appear at all in the libretto of *A Life for the Tsar*, which only hints at the Poles' social status in a stage direction for the scene: "A splendid ball. Along the sides of the stage are seated Polish gentlemen and ladies at a feast; at the back of the stage is a brass band; dancers are in the middle." Instead, the original version of the opera revolves around a seventeenth-century dynastic rivalry, in which the Poles seek to gain control over Muscovy by placing Sigismund's son on the Russian throne. In the words of the Polish noblemen: "We shall bring to Poland everlasting glory / We shall bring Wladislaw to Moscow in victory! / We shall place Poland high above Rus', / Muscovy shall be Poland with a Polish tsar." This political ambition is a recurring theme of the Poles' festivities, and they sing continuously of crushing the obstinate Muscovites, subjugating Muscovy to Poland, and celebrating the glory of their military feats.

In the Soviet version of the libretto, the Poles' dynastic pretensions are replaced by concerns only for exploitation and plunder. From the opening lines of the scene, the Polish noblemen describe the Muscovites as serfs (*kholopy*), as the "chorus of knights" sings, "Pour out the wine! Drink it down! / War brings us booty! / We will soon finish with the Moscow serfs." The Polish warriors and noblewomen revel in their plans to subjugate the slaves (*raby*) and collect tribute, in marked contrast to Rozen's text, where terms like "serfs" and "slaves" are not applied to the Russians at all. Gorodetskii depicts seventeenth-century Muscovy as a land rich in livestock, precious metals, and jewels, where the people dress in furs and silk. The Soviet librettist thus creates a veritable "workers' paradise" in which Russian serfs enjoy lives of luxury, while also demoting the Poles from dynastic political rivals to little more than a gang of brigands.[14]

This new socioeconomic focus was reflected in the Soviet public discussion of the revised opera as well. In his reviews of *Ivan Susanin*, published at the time of the opera's Soviet première, the critic G. N. Khubov asserts that according to the composer's original conception, Glinka's opera depicted the Polish nobility rather than Poland in general, and that in this sharp contrast between the Russian people and the Polish nobility, the genius of Glinka's work was most visible.[15] Khubov claims that through the Polish dances, the composer symbolized the outward brilliance, affected splendor, and boastful arrogance of aristocratic Poland.[16] In a similar vein, the opera's producer, B. A. Mordvinov, published an essay in which he contended that the Polish dances reveal the Poles' "superficial brilliance and inner corruption."[17] Another critic, V. M. Gorodinskii, described the pretentious behavior of the Polish nobles, with their "clatter of spurs, knightly genuflections, and dancing."[18] Thus while Glinka never explicitly attributed any significance to socioeconomic differences dividing the Russians and the Poles, Soviet critics claimed that this was his intent and made class one of the defining aspects of Glinka's opera.[19]

Of course, party ideology gave good reason to amplify the negative characteristics attributed to the Polish nobles, making socioeconomic tensions a primary feature of the revised text. At the Seventeenth Party Congress in 1934 Stalin reminded his audience that although a "classless, socialist society" was within reach, the goal could be attained only by means of expanding class struggle. After the February-March plenum of 1937, Stalin's doctrine of "sharpening class struggle" became one of the justifications for the Great Terror, which culminated just six months before the première of *Ivan Susanin* in February 1939.[20] As is well known, Stalin's theory argued that the closer the Soviet Union came to true socialism, the more intense class struggle would become:

> The further we move forward, the more success we have, the more embittered will the remnants of the destroyed exploiter classes become, the sooner they will resort to extreme forms of struggle, the more they will blacken the

Soviet state, the more they will seize on the most desperate means as the last resort of the doomed.[21]

Gorodetskii's portrayal of the Poles answered Stalin's call for a sharpening of class struggle through an intriguing projection of contemporary politics into a canonical work of art. Nonetheless, despite Gorodetskii's emphasis on class struggle between the Polish aristocracy and the Russian people, he cast remarkably little attention on socioeconomic differences between the Russian nobles and their peasants. In fact, there is only one suggestion of domestic discord in the Soviet libretto: in the first act, the Russian peasants contemptuously place the blame for the loss of Moscow on the Russian nobility: "The boyars have surrendered / Our capital city to the Polish nobles." Apart from this parenthetical remark, the Soviet librettist depicted Muscovites of all social castes as united in their resolve to expel the Polish invaders. In all likelihood, the need to allegorically evoke a Soviet society similarly united in the face of foreign aggression explains this peculiar subordination of class consciousness to national consciousness.

In the late 1930s, Soviet society was rife with discussion of enemies in both the domestic and international spheres. In a sense, the Soviet creators of *Ivan Susanin* could hardly have found a more compelling historical rival than the Poles. During the Time of Troubles, Muscovite forces had frustrated the Poles' covetous desires for the cap of Monomakh. Throughout the seventeenth century, Russia and Poland repeatedly clashed over their Ukrainian and Belorussian borderlands. During the eighteenth century, Russia took a leading role in the partitioning of Poland.[22] The Poles responded with bloody insurrections in 1830–1831 and 1863, and after the resurrection of the Polish state at the end of the First World War, they invaded Ukraine, claiming part of the former tsarist empire for themselves.

Yet while Gorodetskii's portrayal of the Poles created an enemy that Russian-speaking Soviets could relate to, he also hinted at an even more threatening enemy standing in the shadows behind the Poles. The Germans appear in Gorodetskii's libretto as mercenaries in league with the Poles, despite the fact that they are never mentioned in the tsarist text. This fictional alliance emerges when King Sigismund asks, "Where, tell me, are my troops? Where are the German knights?" When a messenger reports that Kuz'ma Minin had crushed the German forces, the noblemen lament that, "The German military detachment / And the knights of the Polish kingdom / Tremble before a handful of serfs!"

Yet this overt, historically absurd appearance of Germans in the libretto is secondary to their oblique, allegorical presence in the text as doubles of the seventeenth-century Poles. There is an obvious symmetry, after all, between the Polish nobles' territorial ambitions in Muscovy and the Nazi slogans of *Drang nach Osten* and *Lebensraum*. This figural connection is strengthened in the first scene of the opera by means of a historical parallel. Appearing on stage for the first time, the Russian militia and peasants harken back to an ancient victory: "We drove the German rabble / Beneath the ice of the blue lake." This transparent allusion to Aleksandr Nevskii's 1242 defeat of the Teutonic knights on Lake Chud' connected the opera and its mobilizational goals with S. M. Eisenstein's well-known 1938 film about the medieval prince, which ends with the words "Whosoever comes at us with the sword shall perish by the sword. Such is the law of the Russian land and such shall it ever be!"[23] Indeed, this sentiment is echoed nearly verbatim in the opening scene of *Ivan Susanin* in several instances, ranging from "Whosoever has made war on Russia / Has always wrought his own destruction there" to "Whosoever has attacked Russia / Has himself perished." After recalling the defeat of the "German rabble" in the thirteenth century, the Soviet libretto then promises the same retribution not only to Russia's seventeenth-century enemies but to anyone else who might dare to invade in the future—a not-so-veiled warning aimed at Nazi Germany.

Such anti-fascist rhetoric permeated the official Soviet reception of *Ivan Susanin* as well. For instance, Khubov's *Sovetskaia muzyka* review of the opera condemns artistic policies being enforced in Nazi Germany. He sets up a contrast between cultural activities in Germany and the USSR in the very first lines of his essay: "The Soviet people are reviving a great work of a national artist according to its true authorial plan, while western culture is enduring a painful, never-ending crisis, a dark period of stagnation." Khubov states that "the fascist barbarians are destroying noteworthy works of art and impudently desecrating the classics of world culture with animalistic malice," banning, among other things, the performance of works by such renowned nineteenth-century Jewish composers as Mendelssohn and Meyerbeer. The author concludes by declaring that although socialist culture has always looked to the classics for everything good and progressive that they could offer, "fascism has brought about only the death and degeneration of culture."[24] Clearly, for Khubov the opera provided an occasion to reflect not only on seventeenth-century Russian-Polish relations but also on the greater threat posed by Nazi Germany.

When the revised version of Glinka's opera premièred on the Soviet stage in early 1939, the threat of war loomed over Europe like a dark cloud, and this sort of anti-fascist rhetoric was becoming increasingly widespread in Soviet mass culture. While the Western powers followed a policy of appeasement in the mid- to late 1930s, the Soviet Union feared standing alone against a possible Nazi onslaught, and propagandists openly discussed the prospect of a showdown with fascist Germany.[25] Such fears inspired the Soviet regime to rally its society to the cause of national defense, and Soviet artists turned to heroes from the Russian past and situations where the Russian people had stood together in order to create an inspirational historical narrative. Clearly, the retelling of Susanin's legend should be viewed in this context of international tension and mobilizational propaganda.[26]

In the libretto of *Ivan Susanin*, the lines between figurative and actual enemy are intentionally blurred. Direct and indirect references to Germany, as well as the allusions to the thirteenth-century Teutonic invaders, instruct the Soviet audience that the Poles should be seen as representing an aggressive and reactionary Germanic culture. The opera's text provides a sort of "instruction manual" for reading the Poles "as Germans." In this sense the libretto of *Ivan Susanin* can be characterized as a "readable text," a work that avoids obscurity or ambiguity and renders figurative language absolutely transparent.[27]

The directness with which *Ivan Susanin* informs its audience about how it is to be read relates closely to the poetics of Socialist Realism. Gorodetskii's libretto also corresponds to the conventions of this aesthetic through a sharp delineation between heroes and villains. Aside from portraying the Poles as depraved exploiters, the Soviet librettist attributes to them an array of other pernicious characteristics. One of the most glaring vices that Gorodetskii imputes to the Poles is insatiable greed, which is woven throughout the libretto like a garishly colored thread. From the very first lines of the Polish act, the Poles relish the thought of the spoils of war: "War brings us booty!" A few lines later, the Polish noblewomen sing the following lines, which the noblemen then echo: "Their whole country is a paradise on earth, / It's time we owned it! / Their furs and silken garments / We alone should be wearing!"

This theme was also reflected in Soviet press accounts of the opera. Mordvinov asserts that when the Polish nobles sought to inflict a blow upon the "unruly Russians," they primarily aimed to amass wealth, to boast of spoils, and to exploit the Russian peasants. According to Mordvinov, for the Polish nobles, war was robbery, an excuse to plunder the Russian land.[28] This account shows that the artists who transformed *Ivan Susanin* deliberately chose to debase the Poles' dynastic ambitions to the level of simple greed, making their aggression seem exceptionally petty and opportunistic.

While Gorodetskii depicted seventeenth-century Polish noblemen as obsessed with greed, he reserved his harshest judgment for the Polish noblewomen, portraying them as even more bloodthirsty and rapacious than the men who actually engaged in battle. This vilification of the Polish noblewomen is one of the most striking alterations in the libretto. In Rozen's original text, the Polish women seem anxious for the hostilities to end, singing, "But soon, of course, all battles will end! / Back to the sacred homeland, heroes! / The homeland is preparing for you myrtle and roses, / And reunions of delight and tears!" War for them is a necessary evil, a tragedy whose conclusion they eagerly anticipate. In *Ivan Susanin*, by contrast, Gorodetskii portrays the Polish noblewomen as purely avaricious. Their desire for material possessions seems insatiable, and throughout the scene their attention returns again and again to the subject of Russian furs and jewels. They exhort their kinsmen to grab as much wealth as possible: "Seize a bit more treasure for Poland! / Seize whatever you can of the tribute of war! / Seize rich tribute wherever you can! / Go! Destroy! Seize! Give it to us! Diamonds, rubies, topazes! All for us!" They seem oblivious to the horrors of war, goading their husbands and brothers into battle in order to accumulate more wealth.

This derogatory portrayal of the Polish noblewomen serves several purposes. Aside from its apparent misogyny, such an attack speaks of a common technique of denigrating entire enemy nations by pillorying its women as surrogates. More specifically, by presenting the Polish women as aggressive and ruthless, the librettist characterizes them as the driving force behind the military incursion, rendering the Polish nobles their weak and ineffectual pawns. Needless to say, this depiction also draws attention to the contrast between their cold-hearted materialism and the newly conservative vision of a woman's role in society that was gaining currency in Soviet mass culture during the mid- to late 1930s. This ideal, which celebrated Soviet women as nurturing housewives and mothers, was the result of an array of new pro-natalist legislation and an aggressive propaganda campaign that reversed earlier, more militantly revolutionary norms.[29]

Other features of the representation of the Poles in *Ivan Susanin*, such as their heavy drinking, may also be linked to the newly puritanical Stalinist social orthodoxy. In the very first line of the Polish scene, the Polish noblemen sing: "Pour the wine! Drink it all down!" Once again, Polish noblewomen are cast in the most unfavorable light as they proclaim how much they love "amusements and luxury, wine and merrymaking," followed by this revealing toast: "We drink a toast to all / Who are bold both in battle and in love! / We drink to boldness! To our nobles! To Poland! / We drain our glasses." In marked contrast, when the Russian peasants sing of merrymaking, there are no references to anything stronger than mead. Clearly, by emphasizing the bacchanalian quality of the Poles' festivities, the Soviet librettist intended to expose the enemy's moral bankruptcy.

Taken as a whole, the Poles are portrayed as petty, opportunistic, greedy, and corrupt, qualities that stood in direct contrast to Socialist Realism's "positive hero," who was generally a brave but modest person, possessing a calm, serious disposition and unwavering determination.[30] According to Mordvinov:

> Glinka found a deeply lyrical, warm, stirring, emotional tone for depicting the positive heroes of the Russian people, but portrays the enemy completely differently. He emphasizes the external brilliance, frivolousness and arrogance of the Polish nobles.[31]

The Soviet composer I. I. Dzerzhinskii concurred with Mordvinov's characterization, noting that the scenes depicting the lyrical beauty of Russia contrasted sharply with the "pomposity of the Polish act."[32] Both of these statements, in turn, echoed what S. A. Samosud, the opera's director, had written in *Pravda* some two years earlier when he distinguished the Poles' unthinking materialism and pretension from the simplicity, sincerity, deep feeling, and genuine goodness of the Russians.[33] This opposition turns out to have been one of the most memorable innovations in the entire production.

∽

While the most obvious change to take place during the Sovietization of *A Life for the Tsar* was the purging of the tsar himself, this was not the only change, nor was it arguably the most significant. During the revival of imperial Russian history that took place during the mid- to late 1930s, Soviet historians selectively restored famous figures and reputations from the Russian national past. Gorodetskii, however, realized that Mikhail Fedorovich was not a viable candidate for rehabilitation and instead focused on a negative characterization of the villains from the drama of 1612–1613. He apparently believed that by amplifying the moral contrast between the Russians and Poles, he could use this historic rivalry to aid in the development of a new sense of Soviet cultural identity that displayed unmistakably Russian overtones.

According to Gorodetskii's vision, the Poles in *Ivan Susanin* were not genuine dynastic rivals; instead, they only strut about on stage, bragging about their nobility, lusting after Russian riches, and drinking wine in a decidedly un-Soviet fashion. Any political ambitions are eclipsed by their materialism and hedonistic pursuits. What is more, as debauched as the Polish noblemen may appear, their negative tendencies were outdone in the librettist's portrayal of the Polish noblewomen, whose cold, uncaring materialism further indicts Polish culture and provides a foil for Soviet mass culture's upright, nurturing, and virtuous feminine ideal.

These changes in the libretto of *Ivan Susanin* contribute to our understanding of this period in several ways. First, the transformations illustrate the way that the Soviet obsession with class struggle changed over time, by the late 1930s becoming subordinate to more conventional national priorities. Also, by drawing direct and indirect connections between the seventeenth-century Polish intervention and the contemporary threat of German invasion, the libretto dovetailed with Soviet anti-fascist rhetoric of the period. Finally, in keeping with the tenets of Socialist Realism, the villainous Poles were held to signify everything antithetical to Soviet society: not only were they class enemies, but their aggression and greed were impulsive and immoral, motivated by unthinking materialism and the aggressive, self-seeking ruthlessness of their women at home.

The extent to which Soviet authorities regarded *Ivan Susanin* as propaganda can be seen in additional changes in the libretto that were made five months after its 1939 debut, when the enemy was reinvented yet again. Perhaps in anticipation of the August 1939 Molotov-Ribbentrop pact, the Soviet creators of *Ivan Susanin* softened their anti-German rhetoric when the opera premièred that June in Leningrad. In particular, Gorodetskii's libretto was stripped of all references to Germans, which were replaced by more generic terms like "foreigner" (*chuzhezemnyi*) and "hireling" (*naemnyi*).[34] Although Gorodetskii had originally highlighted the anti-fascist elements in the opera, on the eve of the signing of the non-aggression pact, *Ivan Susanin* served as a conventionally anti-Polish work, providing historical justification for the Soviet annexation of eastern Poland in the fall of 1939. Then, two years later, after the launch of the Nazi invasion of the USSR, *Ivan Susanin* was once again rewritten in order to return the Germans to their place of notoriety in the text. Although the Soviet creators of *Ivan Susanin* could not have foreseen these eventualities, their flexible approach in producing a composite image of the enemy made the opera an ideal instrument of party propaganda. This same explanation may, in the long run, explain at least part of the lasting success of Glinka's epic work.

Notes

Research for this chapter was supported by grants from the American Council of Teachers of Russian and the University of North Carolina's department of history. I wish to thank E. Willis Brooks, Jeff Jones, Paula Michaels, and Donald J. Raleigh for their helpful comments concerning this essay.

1. RGALI, f. 648, op. 5, d. 658; and f. 648, op. 5, d. 1345, prilozhenie no. 41, pp. 142–43. Compare with fourteen performances of P. I. Tchaikovskii's *Evgenii Onegin* and thirteen of A. P. Borodin's *Kniaz' Igor*.

2. The final production of *A Life for the Tsar* in imperial Russia took place on 6 December 1916, which marked its 600th performance. RGALI, f. 2336, op. 1, d. 150, 1. 89.

3. Although he was not portrayed on stage, the image of the tsar dominated *A Life for the Tsar*. See Richard Taruskin, *Defining Russia Musically: Historical and Hermeneutical Essays* (Princeton, N.J.: Princeton University Press, 1997), 25–47; and Jennifer Baker, "Glinka's *A Life for the Tsar* and 'Official Nationality,'" *Renaissance and Modern Studies* 24 (1980): 92–114.

4. Caryl Emerson, *Boris Godunov: Transpositions of a Russian Theme* (Bloomington: Indiana University Press, 1986), 143. One work that attempts to remedy this disrespect is Patrick Smith, *The Tenth Muse: A Historical Study of the Opera Libretto* (New York: Knopf, 1970).

5. For example, see A. Gozenpud, *Russkii sovetskii opernyi teatr (1917–1941): Ocherk istorii* (Leningrad: Gosudarstvennoe muzykal'noe izdatel'stvo, 1963), 254, 247; E. L. Kachanova, "Ivan Susanin" M. I. Glinki (Moscow: Muzyka, 1986), 39; O. E. Levasheva, *Mikhail Ivanovich Glinka* (Moscow: Muzyka, 1987), 243; V. V. Protopopov, *"Ivan Susanin" Glinki: Muzykal'no-teoreticheskoe issledovanie* (Moscow: Izdatel'stvo Akademii nauk SSSR, 1961), 25–26, 46–48; V. A. Vasina-Grossman, *Mikhail Ivanovich Glinka* (Moscow: Muzyka, 1982), 47; and A. V. Ossovskii, "Dramaturgiia opery M. I. Glinki 'Ivan Susanin,'" in *M. I. Glinka: Issledovaniia i materialy*, ed. A. V. Ossovskii (Leningrad, Moscow: Gosudarstvennoe muzykal'noe izdatel'stvo, 1950), 8, 25, 33–34. The sole extensive English-language biography of the composer merely states that the Soviets rewrote the libretto of *A Life for the Tsar* because of what they considered "'incorrect' sentiments." See David Brown, *Mikhail Glinka: A Biographical and Critical Study* (London: Oxford University Press, 1974), 3.

6. On language as a social-historical phenomenon, see Pierre Bourdieu, *Language and Symbolic Power*, ed. John B. Thompson, trans. Gina Raymond and Matthew

Adamson (Cambridge, Mass.: Harvard University Press, 1991), chap. 1. On sociocultural production and consumption, see Michel de Certeau, *The Practice of Everyday Life*, trans. Steven Rendall (Berkeley: University of California Press, 1984), chap. 3.

7. See Thomas Hodge, "Susanin, Two Glinkas, and Ryleev: History-Making in *A Life for the Tsar*," in *Intersections and Transpositions: Russian Music, Literature, and Society*, ed. Andrew Baruch Wachtel (Evanston, Ill.: Northwestern University Press, 1998), 3–19; Susan Beam Eggers, "Mikhail Ivanovich Glinka's Opera *A Life for the Tsar/Ivan Susanin*: Culture, Politics, and Artistic Representation, 1836–1939" (Ph.D. diss., University of North Carolina, forthcoming), chap. 1.

8. On the power of language and mobilization, see Bourdieu, *Language and Symbolic Power*, chaps. 3, 7.

9. For example, see "Mikhail Fedorovich Romanov," in *Bol'shaia sovetskaia entsiklopediia*, 65 vols. (Moscow: Sovetskaia entsiklopediia, 1926–1954), 27:607. For a more recent interpretation that disputes this dominant view, see L. E. Morozova, "Mikhail Fedorovich," *Voprosy istorii* 1 (1992): 32–47.

10. In this essay, quotations from the prerevolutionary libretto are taken from M. Glinka, *Polnoe sobranie sochinenii: Literaturnye proizvedeniia i perepiska*, 20 vols. (Moscow: Muzyka, 1955–), 1:34–94. Quotations from the Soviet libretto are from the published piano and vocal score: M. I. Glinka, *Ivan Susanin* (Moscow: Muzgiz, 1953).

11. For a recent study on the role of music in this process, see Susannah Lockwood Smith, "Soviet Arts Policy, Folk Music, and National Identity: The Piatnitskii State Russian Folk Choir, 1927–1945" (Ph.D. diss., University of Minnesota, 1997).

12. This observation had been made in Bojan Bujic, "Anti-Polish Propaganda and Russian Opera: The Revised Version of Glinka's *Ivan Susanin*," *European History Quarterly* 15, no. 2 (1985): 175–86. Bujic criticizes Gorodetskii's revisions, describing them as "artistic falsification," without suggesting explanations for the changes.

13. M. I. Glinka, "Zapiski," in *Polnoe sobranie sochinenii*, 1:267. See Kachanova, "*Ivan Susanin*" M. I. Glinki, 21–22; Protopopov, "*Ivan Susanin*" Glinki, 30; Ossovskii, "Dramaturgiia opery M. I. Glinki 'Ivan Susanin,'" 63.

14. Viktor Zhivov, "Ivan Susanin i Petr Velikii: O konstantakh i peremennykh v sostave istoricheskikh personazhei," *Novoe literaturnoe obozrenie* 38, no. 4 (1999): 56–57.

15. Georgii Khubov, "Ivan Susanin," *Sovetskaia muzyka* 2 (1939): 33.

16. Georgii Khubov, "Narodno-geroicheskaia epopeia: 'Ivan Susanin' na stsene Bol'shogo teatra," *Pravda*, 22 February 1939, 4.

17. B. Mordvinov, "'Ivan Susanin' na stsene Bol'shogo teatra," *Pravda*, 7 February 1939, 6.

18. V. Gorodinskii, "Genial'naia opera," *Komsomol'skaia pravda*, 27 February 1939, 3.

19. Despite their obvious exaggeration, it is important to admit that this Soviet emphasis on class is not entirely without interpretive merit. Although the original libretto of *A Life for the Tsar* devotes little attention to the topic of the Poles' nobility, its musical score is somewhat more suggestive. Taruskin has described

the music of the Polish act as a "symbolic battle of styles": the Poles are represented by stereotyped dance genres (typically in triple meter), and they express themselves collectively and impersonally, while the Russian music (usually in a simple duple, or double, time) is highly personal and lyrical. See Taruskin, *Defining Russia Musically*, 29–34. Whether or not Glinka conceived of these differences primarily as socioeconomic, his contrast between the "decadent" music of aristocratic Poland and more simple Russian folk tunes reinforced the Soviet justification for rewriting the libretto.

20. Chris Ward, *Stalin's Russia* (London: Edward Arnold, 1993), 117. In his discussion of the Bolshevik-type organizational model, Pierre Bourdieu argues that this rekindling of the discourse of class struggle could be used to restore the legitimacy of party discipline. Bourdieu, *Language and Symbolic Power*, 201. For a discussion of this phenomenon during the Civil War period, see Donald J. Raleigh, "Language of Power: How the Saratov Bolsheviks Imagined Their Enemies," *Slavic Review* 57, no. 2 (1998): 320–49.

21. Cited in Dmitri Volkogonov, *Stalin: Triumph and Tragedy*, ed. and trans. Harold Shukman (New York: Grove Weidenfeld, 1991), 284.

22. The Soviet opera was much more anti-Polish than *A Life for the Tsar*, perhaps because Poland was a still a Russian imperial possession in 1836. Even so, no less than the tsarist censor, Auguste Ol'dekop, expressed deep concern about the opera's potential for further complicating Russian-Polish relations: "The play is wonderful . . . it raises the national spirit; but on the other hand, the Poles were depicted in this opera in all their hatred of Russia—why was it necessary to arouse again this hatred which was once so pernicious!" RGIA, f. 780, op. 1, d. 12, 1. 198. Ol'dekop's misgivings were ignored.

23. See chapters 14 and 15 in this volume.

24. Khubov, "Ivan Susanin," 32.

25. For example, see "Sviashchenayi dolg," *Pravda*, 11 August 1937, 1, which declared, "we are living in stormy times. Our foreign enemies are preparing to attack us. But we calmly look danger in the eye, certain in our strength and future victory."

26. In addition to the première of the opera *Ivan Susanin*, 1939 witnessed the publication of E. Gerasimov, *Ivan Susanin* (Moscow: Voennoe izd-vo, 1939).

27. See Régine Robin, *Socialist Realism: An Impossible Aesthetic*, trans. Catherine Porter (Stanford, Calif.: Stanford University Press, 1992), 246, 251.

28. B. Mordvinov, "Kak sozdavalsia spektakl' 'Ivan Susanin,'" *Sovetskaia muzyka* 2 (1939): 39.

29. For the editorial "Stalinskaia zabota o materi i detiakh" and associated legislation banning abortion and restricting divorce, see *Pravda*, 28 June 1936, 1. Generally, see Wendy Goldman, *Women, the State and Revolution: Soviet Family Policy and Social Life, 1917–1936* (Cambridge: Cambridge University Press, 1993); Victoria Bonnell, "The Peasant Women in Stalinist Political Art of the 1930s," *American Historical Review* 98, no. 1 (1993): 72–75. Sheila Fitzpatrick discussed the "great retreat" in music in her article "The Lady Macbeth Affair: Shostakovich and the Soviet Puritans," in *The Cultural Front: Power and Culture in Revolutionary Russia*

(Ithaca, N.Y.: Cornell University Press, 1992), 183–215. Susanin's daughter, Antonida, served as an example for Soviet women through her devotion to family. See Susan Beam Eggers, "The Women of Glinka's Opera *Ivan Susanin* on the Soviet Stage," paper presented at the Southern Conference on Slavic Studies, Chapel Hill and Durham, N.C., March 1998.

30. Katerina Clark, *The Soviet Novel: History as Ritual* (Chicago: University of Chicago Press, 1981), 46–47, 57–63, 186–87; Rufus Mathewson Jr., *The Positive Hero in Russian Literature* (Stanford, Calif.: Stanford University Press, 1975); Hans Günther, "Education and Conversion: The Road to the New Man in the Totalitarian *Bildungsroman*," in *The Culture of the Stalin Period*, ed. Hans Günther (New York: St. Martin's, 1990), 210–28.

31. Mordvinov, "Kak sozdavalsia," 38.

32. Iv. Dzerzhinskii, "Zamechatel'nyi spektakl'," *Sovetskoe iskusstvo*, 27 February 1939, 2.

33. S. A. Samosud, "K vershinam mirovogo iskusstva," *Pravda*, 7 June 1937, 3.

34. RGALI, f. 656, op. 3, d. 723, ll. 6, 19, 22–23, 65–68, 73, 84, 89.

18
Official Praise for *Ivan Susanin*

B. A. Mordvinov's feature article on the 1939 debut of *Ivan Susanin* epitomizes the official Soviet line on the rehabilitation of this classic work of nineteenth-century nationalist culture, despite the fact that the author was a famous actor and director rather than a professional journalist or propagandist.[1] Published in *Pravda*, the most authoritative forum in the USSR, this article is instructive for two principle reasons.

Like much of the rest of the official discussion surrounding the restaging of the opera, it describes the preparatory work performed by playwrights like S. M. Gorodetskii and M. A. Bulgakov as more of a restoration that a revision of the original. In an inventive rewriting of the opera's history, Mordvinov claims that Glinka was prevented from realizing his true vision for the opera by the imposition of jingoistic and monarchial themes by its original librettist, G. F. Rozen. In Mordvinov's account, even the original title, *A Life for the Tsar*, was less Glinka's choice than that of Nicholas I. Such historical fictions were necessary in order to allow the Soviet opera establishment to recoup the tendentiousness of the tsarist operatic tradition without compromising its own ideological purity. After all, in the late 1930s, Soviet opera was struggling to distance itself from the "formalist" excesses of the preceding decade, and many believed that a "return to the classics" would restore the authority and prestige of the Soviet stage. Under such conditions, even this mainstay of the pre-revolutionary canon proved to be a viable candidate for rehabilitation once its most disagreeable aspects were discredited as a perversion of Glinka's "true" intentions.

Quite apart from Mordvinov's reading of the opera's history under the old regime, his article is interesting due to its contradictory approach to the historical subject matter itself. At first, the author suggests that, in the interest of historical accuracy, Gorodetskii resisted the urge to recast Susanin as sacrificing himself to defend the common-born militia commander Kuz'ma Minin instead of the future tsar Mikhail Romanov. Such a plot line, avers Mordvinov, would have been a blatant "falsification of history." He acknowledges, however, that in the Soviet version of the opera, Susanin perishes in order to save Moscow rather than the future tsar. Mordvinov clumsily justifies this act of artistic license with the argument that it mirrored analogous episodes from the nation's history. Images of these events, including Nevskii's 1242 defeat of the Teutonic knights on Lake Chud', even form the backdrop for the opera's finale.

Of course, all of Mordvinov's "historical" considerations are moot, insofar as the story of Ivan Susanin is legend and not historical fact. But this only makes the peculiarities of this discussion more glaring. On one hand, he calls for accuracy in historical representation. On the other, he reveals that the driving force behind the Soviet rehabilitation of the tsarist past endorsed a "mythic" approach, in which real events were connected not by the causal flow of historical circumstances but as hypostases of an eternal, recurrent pattern. Thus the final realization of Susanin's pattern of sacrifice is evident in "the feats of hundreds of thousands of Soviet patriots" in the present. This tolerance for what is at base a historiographic mélange, in which legend appears as history and history as legend, testifies to an abiding tension within the Stalinist rehabilitation project as a whole between the specific, "fixed" nature of the past and Soviet authorities' need for a pliable historical narrative that could be adapted to the ever-changing political context of the present.

B. A. MORDVINOV, "*Ivan Susanin* ON THE STAGE OF THE BOLSHOI THEATER"

Pravda, 7 February 1939

The entire collective of the Bolshoi Theater—from its artistic director to the stagehands and carpenters—is working with tremendous creative enthusiasm on Mikhail Glinka's ingenious opera *Ivan Susanin*. The final rehearsals are taking place. Soon the show will be presented to the audience.

All of us working on *Susanin* are united by a common goal: to reveal as fully as possible the inexhaustible musical riches of this opera and to show truthfully on our stage the Russian people's patriotism and heroism, as represented in Glinka's brilliant image of Ivan Susanin.

As is well known, the poet Zhukovskii suggested the subject of the opera to M. I. Glinka and also proposed to write the libretto. However, Zhukovskii wrote only Vania's lines in the epilogue, and the composer had to draft the plan for the libretto himself. He composed the music according to this plan, but the poetic content of the opera was produced by an incompetent rhymester—a certain Baron Rozen. Contradicting the composer's conception, Rozen replaced the original theme of a folk movement against foreign invaders with an utterly false monarchical theme. *Ivan Susanin* also received a new "official" title: at first, *A Death for the Tsar*, which was corrected to *A Life for the Tsar* on the order of Nicholas I.

Following this long-standing falsification of the opera and the twenty-two years that have elapsed since its last production on the stage of the Bolshoi Theater, our collective has taken upon itself the task of reviving *Ivan Susanin* in all the greatness of its brilliant author's original conception.

We began our work with a search for the correct dramatic formula. The theme of the opera is the salvation of the motherland. But how were we to approach this subject? According to Rozen, Susanin leads the Poles off into the forest in order to save Mikhail Romanov. In the first version of the opera's revival, it was proposed that Susanin would save Minin. But this mechanical alteration of the plot would have been, first of all, a falsification of history, and second of all, dramatically unconvincing.

The authors of the new edition of the libretto (S. Gorodetskii, S. Samosud, and B. Mordvinov) came to the following decision: Susanin accomplishes his feat in the name of the salvation of the motherland and its symbolic center—Moscow. Detachments of Poles are marching on Moscow to unite with their garrison, which has remained in the capital. Susanin, by leading the Poles away into the woods where death awaits them, saves Moscow and thus the motherland.

This treatment of the subject matter is completely justified both historically and dramatically. Our historical consultants have identified a series of analogous circumstances in the Russian national past—both during the period of the Polish intervention and during the Patriotic War of 1812.

In our new libretto we transferred action originally set in Kostroma to a village near Moscow. Why? Because Susanin is a collective image of the Russian patriot. He represents the thousands of Russian Susanins who have lived throughout the ages and in all corners of our homeland and whose spirit lives on today in the feats of hundreds of thousands of Soviet patriots.

With an infinitely rich array of musical tonality, Glinka depicts the joys and sorrows of the Russian people. His choruses, in particular, are marvelous: those of the prologue, full of the deepest lyricism, saturated with resoluteness and faith in victory; those of the first act and the monastery scene; and finally the majestic folk hymn—the hymn of power and invincibility in the opera's finale.

The best traits of the great Russian people—their humility, moral purity, and strength and determination in realizing their goals—are combined in the central hero of the opera, Ivan Susanin.

And he raises his children to possess these same virtues. Susanin's family has a deep love of the motherland and great faith in it. Antonida is a remarkable Russian girl; Vania is a brave and energetic youth, Susanin's worthy heir; and Sobinin is an honorable, stalwart warrior, who rouses his fellow countrymen for battle with the enemy. They all place duty to the motherland above all else.

In complete contrast to the profound, multifaceted image of the Russian people's patriotism and nobility, Glinka portrayed the Polish nobles using the distinctive medium of dance. The themes of the polonaise and mazurka subtly emphasize the superficial brilliance and inner corruption of the Polish aristocracy, as well as its boastful saber-rattling.

The monumental epilogue is really the organic conclusion to the show. It is to be staged on a set composed of enormous panels, depicting the remarkable events of Russian history: the battle on Lake Chud' and the expulsion of the Poles from Russia. A third panel shows the Moscow Kremlin and the monument to Minin and Pozharskii. The opera closes with a heroic hymn to the glory of Russian military might and the greatness and invincibility of the Russian people.

The key to our resolution of the fundamental issues of this production was found in Glinka's brilliant score. For the set designer, the music suggested a specific style and manner, calling for a reproduction of the Russian countryside in tender, lyric tones. It gave direction to our imagination and prevented us from weighing down the plot or psychologically overburdening any of the separate episodes. Glinka's music steered us toward a grand sweep of passion informed by broad generalizations and high drama. This is a show about profound and noble feelings, about great individuals, and about the magnificent Russian people.

The complexities we encountered in our production of *Ivan Susanin* were so critical and involved that they demanded a new approach to operatic direction and work with designers and actors. For example, we made initial assessments of set designs using a specially constructed model of the stage. This huge model—three meters in length—exactly reproduces the stage of the Bolshoi Theater, including all the mechanical equipment, wings, and lighting. Prior to rehearsals, we used this model to work out preliminary plans for the staging of the opera.

Our dramatic score is yet another innovation for operatic production work. This score presents an exact "photographic reproduction" of the show. It serves to protect the production from future degradation and facilitates the introduction of new performers.

The Soviet operatic theater is experiencing a genuine renaissance. A combination of a demanding audience and new topical subject matter is rendering our operatic art truly dynamic, transforming opera from a magnificent yet ideologically empty spectacle into a profound performance with stirring content. Our strict and just spectator—the Soviet public—will judge the outcome of our work on *Ivan Susanin*.

Ultimately, in our production of the opera *Ivan Susanin*, the working collective of the Bolshoi Theater desires to sing a marvelous song with all of its might about the Russian people—an epic-hero people.

Note

1. B. A. Mordvinov, "'Ivan Susanin' na stsene Bol'shogo teatra," *Pravda*, 7 February 1939, 6.

Mikhail Lermontov

19
Fashioning "Our Lermontov"
Canonization and Conflict in the Stalinist 1930s

ᠵ᠊ DAVID POWELSTOCK

The Stalinist regime inducted pre-revolutionary literary "classics" such as M. Iu. Lermontov (1814–1841) into the Soviet literary canon during the 1930s in an attempt to use tsarist-era culture to legitimize itself both historically and politically. Such a revised narrative of the past represented the Soviet state as a historical inevitability and allowed the regime to flatter its subjects by asserting their right to inherit the pre-revolutionary cultural legacy. Moreover, the canonization process emphasized the cultural superiority of the Soviet regime and people, as evidenced by their ability to discover once and for all a single, correct interpretation of the past. Finally, canonization of the classics helped to forge a coherent identity for the new Soviet society by placing a reinterpreted Russian cultural narrative at its core. All of these aims emphasized unity and unanimity, the distinctive desiderata of high Stalinist social policy.

Leaving behind the divisive politics of the chaotic Cultural Revolution (1928–1932), the regime sought during the mid-1930s to promote a unified political program in many areas of Soviet life, among which culture was especially prominent. The formation of the Soviet Writers' Union (1934) and the conclusion of a campaign against "vulgar sociology" in literary criticism (ca. 1936–1938) reflected the regime's official rejection of class-based attacks on all but a few pre-revolutionary writers.[1] In a startling turnabout, the regime now aimed to build unity in the cultural sphere by mounting massive union-wide celebrations of particular classics deemed worthy of canonization.[2] Although the selection of candidates for rehabilitation took place within the highest echelons of power, it fell to the literary intelligentsia—scholars, journalists, and writers—to produce ideologically "cleansed" interpretations of the individual authors and their works. Their task, it would seem, was crystal clear, the outcome overdetermined. The goals dictated the necessary methods, leaving little room for disagreement: accentuate the positive and eliminate the negative. Ultimately, the banal interchangeability and ideological blandness of the "cleansed" classics that emerged from the 1930s—the revolutionized avatars of such diverse authors as Pushkin, Lermontov, Gogol', and Tolstoi—also suggest a process that was, if anything, too unanimous and glib. Each author was revealed to be a "humanitarian," a true friend of "the people," a critic of bourgeois social vices and injustice, and a "realist." According to the official Stalinist vision, the classic authors emerged as fundamentally sympathetic to the progressive values of the Revolution, despite having had the misfortune of living and writing in the reactionary Russia of the past.

Yet as several contributions to this volume suggest, such a matter-of-fact account of Stalinist cultural processes obscures as much as it reveals. A close examination of Lermontov's canonization shows that the production of these revolutionized classics could be surprisingly contentious and chaotic in ways that had more to do with the political realities of the present than with either the literature of the past or the process of canonization itself. Although conflicts usually remained hidden beneath the surface discourse of such all-Soviet celebrations of unity, traces of these disagreements occasionally surfaced in the public record, at times with explosive hostility. In such instances, arguments nominally concerning literary issues actually reflected deeper political tensions and rivalries, often exacerbated by unstated cultural policies of the regime. These outbursts provide useful insights into the conflicts, concerns, and anxieties that beset the literary intelligentsia and shaped the canonization process during the 1930s.

An Insult to Lermontov's Memory

On 26 July 1937, *Literaturnaia gazeta* observed under its "Literary Calendar" rubric that the following day would mark the anniversary of Lermontov's fatal duel, and quoted at length from an eyewitness account of that event by Prince A. I. Vasil'chikov, Lermontov's friend and one of the seconds.[3] The entry stuck largely to facts and direct quotation, editorializing very little. But this seemingly innocuous little article drew a surprisingly impassioned attack from one P. Litoshenko, a reader from Novocherkassk, whose letter to the editor was published by *Komsomol'skaia pravda* under the provocative title "An Insult to Lermontov's Memory."[4] According to Litoshenko, everyone knew that Vasil'chikov had been a secret enemy of the poet and had "unconscionably distorted reality" in order to "cover the tracks of the crime that he had committed with N. S. Martynov," Lermontov's opponent in the duel. Citing another account of the duel by P. K. Mart'ianov, Litoshenko argued that Vasil'chikov had been known in society as "Prince good-for-nothing" and "the Don Quixote of Jesuitism," and was "one of those who provoked the duel." "And now it is the testimony of this scoundrel—one of Lermontov's murderers—that *Literaturnaia gazeta* cites!" "It is strange," the letter concluded darkly, "that *Literaturnaia gazeta* has passed over other sources in silence and limited itself to a reprint that insults Lermontov's memory."

Literaturnaia gazeta promptly published a response. Conceding that some details of Vasil'chikov's account had been challenged by his contemporaries, the editors of *Literaturnaia gazeta* noted that the section of the account quoted in the original article had been purely factual; moreover, Vasil'chikov's description was the only known eyewitness account of the duel and was generally regarded as more or less accurate.[5] The response added, peevishly, that no one except for *Komsomol'skaia pravda* and Litoshenko had ever seen any "insult to Lermontov's memory" in the cited portions of Vasil'chikov's account.

By any reasonable standard of argument, this should have sufficed to defend the original publication. But these were not reasonable times, and the response in *Literaturnaia gazeta* then escalated into a counterattack. Seizing upon *Komsomol'skaia pravda*'s quotation of Mart'ianov's account, *Literaturnaia gazeta* accused the editors of unwittingly assisting "'readers' such as Litoshenko" in "propagandizing the filthy, slanderous writings of bards of the autocracy." Mart'ianov, after all, had attempted to cover up Nicholas I's hostility toward Lermontov by claiming that the tsar and his family had reacted with sadness to the news of the poet's death. "Is it not clear," asked *Literaturnaia gazeta*, "that this citation of the tsar's lackey Mart'ianov represents the real insult to Lermontov's memory?"[6] Nor was this the end of the matter. *Komsomol'skaia pravda* unleashed yet another volley, signed by one V. Pavlova, accusing *Literaturnaia gazeta* of attempting to "cover [its] tracks,"[7] echoing the language of Litoshenko's original accusation against Vasil'chikov. Pavlova took *Literaturnaia gazeta* to task for its disrespectful treatment of Litoshenko, a respected pedagogue, as well as for its failure to address his original point, for being "intolerant of criticism," and for "raising a clamor" about Mart'ianov in order to "distract attention away from the heart of the matter."

By this point, an uninformed reader would have to be forgiven for wondering exactly what the "heart of the matter" had been in the first place. In the curious vacuousness of the debate, one discerns an unspoken commonality uniting all parties: *Literaturnaia gazeta* and *Komsomol'skaia pravda* were more concerned with discrediting each other than with discussing Lermontov's memory. Indeed, *Komsomol'skaia pravda*'s final sally concluded with a broadside that failed even to mention Lermontov: "It has long been known that *Literaturnaia gazeta* displays the greatest vehemence precisely where it is least necessary. Avoiding direct answers to the question in order to save itself from its own monstrous blunders; hemming and hawing, looking for a way out of its dead-end position—it's not an envious lot! One can only express pity that intolerance of criticism still remains a distinctive characteristic of *Literaturnaia gazeta*."

But what can explain such bitter sarcasm, such acrimony, between two periodicals that were both official party organs, ostensibly united in the goal of promoting the new Soviet culture? And why should this mutual belligerence, whatever its hidden causes, have flared up around Lermontov, a refractory, aristocratic, apolitical Romantic poet? What was at stake in this ardent "defense" of Lermontov and these accusations of "insult" to his memory? If Lermontov's legacy was so vitally important, how is it that the debate unfolded not around his life, personality, or works, but around the obscure figures of Vasil'chikov and Mart'ianov and their alleged roles in his death? Neither newspaper ever even referred to a single one of Lermontov's works! What can explain this fervid hunt for the perpetrators of a century-old "murder," especially given that there was no credible evidence that there had been a murder in the first place?

Part of the answer stems from the exigencies of ideologically cleansing problematic figures such as Lermontov for consumption by the Soviet reading public. Lermontov was a rebellious young man, but his rebelliousness was deeply individualistic, politically incoherent, and intellectually indifferent, if not outright anti-intellectual. The poet was pointedly uninterested in discussions current in the salons of his day. N. P. Ogarev recalled that Lermontov was no philosopher: "he did not seek the answer to life's mysteries, and the explanation of its principles was a matter of indifference to him." Indeed, according to Ogarev, the poet referred to gatherings of a "learned or literary cast" as "literary masturbation."[8] Certain episodes in the poet's biography and oeuvre suggest vengefulness and an almost sadistic cruelty.[9] Lermontov was in almost every way closer to Byron's—or even Childe Harold's—aristocratic Romantic individualism (sans Byron's philosophical and political commitments) than to the progressive democratic sentiments espoused by contemporaries like A. I. Herzen and V. G. Belinskii.[10]

Short on the "raw material" necessary to construct a convincing portrait of the poet as a political progressive, Lermontov's Soviet "handlers" seized upon his run-ins with the tsarist authorities. Lermontov's lack of a political program did not, after all, exempt him from Nicholas's reactionary paranoia or his gendarmes' legendary surveillance. And even if Lermontov had never articulated a political challenge to the regime, his general rebelliousness still earned him two terms of exile to the Caucasus. One such sentence was for dueling. The other came as the result of "The Poet's Death" ("Smert' poeta," 1837), Lermontov's poetic response, elegiac and outraged by turns, to the death of Pushkin. The poem's offense stemmed from its harsh indictment of foreign toadies at court who, the poem asserted, were abusing their positions to cover up various heinous crimes. The poem's epigraph begs the tsar for justice, and for the punishment of Georges D'Anthès, the man who had just killed Pushkin in a duel. During the centennial of Pushkin's death in 1937, Lermontov's poem was tendentiously invoked to support the claim that highly placed members of Petersburg court society, perhaps including the tsar himself, had conspired to bring about Pushkin's duel for political reasons. ("The Poet's Death" falls far short of actually making such a charge, which would have certainly elicited a much harsher sanction than simple exile.) As we have already seen, allegations of Vasil'chikov's perfidy led Lermontov's "handlers" to describe that poet's death in 1941 in similarly conspiratorial terms during the mid- to late 1930s.[11]

Thus, although Pushkin and Lermontov never met, the two poets became allied in the eyes of the canonizers due to the similarity of their fates. By the same token—and via the politically expedient reasoning that "my enemy's enemy is my friend"—they also became allies of the Revolution. The discourse of the Lermontov celebrations in 1939 and 1941 relied heavily on this logic, which encouraged the unmasking of hidden enemies among the poet's supposed friends at the same time that it continuously exaggerated his persecution at the hands of the tsarist authorities. The production of conspiracy theories surrounding Lermontov's death ultimately became something of a cottage industry among both journalists and scholars.

(Indeed, there is a morbid irony in the extent to which the 1939 celebration of the 125th anniversary of Lermontov's birth focused on his demise, despite the imminence of the 100th anniversary of his death, which would be marked by another jubilee less than two years later.)

The genius of this tactic lay in its appeal to the public's taste for the scandalous, the venial, and the dramatic. It was not necessary to be a card-carrying Stalinist to appreciate such a juicy tale of conspiracy.[12] Moreover, this plangent narrative encouraged sympathy for Lermontov's plight, portraying him as a martyr of sorts and forging a bond between reader and poet that did not depend on the ideologically problematic content of his literary works. This emphasis on biography over oeuvre replicated the general pattern of celebrating the classics under Stalin: a given figure first had to be declared worthy, and only then, with the "correct" interpretive conclusion foretold, could the interpretation itself proceed. The 1937 exchange between *Literaturnaia gazeta* and *Komsomol'skaia pravda*, taking place a year and a half before the launch of the official Lermontov campaign, represents an early attempt to identify the "correct" Lermontov while skirting the treacherous territory of his literary and ideological legacy. As the two papers jockeyed for position, neither one strayed far from the safe subject of Lermontov's difficulties with the tsarist regime, each striving to depict itself as the more "vigilant" in uncovering the nature and extent of the plot against Lermontov.

Yet even when the call was sounded for an explicitly ideological characterization of the poet in early 1939, Lermontov's canonizers hesitated in defining the specific nature of his progressivism. This was due in part to the ideological ambiguity of Lermontov's legacy. But a major role was also played by the regime's changing policies in the 1930s, which rendered ideological correctness (*ideinost'*) a moving target. The critical terms of canonization were drifting from the rigid and rigorous criteria of *klassovost'* (class origin) and *partiinost'* (party-mindedness) to considerably more vague and less ideologically precise terms such as "Soviet patriotism," *narodnost'* (orientation toward "the people"), *zhizneutverzhdenie* (life-affirming optimism), and *sovremennost'* (relevance to "our day").[13] This occurred in the context of a general redrawing of social and political battle lines, wherein ideological labels increasingly became axiological ones, virtually stripped of specific meaning. The driving force behind the canonization rhetoric can be identified as the push to define Soviet social identity in terms of the paranoiac dichotomy between "us" and "them." This distinction elided subtler ideological shadings, eclipsed class divisions that had defined Soviet propaganda for two decades, and emphasized loyalty in its rawest, most politically pragmatic sense.

Such terms were ideal for the purposes of canonization, as they were vague enough to allow for the rehabilitation of virtually any well-known pre-revolutionary figure. But if such language was designed to promote unity and consensus, it also worked to erode the value of argumentation in literary discussions, giving rise to debates in which fundamental distinctions ceased to reflect meaningful intellectual disagreement. The "us versus them" principle also implicitly encouraged the hyperbole of the "enemy's enemy" logic, for only when overdefined in this way could the enemy's enemy become not only a friend but—as was frequently claimed regarding Lermontov in the jubilee literature—"one of us," "our Lermontov."[14] Furthermore, whereas earlier political discourse had defined "us" as "the working class" and "the peoples of the Soviet Union," the implied meaning of this rhetoric expanded during the mid- to late 1930s under the influence of terms like *narodnost'* and *sovremennost'* to include a genealogy of "our great ancestors" as well. Figures like Belinskii and Herzen came to be seen as representatives of a shadow culture during the tsarist era that had been "infinitely richer and brighter than the 'culture' of the open defenders of the yoke and exploitation." This retrospectively defined tradition, which "grew on the soil of the defense of the people's interests and was persecuted to the utmost by the tsarist government," was now to be taken as a central component of "our" Soviet culture.[15]

Lermontov's membership in "our" past was established primarily by linking him, however tenuously, to historical figures with less questionable progressive credentials, including Belinskii, Herzen, N. G. Chernyshevskii, and N. A. Dobroliubov. Belinskii was especially important, as he had known Lermontov personally and served as his greatest critical exponent during the poet's lifetime. Soviet readers were repeatedly reminded of Belinskii's characterization of Lermontov, following a visit to him in detention in 1840, as a "great and mighty spirit."[16] Even if ideologically vague, such endorsements sufficed to assert that the poet belonged to "our" tradition, especially when bolstered by his tense relationship with the tsar. Association with "us"—"our" progressive ancestors—thus amplified and complemented dissociation from "them"—"our" ancestors' enemies.

These tactics of association and dissociation were themselves embedded in a strategy that sought to place Lermontov in a Russian progressive tradition, unfolding from A. N. Radishchev to the Decembrists, and then through Belinskii, Herzen, Chernyshevskii, and Dobroliubov to culminate directly (and inevitably) with the Bolsheviks themselves. This was a whiggish history of Russian political thought, a "success stor[y] marching inexorably toward the glorious present with wrong turnings and failures erased."[17] By writing Lermontov into this narrative via his "inspiration" of the so-called revolutionary democrats, canonizers sought to demonstrate his works' "objectively" progressive character and "practical significance for the elimination of the actual causes of social disharmony."[18] Given the poet's lack of participation in revolutionary groups or political debates, the canonizers had to rely here more than ever on vaguely positive terms of praise to assert that Lermontov's "great and mighty spirit" was fundamentally progressive, and that "only external circumstances . . . had isolated Lermontov like a 'Chinese wall' from the 'thinking milieu,' [and] prevented him from organically merging with the leading social movement of the 1840s."[19] Despite their spuriousness, such arguments found favor because they resonated with the foundational myth of Stalinism itself, which framed the party and the New Soviet Man as the organic, inevitable, and triumphant culmination of history.

This revisionist history facilitated a primary goal of canonizing the classics—to root Soviet social identity deeply in Russian national history. It also framed the fight against hidden enemies of the people in the present as the continuation of a struggle already underway in Lermontov's time, thus extending the categories of "us" and "them" into the past as well. Enmeshing Lermontov in this timeless conflict conveniently placed the "tragedy" of his persecution and death in the foreground, ahead of more troubling aspects of his legacy, such as his class origin and political worldview. At the same time, it mandated the unmasking of enemies in the past—the enemies of "our Lermontov"—just as socialist construction in the present necessitated the exposure and elimination of hidden domestic spy rings and "their" insidious conspiracies against the new society.

Other dynamics also linked Lermontov to the present. Indeed the process of canonization revealed that Lermontov's hounding by evildoers had not ended with his death. Instead, the struggle against his enemies became a struggle over his legacy, for if the revolutionary democrats had presciently understood him to be a representative of progress, many of his contemporaries considered him esoteric and "persecuted him like a prophet who had come to deliver a new word to the world."[20] Such pre-revolutionary "bourgeois" critics had not merely misunderstood Lermontov but had "slandered" him. Carrying this polarized narrative forward into the 1930s raised the stakes of interpreting Lermontov in the present, for the canonizers were required to unmask not only the bourgeois slanderers of the past but also those in the present who continued to propagate their lies. This simultaneous application of the "us versus them" principle to both Lermontov's day and the Stalinist 1930s collapsed history into a single, epic struggle between the poet's enemies and his defenders.

Lermontov's canonization thus called less for interpretation of his works than for vigilant defense of his newly confabulated political legacy. Litoshenko ostentatiously assumed this role in his letter to *Komsomol'skaia pravda*. When he accused *Literaturnaia gazeta* of "insulting Lermontov's memory," he based his indictment solely on the notion that Vasil'chikov was the poet's secret enemy and part of a conspiracy to kill him. He produced no specific evidence of Vasil'chikov's enmity, nor did he specifically identify anything in Vasil'chikov's account that might be considered "insulting."[21] Rather, because Vasil'chikov had been labeled as an enemy, his testimony as a whole was suspect—as were the editors who reprinted it in *Literaturnaia gazeta*. In its response, *Literaturnaia gazeta* agreed that Vasil'chikov was an enemy and attempted merely to distinguish between the usable and unusable parts of his account. The paper was not about to defend him or deny the master narrative of conspiracy. On the contrary, its editors readily acknowledged that Vasil'chikov was "one of the co-participants in Lermontov's murder," casually characterizing this fact as "well-known." Indeed, by conceding this, *Literaturnaia gazeta* suggested that *Komsomol'skaia pravda* was merely stating the obvious in its "unmasking" of Vasil'chikov. Moreover, it was *Komsomol'skaia pravda* and Litoshenko who had smuggled a hidden enemy into print: the "tsarist lackey" Mart'ianov. "Is it not clear," the editors of *Literaturnaia gazeta* asked rhetorically, that this represented the "real insult" to Lermontov's memory?

By this point the newspapers had abandoned all semblance of reason, along with any concern for the historical record—or for Lermontov, for that matter. The debate had become a reciprocal exchange of insults, each paper striving to appear more vigilant and to prove that the other publication was defending Lermontov's enemies, and thus "our" enemies. Meanwhile Lermontov's status as "one of us," ordained from on high, had become an absolute ideological constant for both papers, causing the poet and his works to drop out of the discussion, like an expression that appears on both sides of an algebraic equation. The rivals committed themselves instead to repeating empty rhetorical formulas, endlessly producing and affirming the revolutionized Lermontov by whatever means possible in an anachronistic hash of signifiers drawn from both past and present. This ritualistic discourse had little substantive meaning, but it reflected the aspirations, anxieties, and resentments of the Soviet literary establishment at this particular moment in history.

It is often difficult to grasp fully the tensions beneath the surface of the canonization discourse. Unsigned editorials were common, and many of those authors and editors whose names do appear in print are obscure figures, about whom we know very little. What is more, because the canonization process emphasized the production of a single, unquestionable, ideologically cleansed image, internecine disputes such as the 1937 exchange were rarely aired in public. At the first planning session for Lermontov's quasquicentennial in 1939, emphasis was placed on establishing "a comprehensive and precise plan" and on "consolidat[ing] forces," according to *Literaturnaia gazeta*. This "great and complex undertaking," the report continued, "must proceed on the highest level of ideological correctness [*na samom vysokom ideinom urovene*]."[22] A headline in the middle of the page echoed this declaration: "[Let us take] the study of Lermontov to the heights of ideological correctness [*na ideinuiu vysotu*]."[23] The article that appeared under this exhortation reminded readers and fellow critics that "the people want to receive the correct elucidation of Lermontov's works" and that "we must not for a moment forget the responsibility that rests upon us." The sort of bickering that had broken out in 1937 did not befit those who shared such a responsibility.

What, then was at stake in the debate between *Literaturnaia gazeta* and *Komsomol'skaia pravda*? At base, the 1937 exchange suggests a conflict between two distinct and competing models of discursive authority in Soviet public life. The first was that of a political imperative, devoted to the articulation and dissemination of ideologically correct rhetoric. This discursive mode dictated that contributions to the Lermontov campaign carried weight only in so far as they answered the establishment's demand for a usable past and served contemporary state interests, broadly defined. The dominance of the "enemy's enemy" logic in the campaign was a reflection of this base of authority, geared more toward the instrumental construction of political identity by the exclusion of the "impure" from the social body than toward serious inquiry into the poet's biography or works. Those who advanced claims of legitimacy according to this frame of reference amassed political capital precisely by questioning the ideological purity of "others," past and present. Moreover, such dutiful unmasking and denunciation of others likely appeared to diminish the chances of being accused oneself: the best defense was often a good offense. This tendency toward the exaggerated politicization of public discourse clashed with the second model of authority advanced during the canonization process: that of scholarship itself, which aspired to create a historically defensible Soviet vision of the past through the production of verifiable knowledge. To be sure, much of this scholarship was highly partisan and subordinated to the advancement of a political agenda and an overtly whiggish historical narrative.[24] That said, it took a somewhat more restrained and reasoned approach to winning the hearts and minds of Soviet society than the shrill propaganda epitomized by the political mode of popular mobilization.

The tension between these two models of authority may be loosely associated with the generational conflict that divided the Soviet intelligentsia during the Cultural Revolution, pitting young, upwardly mobile cadres educated by the Soviet regime (the *vydvizhentsy*) against older, better trained "bourgeois specialists." Moreover, the persistence of this generational conflict suggests a linkage in general terms of these two models of authority with the two print organs relevant to the episode under analysis here. *Komsomol'skaia pravda* was the newspaper of the Communist Party's youth wing and therefore may be said to represent the voice of the younger generation—a cohort born under Soviet rule, ideologically untainted by the pre-revolutionary past and closely identified with the state's politicized public discourse and brinkmanship. In contrast, *Literaturnaia gazeta*, the official organ of the Writers' Union and the "creative intelligentsia," may be connected with the older generation and its greater affinity for the authority of scholarship and the integrity of historical inquiry. These generational and institutional affiliations should not be exaggerated: if during the Cultural Revolution party authorities had supported the young Turks in their attacks on the "establishment," by the mid-1930s they had put an end to the stand-off and forced them into an uneasy reconciliation under the umbrella of a single, official party line.[25] Furthermore, these two models of discursive authority were not as mutually exclusive as they might appear—Soviet scholarship (especially the publicistic writing published in *Literaturnaia gazeta*) was hardly immune to politicization. Conversely, far from "peddling cant," Soviet propagandists (such as the editors of *Komsomol'skaia pravda*) took their own pronouncements quite seriously, viewing their work as part of a public culture legitimated by the authority of scientific Marxism.

From the 1937 exchange, it is readily apparent that each paper was laying claim to both forms of discursive authority, and that one of the key issues at stake was sorting out the relative weight of instrumental political concerns versus the demands of historical accuracy. Litoshenko accused *Literaturnaia gazeta* of lacking political vigilance. *Literaturnaia gazeta* replied, rather baldly, that the letter writer was himself a reactionary enemy and that the "aims" of such "readers" were "all too clear."[26] But the paper reserved a special barb for the editors at *Komsomol'skaia pravda* responsible for publishing Litoshenko's letter. Not only had these editors been insufficiently vigilant in a political sense, but they were also poorly informed with regard to historical facts. They had been effectively duped by Litoshenko, who sent his letter to *Komsomol'skaia pravda*, "reckoning on the ignorance of some of its editorial workers." In effect, *Literaturnaia gazeta* rested its case only after accusing *Komsomol'skaia pravda* of intellectual incompetence. *Komsomol'skaia pravda*, for its part, took great offense at both the accusations of "ignorance" and of ideological laxity. It denounced *Literaturnaia gazeta* for "taking a high tone" by casting doubt upon Litoshenko's character and for "losing its head from delight in its own cleverness," while "brandishing every possible reference book." Yet readers were also instructed not to mistake *Literaturnaia gazeta*'s counterattack as "disinterested scholarly argument." It was, rather, the editors' effort to "cover their tracks"—to divert attention from their inability to defend themselves against the original charge of political heterodoxy. *Komsomol'skaia pravda* then tried to beat *Literaturnaia gazeta* at its own game by pointing out a major factual lapse committed by its opponent: "Flaunting the most shameless ignorance," an item in *Literaturnaia gazeta* had mistakenly referred to a particular estate as belonging to Lermontov's maternal grandmother, when it had fact been part of his father's estate. "What Pioneers, and indeed all literate citizens of our country know, is beyond the ken of the specialist 'literary scholars' at *Literaturnaia gazeta*." In sum, neither side was willing to cede the other a monopoly on either type of authority, and so each paper attacked the other as both ignorant and politically suspect.

Politicizing the Poet

This tension between political and scholarly authority was to persist in public discourse around Lermontov in subsequent years as the canonization process progressed. Early in 1939 *Literaturnaia gazeta* acknowledged the difference in approaches in a diplomatic manner: "there is nothing bad in the fact that scholarship voices differing views, and that there are fruitful arguments and discussions." "For the mass audience," however, "we must present only that which is indisputable and makes Lermontov dear and close to us."²⁷ In the same issue V. I. Kirpotin, a scholar central to the Lermontov celebrations, acknowledged behind-the-scenes disagreements that some must have found troubling. "Sometimes [in the Gor'kii Institute of World Literature's Lermontov Group] we mercilessly criticize one another," he observed. "In these discussions and arguments we are working out consensus views on Lermontov's works."²⁸ Kirpotin's slightly defensive tone acknowledged the clash of discursive modes that threatened the consensus-building process at the same time that he called upon his colleagues to recognize that there was a time and a place for each approach.

No single individual involved in the Lermontov celebrations exemplified the high stakes and dual imperatives of canonization better than Valerian Iakovlevich Kirpotin. Born in 1898, a party member from 1918, and a 1925 graduate of the Institute of Red Professors, he was one of the first and most successful working-class promotees in the field of literary scholarship. By the 1930s, he occupied several powerful posts in party cultural organizations, including the Soviet Writers' Union and the Literary Sector of the Central Committee, in addition to academic posts at the Communist Academy and the Gor'kii Institute of World Literature.²⁹ During Lermontov's jubilee years, Kirpotin served as a secretary of the Writers' Union, chaired the Gor'kii Institute's Lermontov Group, and headed the 1941 Lermontov Jubilee Committee.

Aside from holding such prestigious posts, Kirpotin played a leading role in developing a comprehensive ideological interpretation of the poet's works. Yet he also issued a call in early 1939 for critical and scholarly "responsibility" in presenting the "correct elucidation of Lermontov's creative work" to the people.³⁰ As a representative of the official line, Kirpotin strove to combine and embody the roles of both scholar and propagandist in his work. Reflecting this imperative, his *Political Motifs in Lermontov's Works* (1939), the first systematic ideological interpretation of Lermontov's works, was published in multiple formats: as an academic monograph (complete with scholarly apparatus), as a long article in the literary journal *Novyi mir* (abridged and without footnotes), and as a highly condensed propagandistic editorial in the popular cultural journal *Rezets* (*The Chisel*).³¹ Kirpotin's efforts and the polemics that they spawned epitomized the objectives and obstacles involved in synthesizing scholarly and politicized approaches to Lermontov.

Kirpotin was a fitting figure to attempt the rapprochement between these discrete discursive styles. As a member of the first generation of *vydvizhentsy*, he had been trained in both pre-revolutionary and post-revolutionary institutions. He had entered the party at the relatively young age of twenty but did not wear the stripes of the doomed Old Bolsheviks or fellow travelers, whom the *vydvizhentsy* were being groomed to replace. At the same time, as an early conscript into official Soviet cultural institutions, he had avoided developing a reputation for shrill ideological rhetoric during the radical debates of the Cultural Revolution. Instead, his was a voice of moderation, and he made it clear that he understood and supported both the values of scholarship and the propagandistic function of the Lermontov celebrations. He also emphasized the importance of inter-generational collaboration in the work he led at the Gor'kii Institute, boasting on one occasion: "Working with us, alongside scholars with established reputations, are young specialists who have already demonstrated their worth in scholarship, as well as youth who will be contributing their first work" to the Lermontov jubilee.[32]

Whatever Kirpotin's qualifications, the reception of his work illustrates the delicate balance entailed by synthesizing scholarly and politicized approaches. Kirpotin's prominence ensured that none of the fellow-traveling members of the "old" intelligentsia would dare disparage his scholarship, even behind closed doors. True, some senior Lermontov scholars such as Sergei Durylin and Boris Eikhenbaum did include ginger but substantive criticisms in their otherwise positive reviews of Kirpotin's work.[33] Yet they generally seem to have appreciated Kirpotin's sincere efforts to grapple directly and systematically with some, if not all, of the difficult ambiguities and contradictions of Lermontov's political outlook. There can be little doubt that Kirpotin likewise valued the opinions of such established professors.

But it was precisely when Kirpotin carried such scholarly nuance into his articles meant for popular consumption that he came under sharp attack from more politically motivated interpreters. The editorial "Lermontov's Historical Significance," published in *Literaturnaia gazeta* a year before *Political Motifs*, can serve as a good example.[34] Kirpotin's piece sought to describe Lermontov's political worldview, explaining why the rebellious poet never articulated a political program like that of revolutionary democrats such as Belinskii and Chernyshevskii. To do this, Kirpotin sketched three stages in the evolution of Lermontov's political worldview. The poet's thinking moved from a stage of "idealist romanticism," in which good and evil engaged in a divinely ordained "eternal irresoluble struggle," and in which people, "regardless of their political and social roles," became an "object of contempt," to a second stage, a "return to earth" and "ideological crisis," in which he was paralyzed by the "helplessness of a personality who fancies himself a titanic warrior for the fullness of life and the victory of the ideal," to a final stage, in which the poet began to recognize that "people, mores and the social structure" are the cause of "evil and injustice." At this point, Lermontov recalled "the social purpose of the poet" as a "prophet," "tribune" of the people, and "exposer" of social and political evils. Kirpotin concluded that during this third period Lermontov's role as social critic, manifested by "the realistic and satirical principle in his work," should be viewed as "essentially . . . the only possible realization of his early dreams."

Critics like M. Rozental' at the highly independent monthly *Literaturnyi kritik* objected to Kirpotin's depiction on four counts.[35] First, they denied that Lermontov had ever "struggled" with God, for struggle implies belief. Second, they disputed Kirpotin's claim that Lermontov's "furious rebellion" against God's world engendered in him "contempt" for the people. Far from being an elitist, Lermontov had actually been a class warrior and had directed his contempt toward "the high-society mob . . . , the aristocracy." Toward "the people, the people of labor," the poet felt only love.[36] Third, the critics rejected Kirpotin's evolutionary account of Lermontov's political views in toto. Denying that Lermontov might have experienced any sort of "ideological crisis" they saw Lermontov's oeuvre as entirely consistent: "the entire pathos of Lermontov's poetry, from start to finish, consists in the merciless exposure of those who are to blame for the misfortune that exists on earth."[37] Fourth, Kirpotin's critics attacked him for undermining Lermontov's propaganda value. With the Soviet mass reader in mind, Rozental' worried that Kirpotin's politically tentative Lermontov "can only introduce confusion and lead to the conclusion that Lermontov's poetry had no practical significance for the elimination of the actual causes of social disorder."[38] Another critic, B. Zan'ko, added that Kirpotin's opinions led to "utterly mistaken conclusions," insofar as they "reconstituted the myths" about Lermontov propagated before the Revolution by bourgeois scholars and failed to reconstruct the poet's "authentic political make-up."[39] Although the attacks in *Literaturnyi kritik* and elsewhere were quite specific about the lapses in Kirpotin's works, every criticism also implied a single overarching political critique: Kirpotin's Lermontov was too ideologically complex, equivocal, and ambiguous for public consumption. Whereas Kirpotin seemed to feel it necessary to apologize for Lermontov's lack of revolutionary engagement and well-defined social program, the scholar's more doctrinaire critics denied that the poet required such a defense in the first place.

Kirpotin responded to Rozental's politicized attacks by stubbornly defending his scholarly investigation of the poet's "worldview" and of "the contradictions in Lermontov's works [and] the fact that the great poet together with his contemporaries failed to discover an immediate and conclusive program for social struggle." He condemned Rozental's views as a "linear and impoverished simplification" of Lermontov's legacy and denied that his own approach in any way "degraded" the poet. Lermontov "expressed the searchings of his time," Kirpotin asserted, citing Belinskii; moreover, there is "nothing shameful" in the poet's failure to find a definitive answer, for "his works did help in finding this answer" through their inspirational influence on the revolutionary democrats. Kirpotin found it incomprehensible that anyone could find in his work grounds for "declaring a campaign 'in defense of Lermontov,'" and rebuffed Rozental's barely veiled charges of "vulgar sociology" and conspiracy. Speaking with the authority of an apparatchik, he characterized Rozental's article as "pretentious and tasteless" and accused its author of "straining with all his might to stand on his tiptoes, in order to reach a height from which he might correct and lecture others."[40] Thus, while Kirpotin briefly addressed some specific criticisms of his work, his response focused on defending the principle of scholarly nuance and decrying *Literaturnyi kritik*'s shrill partisanship.

Literaturnyi kritik probably showed undue recklessness in repeatedly attacking a figure as powerful as Kirpotin, inasmuch as this kind of bellicose rhetoric had gone out of style by the late 1930s and was particularly unwelcome in celebration discourse. What is more, although Rozental' and his journal had played a major role in the savage campaign against "vulgar sociology" in literary studies (ca. 1936–1938), the campaign had been suspended by the time he began firing his salvos at Kirpotin.[41] Of course, Rozental' did not help his case by reviving intergenerational tensions, flagrantly contradicting the party's emphasis on unity with statements to the effect that "genuine prehistoric fossils" still exist, "against whom it is necessary to defend the great Russian poet, whose works represent the legitimate pride of the Soviet people."[42] Irritated with Rozental' and his colleagues, Kirpotin and A. A. Fadeev used their positions as cosecretaries of the Soviet Writers' Union to accuse the *Literaturnyi kritik* group of "anti-party" and "un-Marxist" positions in a secret denunciation to the Central Committee in February 1940.[43] In November of that year the Central Committee declared the journal to be "isolated from readers and [Soviet] literature" and ordered its closure.⁴⁴

If *Literaturnyi kritik* contributed to its own downfall by engaging in rhetorical overkill, Kirpotin's position nevertheless obliged him to accommodate aspects of the more politicized approach to Lermontov. Even as he defended scholarly standards, he quietly adjusted some of his positions as well, as is already apparent in his *Political Motifs*. Here, Kirpotin retained his main thesis that Lermontov was a poet of "enormous political passion," whose "political convictions did not succeed in fully forming," not because of an "absence of political interest," but due to the "circumstances of his time," including his own aristocratic background.⁴⁵ That said, the scholar now backed away from many of his more specific ideological terms and analyses. Instead of "crises" and "stages" he now addressed "motifs," "sentiments," and "feelings" in Lermontov's works, which he took to reflect the poet's political ideas. *Political Motifs* also took advantage of vague and malleable shibboleths that increasingly dominated cultural discourse: *narodnost'*, patriotism, love of freedom, and equality. Finally, Kirpotin simply omitted many passages dealing with especially problematic "contradictions" in Lermontov's worldview from the abridged version of the monograph published for a mass readership in *Novyi mir*.⁴⁶

Kirpotin's last two celebration-era essays about Lermontov, both published in 1941, demonstrated this adoption of politicized discourse even more clearly. A scholarly article arrived at a much more assertive conclusion regarding Lermontov's political commitment and significance than had *Political Motifs* and employed the "enemy's enemy" logic as well:

> Lermontov did not achieve all that he could have; he did not develop to full measure his grand powers. But he did not die in obscurity, or in insignificance. He died accompanied by the hatred of Nicholas and his retinue, as an enemy of the regime. He died as warrior of the progressive camp, as a poet-tribune, as a poet-citizen.⁴⁷

Kirpotin outdid even this stridently political language in *Komsomol'skaia pravda*, concluding that

> the Soviet reader fully shares Lermontov's patriotism, his selfless love for the motherland, his faith in the glorious future of the Russian people, his fraternal feelings toward other peoples connected with the Russians by a common historical fate, his respect for the dignity of a man, regardless of national affiliation and racial origin.⁴⁸

These words appeared in print a day before the German invasion of the USSR on 22 June 1941, an event that would nearly completely eclipse the Lermontov jubilee scheduled for the following month. By this time, all that remained in Kirpotin's writings of Lermontov's "ideological crisis" and "distance from the masses" is a reference to "bitter thoughts about the people's [political] immaturity." Kirpotin had finally acceded to a didactically puerile style of politicized rhetoric. Perhaps it was in recognition of this accomplishment that he was appointed chairman of the 1941 Lermontov Jubilee Commission.[49]

Although Kirpotin succeeded in modulating his views on Lermontov without damaging his career, the Stalinist enemy mindset remained deeply skeptical of self-improvement and personal political transformation. Political identity was seen as the unchanging essence of the individual, awaiting discovery, even in literary criticism, and some of Kirpotin's critics refused to accept the evolution of his views. As an epigraph to a mid-1940 review of *Political Motifs*, Zan'ko quoted from the Russian fabulist I. A. Krylov: "Although you wear a different skin, / Your heart remains the same."[50] S. Ivanov's review of recent literature about Lermontov in 1941 presented a more subtle but no less striking example of this unwillingness to forgive Kirpotin for his earlier sins. Ivanov dedicated nearly a fifth of his review to Kirpotin's work—within which he devoted three times as much space to the brief "Historical Significance" piece as he did to the later and much more substantial *Political Motifs*.[51] What is more, he largely repeated Rozental's and Zan'ko's criticisms of the earlier piece, even though few of these points were relevant to his discussion of *Political Motifs*. Indeed, Ivanov's extensive quotation of the nearly three-year-old article seems to have been intended to embarrass Kirpotin with views that he had quietly discarded. Apparently aware of the risk he was taking with this vein of criticism, Ivanov ended his treatment of Kirpotin's work with a brief congratulatory statement about *Political Motifs* that damned with faint praise. Despite "flaws and several mistakes [that] in some cases derive from Kirpotin's first article," Ivanov wrote, this work "produces a different impression; it is exceptionally valuable."[52]

Such suspicion of self-improvement seems to reflect the same essentialism that lay behind assertions that Lermontov was not only revolutionary in spirit from start to finish, but that to suggest otherwise was an insult. The distinction between "ours" and "theirs" was apparently an eternal one, stretching back to the early nineteenth century. This denial of man's ability to change is surprising, given the doctrinal Bolshevik belief in the perfectibility of human nature. But amid the social paranoia of the 1930s, half-forgotten sins and errors were seen as signs of essential enmity, cleverly hidden but unchanged and unchanging. Of course, rhetorical accusations of disloyalty often had nothing to do with the actual loyalties of the accused. This was especially true in the sphere of culture, where the ideological campaigns and slogans of the moment, even if removed from the actual currency of power, could be invested with political value by means of rhetorical shibboleths. The ideological demands placed on cultural agents, vaguely defined from the outset, could shift very rapidly. Kirpotin's role in the Lermontov jubilees reveals how members of the creative intelligentsia recast their own scholarly autobiographies even as they canonized great names from the Russian national past.[53]

The brief clashes examined here reveal tensions that lurked beneath the officially promoted unanimity of the canonization campaigns. The question of how best to balance scholarly and political imperatives was of central concern to those engaged in updating and cleansing pre-revolutionary figures. The very fact that Lermontov's canonizers struggled with this problem reminds us that scholarship still carried a certain inherent cachet, despite the overwhelming tide of politicization affecting nearly every sphere of Stalinist society. But while the tension between historicizing and contemporizing perspectives represents, even today, a hermeneutic question of great importance and subtlety, the canonizers of the 1930s were not free to address it explicitly (or even implicitly) as a theoretical problem. To do so would have implied the possibility of discrepancy between Soviet historiography and the political exigencies of the Soviet present, thus undercutting the regime's most basic claim to legitimacy. Rather, participants in the canonization process exploited the inherent theoretical difficulties of this delicate balancing act for rhetorical purposes. It was all too easy to leave one's political flank open while attending to scholarly imperatives (like Kirpotin), or vice versa (like Rozental'); and as we have seen, at least some players, jockeying for position in the still relatively new literary institutions, were eager to pounce at the slightest misstep.

At the same time, it is hard not to see in this dynamic an element of Stalinist design. Competition and mutual criticism among participants, if kept within bounds, served as useful channels for the self-policing among the intelligentsia that the regime seems to have encouraged. Peer pressure helped to identify "us" and "them," to correct what could be corrected, and to identify persistent problems requiring attention from the authorities. Meanwhile, the clear official preference for reconciling scholarly and political discourses, rather than emphasizing their divergence, succeeded in containing disagreements within certain bounds of propriety—most of the time. Ultimately, by drawing scholars into political discourse, the canonization of figures like Lermontov precipitated a controlled lustration of existing literary institutions and agents. Resembling the social and political dynamic encouraged by various other Stalinist policies of the period, the canonization of the classics lured the specialized and relatively independent discourse of literary scholarship out into the light of public attention for ritualistic cleansing and selective assimilation.

Notes

1. "Vulgar sociology in literary studies—a system of views stemming from a one-sided interpretation of the Marxist position regarding the class determination of ideology and leading to a simplification and schematization of the historico-literary process." V. V. Kozhinov, "Vul'garnyi sotsiologizm," in *Kratkaia literaturnaia entsiklopediia*, ed. A. A. Surkov, 9 vols. (Moscow: Sovetskaia entsiklopediia, 1962–1978), 1:1062–63.

2. See, for example, Karen Petrone's treatment of Stalinist "celebration culture" and "celebration discourse" in a variety of spheres: *Life Has Become More Joyous, Comrades: Celebrations in the Time of Stalin* (Bloomington: Indiana University Press, 2000). See also the first systematic examination of Maiakovskii's Soviet canonization, which also includes an excellent discussion of the 1937 Pushkin commemoration: Laura Shear Urbaszewski, "Creating the First Classic Poet of Socialist Realism: Mayakovsky as a Subject of 'Celebration Culture,' 1935–1940" (Ph.D. diss., University of Chicago, 2002).

3. "1841 god. Duel' i smert' Lermontova," *Literaturnaia gazeta*, 26 July 1937, 6. Vasil'chikov's alleged perfidy was in part supported by accounts that he served as Martynov's second in the fatal duel. Even if true, this fact in itself is of little import, for the role of second was frequently played by a disinterested yet honorable gentleman of appropriate social status, on whom the mutual combatants could agree. But accounts of the duel differ as to whose second Vasil'chikov really was, if anyone's. See L. M. Arinshtein and V. A. Manuilov, "Duel' Lermontova s N. S. Martynovym," in *Lermontovskaia entsiklopediia*, ed. V. A. Manuilov et al. (Moscow: Sovetskaia entsiklopediia, 1981), 150–54, esp. 152.

4. P. Litoshenko, "Oskorblenie pamiati Lermontova," *Komsomol'skaia pravda*, 20 August 1937, 3.

5. "Oskorblenie pamiati Lermontova ili 'Bum-bum' na stranitsakh 'Komsomol'skoi pravdy,'" *Literaturnaia gazeta*, 26 August 1937, 6. The title is a pun. 'Bum-bum' means something like "hullabaloo," often with implications of sensationalism or scandal-mongering; but, according to *Literaturnaia gazeta*, it was also a pseudonym used by Mart'ianov in reactionary journals. In fact, there were other accounts

of the duel, but presumably the editors at *Literaturnaia gazeta* considered that of N. S. Martynov, Lermontov's victorious opponent, unworthy of mention. Moreover, neither they nor Litoshenko seem to have been aware of the official military investigation file, including the testimony of another second, M. P. Glebov. V. Nechaeva seems to be speaking of these documents in "Novye dannye ob ubiistve Lermontova," *Pravda*, 4 October 1938, 4; and "Novoe o Lermontove," *Pravda*, 29 September 1939, 4. Also see "Delo o poedinke," *Komsomol'skaia pravda*, 14 October 1939, 3. Nechaeva first published parts of the file in "Sud nad ubiitsami Lermontova: 'Delo shtaba otdel'nogo kavkazskogo korpusa' i pokazaniia N. S. Martynova," in *M. Iu. Lermontov: Stat'i i materialy* (Moscow: Gos. sotsekiz, 1939), 16–63. Arinshtein and Manuilov discuss Glebov's testimony in "Duel' Lermontova," 150, 152–53.

6. Other sources attributed to Nicholas caustic words in response to news of Lermontov's passing, e.g., "a dog's death for the dog."

7. V. Pavlova, "Nezavidnaia uchast': 'Literaturnaia gazeta' zametaet␣sledy," *Komsomol'skaia pravda*, 2 September 1937, 3.

8. Foreword to *Russkaia potaennaia literatura XIX stoletiia*, ed. N. P. Ogarev (London: Trübner, 1861), quoted in his *Izbrannye proizvedeniia*, 2 vols. (Moscow: Khudozhestvennaia literatura, 1956), 2:487. This testimony was *never* mentioned in the canonization discourse, although it appeared in an oft-quoted text by a notable revolutionary democrat.

9. See, in particular, his manipulative seduction of Ekaterina Sushkova, as recounted both by the victim and, without remorse, by Lermontov himself: Ekaterina Sushkova [E. A. Khvostova], *Zapiski, 1812–1841* (Leningrad: Academia, 1928); letter to Sasha Vereshchagina, dated Spring 1835, in M. Iu. Lermontov, *Polnoe sobranie sochinenii v shesti tomakh*, 6 vols. (Moscow: Akademiia nauk, 1954–1957), 4:429–32.

10. I argue that Romantic individualism informed Lermontov's life and works from beginning to end in my *Becoming Mikhail Lermontov: The Ironies of Romantic Individualism in Russia* (Evanston, Ill.: Northwestern University Press, 2005).

11. Arinshtein and Manuilov point out that versions of the duel implicating Nicholas I were popular "toward the end of the 1920s and especially in the 1930s and 1940s," but that "no reliable materials supporting such versions have been discovered." However, as these same two scholars dryly observe, these theories' "proponents discerned evidence of the conspiracy in the very absence of documents" ("Duel' Lermontova," 151).

12. Emma Gershtein later made a more systematic, yet nevertheless speculative, argument that Vasil'chikov was Lermontov's "secret enemy." See her *Sud'ba Lermontova* (Moscow: Sovetskii pisatel', 1964), 161–80. With the tact appropriate in dealing with the work of a respected colleague, M. I. Gillel'son remarked in 1981 only that Gershtein's thesis "warrants further study"—see his "Vasil'chikov," in *Lermontovskaia entsiklopediia*, 80.

13. As A. A. Zhdanov declared at the First Congress of the Soviet Writers' Union in 1934, Soviet literature is "the most ideologically correct [*ideinaia*], the most progressive revolutionary literature of all peoples and countries." See Marina Balina,

"Ideinost'—Klassovost'—Partiinost'," in *Sotsrealisticheskii kanon*, ed. Hans Günther and Evgenii Dobrenko (St. Petersburg: Akademicheskii proekt: 2000), 362–76.

14. See, for example, V. Kirpotin, "Nash Lermontov: K 125-letiiu so dnia rozhdeniia," *Komsomol'skaia pravda*, 12 October 1939, 3.

15. This and the immediately preceding quotation: "Iubilei Lermontova," *Literaturnaia gazeta*, 5 October 1939, 1. The piece argued that the USSR had inherited this formerly repressed tradition and was transmitting it to the masses as part of the new, "free" official culture. Accordingly, the Lermontov jubilee "represents a manifestation of the great cultural growth experienced by the happy and free Soviet republics under the leadership of the great party of Lenin-Stalin." Although unsigned, this piece appears to have been written by V. Ia. Kirpotin, a highly placed official in the Writers' Union and prominent member of the Lermontov Jubilee Committee.

16. Even the associative method sometimes demanded historical censorship. Like Ogarev's testimony regarding Lermontov's anti-intellectualism, Belinskii's first, much less felicitous impression of the poet in 1837 was generally avoided. Lermontov and Belinskii were introduced at the apartment of N. M. Satin in Piatigorsk in June of that year. After some small talk—during which the two men discovered that they had both grown up near the provincial town of Chembar—the ever-earnest Belinskii turned the conversation toward the French Encyclopedists and Voltaire in particular. Lermontov "began to answer Belinskii's serious opinions with various jokes," concluding finally, "well, here's what I have to say about your Voltaire ... Were he to appear in our Chembar, not a single decent household would take him on as a tutor." Dumbfounded, Belinskii stared silently at Lermontov for a moment before picking up his hat and leaving in a huff. Satin recalls that in the wake of this scene Belinskii "never referred to Lermontov other than as that *vulgarian* [*poshliak*]." See N. M. Satin, "Otryvki iz vospominanii," in *M. Iu. Lermontov v vospominaniiakh sovremennikov*, ed. V. E. Vatsuro et al. (Moscow: Khudozhestvennaia literatura, 1989), 251. To my knowledge, this episode is mentioned only twice in the jubilee literature: S. Durylin, "Nastoiashchii Lermontov," and D. Blagoi, "Poet i kritik," both in *Literaturnaia gazeta*, 15 October 1939, 4 and 5, respectively. Characteristically, it was scholars, rather than journalists, who raised the episode; journalists tended to ignore such problematic facts entirely.

17. Christopher Kent, "Historiography and Postmodernism," *Canadian Journal of History* 34, no. 3 (1999): 409.

18. "V zashchitu Lermontova!" *Literaturnyi kritik* 9–10 (1938): 74–84, esp. 75.

19. V. Zhdanov, "Revoliutsionnye demokraty o Lermontove," *Pravda*, 14 October 1939, 4. This claim seems to come from Chernyshevskii, who wrote that "Lermontov ... by his independent sympathies, belonged to the new direction, and it was only because he spent the last period of his life in the Caucasus that he could not share the friendly conversations of Belinskii and his friends." Quoted without citation by V. Ia. Kirpotin, *Politicheskie motivy v tvorchestve Lermontova* (Moscow: Khudozhestvennaia literatura, 1939), 166.

20. "Lermontov," *Pravda*, 14 October 1939, 1. In contrast, the enlightened "Soviet reader loves, knows, appreciates the great poet" as no reader ever had.

21. The idea of Vasil'chikov as Lermontov's secret enemy stemmed from two aspects of his testimony, neither quoted in the original article by *Literaturnaia gazeta*. First, Vasil'chikov identified Lermontov's "obstinate and turbulent" character as one factor contributing to the duel. Second, he (like the other seconds) concealed certain details in order to protect Martynov from prosecution. This need not be construed as a sign of conspiracy, however, for such secrecy was part of the dueling code. See *M. Iu. Lermontov v vospominaniiakh*, 466–75, 625–28.

22. "Dve godovshchiny," *Literaturnaia gazeta*, 15 January 1939, 4. *Ideinost'* was a major Soviet desideratum in literary criticism during the 1930s, although its meaning changed over time. At its most neutral, *ideinost'*, as applied to literature, simply referred to the presence of political ideas in a work, as opposed to their absence in the decadent tradition of "art for art's sake." However, the concept of art's "objective function"—the idea that it should be tendentious, that it should influence the reader and thereby manifest social utility—took hold among Russian writers and critics of the nineteenth century even prior to the advent of Marxism. Literary *ideinost'* in its strictest sense, as the explicit and thoroughly intentional ideological tendentiousness of art, came to be fully articulated only with the declaration of normative Socialist Realism in 1934. At this point, the term acquired its adjectival form, *ideinyi*, meaning simultaneously "containing ideas" and "ideologically correct." See Balina, "Ideinost'—Klassovost'—Partiinost'," 367.

23. "Izuchenie Lermontova—na ideinuiu vysotu," *Literaturnaia gazeta*, 15 January 1939, 4. The article is a synopsis of V. Kirpotin's report to a joint meeting of the cultural institutions that would participate in planning the celebrations.

24. Kent contrasts "the Toryism of historicism, history for its own sake, and suspicion of social scientism" with "Whiggism, with its presentist and determinist tendencies." See his "Historiography and Postmodernism," 386.

25. Sheila Fitzpatrick, "Introduction: On Power and Culture," in *The Cultural Front: Power and Culture in Revolutionary Russia* (Ithaca, N.Y.: Cornell University Press, 1992), 10. Article One of the 1936 Soviet Constitution declared the Soviet Union to be "a socialist state of workers and peasants," with the intelligentsia forming a special service stratum (*prosloika*). See Robert C. Tucker, *Stalin in Power: Revolution from Above, 1928–1941* (New York: Norton, 1990), 325. This role required that the intelligentsia be represented by a unified cultural stance.

26. *Literaturnaia gazeta*'s rhetorical flourish of repeatedly placing the word "reader" in quotes suggests that it was either questioning the literacy of *Komsomol'skaia pravda*'s readers or insinuating that Litoshenko's letter was a cover for the editors' own self-serving attack.

27. "Pochetnaia i otvetstvennaia zadacha," *Literaturnaia gazeta*, 15 January 1939, 4.

28. As reported in "Izuchenie Lermontova."

29. V. A. Kalashnikov, "Kirpotin," in *Kratkaia literaturnaia entsiklopediia*, 3:541–42; and "Kirpotin," in *Biographic Directory of the USSR*, ed. V. S. Mertsalov (New York: Scarecrow Press, 1958), 277–78.

30. "Izuchenie Lermontova."

31. Respectively: *Politicheskie motivy v tvorchestve Lermontova* (Moscow: Khudozhestvennaia literatura, 1939); "Politicheskie motivy v tvorchestve Lermontova," *Novyi mir* 10–11 (1939): 306–54; and "Politicheskie motivy v tvorchestve Lermontova," *Rezets: Zhurnal proletarskoi literatury* 19–20 (1939): 22–23.

32. "Izuchenie Lermontova."

33. Boris Eikhenbaum, "V. Ia. Kirpotin. Politicheskie motivy v tvorchestve Lermontova," *Krasnaia nov'* 10–11 (1940): 346–47; S. Durylin, "Slozhnaia i vazhnaia zadacha," *Literaturnaia gazeta*, 10 June 1940, 3. Both reviewers tactfully characterized scholarly flaws in Kirpotin's monograph as minor. Eikhenbaum questioned only one element of Kirpotin's rather dubious chronology. Durylin wondered why certain important works were not treated. If closely pondered, these criticisms seriously undermine the entire structure of the book's argument.

34. V. Kirpotin, "Istoricheskoe znachenie Lermontova," *Literaturnaia gazeta*, 26 August 1939, 4.

35. The first attack was signed by M. Rozental', the editor of the journal: "V zashchitu Lermontova!" *Literaturnyi kritik* 9–10 (1938): 74–84. It seems that Kirpotin also sat on the editorial board of *Literaturnyi kritik*, at least in name, but I have found nothing to suggest a concrete personal or professional cause for their enmity, beyond ideological differences and institutional competition. Kirpotin defended himself in "Moi otvet M. Rozentaliu," *Literaturnaia gazeta*, 5 January 1939, 4. Later, in a review of *Political Motifs*, published in the "Readers' Comments" section over the name of B. Zan'ko (identified as "a middle-school teacher in Vinnitskii province"), *Literaturnyi kritik* renewed its vicious campaign against Kirpotin: "Lermontov v obrabotke V. Kirpotina," *Literaturnyi kritik* 3–4 (1940): 209–22. Zan'ko argued that "under a new guise ('political motifs') Kirpotin has presented his old vulgarizing theory about Lermontov" (222).

36. Rozental', "V zashchitu Lemontova!" 79.

37. Ibid., 76. Rozental' and especially Zan'ko invoked an interesting theory to explain away any notion of crisis, doubt, or pessimism in Lermontov's worldview. Rozental' laid the groundwork by asserting, with reference to Belinskii, that the poet's sadness arose out of the conflict between the status quo and Lermontov's "terrible thirst for life, his great love for everything earthly and genuinely human, his enormous longing for life." Thus Kirpotin's interpretation of this contradiction—casting Lermontov's pessimism as a phase to be overcome—"sucks the living soul out of the poet, the very basis of his works" (ibid., 80–81; see also B. Eikhenbaum, "Nenavist' iz liubvi," *Leningradskaia pravda*, 15 October 1939, 4). Thus in the eyes of *Literaturnyi kritik*, Kirpotin's interpretation marked him as another of Lermontov's murderers! Rozental' and Zan'ko correctly understood that in order for the poet to serve as a symbol of Soviet society, it was necessary somehow to obfuscate or rationalize the pessimism, disillusionment, and loneliness that pervade Lermontov's works. By the autumn of 1939, Lermontov's "love of life" and "affirmation of life" (*zhizneutverzhdenie*) had entered the poet's canonical image as a central feature, eclipsing all others. For a particularly florid treatment of this type, see P. Antokol'skii, "Zhivoi Lermontov," *Pravda*, 14 October 1939, 4.

38. Rozental', "V zashchitu Lermontova!" 75.
39. Zan'ko, "Lermontov v obrabotke V. Kirpotina," 210, 215, 222.
40. Kirpotin, "Moi otvet M. Rozentaliu."
41. Rozental' authored the screed *Protiv vul'garnoi sotsiologii v literaturnoi teorii* (Moscow: Khudozhestvennaia literatura, 1936).
42. Rozental', "V zashchitu Lermontova!" 74.
43. A. A. Fadeev and V. Ia. Kirpotin, "Ob antipartiinoi gruppirovke v sovetskoi kritike," published in *Vlast' i khudozhestvennaia intelligentsiia: Dokumenty TsK RKP(b)-VKP (b), VChK-OGPU-NKVD o kul'turnoi politike. 1917–1953 gg.*, ed. A. N. Iakovlev, A. Artizov, and O. Naumov (Moscow: Demokratiia, 1999), 440.
44. "V Tsentral'nom komitete VKP(b): O literaturnoi kritike i bibliografii," *Partiinoe stroitel'stvo* 22 (1940): 62–64.
45. Kirpotin, "Politicheskie motivy," 306.
46. Most of the passages that Kirpotin (or his editors) cut were likely to raise questions regarding the ideological correctness of his interpretation of Lermontov. These included treatments of the vagueness of Lermontov's political ideas, his imitation of Byron, his nostalgia and pessimism, his Romantic idealism, his mixed feelings about Pushkin, his elitism and Romantic individualism, and his lack of engagement with the democratic intellectuals of his generation. Some of the omissions can be seen as addressing the criticisms of Rozental' and others.
47. V. Kirpotin, "Nevedomyi izbrannik," in *Zhizn' i tvorchestvo M. Iu. Lermontova: Sbornik pervyi—issledovaniia i materialy*, ed. N. L. Brodskii, V. Ia Kirpotin, E. N. Mikhailova, and A. N. Tolstoi (Moscow: Khudozhestvennaia literatura, 1941), 39.
48. V. Kirpotin, "Mikhail Iur'evich Lermontov (K 100-letiiu so dnia gibeli)," *Komsomol'skaia pravda*, 21 June 1941, 3.
49. For a fascinating firsthand account of Kirpotin's vigilant execution of this role, see Emma Gershtein, *Memuary* (St. Petersburg: Inapress, 1998), 292–93. Kirpotin ordered Gershtein to take down a display in which Lermontov was surrounded by the obscure freethinkers known to scholars as the "The Circle of Sixteen" and replace it with the poet flanked by well-known revolutionary democrats. "What are all these aristocrats doing here?" Gershtein reports him as saying. "Where is Belinskii? Where is Herzen? Where is *Notes of the Fatherland?*"
50. Zan'ko, "Lermontov v obrabotke V. Kirpotina," 209.
51. S. Ivanov, "Noveishaia literatura o Lermontove (Kriticheskii obzor)," *Novyi mir* 7–8 (1941): 203–18. Kirpotin's works are discussed on 211–14.
52. Ibid., 214.
53. Kirpotin's later fate illustrates how fragile a scholarly career could be. As both a Jew and an erstwhile comparativist, he fell victim to the jingoistic and anti-Semitic campaign against "cosmopolitanism" of the late 1940s, even though he himself helped launch the campaign. Publicly denounced, he was dismissed from his posts as professor and assistant director of the Gor'kii Institute in 1949. His professorship was restored in 1956, and he remained highly respected until his death in 1990. On this campaign, see Konstantin Azadovskii and Boris Egorov, "From Anti-Westernism to Anti-Semitism," *Journal of Cold War Studies* 4, no. 1 (2002): 66–80.

20
A Rare Voice of Caution

This book review appeared in 1939 on the eve of celebrations marking the 125th anniversary of Lermontov's birth and is remarkable for its dissonant tone. At a time when canonizers were straining to fit Lermontov into a palatable ideological model (primarily by declaring him a "poet of the people"),[1] A. Ragozin dared to challenge the promiscuous application of this title. He did so in *Pravda*, no less.[2]

The book under review, S. Ivanov's *Lermontov*, is a thick and tendentious hash of fact and fiction written by an incompetent, prolific hack. Boris Eikhenbaum took Ivanov to task not only for filling his putatively scholarly tome with "invention" more appropriate to a "biographical novel" but also for plagiarizing all of this material from Eikhenbaum's own, explicitly fictionalized children's biography of Lermontov![3] (Ironically, Ivanov had written a negative review of Eikhenbaum's book, criticizing it for presenting an "incorrect," i.e., insufficiently heroic, image of the poet.[4]) Two years later, Ivanov fared little better when he published another biography of Lermontov. Although this new book won third prize in a competition sponsored by the All-Union Lermontov Committee in 1941, it was competing against a field of submissions that was apparently so weak that the jury declined to award either a first or a second prize at all.[5]

Ragozin's 1939 *Pravda* piece is of interest for its open espousal of liberal humanistic values and its candid assessment of the boilerplate rhetoric often employed in Bolshevizing the classics. It may also serve as an epitaph for Ragozin himself, who was arrested shortly after it was published.[6]

A. Ragozin, "In the Poet's Defense"

Pravda, 25 August 1939

Almost a hundred years have passed since Lermontov's tragic death, and to this day we do not have a single major, exhaustive study of his life and oeuvre. The works of Viskovatyi and Kotliarevskii, which appeared at the end of the last century, are hopelessly outdated.[7] And no substantial new works have appeared.

Is it even necessary to say how greatly such a study is needed? Millions of people love Lermontov. They read and reread him. They want to know more about his life. This interest will only grow with the approach of the 125-year jubilee of the poet's birth (in October of this year) and the 100th anniversary of his death (in 1941).

And now, finally, the long-awaited *Lermontov* has appeared. Or so it would seem. S. Ivanov's work appears as part of the "Lives of Remarkable People" series.[8] Three hundred pages of text, a chronology, bibliography, and index—all of this might lead one to believe that a valuable contribution has been made to the Lermontov literature, as the expression goes.

Alas! Upon closer inspection, this contribution turns out to be counterfeit.

For a number of years there existed in Soviet literary studies something called the school of "vulgar sociology."[9] The followers of this school hunted in every writer's works for blatant reflections of the interests of one or another social class or stratum, and nothing else. The greatest Russian writers were declared to be nothing more than mouthpieces for the provincial gentry or the educated service class.

Now the vulgarizers have abruptly switched to a new front. They liberally shower the title "writer of the people" on authors and describe each and every one of them with exactly the same words: "he loved the many-millioned masses," "he hated the autocracy," "he suffocated under tsarism," "he couldn't find a way out."

To be sure, Russian writers, as genuine artists and thinkers, felt a connection with the people, loved the people, and hated the autocracy. But each writer experienced these feelings in his own particular way and expressed them according to his own individual artistic means. Herein lies the scholar's task: to penetrate the epoch, the milieu, the confluence of class interests and various ideological influences in order to reveal the individual world of the artist—to capture the uniqueness of his worldview, artistic manner and style; to make sense of the intricate complexity of his hopes, strivings, and mistakes. Any time the scholar attempts to "improve" the writer, to select from his work only those passages and thoughts that accord with the scholar's taste, he simply vulgarizes and impoverishes the writer's image.

Ivanov's book is a case study in the vulgarization of a poet's image. It is essentially the biography of an officer who occasionally scribbled verses, but in no way is it the biography of a great writer. Ivanov presents all the external facts of Lermontov's life: his relations with his relatives, his love affairs, his career in the service, his duels. He vividly describes the officer's uniform of the Nizhnii Novgorod Dragoon Regiment and gives the dates when various works were written. But the most important thing is missing: the book tells nothing of the evolution of the writer's worldview, of his anxious quest for truth, of his joy of discovery. Ivanov expresses the entirety of the poet's rich worldview with standard formulas: he "hated" this, "struggled" against that, "condemned" this, "protested" against that, and so on. Amid all these impersonal clichés, one barely recognizes the living, inimitable image of Lermontov.

The only way to understand a writer is to understand his works. In a book about Lermontov it is unthinkable to limit oneself to cursory or superficial analyses of works like *The Demon* or *A Hero of Our Time*. It is in precisely these works that the poet's entire system of thoughts, feelings and attitudes found their fullest and clearest expression.

But the Demon himself is not to Ivanov's taste: "The incorporeal spirit of evil is not entirely convincing." How is one to understand this profound observation? Does it mean that Lermontov has failed to convince his biographer of the actual existence of his incorporeal spirit of evil? Or that in the Demon's shoes, Ivanov would have acted differently?

Ivanov is not satisfied with *A Hero of Our Time* either. "Pechorin came out insufficiently tragic," he laments. "He has too little passion, no genuine feelings." It goes without saying that no writer will ever satisfy every reader in the world. There will always be readers who find this or that character insufficiently tragic or insufficiently cheerful. But a literary scholar ought to understand that Pechorin "came out" as he did precisely because Lermontov intended to depict in him a contemporary character, a hero of his time and not some villain in a melodrama.

There is no need to reproduce here Ivanov's dubious commentary concerning other examples of Lermontov's works.

But perhaps Ivanov's book is useful for its presentation of factual information? By way of an answer let us examine two passages.

Speaking of the Stankevich and Herzen circles, the author states: "It was precisely these circles that gave rise to the glorious men of the 'forties, not only Lermontov and Belinskii, but also Herzen, Chernyshevskii, and Dobroliubov."[10] One has a hard time picturing Chernyshevskii and Dobroliubov as participants in these circles, if only because Chernyshevskii was five years old at the time and Dobroliubov had yet to be born.

Regarding *The Song of the Merchant Kalashnikov*, the poet's biographer notes that "Lermontov made extensive use of folk *bylinas*, Kirsha Danilov's anthologies, Afanas'ev's fairytales and Karamzin's *History of the Russian State*." This single sentence is triply bewildering. Karamzin's history was not used "extensively;" it was barely used at all. Kirsha Danilov's "anthologies" do not exist—there is only a single anthology. Afanas'ev's fairytales could not have been used, inasmuch as Afanas'ev was a twelve-year-old boy at the time, and his collection of fairytales was first published fourteen years after Lermontov's death.[11]

It is not necessary to provide further examples before asking what is going on here. Are these misprints, innocent mistakes, or the result of simple ignorance?

S. Ivanov's *Lermontov* trivializes the image of a Russian writer of genius. It's a shame that "Molodaia gvardiia" rushed this manuscript into print.[12]

Notes

1. On the use of *narodnost'* (an orientation toward "the people") in Lermontov's Soviet canonization, see chapter 19 in this volume.

2. A. Ragozin, "V zashchitu poeta," *Pravda*, 25 August 1939, 4. The piece's appearance in *Pravda* may have been due to S. A. Tregub (b. 1907), the assistant head of the paper's department of literature and art. In 1940, V. Ia. Kirpotin and A. A. Fadeev accused Tregub of patronizing members of the "anti-party" *Literaturnyi kritik* group, which apparently included Ragozin. See "Ob antipartiinoi gruppirovke v sovetskoi kritike," in *Vlast' i khudozhestvennaia intelligentsiia: Dokumenty TsK RKP(b)-VKP (b), VChK-OGPU-NKVD o kul'turnoi politike, 1917–1953 gg.*, ed. A. N. Iakovlev, A. Artizov, and O. Naumov (Moscow: Demokratiia, 1999), 439–44. See also I. I. Petrova, "Tregub, Semen Adol'fovich," in *Kratkaia literaturnaia entsiklopediia*, ed. A. A. Surkov, 9 vols. (Moscow: Sovetskaia entsiklopediia, 1962–1978), 7:607.

3. "Either S. Ivanov is so little versed in the literature about Lermontov that he fell, so to speak, into a trap, or he simply used my story, wishing to embellish his book with details he found to his liking." B. Eikhenbaum, "Novaia biografiia Lermontova," *Literaturnoe obozrenie* 22 (1939): 45–47.

4. S. V. Ivanov: "'Lermontov' Eikhenbauma," *Literaturnaia gazeta*, 15 August 1937, 4.

5. See "Zakonchilsia konkurs na populiarnuiu biografiiu M. Iu. Lermontova," *Pravda*, 19 March 1941, 6; "Konkurs na biografiiu Lermontova," *Izvestiia*, 19 March 1941, 4.

6. Ragozin was arrested between 25 August 1939 and 10 February 1940. The latter is the date of Fadeev's and Kirpotin's denunciation of the *Literaturnyi kritik* group, which mentions Ragozin's "recent" arrest in passing. See "Ob antipartiinoi gruppirovke v sovetskoi kritike," 439.

7. N. A. Kotliarevskii, *Mikhail Iur'evich Lermontov: Lichnost' poeta i ego proizvedeniia* (St. Petersburg: M. M. Stasiulevich, 1915); P. A. Viskovatyi [Viskovatov], *Mikhail Iur'evich Lermontov: Zhizn' i tvorchestvo*, vol. 6, *Sobranie sochinenii M. Iu. Lermontova* (Moscow: V. F. Rikhter, 1889–1891).

8. The pre-revolutionary series "Lives of Remarkable People" had been revived by Gor'kii in 1933.

9. On "vulgar sociology" in literature, see chapter 13 in this volume. Attacks against this "tendency" in literary studies ran parallel to a similar campaign against the Pokrovskii "school" in history—see chapter 3.

10. Semi-legal salon circles during the 1830s and 1840s that discussed European philosophical trends and debated the relevancy of such "democratic" ideas to Russian society.

11. N. M. Karamzin, *Istoriia gosudarstva rossiiskogo* (St. Petersburg: Voennaia tipografiia Glavnogo shtaba, 1816–1829); *Drevnie russkie stikhotvoreniia*, ed. Kirsha Danilov (Moscow: S. Selivanovskogo, 1804); *Narodnye russkie skazki*, ed. A. N. Afanas'ev (Moscow: V. Grachev, 1855–1863).

12. Ragozin implies here that the book was rushed to press in order to appear in time for the Lermontov jubilee.

Epilogue

21
An Internationalist's Complaint to Stalin and the Ensuing Scandal

As the contents of this volume have argued, Russian national heroes, imagery, and iconography were deployed during the mid-to-late 1930s to enhance the effectiveness of Soviet propaganda, despite the fact that this strategy threatened to eclipse the stress on internationalism and class-consciousness that had characterized nearly two decades of Soviet mass culture. Celebrations of Russian history and the arts that were only moderately unorthodox, like the events marking the 1937 commemoration of Pushkin's death, quickly gave way to more explicitly russocentric propaganda revolving around Peter the Great, Aleksandr Nevskii, and even Ivan the Terrible.

In hindsight, this approach to propaganda was perhaps not an unreasonable way to court and mobilize a society whose members were often too poorly educated to grasp the abstract, philosophical dimensions of Marxism-Leninism. That said, the volte-face surprised many observers abroad, from Nicholas Berdiaev to *Sotsialisticheskii vestnik* critic Vera Aleksandrova.[1] At home, although a few Old Bolsheviks raised their voices in protest, more opposition to the new line emanated from members of the left-leaning creative intelligentsia.[2] As noted in previous chapters, executives at the Leningrad film studios attempted to rein in the triumphalism of V. M. Petrov's and A. N. Tolstoi's *Peter I*, while others attacked S. M. Eisenstein's and P. A. Pavlenko's *Aleksandr Nevskii*. Projects like S. Sergeev-Tsenskii's Crimean War novel *The Ordeal of Sevastopol'* and A. E. Korneichuk's play *Bogdan Khmel'nitskii* likewise faced dogged criticism from behind the scenes in 1937–1938.[3] But perhaps the most articulate domestic critique of this ideological turnabout is to be found in a personal letter that was addressed to Stalin by the literary critic V. I. Blium in January 1939.

Although not an Old Bolshevik, Vladimir Ivanovich Blium was a veteran of the Soviet order. A party member and journalist since mid-1917, Blium acquired the reputation of a diehard radical during the Civil War and early 1920s while editing *Teatral'nyi vestnik* and *Novyi zritel'*. During the second half of the 1920s, Blium served in organizations like the RSFSR's Main Repertory Committee, where he did his best in 1926 to prevent the Moscow Art Theater from staging M. A. Bulgakov's *The Days of the Turbins*, a play he referred to as "a blatant apology for the White Guards."[4]

After the reorganization of the arts in the early 1930s, Blium worked in the Dramaturgy Section of the Soviet Writers' Union and the Group Committee of Playwrights (Gruppkom dramaturgov), where he grew increasingly frustrated over the priorities the party was pursuing in its search for a usable past. By the late 1930s, he had apparently had enough and spoke out at a December 1938 meeting of the Dramaturgy Section against the proliferation of patriotic mobilizational plays like Korneichuk's *Bogdan Khmel'nitskii* and K. Finn's and M. Gus's *Keys to Berlin*, which he felt were inappropriate for socialist audiences.[5] Invoking M. N. Pokrovskii's famous maxim that "history is politics projected into the past," Blium denounced the Soviet rehabilitation of tsarist-era heroes as ideological heresy.[6] About three weeks later, Blium rose to his feet again at a meeting of the Critics' and Theater Specialists' Section of the All-Union Theatrical Society to attack the film *Aleksandr Nevskii* in addition to the plays by Korneichuk and by Finn and Gus, comparing them all to tsarist propaganda under Nicholas II.[7] Such inflamatory rhetoric precipitated the publication of several articles in *Literaturnaia gazeta* and *Vecherniaia Moskva* during January 1939 that rebuked him in no uncertain terms for his apparent lack of patriotic sensibilities. A. V. Shestakov was even recruited to refute Blium's erroneous invocation of Pokrovskii's discredited formula and to reproach him for his failure to appreciate the nature of the new historical line.[8] Shortly thereafter, Blium lost his seat on the Dramaturgy Section and was formally censured for his stubborn refusal to conform to official positions.[9]

Insulted by this treatment at the hands of his erstwhile colleagues and convinced of the waywardness of Soviet mass culture, Blium appealed his case both to the Party Control Commission and to Stalin himself. In the latter letter, which is reproduced below, Blium detailed his principled objections to the emerging populist line.[10] He also enclosed copies of lengthy reviews he had written concerning *Bogdan Khmel'nitskii* and *The Keys to Berlin*, which assail these plays for a lack of anything resembling communist idealism or proletarian internationalism.[11]

Although it is unclear whether Stalin himself ever read Blium's missive, it did elicit a swift response from high-ranking ideological authorities. On Zhdanov's orders, Blium was summoned to Agitprop in mid-February 1939 for a thorough dressing-down. Despite such unusual measures, however, Blium proved unwilling to abandon his doctrinaire internationalist position. Perhaps due to this recalcitrance, he continued to be pilloried in the press during the following months. Intriguingly, an article in *Vecherniaia Moskva* on 8 May 1939 revealed that he was just one of a number of critics who were resisting the new orientation of Soviet propaganda.[12] This backlash culminated in an August 1939 Central Committee resolution that denounced communist-idealists like Blium for their inability to differentiate between a historically grounded sense of Soviet patriotism and the knee-jerk jingoism of the tsarist period.[13] This resolution can be seen as the apogee of the party hierarchs' efforts in 1939 to silence opposition to their new ideological pragmatism. Blium's letter, in turn, illustrates the discomfort with which communist-idealists viewed the party hierarchy's decision to rehabilitate elements of the Russian national past.

Letter to Stalin

Moscow, 31/I-39
Most Esteemed Iosif Vissarionovich!
Some time ago, the party leadership stimulated a strong interest in the study of history within Soviet society by issuing several valuable instructions that were to provide for the Marxist character of future Soviet historical philosophy.[14] At the time, one of these instructions seemed to be especially critical in importance and well grounded in scientific principle—the one concerning the role of the progressive moment in the struggle of conflicting historical forces.

However, as is frequently the case for us, "excesses" immediately became apparent in the realization of this slogan—in journalism, criticism, art and public opinion—and the path of least resistance gained the upper hand. An absolutely nondialectical approach now governs the question of progressive forces in the historical past. The valuable and scientific theoretical tenets of these instructions have been simplified, vulgarized and perverted, sometimes to the point that they become unrecognizable or contradict one another.

In connection with all of this, the character of Soviet patriotism has also been distorted and nowadays is sometimes beginning to display all the characteristics of racial nationalism. It seems to me that this situation is all the more serious because people of the new generations—those who have grown up within the context of Soviet culture and who have never "seen" for themselves the bourgeois patriotism of the Guchkovs, Stolypins and Miliukovs[15]—simply cannot differentiate between these two sorts of patriotism.

This all began (that is, in the arts, and in particular, in dramaturgy) with a search for "our" heroes of the bygone ages, a hasty, blind search for historical "analogies." Publishing houses and the All-Union Committee for Artistic Affairs are interested in all kinds of "anti-Polish" and "anti-German" material,[16] and authors are throwing themselves at the task of fulfilling this "social commission."

All this is going on despite that fact that, as E. Genri has noted, *anti-Polonism* is a Ukrainian fascist tendency, and despite the fact that we witnessed an *anti-German* character within our White Guard counter-revolutionary movement![17]

People of your and my generation matured in the midst of the struggle for internationalist ideals, and we are not capable of harboring animosity toward other races and peoples. We will always count as "our own" the Polish peasant, Copernicus, Mickiewicz, Chopin, Heine, Helmholtz, Curie-Sklodowska, the German worker, Kant, Beethoven, and many, many others.[18] This is the basis of your teachings on nationality.

But during a discussion I recently initiated on historical drama,[19] I personally collided with the widespread but unacknowledged contradiction between the propagandizing of bourgeois, racial patriotism and the patriotism that we've learned from the enlightened minds of the past, the party, and from you yourself.

This contradiction torments me, tearing me apart with doubt, and I am sure that I am not the only one who feels this way.

Today's report about Bartlett's article in the *News Chronicle* was profoundly moving and it cheered me up, as it undoubtedly has the character of some sort of an oblique, veiled "official communiqué" about the essence of your wise and genuinely internationalist foreign policy. . . .[20] This article must really frustrate and stymie our newfound German-, Polish- and Japanese-eating cannibal-crusaders and the like, with their pseudo-socialist racism! . . . They don't understand that we ought to beat the fascist enemy not with his own weapon (racism), but with one that is far superior—internationalist socialism.

Alien, bourgeois chords have begun to resonate audibly throughout our young Soviet culture—so much so that people of my generation feel 24 years "younger," recalling 1914's idealistic mood and the sloganeering in the legal press, literature and the arts![21]

Such are the fruits of the vulgarization and perversion of the party's instructions and directives.

As a critic and a specialist in the arts, I believe the new Soviet dramaturgy on historical themes falls into my orbit of expertise. And I believe it has to be said that this agitation does not resemble our own socialist mobilizational literature so much as it displays all the telltale signs of the bourgeois and racist Kadet[22] mobilizational literature from 1914.

As an illustration of this situation, I am taking the liberty of sending to you my reviews of two typical examples of contemporary historical drama (which I did for the Dramaturgy Section of the Soviet Writers' Union).[23] From them, you will see how far nowadays minds are sometimes "wandering. . . ." Note in particular with regard to these plays: one of them, which the Malyi Theater is preparing to stage as a present to the Eighteenth Party Congress, is from the pen of a deputy in the Supreme Soviet;[24] the other has won the approval of the [All-Union] Committee for Artistic Affairs. All of this can only increase the dosage and effect of the racist, chauvinist poison that they contain.

Dear Iosif Vissarionovich, I would be grateful if you would agree with me that the issues that I have raised require *a word or two from you*, in whatever style and form that you, with your characteristic insightfulness, deem to be the most appropriate, precise and comprehensive.

I have bypassed all the normal ideological authorities in order to appeal directly to you with my confusion because what is in my view an unhealthy current in the Soviet patriotic mood scandalously contradicts, first and foremost, your theories on the national question. Likewise, it contradicts the general resonance of our stunning third Five-Year Plan and the victorious development of the cultural revolution.

Or am I mistaken? Is there something that I haven't taken into account?

With communist greetings,

[signed:] V. Blium, member of the Soviet Writers' Union

address: Moscow, 19. Frunze St., no. 13, apt. 64

tel. 2.99.22[25]

To Central Committee Secretary Comrade A. A. Zhdanov

Memo[26]
re: No. 57214.[27]

Com[rade] V. Blium was summoned to the Central Committee's Department of Propaganda and Agitation. He believes that Pokrovskii's thesis—"history is politics projected back into the past"—is erroneous only in relation to history, and that it is fully applicable to the arts. On the basis of this incorrect assumption, V. Blium believes that all works of Soviet art connected with historical themes—the films *Aleksandr Nevskii* and *Peter I*, the opera *Ivan Susanin*, the play *Bogdan Khmel'nitskii*, and others—illuminate historical events in a distorted way, twisting them to fit contemporary events.

This erroneous thesis that Blium has applied to the arts was criticized in a special article by Prof. Shestakov as well as in an array of other articles published in *Literaturnaia gazeta*.

V. Blium does not agree with this fair critique of his incorrect thesis.

V. Blium believes that propaganda in the arts promoting Soviet patriotism is being replaced by propaganda promoting racism and nationalism at the expense of internationalism; he mentions A. Korneichuk's *Bogdan Khmel'nitskii* as an example.

V. Blium denies the progressive significance of Ukraine's liberation from the rule of the Polish nobles and its unification with Russia. He sees this historical fact in a one-sided way in which Ukraine was liberated from oppression by Poland only to fall under the yoke of tsarist Russia.

In Blium's opinion, Khmel'nitskii cannot be represented in the arts from a more positive angle due the fact that the real, historical Khmel'nitskii suppressed peasant uprisings and organized Jewish pogroms. Here, again, Blium takes a one-sided approach to characterizing Khmel'nitskii.

It might, of course, be possible to agree with V. Blium if this were simply a matter of individual shortcomings of the above-mentioned works of art, or a matter of calling attention to and correcting these shortcomings by means of discussion and criticism. But V. Blium rejects in principle the very idea and intent that lie behind the above-mentioned works of art in the form in which they have been presented to the viewer.

Finally, V. Blium is puzzled about why there is so much talk these days about the historic power of Russian military might, insofar as it served as a means of conquering and oppressing other peoples. Again, he chooses to see only one side of the past, not taking into account the significance of the Russian people's struggle for their independence with armed invaders from abroad.

The erroneous nature of V. Blium's theoretical propositions was explained to him at the Central Committee's Department of Propaganda and Agitation, as was the erroneousness of his conclusions regarding the Soviet arts' use of historical thematics. V. Blium refused to accept this explanation.[28]

Consultant of the Central Committee's
Department of Propaganda and Agitation
[signed:] V. Stepanov[29]
16/II-39.

Notes

For the Russian-language version of this set of documents, see D. L. Brandenberger and Karen Petrone, "'Vse cherty rasovogo natsionalizma . . . ': Internatsionalist zhaluetsia Stalinu (ianvar' 1939 g.)," *Voprosy istorii* 1 (2000): 128–33.

1. Nicolas Berdyaev, *The Origin of Russian Communism*, trans. R. M. French (London: Centenary Press, 1937), 171–77; V. Aleksandrova, "Ideologicheskie metamorfozy," *Sotsialisticheskii vestnik*, 27 April 1937, 14.

2. See, for example, E. Iaroslavskii, "Nevypolnennye zadachi istoricheskogo fronta," *Istoricheskii zhurnal* 4 (1939): 4–5; "K 120-letiiu so dnia rozhdeniia N. K. Krupskoi," *Izvestiia TsK KPSS* 3 (1989): 179.

3. On Sergeev-Tsenskii, see V. Surganov, "Slovo o Fedore Panferove: K 90-letiiu so dnia rozhdeniia," *Moskva* 10 (1986): 194; S. Sergeev-Tsenskii, "Sevastopol'skaia strada," *Oktiabr'* 7–9 (1937); 1–3 (1938); on Korneichuk, see Serhy Yekelchyk, *Stalin's Empire of Memory: Russian-Ukrainian Relations in the Soviet Historical Imagination* (Toronto: University of Toronto Press, 2004), 20–21.

4. "Vypiska iz protokola soveshchaniia Glavnogo repertuarnogo komiteta s predstaviteliami MKhAT 1-go ot 25 iiunia 1926 goda," in *Neizdannyi Bulgakov: Teksty i materialy*, ed. Ellendea Proffer (Ann Arbor, Mich.: Ardis, 1977), 82; A. Smelianskii, *Mikhail Bulgakov v Khudozhestvennom teatre* (Moscow: Iskusstvo, 1986), 143–44.

5. V. Golubeva, "Neudavshiisia razgovor: v Sektsii dramaturgii," *Literaturnaia gazeta*, 20 December 1938, 5; see also the resulting letter to the editor and reply: "O 'Neudavshemsia razgovore,'" and "Ot redaktsii," *Literaturnaia gazeta*, 5 January 1939, 5. On *Bogdan Khmel'nitskii*, see A. Fonshtein, "Bogdan Khmel'nitskii v Malom teatre," *Literaturnaia gazeta*, 15 April 1939, 3. On K. Finn's and M. Gus's *Kliuchi Berlina*, which was staged only in September 1941, see I. Kruti, "V gody Otechestvennoi voiny," in *Sovetskii teatr*, ed. M. S. Grigor'ev (Moscow: Vserossiiskoe teatral'noe ob-vo, 1947), 199. The delay was likely a result of the signing of the Molotov-Ribbentrop Treaty in August 1939, which precluded the staging of anti-German material.

6. "Khudozhestvennaia i istoricheskaia pravda," *Literaturnaia gazeta,* 10 January 1939, 1; A. Shestakov, "Propaganda vrednogo tezisa," *Literaturnaia gazeta,* 10 January 1939, 5. On the wax and wane of Pokrovskyian materialist historiography, see the introduction and chapter 3 in this volume.

7. "Snova Blium . . . ," *Literaturnaia gazeta,* 26 January 1939, 5; A. Shin, "Na sobranii dramaturgov Moskvy," *Vecherniaia Moskva,* 20 January 1939, 2.

8. Shestakov, "Propaganda vrednogo tezisa," 5.

9. RGALI, f. 631, op. 2, d. 349, l. 9.

10. RGASPI, f. 17, op. 120, d. 348, ll. 63–67.

11. See RGASPI, f. 17, op. 120, d. 348, ll. 68–710b; ll. 72–750b.

12. B. M., "Vladimir Blium i Il'ia Muromets, Boris Baks i Mikhail Lermontov," *Teatr* 4 (1939): 143; A. Fonshtein, "O chuvstve mery," *Vecherniaia Moskva,* 8 May 1939, 3.

13. Jingoism, or *kvasnoi patriotizm,* was also referred to as *kuz'makriuchkovshchina* after the tsarist regime's agitational campaign surrounding Kuz'ma Kriuchkov, a Cossack hero during the First World War. While the resolution was not published, it was described in "O nekotorykh literaturno-khudozhestvennykh zhurnalakh," *Bol'shevik* 17 (1939): 51–57. The article seems to stem from a 20 August 1939 Central Committee resolution, although only the resolution's supporting materials mention controversy over the meaning of "Soviet patriotism." See "O redaktsiiakh literaturno-khudozhestvennykh zhurnalov," at RGASPI, f. 17, op. 116, d. 9, ll. 2–3; op. 117, d. 19, ll. 54–58. Both are published in *"Literaturnyi front": Istoriia politicheskoi tsenzury, 1932–1946—sbornik dokumentov,* ed. D. L. Babichenko (Moscow: Entsiklopediia rossiiskikh dereven', 1994), 40–44.

14. See *K izucheniiu istorii: Sbornik* (Moscow: Partizdat, 1937); "Ob uchebnike istorii VKP(b): Pis'mo sostaviteliam uchebnika istorii VKP(b)," *Bol'shevik* 9 (1937): 8–10.

15. A. I. Guchkov (1862–1936), leader of the pre-revolutionary monarchist Octoberist Party; P. A. Stolypin (1862–1911), chair of the Council of Ministers; P. N. Miliukov (1859–1943), leading member of the liberal Kadet Party.

16. An oblique reference to *Ivan Susanin* and *Aleksandr Nevskii.*

17. E. Genri, *Hitler over Russia? The Coming Fight between the Fascist and Socialist Armies,* trans. Michael Davidson (New York: Simon and Schuster, 1936), 162–67.

18. A German and Polish cast of popular heroes that includes Nicolaus Copernicus/Mikolaj Kopernik (1473–1543), early Polish astronomer Adam Mickiewicz (1798–1855), Polish poet and champion of Polish liberty; Frederic Chopin/Fryderyk Franciszek Szopen (1810–1849), Polish composer and pianist of the Romantic period; Heinrich Heine (1797–1856), German poet of Jewish ancestry; Hermann von Helmholtz (1821–1894), German scientist and philosopher; Marie Curie (neé Sklodowska, 1867–1934), Polish chemist credited with discovering radium; Immanuel Kant (1724–1804), German philosopher; Ludwig van Beethoven (1727–1807), German composer.

19. Blium inserted the following footnote here: "Having adopted a hostile attitude toward this discussion, *Literaturnaia gazeta* and *Vecherniaia Moskva* have

maliciously distorted its entire nature and content. I have filed a petition with the Party Control Commission in regard to this."

20. "'N'ius Kronikl' o sovetsko-germanskom sblizhenii," *Pravda*, 31 January 1939, 5.

21. On World War I Russian propaganda, see Hubertus Jahn, *Patriotic Culture in Russia during World War I* (Ithaca, N.Y.: Cornell University Press, 1995), passim.

22. The Kadets, or Constitutional Democrats, were a liberal pre-revolutionary party.

23. For Blium's reviews of Korneichuk's *Bogdan Khmel'nitskii* and Finn's and Gus's *Keys to Berlin*, see RGASPI, f. 17, op. 120, d. 348, ll. 68–71ob; ll. 72–75ob.

24. A. E. Korneichuk.

25. Under his signature, Blium attached the following postscript: "For the sake of convenience, I will provide some brief information about myself. I am 62 years old. I have been a party member since July 1917 (and not since 1920, as A. P. Smirnov once lied to you about me 10 years ago, nor was I ever an 'interloper,' as he characterized me at that time, and as my former student N. A. Bulganin can confirm). I have been involved in journalism and criticism since 1908; aside from that, until the end of 1917, I taught history in high school. After 1917, I worked in Soviet journalism as a social commentator and critic. I have specialized in criticism in the arts since the mid-1920s and, prior to 1933, I worked in administrative posts connected with the arts, e.g., theater, music and radio. Until recently (until the election of the new board), I was a board member of the Dramaturgy Section of the Soviet Writers' Union and remain a board member of the Group Committee of Playwrights." Blium probably knew as he wrote these lines that A. P. Smirnov had recently been purged from his position in the state and party bureaucracy; N. A. Bulganin went on to have a prominent career in the Soviet leadership.

26. RGASPI, f. 17, op. 120, d. 348, ll. 76–77. The remark "Into the archive" (*V arkhiv*) is written at the top of the page in the left margin over the initials of A. Kuznetsov, Zhdanov's personal secretary.

27. A reference number for the Agitprop investigation.

28. Although this memorandum might give the impression that Blium risked an array of punitive sanctions such as administrative exile or imprisonment on charges of "anti-Soviet agitation," he merely seems to have been forced into early retirement. According to the 1940 almanac *Teatral'naia Moskva*, Blium still resided at his previous Moscow address (p. 176); in 1941, he became the subject of a petition sent to the Central Committee of the Press Workers' Union requesting that his pension be increased due to disability. See RGALI, f. 631, op. 15, d. 539, ll. 181–82.

29. Probably V. P. Stepanov, a propaganda consultant who rose up through the Agitprop ranks to head Gospolitizdat in the early postwar years, ultimately working as a deputy editor at *Kul'tura i zhizn'* in 1949. By the early 1960s, he was editor-in-chief of *Pravda* and *Kommunist*.

Conclusion

Epic Revisionism and the Crafting of a Soviet Public

◯ JAMES VON GELDERN

The late 1930s were turbulent for the USSR. Fascist Germany loomed to the west; Old Bolsheviks were accused of treachery and executed; peasants migrated to the city in waves, driven by fear and opportunity. On the positive side, a new constitution was adopted, Soviet explorers investigated the polar wastelands, and massive construction projects went up throughout the country. Atop and seemingly in control of this maelstrom was Stalin, general secretary of the communist party and the most powerful man in the land. Demands on Stalin's time were overwhelming, whether he was reviewing the budget of a construction project, receiving foreign dignitaries, or approving a list of party members to be purged. Yet near the top of his agenda for half a decade remained a task that few other statesmen would have considered worthy of their time: the development of a state-endorsed historiography, and its dissemination to popular audiences. In aggregate and in context, the time that Stalin devoted to the project is impressive. He read a stream of scholarship on various figures of Russian history, wrote detailed and often harsh critiques of many books, reviewed plans for curricular materials and textbooks, and even attended scholarly conferences. Far from a historian himself, Stalin was nevertheless articulate and well-informed on historical issues. Even if we bemoan many of his opinions, we cannot label him a dilettante. Why then did Stalin, a statesman as versed in *realpolitik* as any in the twentieth century, devote so much energy to the phantoms of the past at a time of such political turmoil?

As the chapters in this book demonstrate convincingly, history was statecraft for Stalin, a statecraft that enlisted the efforts of thousands of historians, teachers, journalists, writers, and artists throughout the USSR, and that reached millions of readers and spectators. Complex historical figures such as Ivan the Terrible and Peter the Great, state builders and breakers of men who had been dismissed outright by the simplistic Marxism of early Soviet historians, were lionized during the mid- to late 1930s. Plays, poems, movies, and novels were devoted to their state-building skills, to their campaigns against invaders from abroad and dissent at home. Readers will note the obvious echoes with Stalin's own program, as he consolidated his personal power, as well as the power of the public over the private, of the capital over the periphery, and rid Soviet Russia of its deference to foreign ideas and cultures.

History in such a context became a system of communication within a society in which the public sphere had ceased to exist. While the authors of this volume detail the involvement of the Soviet hierarchs, they insist on looking at the actions of less exalted citizens as well. If practical politics were at the foundation of Stalin's new history, what motivated the writers and historians who produced it? Was it simply fear and ambition, or, as seems to be the case, was their participation keener? And what about the audiences and readers? Surely the tools of statecraft did not elicit their responses, which were enviably positive. There was a deeper resonance, as they recognized something familiar and appealing—a greater good—in the principles inscribed in the new history. By charting the flow of information and communication through the system, this collection provides a sense of what constituted the Soviet public in the late 1930s and how it functioned.

One of the ironies of the 1930s is that public culture boomed just as the public sphere, the somewhat utopian field of autonomous nonstate discourse described by Jürgen Habermas, was being closed down.[1] The harshness of the time cannot be discounted. Poets and writers were shackled by the canon of Socialist Realism, silenced by the censor, or condemned to even worse fates at the hands of the NKVD. Political alternatives were extirpated, and even the most loyal of the Old Bolsheviks were subject to repression. Schoolchildren were presented with a newly regimented educational system, in which the teacher was a master who offered unquestioned facts and figures to be memorized. Their role model was the young peasant Pavlik Morozov, who denounced his father to the authorities, a frightening prospect for millions of Soviet parents. Healthy dialogue was slowly excluded from the public sphere (and often from the private sphere as well), leaving a vacuum of silence and fear in its place.

Yet few visitors to the Soviet Union noticed the silence amid the noise and energy of official public culture. Movies lit silver screens across the land. Songs filled the airwaves for those who owned radio sets, and could be heard from phonographs and on the lips of common folk. Many of these songs were upbeat and inspiring, one of the most famous declaiming that "Life's Getting Better, and Happier Too!"[2] There were books (fiction and nonfiction), tales, posters, paintings, symphonies, and a host of other entertainments available to the common man, and public places accessible to all. Evidence suggests that Soviet citizens consumed public culture avidly, responding to it in a way that would have made artists in the West envious. They read, watched, and listened, interpreting the embedded political and social messages in their own ways, and shared their impressions with fellow citizens in public and private discussions.

The editors of this volume contend that the reconfigured heroes of Russian history became a defining feature of this Soviet public culture. As public culture expanded, Russian history provided its sponsors with compelling characters, intriguing plots, and sentiments to please and unite their audiences. Writers and artists found that choosing certain historical characters, most notably state-builders such as Peter the Great and Ivan the Terrible, diminished the risk of official displeasure. By 1937 public culture was characterized by a respect for Russian-centered state authority that would have made the pre-1917 revolutionaries gasp. Commendably, the authors in this volume have chosen not to scan these texts for dissident "gaps" and echoes, or to critique their perversions of history, but rather to describe the effective creation of an integral new world for Soviet audiences. The texts offered an overwhelming sense of authority, and Soviet consumers (at least Russian speakers) seem to have responded positively. We can only wonder how subjects of the non-Russian republics received this culture, a subject in need of a study of its own.

If the consolidation of the Russian state was a common theme, its subtext was power, the ability of the Soviet state to enforce its desires on the creators and consumers of culture. On this count, the record is mixed: for all its willingness to use coercion, the state could never ensure that audiences understood public culture precisely as they were meant to. This was not for lack of trying. When Lev Tolstoi's one-hundredth birthday was celebrated in 1928, a lively contestation ensued between center and periphery over interpretation of the writer. Was he a nobleman or a fighter for the people; a proto-socialist or steadfast Christian? The center held sway, but with difficulty. Future years would see the party exert more control over the academy, allowing true orchestration to become possible. When the Pushkin centennial was organized in 1937, a vast machine encompassing institutions throughout the USSR was mobilized. This campaign was much more successful in producing a single message, in which Pushkin was described as the great Russian national poet (an uncontroversial claim) and a revolutionary who would have readily accepted his adoption as mascot by the socialist state (a considerably less likely contention). The message was projected in public meetings, in classroom recitations, in plays, operas, paintings and hundreds of other public events.

The Pushkin celebration might lead us to see a hegemonic cultural machine, exercising top-down control over cultural production, yet this volume provides an excellent picture of how complex and contested such enterprises could be. Even the monolith of the Pushkin celebration, which struck a deep popular chord among Russian-speakers, was accompanied by a blizzard of jokes that undermined the pomposity of the event. Elsewhere the tensions are clearer. We see censors puzzled by the literary turns of Mikhail Bulgakov, determined to protect the official line from his satiric barbs and yet unsure of what the official line actually was! Stalin himself intervened when Dem'ian Bednyi, who had been Lenin's court poet and was as adept at Soviet cultural politics as anyone, violated the as-yet unarticulated imperative of Russian national pride. Stalin chastised the stunned Bednyi, who never regained his feel for Soviet mass culture, a fate symptomatic of a public culture riddled with inconsistencies, conflicting mandates, and shifting needs. Historians and novelists who helped the state rewrite history were often at odds with each other and with state authorities. They saw their task less as serving the party than as guiding a realignment of Soviet society. Others who wished only to serve their masters found themselves forsaken as the official line shifted. Still others such as Aleksei Tolstoi, the novelist whom history has branded a Stalinist toady, were in fact innovators who not only refused to follow the official line but also managed to reach its most stable positions before the cultural bureaucracy did.

The Soviet government was surely alone in the world in placing hermeneutics (the science of interpretation) at the center of state policy. Concern for the emergence of a new Soviet man, a model citizen whose behavior and innermost mental processes were shaped by socialist society, had been paramount since the October Revolution. Reading stood as a metaphor and catalyst for this model citizen. Such people were to consume the classic texts of Russian and Soviet culture, gleaning from them ideas that would guide them throughout their lives. Training writers to adopt the style of

Socialist Realism and ensuring that these works were read at school and in the home were great institutional accomplishments. Even more impressive was the creation of a new style of reading, in which readers responded properly to cues embedded in the texts, making the appropriate leaps of imagination and ignoring inconvenient gaps. Perhaps most important was that readers read the new literary material as if it were part of a tradition that stretched back to the classics of Russian literature. By celebrating the anniversaries of the classics, cultural authorities were able to convey to readers a sense of continuity and the conviction that the heritage was unbroken.

What were the rules of this new hermeneutic, and what habits did it ingrain? What did it teach Soviet readers about the world around them? The new hermeneutic was riddled with contradictions, which readers were taught to overcome. Fundamental were two historical contexts, that of the writer and that of the reader, with the reader's context ascendant. Any literary text could be salvaged, just as any could be erased. Thus, the adolescent rebelliousness of Lermontov could be transformed (albeit cautiously) into a harbinger of revolution; Pushkin's defiance of the tsar could become a glimmering of class struggle. The Poles invading Muscovy during the Time of Troubles could stand in for Pilsudski's interwar Polish legions. D'Anthès, who hounded Pushkin to his grave, could even merge with the figure of Trotskii, denounced as a foreign hireling on the same front pages in 1937 that commemorated the centennial of Pushkin's death. Remarkable was the willingness both of writers to draw these analogies and of the readers to understand and accept them.

The willingness of Soviet readers to sense history in the present, and the present in history, needs some explaining. A society that had undergone a decade and a half of flux, during which the anchor of history had been raised and the ship of state cast adrift, was surely glad to recover its sense of the past. Evidence shows how deeply Russian readers absorbed the lessons being offered them, and how avidly they responded to historical heroes and villains. It was one thing for them to sense and even accept the implied symmetry between Stalin and Ivan the Terrible. Stalin had practical reasons for sanctioning such an analogy, and readers knew not to question it in the time of terror. It was quite another thing for readers to sense parallels between princes, poets, and themselves, and yet they did. When they celebrated Aleksandr Pushkin, they celebrated the supreme bearer of their own culture and language, finding comfort in continuities and ignoring the discontinuities that were quite striking after two decades of Soviet rule. Celebration of the past had a direct effect on their understanding of themselves as Russians; and in many cases, they transformed this newly russocentric vision of the past into legitimacy for the Soviet state. When the trials of war arrived a few years later, their understanding of history gave them a confidence that the present could not possibly sustain. Thus in the grim winter of 1941–1942, as the Soviet Army retreated before the Germans, readers could reflect back on the battle tactics of Kutuzov against Napoleon, or Nevskii against the Teutonic knights, and discern a brilliant deception in the chaos.

Celebrations of Russian culture and history also emphasized their unitary nature. Russian history was a single thing, the meaning of which could be debated, but which brooked no ambiguity in the end. The ultimate arbiter of the meaning of culture was the state, but citizens were invited to participate in a secondary capacity. The vast machinery set in place for the Pushkin celebration, which created a single image of the great national poet, emphasized that all people could read Pushkin, and made volumes of his work accessible to the public and schools. In the state interpretation, the primary object of Russian culture and history was the creation of the great Russian state—a state in which many diverse peoples resided, united by Russian military might. Imperial Russia was, in this sense, the direct antecedent of the great multicultural state that would become the Soviet Union, an empire constructed through the iron wills of great individuals, from Aleksandr Nevskii to Ivan the Terrible and Peter the Great. Readers were encouraged to take "revolutionary national pride" in these leaders, and they noted that Stalin himself sensed the links and was proud of them. Only the most ideologically conscious readers felt uncomfortable at the formulation.

For all the publicity given the great Russian state-builders, one absence went unnoticed—that of the greatest state-builder of modern Russian history, Nicholas I, whose experience policing society was surely relevant to Soviet authorities. Yet he rarely appeared in histories, and then only in a negative light, as the tsar who crushed the Decembrists' uprising and censored Pushkin. As a rule, the Soviet reader, who was so sensitive to implied analogies, seemed wholly obtuse when confronted with blank spaces in the record. Readers seemed comfortable with a history of the communist party, *The Short Course,* in which most leading revolutionaries were missing. They could glow with pride when reading Russian classics such as Pushkin, Lermontov, and Tolstoi, not noticing the exclusion of Fedor Dostoevskii (who was actually more concerned with Russian national identity than the rest of these writers). Indeed, readers were not encouraged to think too deeply about the biographies of their new heroes. They were to ignore the fact that the princes had been minimally concerned with the life of the lower classes, and that the new interest in individual heroes fit poorly with the collectivism that was still the stated philosophy of the party. Readers were often encouraged not to notice the contradictions and ambiguities of the personalities they honored. Lev Tolstoi, whose character had accommodated all varieties of experience, was flattened into a single shade of being, positive or negative according to the needs of the moment. Commentaries that described the contradictory Tolstoi, such as Maksim Gor'kii's masterful *Reminiscences,* were subjected to similar simplification.

In a culture where the primary language of social communication had been dismembered, the historical figures detailed in this volume became one of the sole "languages" of political discourse. Questions central to Soviet society were not discussed openly in the late 1930s, and were often not even raised. Should a single unchallenged leader direct Soviet democracy? Why had so many leaders of the October Revolution been unmasked as traitors? Could the Soviet Union survive in isolation despite the rise of fascism? By reading about and discussing the great figures of Russian history, ordinary citizens could make sense of important contemporary issues; and in their responses to their readings, they could express a variety of opinions about the present. By refusing to accept Dem'ian Bednyi's contempt for the medieval Russian knights, spectators could limit the Marxist attack on national identity. By cheering Eisenstein's Ivan the Terrible as he struggled against the boyars, they could express support for strong executive power. They could hiss at the primping, traitorous Andrei Kurbskii as he fled to the Kingdom of Poland; in doing so, they denounced the treachery of Trotskii and others.

What is less clear is how dialogic, or accommodating of multivocal expression, this language was. It is apparent that the audiences cheering Aleksander Nevskii's victory over the Teutonic knights were also cheering their own armies in an upcoming battle against the Germans. Yet a writer or audience that attempted to use the same language of historical analogy to suggest that Soviet leaders listen to ordinary citizens as closely as Nevskii did on the eve of his battle in 1242 would not likely have received a positive response. Could artists and citizens use history to "talk back" to their leaders? If the experience of Sergei Eisenstein is indicative, the language could not accommodate two-way communication. The final two parts of his three-part *Ivan the Terrible,* those that dealt with the years of *oprichnina* terror, encountered troubles precisely because Eisenstein tried to do just that.

In many ways, institutional support for the new Soviet reader was as impressive as that for the new Soviet writer. Though there was no single institution such as the Soviet Writers' Union to enunciate the rules of Stalinist readership, readers were constantly cued as to what they should find in historical texts. In classrooms, children were drilled about the meanings of their history, reinforcing the messages they found in films and books. Those children who saw Eisenstein's *Aleksandr Nevskii* (and there were many) repeated in their schools the lesson that this signified the rise of Russian military might.[3] Those few children who missed the film, or whose teachers ignored the lesson plans sent by Moscow, could still find the message in posters, newsreels, or newspapers. Elaborate "media events" accompanied the publication of new historical texts, supporting a state-endorsed interpretative apparatus that few could escape.

So much of the interaction between the Soviet reader and the state was scripted—even ritualized—that it becomes difficult to speak of the relationship in terms of dialogue. Authorities who wished to use readers' responses as a form of citizen-state communication never quite knew whether these expressions of public opinion reflected the innermost thoughts of readers, or whether they were simply hearing their own words parroted back. This uncertainty, amplified by the authority of the words themselves, created an atmosphere of tremendous anxiety. Even when there were more than enough directives and instructions available, Soviet citizens relied less on what they were told than on what they imagined their interlocutors wanted. And they were correct to do so, for Soviet cultural history is littered with individuals who thought they were working within official cultural values, unaware that the rules had undergone major transformation. Dem'ian Bednyi, hearing long-time echoes of Bolshevik atheism and hostility to the Russian past, composed a wicked mockery of the medieval Russian epics in *The Epic Heroes* in 1936. His director, Aleksandr Tairov, dismissed all objections, including his own personal qualms, trusting Bednyi's judgment and believing that this was what Platon Kerzhentsev wanted as chairman of the All-Union Committee for Artistic Affairs. For Bednyi, it was a career-ending mistake.

Though proper Soviet readings did not allow for true and open dialogue, there was still enough give-and-take in the process to allow for an open-ended conversation of sorts. The Soviet reader grew less and less autonomous yet remained to the end unpredictable. There were several varieties of uncertainty in the process. One element that only slowly came under control was the creative impulse of the artistic intelligentsia. In their reinterpretation of the Russian past and classics, artists tested and often crossed the boundaries of officially sanctioned expression. This happened to both loyal and disloyal artists. Bednyi fell when he mocked mythical Russian heroes. Dmitrii Shostakovich, the young composer who identified with the revolutionary impulse, dared to reinterpret a Russian classic, Nikolai Leskov, from politically suspect conservative into a herald of revolution. He took the protagonist of Leskov's "Lady Macbeth of Mtsensk District" and made her into the equivalent of a Socialist-Realist heroine. Although the production enjoyed two years of critical acceptance, the shifting currents of Soviet taste eventually shipwrecked it by declaring its eroticism intolerable. A more familiar form of uncertainty came from the satirical genius of Mikhail Bulgakov, whose Molière in the stage production of the same name could have been many things to many readers, ranging from a castigation of the philistine Soviet cultural agenda to a defense of the free artist against the state. Soviet authorities became increasingly sensitive to the dangers of multiple meanings, a fear that eventually led to the flattening of such texts into unambiguous monovocality.

Springing from these anxieties came perhaps the greatest accomplishment of institutional Soviet culture: the assumption that culture is a single thing, and not an aggregate of diverse meanings and values. Although debate continued about which texts best represented Soviet culture, and what meanings were proper for classic and contemporary texts, there ceased to be much doubt that every text had a single, fixed, "proper" reading. Needless to say, this reading was the one generated and endorsed by official institutions, from the Academy to literary unions to institutions of higher learning to journals and newspapers. The Tolstoi centenary was an early instance of such a campaign, focused on a writer whose work was filled with contradictions. Debates over the good and bad Tolstoi described in this volume were driven by the fear that readers, particularly working-class readers, befuddled by uncertainty, would be infected by the bad Tolstoi, whose Christianity was unacceptable to an atheist state. Organizers of the celebration took preemptive measures to protect worker-readers from this Tolstoi, attempting to flatten his complex figure into a single, unthreatening classic. Although such a measure evoked great controversy in 1928, when Soviet culture still accommodated many voices, by the time of the Pushkin commemoration of 1937, there was no protest when the Writers' Union passed a much more radical measure, forbidding any organization to use Pushkin materials without official permission.

The historiographic debates of the mid-1930s, which settled controversies over great leaders such as Peter I and Ivan IV, featured a similar attention to imagined readers, as historians tried to anticipate how the official line would evolve over time. The evidence presented in this volume suggests a surprising degree of forthright contention in the process, in which tensions were heightened by the great rewards garnered by the winners and the misfortunes suffered by the losers. This controversy was resolved by the intervention of Stalin, the USSR's "ideal reader," who took his responsibilities very seriously. The presence and participation of Stalin allowed for the creation of authoritative readings, providing an interpretation that was beyond debate and would not be swept aside by the next purge or campaign. With the intervention of Stalin, new histories could be approved and published, movie scripts could be approved and produced, and schoolchildren could recite their lessons by rote. Stalin was an extremely demanding reader, who paid close attention to texts, provided detailed responses, and objected to all manner of impropriety. His public appearances became media events in themselves, and like a Roman emperor, his thumb pointed upward or downward determined the fate of books, musical compositions, and entire productions. His appearance at Shostakovich's opera boded its downfall; and when his minion Viacheslav Molotov stormed out of Bednyi's *The Epic Heroes*, much the same fate could be expected for that show. Stalin had become the sole authoritative reader in the Soviet Union, one who fixed the final meaning for each text. Although we might find this situation arbitrary and unconducive to cultural exchange, there is considerable evidence that the "victims" of the process reconciled themselves to the rules of the game. Bednyi, Aleksei Tolstoi, and Eisenstein all solicited and heeded the opinions of their leader, even before his participation was standard practice; artists as unpredictable as Bulgakov also showed some willingness to follow the practice. What is most striking in this volume is not the evidence concerning the artists, but the responses of simple Soviet readers themselves. In the letters they wrote to Eisenstein in praise of *Nevskii*, they show that they too heeded and absorbed the readings prescribed in the mass media, and that they had been trained to yearn for authority. Many seemed to enjoy reading and watching much more when they did not have to confront the anxieties caused by competing interpretations.

What is the condition of a public culture in which authorities constrict open debate and provide the only legitimate forums for public expression? How can we speak of a public sphere when artists and average citizens are arrested and even executed for merely voicing their thoughts? Can we call an interaction dialogic when the ultimate product is a single reading endorsed by the state? Put this way, of course, the existence of a Soviet public in 1930s seems unlikely.

Even so, this volume demonstrates that state and party did not fully control public culture in the 1930s, and that loyal Soviet readers and artists themselves caused much of the volatility. Historians and writers struggled with their material to find its inner mechanisms, to reach their own understandings of the past and through it of the present. Some were willing to provide state authorities with predetermined answers, but others were not; even the most pliant artists at times failed to please their patrons. State commissions were riddled with indeterminacy and contradiction. Ambiguity should not be confused with openness, nor unresolved issues with free speech, yet we must note that Soviet public culture did allow for a surprising degree of interplay and exchange.

It is the role of the audience that evokes the greatest interest here and is most suggestive of the shape of the Soviet public. There can be little mistake as to the positive response evoked by many products of public culture. Readers bought the books, borrowed them from libraries, went to discussion groups, and wrote letters to the authors. Audiences bought tickets and flocked to theaters, gossiped, and narrated the plots to each other in ways that showed they had absorbed the lessons that state authorities wished to implant. Most remarkably, consumers showed the same aversion for indeterminacy that the state demonstrated. Can we speak of dialogue when the state, in response to the desires of readers, relieves them of interpretive uncertainty and provides them with comforting readings? Is this a dialogue of state and audience, or of the state and its own created audience? There can be no final answer for a question in which there is no credible utterance, text, or archival resource. Yet the evidence offered in this volume suggests that Soviet public culture in the mid- to late 1930s was consonant with the tastes of its intended audiences, perhaps more so than at any other time in Soviet history, and that it responded to the perceived needs of its consumers. Indeed, it is possible to say that Soviet public culture essentially created the needs of its viewers and readers, shaping them in a way that helped give birth to the new Soviet man.

The two intertwining themes that dominated the debate on history go to the heart of state-citizen relations in Stalinist society. One was the rise of a Russian national identity centered on the classics of literature, notably Pushkin, Tolstoi, and Lermontov, and on its great empire-builders, foremost Ivan the Terrible and Peter the Great. The second theme emphasized the need for vigorous central authority to organize citizens into a coherent whole and to resist the incursions of internal and external enemies. That both themes discounted the role of the common man in whose name the October Revolution had been waged was apparent to some observers. Yet the great merit of this volume is that it demonstrates how the principles of etatist nationalism and central authority could also have a populist tinge and could be used to bring a society together. We cannot ignore the tensions involved in rallying the multinational Soviet citizenry around the history of Russian empire-building, or in asking citizens of the non-Russian republics to celebrate their own cultures within a pantheon that placed them beneath the Russian classics. Yet neither can we ignore popular affirmation of these themes, witnessed in structured environments such as the classroom or reading club, and in less controlled environments such as darkened movie theaters or the kitchen tables from which consumers wrote to their favorite artists. Many of the books and films discussed in this volume met with critical acclaim and remain popular to the present day.

Perhaps most remarkably, many of the themes discussed here outlived both Stalin and their individual creators to be subjected to reinterpretation by subsequent generations, emerging in many cases as stronger works of art in which multiple messages can be found. Eisenstein's films and Aleksei Tolstoi's novels are still compelling to many audiences; and the classics of Russian literature are still read avidly. The flush of Russian national pride and the strong desire for central authority move Russian audiences even today, long after the fall of the Soviet Union. Texts created in the 1930s still speak to readers in ways that enlighten them. Thus we must conclude that the historical debates that began their lives as a simulation of public culture, directed toward a semi-fictional audience, ultimately created that audience, giving life to an increasingly vital and genuine public culture during the Stalin and post-Stalin eras.

Notes

1. Jürgen Habermas, "The Public Sphere: An Encyclopedia Article (1964)," *New German Critique* 1, no. 3 (1974): 49–55.

2. A comment attributed to Stalin during the preparations for the 1936 constitution that quickly became the central refrain of V. Lebedev-Kumach and A. Aleksandrov's popular song. See L. Gurevich, *Pesni sovetskoi molodezhi* (Moscow: "Molodaia gvardiia," 1937).

3. See, for instance, the 1938 newsreel "Urok istorii v 6 klasse 114-i Moskovskoi shkole," RGAKFD, *Pioneriia* no. 12, catalog no. 3318, production no. 1–4595.

ARCHIVAL REPOSITORY ABBREVIATIONS

CONTRIBUTORS

INDEX

Archival Repository Abbreviations

Arkhiv RAN — Arkhiv Rossiiskoi akademii nauk (Archive of the Russian Academy of Sciences)

Arkhiv UFSB--g.SPbLO — Arkhiv Upravleniia Federal'noi sluzhby bezopasnosti po g. Sankt-Peterburgu i Leningradskoi oblasti (the former secret police archive of Leningrad Province, presently the St. Petersburg Archive of the Federal Security Service)

GAIO — Gosudarstvennyi arkhiv Irkutskoi oblasti (State Archive of Irkutsk Province)

GARF — Gosudarstvennyi arkhiv Rossiiskoi federatsii (former Central State Archive of the October Revolution and former Central State Archive of the RSFSR, presently the State Archive of the Russian Federation)

NA IRI RAN — Nauchnyi arkhiv instituta Rossiiskoi istorii Rossiiskoi akademii nauk (Scholarly Archive of the Russian Academy of Sciences' Institute of Russian History)

RGAKFD — Rossiiskii gosudarstvennyi arkhiv kinofotograficheskikh dokumentov (Russian State Archive of Documentary Films and Photographs)

RGALI — Rossiiskii gosudarstvennyi arkhiv literatury i iskusstva (Russian State Archive of Literature and Art)

RGASPI — Rossiiskii gosudarstvennyi arkhiv sotsial'no-politicheskoi istorii (the former Central Party Archive, presently the Russian State Archive of Social and Political History)

RGIA — Rossiiskii gosudarstvennyi istoricheskii arkhiv (Russian State History Archive)

RGVA	Rossiiskii gosudarstvennyi voennyi arkhiv (Russian State Military Archive)
TsA FSB RF	Tsentral'nyi arkhiv Federal'noi sluzhby bezopasnosti Rossiiskoi federatsii (the former central archive of the secret police, presently the Central Archive of the Federal Security Service)
TsAODM	Tsentral'nyi arkhiv obshchestvennykh dvizhenii g. Moskvy (the former Moscow party archive, presently the Central Archive of Social Movements of the City of Moscow)
TsGAIPD SPb	Tsentral'nyi gosudarstvennyi arkhiv istoriko-politicheskikh dokumentov v Sankt-Peterburge (the former Leningrad party archive, presently the Central State Archive of Historical and Political Documents of the City of St. Petersburg)

Contributors

DAVID BRANDENBERGER is assistant professor of history at the University of Richmond. He has written on Stalin-era ideology and nationalism in journals like *Europe-Asia Studies, Jahrbücher für Geschichte Osteuropas,* and *Voprosy istorii;* his *National Bolshevism: Stalinist Mass Culture and the Formation of Modern Russian National Identity, 1931–1956,* was published by Harvard University Press in 2002.

ALEXANDER MIKHAILOVICH DUBROVSKY is docent in the History Department of Briansk State Pedagogical University (Russian Federation). A specialist in historiography and the socio-cultural milieu surrounding Russo-Soviet historians during the past century, he has published dozens of articles in addition to the definitive biography of S. V. Bakhrushin. He has just completed a second major book, titled *The Historian and Power* (BGU, 2005) (in Russian).

SUSAN BEAM EGGERS is a Ph.D. candidate in the Department of History at the University of North Carolina. She is currently writing a dissertation entitled "Mikhail Ivanovich Glinka's Opera *A Life for the Tsar/ Ivan Susanin:* Culture, Politics, and Artistic Representation, 1836–1939." She has published "Culture and Nationalism: Tchaikovsky's Visions of Russia in *The Oprichnik,*" in *Tchaikovsky and His Contemporaries: A Centennial Symposium,* edited by Alexander Mihailovic (Greenwood Press, 1999).

WILLIAM NICKELL received his Ph.D. from U.C. Berkeley and is lecturer in Russian Language and Literature at U.C. Santa Cruz. He has published articles and reviews in the *Tolstoy Studies Journal, Novoe literaturnoe obozrenie, Slavic and East European Journal,* and *Slavic Review.* He is currently revising a monograph on Tolstoi's death, *Tolstoy in the Public Domain.*

MAUREEN PERRIE is emeritus professor of Russian History in the Centre for Russian and East European Studies, University of Birmingham (UK). She has published extensively on Russian history from the sixteenth to the twentieth centuries; her books include *The Agrarian Policy of the Russian Socialist-Revolutionary Party* (Cambridge University Press, 1976); *The Image of Ivan the Terrible in Russian Folklore* (Cambridge University Press, 1987); *Pretenders and Popular Monarchism in Early Modern Russia* (Cambridge University Press, 1995); *The Cult of Ivan the Terrible in Stalin's Russia* (Palgrave, 2002), and, with Andrei Pavlov, *Ivan the Terrible* (Longman Profiles in Power series, 2003). She is editor of the first (pre-Petrine) volume of the three-volume *Cambridge History of Russia,* currently in preparation. She was president of the British Association for Slavonic and East European Studies (BASEES) from 2001 to 2004.

KEVIN M. F. PLATT is associate professor and chair of the Department of Slavic Languages and Literatures at the University of Pennsylvania. He is the author of *History in a Grotesque Key: Russian Literature and the Idea of Revolution* (Stanford University Press, 1997), as well as articles on Russian history and literature in journals such as *Common Knowledge, Russian Review, Novoe literaturnoe obozrenie,* and *Rethinking History.* He is currently completing a manuscript entitled *Ivan, Peter, Russia: Nation (A Cultural Historiography).*

DAVID POWELSTOCK is assistant professor of Russian and East European Literatures and chair of the Program in Russian and East European Studies at Brandeis University. His book is *Becoming Mikhail Lermontov: The Ironies of Romantic Individualism in Russia* (Northwestern University Press, 2005). He has published articles on Lermontov, Aleksandr Pushkin, Mikhail Bakhtin, and Iurii Olesha and has translated poetry and prose from the Czech and Russian, including two novels by the contemporary Czech writer Iva Pekárková.

STEPHANIE SANDLER is professor of Slavic Languages and Literatures at Harvard University. She is the author of *Alexander Pushkin and the Writing of Exile* (Stanford University Press, 1989) and *Commemorating Pushkin: Russia's Myth of a National Poet* (Stanford University Press, 2004), and has edited *Rereading Russian Poetry* (Yale University Press, 1999) and, with Laura Engelstein, *Self and Story in Russian History* (Cornell University Press, 2000).

JAMES VON GELDERN is professor of Russian and International Studies at Macalester College. He is author of *Bolshevik Festivals, 1917–1920* (University of California Press, 1993) and co-editor of complementary anthologies of popular culture, *Mass Culture in Soviet Russia: Tales, Poems, Songs, Movies, Plays and Folklore, 1917–1953* (1995) and *Entertaining Tsarist Russia: Tales, Songs, Plays, Movies, Jokes, Ads, and Images from Russian Urban Life, 1779–1917* (1998), both published by Indiana University Press. He and Lewis Siegelbaum have compiled a digital sourcebook entitled "Seventeen Moments in Soviet History" accessible at www.soviethistory.org.

ANDREW B. WACHTEL is Bertha and Max Dressler Professor in the Humanities, director of the Center for Comparative and International Studies, and dean of the Graduate School at Northwestern University. He is the author or editor of ten books and more than fifty articles on Russian and South Slavic literature, culture, history and society. His most recently published book is *Making a Nation, Breaking a Nation: Literature and Cultural Politics in Yugoslavia* (Stanford University Press, 1998). Earlier books include *The Battle for Childhood: Creation of a Russian Myth* (Stanford University Press, 1990), *An Obsession with History: Russian Writers Confront the Past* (Stanford University Press, 1994) and *Petrushka: Sources and Contexts* (Northwestern University Press, 1998). Forthcoming books include *Remaining Relevant after Communism? Writers and Society in Eastern Europe since 1989* and *A History of the Balkans*. In recognition of his academic work in the area of literary criticism he was elected to membership in the American Academy of Arts and Sciences in 2003.

Index

agitation. *See* propaganda
Aleksandr Nevskii (1220–1263, prince), 5, 10, 150, 158, 227, 234–36, 238–39, 243–46, 249–50n29, 251n49, 251n54, 254, 257, 262, 267, 277, 315, 330. *See also* Battle on the Ice; Eisenstein
All-Union Committee for Artistic Affairs (KDI), 88, 93, 97n37, 97n44, 97n50, 98n55, 100–102, 105, 107, 109, 111, 112n10, 114n58, 144, 146, 174n26, 179–80, 183, 188n6, 318–19, 332
Angarov, A. I. (1898–1939, deputy chief of Kul'tprop), 57–58, 108, 146
anniversary. *See* commemoration
atheism. *See* ideology
avant-garde, 8, 19, 35n26. *See also* modernism

Bakhrushin, S. V. (1882–1950, historian), 143, 159, 164–65, 174–75n26, 176n39
Battle of Kulikovo Field (1380 clash with Tatars), 235, 242, 248n12. *See also* Dmitrii Donskoi
Battle on the Ice (1242 clash with Teutonic Knights), 236–39, 243, 248n11, 248n17, 251n48, 256–57, 267. *See also* Aleksandr Nevskii; Eisenstein

Bednyi (Pridvorov), Dem'ian (1883–1945, poet), 6, 74, 77–79, 82–84, 86, 88, 94–95, 228n16, 328, 332, 334; *Epic Heroes, The*, 88–94, 98n57, 98n59, 99–111, 112n20, 147, 150, 152, 257n10, 331–34; "Get Down off the Hearth," 79–83; "Let's Straighten It Out," 86–87; "On the Heroic," 84–86, 96n26; "Pererva," 80–81; "Without Mercy," 80–82
Belinskii, V. G. (1811–1848, social critic), 287, 289, 296, 298, 304n16, 304n19, 306n37, 307n49, 311
Blium, V. I. (theater critic), 5, 241, 258n13, 315–21. *See also* communist idealists
Boiarskii (Shimshelevich, Ia. O.), Ia. I. (deputy chief of All-Union Committee on Artistic Affairs), 91, 97n44, 102, 104, 111, 112n10
Borodin, A. P. (1833–1887, composer), 88, 91, 101, 103–4
Bukharin, N. I. (1888–1938, Old Bolshevik), 19, 71
Bulgakov, M. A. (1891–1940, playwright), 98n57, 111, 112nn15–16, 114n53, 114n56, 114n64, 144–45,

Bulgakov, M. A. (*continued*)
156n63, 276, 328, 333–34; *Ivan Vasil'evich*, 6–7, 98n57, 111, 112nn15–16, 114n53, 114n56, 114n64, 143–52, 154n25, 155n42, 155–56n61, 158, 328, 333–34; *The Last Days*, 193, 200–205, 211n47, 212n54

censor, 14n17, 18, 39, 74n5, 97n37, 105–6, 108, 147–49, 194, 208–9n10, 220, 304n16, 326, 328; prerevolutionary, 25, 110, 215, 274n22, 330. *See also* Glaviskusstvo; Glavrepertkom
Chapaev, V. I. (1887–1919, civil war hero), 4, 236, 238
Cherkasov, N. K. (1903–1966, actor), 58, 73, 114, 167–68, 177n49, 181, 239, 251n49, 254, 257n7
Chernyshevskii, N. G. (1828–1889, social critic), 20–21, 42–43, 43n8, 117, 289, 296, 304n19, 311
christening of Rus' (ca. 988), 89–93, 97n40, 101, 106, 110. *See also* Russian Orthodox Church
civil war (1918–1921), 9, 113n25, 113n30, 113n48, 151, 165, 249n22, 255, 258n11, 274n20
class consciousness, 12n7, 23–24, 29, 32, 95–96n14, 266
commemoration: in Imperial Russia, 18–19, 198, 209n20; Soviet commemoration of "Soviet" figures and events, 5, 20–21, 42, 84, 86, 234, 236; Soviet commemoration of tsarist figures, 6, 17–33, 36n33, 37n39, 38n53, 39–43, 193–94, 196, 199–200, 205, 207, 209n18, 214, 216, 250n37, 251n49, 284, 288–89, 295–96, 300–301, 302n2, 304nn15–16, 308–9, 312n12, 315, 329; unofficial commemorations, 17, 21, 23, 30, 35n16, 38n51, 40, 200–207, 221
Committee for Artistic Affairs. *See* All-Union Committee for Artistic Affairs

communist idealists, 17–18, 20–23, 25–26, 235, 316–17
creative intelligentsia. *See* intelligentsia
cult of personality. *See* Stalin
Cultural Revolution (1928–1932), 24, 28, 40, 42, 86, 88–89, 283, 293, 296

D'Anthès, Georges Charles (1812–1895, Pushkin's killer), 200, 202–4, 215, 224, 226, 287, 329
Decembrists (participants in 1825 rebellion), 4, 214, 216, 289, 330
Derzhavin, G. R. (1743–1816, poet), 206–7, 229n20
dissent, 5–7, 41, 308–11, 316–20, 326. *See also* communist idealists
Dmitrii Donskoi (1350–1389, grand prince), 10, 235, 242, 251n54. *See also* Battle of Kulikovo Field
Dobroliubov, N. A. (1836–1861, critic), 289, 311
Dostoevskii, F. M. (1821–1881, writer), 219n10, 330

educational level, low, 9, 246, 315
Egorov, A. I. (1883–1939, Red Army marshal), 10–11
Eikhenbaum, B. M. (1886–1959, critic), 296, 306n33, 308
Eisenstein (Eizenshtein), S. M. (1898–1948, film director), 4, 60, 107, 169, 234, 334, 336; *Aleksandr Nevskii* (1938), 5–6, 233–46, 247n4, 248n12, 248n14, 248nn16–17, 248–50n19, 250n32, 251n48, 252n59, 253–57, 257n1, 257nn7–8, 267, 315–16, 320, 322n16, 334; *Ivan the Terrible* (1944–1946), 143, 162–63, 166–69, 174–75n26, 175nn31–32, 176n44, 177n45, 177n49, 178n54, 181, 242, 257, 257n7, 331–32
Enukidze, A. S. (1877–1937, party hierarch), 10–11

Epic Heroes, The. See Bednyi; Borodin; Tairov
etatism. *See* ideology
Evgenii Onegin. See Pushkin
Ezhov, N. I. (1895–1940, secret police chief), 10–11, 257n1

Fadeev, A. A. (1901–1956, writer), 59, 94, 298, 311n2, 312n6
film, 5, 17, 29, 161–62, 170, 196, 200, 241–43, 332, 336. *See also* Eisenstein, mass culture; Tolstoi, A. N.
First Five-Year Plan (1928–1932), 9, 24, 32, 225
First World War (1914–1918), 221, 249n22, 254–55, 258n13, 266, 318–19, 322n13, 323n21
folklore, 8–9, 48, 88–91, 104–5, 112n20, 113n28, 114n60, 118, 120, 124, 132n5, 133n22, 149, 154n32, 155n42, 158, 173n6, 183, 228n6, 239, 243, 274, 278–79, 311
Formalism: theoretical school, 20, 133n5, 193; campaign against "formalism in the arts," 102–3, 137–38, 139n4, 143–44, 146, 150, 152, 199, 276
Friche, V. M. (1870–1929, critic), 20, 37–38n49

Germany, 3–5, 7, 97n40, 147, 160, 164–65, 221, 234–36, 238, 240–46, 248n11, 251n53, 253, 254–57, 258n11, 258n15, 261, 266–68, 271, 300, 318–19, 321n5, 325, 330, 332
Glaviskusstvo (Main Directorate for Literary and Artistic Affairs), 18, 92, 112n10. *See also* censor
Glavrepertkom (Main Repertory Committee), 97n37, 112n10, 144–45. *See also* censor
Glinka, M. I. (1804–1857, composer), 5, 7, 151, 261–72, 274n19, 276, 322n16
Gogol', N. V. (1809–1852, writer), 86, 97n35, 220, 222, 261

Gor'kii, M. (A. M. Peshkov) (1868–1936, writer), 9, 20–21, 32, 34n14, 35–36n30, 37n40, 38n53, 39, 54, 66–67n20, 149, 158, 173nn6–7, 196, 217, 227n1, 312n8, 331
Gorodetskii, S. M. (1884–1967, playwright), 105, 113n28, 151
"Great Break, the" (*Velikii perelom*). *See* First Five-Year Plan
"Great Retreat, the," 5, 12, 274n29
"Great Terror, the." *See* purges

heroes, 3–5, 9–11, 12n7, 14n13, 14nn18–19, 21, 52–54, 64, 68n37, 119–21, 147, 150, 157–58, 164–65, 169, 178n51, 194–95, 206, 209n16, 239, 263, 268, 331; embrace of Russian historical heroes, 10–11, 12n7, 14n18, 21, 52–54, 64, 68n37, 94, 144, 147–48, 150–52, 156n65, 157–58, 164–65, 166, 169–70, 173n7, 178n51, 180, 184, 194–95, 205, 234–35, 238, 242–45, 251n54, 253, 268–70, 277, 286, 315, 327, 329–31; materialists' rejection of, 3–5, 148, 157–58, 164–65, 169, 241, 316; purge of Soviet heroes, 10–11, 330; revival of the positive hero, 4–6, 9–11, 14n13, 54, 64, 68n37, 120, 133n11, 270, 331; Soviet heroes as role models, 4, 9–10, 42, 53, 64, 83–84. *See also* ideology; Socialist Realism
Herzen, A. I. (1812–1870, critic), 287, 289, 307n49, 311
history, 3–4, 47–48, 51–52, 262, 276–79, 290, 325; "great men of history," 3, 20–21; propagandistic vs. scholarly, 292–93, 295–96; the "usable past," 3–9, 12n3, 13n10, 19, 47–48, 55, 57–59, 64, 71–72, 144, 150, 156n65, 157–59, 165–66, 169–70, 175n27, 176n41, 178n51, 180, 218, 233, 235, 242, 253, 278, 290–92, 316, 325–30, 336. *See also* ideology; Pokrovskii

ideology, 3, 5–6, 20–26, 29–31, 54, 57, 63, 68n37, 77, 93, 117, 119, 121, 132–33n7, 157, 199, 221, 285–86, 288, 292, 301, 303n13, 305n22, 306n35, 307n46, 308, 330; atheism, 21–23, 34n6, 89, 91, 93, 254, 332–33; deviation, 20, 25, 29, 32, 294; etatism, 4–6, 77, 87–88, 94, 157–71, 233, 236, 330; materialism, 3–4, 52, 57, 67n23, 148, 150, 302n1, 316, 320, 322n6; Marxism-Leninism, 3–4, 18–23, 30–33, 34n5–6, 35n26, 40, 47, 63, 84, 87, 148, 150, 246; proletarian internationalism, 5, 12n7, 77, 246; populism, 6, 233, 235, 246, 330; russocentrism, 4–6, 9, 14n13, 14n18, 93–94, 233, 242–44, 330. *See also* propaganda
intelligentsia, 12, 14, 39, 59, 77–78, 99, 111–12n1, 117, 120, 149, 155n49, 164, 169, 214, 255, 257n1, 283–84, 293, 301, 305n25, 328, 333; generational conflict within, 293, 296; ideological confusion within, 6, 10, 19–20, 34n12, 39, 80–88, 94, 160, 169–70, 235, 284, 287–89, 301, 315–16, 330, 332. *See also* communist idealists
internationalism. *See* ideology
Ivan III, "the Great" (1440–1505, grand prince), 160, 180
Ivan IV, "the Terrible" (1530–1584, tsar), 5–6, 143, 145, 147–49, 152n1, 154n32, 155n42, 156n63, 157–71, 173nn6–7, 174n19, 174n21, 174n26, 175n27, 177n47, 178n51, 178n56, 178n58, 179–87, 315, 326–27, 329–30, 334, 336. *See also* Eisenstein
Ivanov, S. V. (author, critic), 300, 308–11

journalism. *See* press
jubilee. *See* commemoration

Karamzin, M. N. (1766–1826, historian, writer), 173n6, 182, 188n9, 311

Kharms (Iuvachev), D. I. (1906–1942), 193, 205–7, 212n59, 212–13n60, 213n64
Khrennikov, T. M. (1913–, composer), 162, 175n27
Khubov, G. N. (1902–1981, author, critic), 265, 267
Kievan Rus' (9–12th cent. Slavic state), 5, 61, 72–73, 80, 85, 87–95, 113n27, 234, 243–46, 331–33. *See also* christening of Rus'
Kirpotin, V. I. (1898–1990, critic), 295–302, 304n15, 305n23, 306n33, 306nn35–37, 307n46, 307n49, 307n51, 311n2, 312n6
Kliuchevskii, V. O. (1841–1911, historian), 51, 65n4, 182, 184
Komsomol (Communist Youth League), 9–10, 23, 31, 35n24, 37n39, 41–42, 255, 257
Korneichuk, A. E. (1905–1972, Ukrainian playwright), 5, 48n15, 315–16, 319–20, 323n24
Kosarev, A. V. (1903–1939, Komsomol chief), 10–11
Krupskaia, N. K. (1869–1939, Lenin's widow, deputy Commissar of Education), 21
Krylov, I. A. (1768–1844, writer), 78, 88, 91, 300
Kurbskii, A. M. (1528–1583), 155n42, 182, 185, 188n8, 331
Kustodiev, B. M. (1878–1927, artist), 122–31, 133nn17–18, 133n21, 133n23
Kutuzov, M. I. (1745–1813, marshal), 5, 10, 242, 250n45, 251n54, 330

Lady Macbeth of Mtsensk District. See Leskov; Shostakovich
Lake Chud'. *See* Battle on the Ice
Larionov, M. F. (1881–1964, artist), 128–31
League of the Militant Godless, 21–23, 34n6

Index

"leftist internationalism." *See* communist idealist
Lenin (Ul'ianov), V. I. (1870–1924), 3–4, 12n2, 18–33, 34n5, 35n26, 36n33, 36nn35–36, 37n40, 37n45, 38n53–54, 39–42, 43n5, 66n9, 77–78, 82, 84, 87, 96n15, 119, 195, 196, 209n16, 211n38, 218, 240, 257, 304n15, 328
Lermontov, M. Iu. (1799–1841, writer, poet), 6, 10, 96n17, 198, 204, 212n55, 222–23, 226, 283–312, 329, 330, 336
Leskov, N. A. (1831–1895, writer), 220; *Lady Macbeth of Mtsensk District*, 7, 117–39, 333
Libedinskii, Iu. N. (1898–1959, critic), 17
literature, 7–11, 14n17, 31, 38n50, 74n3, 90, 161–62, 182–83, 187, 199, 302n1, 308–11, 312n9, 326–33; and social identity, 18–20, 22–23, 25, 29, 193–97, 205, 207, 283, 286–90, 328–33; "classics," 10, 19–20, 25, 35n26, 39, 40, 117–18, 130–31, 193–95, 196, 256, 283–84, 301–2, 333–34; historical subjects, 47–48, 319, 320–21. *See also* mass culture; readers and readership; Socialist Realism
Ludwig, Emil (1881–1948, German biographer), 3–5
Lunacharskii, A. V. (1875–1933, Commissar of Education), 21, 22, 26–31, 33n1, 35n28, 36n33, 36n35, 37nn38–39, 43n5
Luxembourg, Rosa (1871–1919, Polish-German communist), 20, 37–38n49

Maiakovskii, V. V. (1893–1930, poet), 196, 302n2
Marx, Karl (1818–1883), 56, 245, 249n26
Marxism-Leninism. *See* ideology
mass culture, 5–11, 20–24, 28–33, 33nn1–3, 35n20, 35n24, 39, 42–43, 69–70, 136–37, 161–62, 193–200, 204–5, 209n16, 209n18, 209n20, 210n23, 210n26, 210n29, 210–11n36, 233–52, 268–71, 283–84, 294–95, 297, 315–17, 325–37. *See also* film; literature; opera; press; theater
materialism. *See* ideology
McLean, Hugh, 118, 133n6, 220
Mekhlis, L. Z. (1889–1953, party official), 81, 98n58
Meyerhold (Meierkhol'd), V. E. (1874–1940, director), 103–4, 109, 114n55, 114n58, 136–37
Mikhail Fedorovich (1596–1645, tsar), 262–63, 270, 272n3, 277–78
Miliukov, P. N. (1859–1943, tsarist-era historian, politician), 51, 65n4, 318
Minin, Kuz'ma (d. 1616, merchant, militia commander), 5, 10, 81, 105, 150, 151, 156nn65–66, 162, 242, 251n54, 266, 277–79. *See also* Pozharskii; Time of Troubles
mobilization, 9, 47, 152, 164, 194, 233, 238, 246, 253, 262, 263, 267, 268, 273n8, 293, 315–16, 319
modernism, 32n26, 122, 128, 130–31. *See also* avant-garde
Molotov (Skriabin), V. M. (1890–1986, party hierarch), 19, 80–83, 92, 96n20, 96n26, 107, 168, 234, 334
Molotov-Ribbentrop Treaty, 160, 243, 271, 321n5
Mongrel Knights. *See* Teutonic Knights
Mordvinov (Sheftel'), B. A. (1899–1953, director), 265, 268, 270, 276–80

Nechkina, M. V. (1901–1985, historian), 56, 148, 174–75n26
Nicholas I (1796–1855, emperor), 214, 225, 228n14, 261, 276, 278, 285, 287, 299, 303n6, 303n11, 330
Nicholas II (1868–1918, emperor), 19, 22, 77, 110, 316
NKVD. *See* secret police
Novgorod, 236, 240, 241, 244–45, 255–57. *See also* Aleksandr Nevskii

Ogarev, N. P. (1813–1877, poet, critic), 286, 303n8, 304n16
OGPU. *See* secret police
Old Bolsheviks, 4, 9, 10, 21, 23, 114n51, 296, 315, 316
Ol'minskii, M. (M. S. Aleksandrov) (1863–1933, critic), 22, 25–28, 36nn32–33, 36n35
opera, 5, 7, 88–95, 99–114, 117–39, 145, 146, 147, 150, 151, 156n66, 162, 174–75n26, 226, 228n17, 254, 261–80, 320, 328, 334. *See also* mass culture
Oprichnina (privy council guard blamed for Ivan IV's terror), 147–49, 151, 155n42, 159–63, 167–71, 185, 331–32. *See also* Ivan IV

Pankratova, A. M. (1897–1957, historian), 56, 174n17, 176n44, 178n58
Pavlenko, P. A. (1899–1951, writer), 234–39, 254, 315
Peter I, "the Great" (1672–1725, emperor), 3–6, 10–11, 12n7, 14n18, 47–74, 147, 150, 151, 156nn65–66, 158, 173n7, 233, 262, 315, 320, 326, 327, 330, 334, 336
Petrov, V. M. (1896–1966, director), 58, 70–73, 74n10, 233
Piatakov, Iu. (G.) L. (1890–1937, Bol'shevik leader), 10–11, 199
Plekhanov, G. V. (1856–1918, Marxist critic), 12n2, 18, 20–22, 31, 39–42, 182
Pokrovskii, M. N. (1868–1932, historian), 4, 34n4, 52–59, 66n9, 67n23, 72, 98n59, 148, 150, 312n9, 316, 320, 322n6. *See also* materialism; "vulgar sociology"
Poland, 7, 150, 165, 182, 188n8, 261–75, 318–20, 322n18, 329, 331. *See also* Susanin; Time of Troubles
Politburo (Central Committee Political Bureau), 55, 93, 95n8, 148, 228n4
populism. *See* ideology
Pozharskii, Dmitrii (1578–1642, prince), 5, 10, 81, 105, 150, 151, 156nn65–66, 162, 242, 251n54, 266, 277–79. *See also* Minin; Time of Troubles
press, 5, 9, 20–28, 33n3, 39–43, 57, 67n1, 69–70, 79–87, 91–92, 94, 98n58, 99, 100, 105, 107, 150, 151, 156n65, 165, 187, 196–200, 210n23, 210n26, 210n29, 210n35, 219n12, 225, 235–36, 240, 250n38, 251n48, 268, 283–94, 304n16, 317, 323n27, 326, 332–33. *See also* mass culture
Prokof'ev, S. S. (1891–1953, composer), 177n49, 254
proletarian internationalism. *See* ideology
proletarians. *See* workers
propaganda, 3–14, 21, 34n4, 37n40, 53, 69, 79, 81, 101, 110, 157–78, 215, 233–34, 242–46, 248n15, 253–54, 258n11, 262–63, 268–72, 276, 283–85, 288–93, 297–301, 315–24. *See also* heroes; history; ideology; mass culture; press; "Soviet patriotism"
public opinion, 99–100, 111–12n1, 234–52, 317, 331–32. *See also* reception
Pugachev, Emel'ian (1742–1775, peasant rebel), 4, 10, 109, 113, 151, 156n63
purges, 10–11, 14n18, 136, 148, 166, 193–213, 234, 257n1, 265–66, 323n25, 325, 329, 334. *See also* secret police
Pushkin, A. S. (1799–1837, writer, poet), 5, 10–11, 14n18, 96n17, 144, 151–52, 156n63, 261, 284, 287, 307n46, 329–30, 336; commemoration of, 6, 18, 193–229, 233, 250n37, 287, 302n2, 315, 328–30, 334; "Bacchic Song," 194, 218, 219n11; "The Countryside," 216, 219n4; "Exegi Monumentum" ("Ia pamiatnik sebe vozdvig nerukotvornyi"), 218, 219n9; *Evgenii Onegin*, 198, 216, 219n2, 223–26, 228n9; *Feast in a Time of Plague*, 195; "Freedom: An Ode," 208n10;

"... I visited once again," 216, 219n3; "My Ruddy-Faced Critic," 194; "The Queen of Spades," 198, 227; "Remembrances in Tsarskoe Selo," 206; "Triumph of Bacchus," 224, 228n13; "Winter Evening," 202

Ragozin, A. (critic), 308–12
RAPP (Russian Association of Proletarian Writers), 17, 54–58, 67n22, 70–72, 73n2
Raskol'nikov, F. (critic), 20, 22, 31, 36n35, 37–38n49
Razin, S. T. (1630–1671, peasant rebel), 4, 10
readers and readership, 18–19, 22–23, 29, 31–32, 34n6, 39–43, 62–63, 69–70, 85–87, 135, 196, 198, 206, 215–16, 284–85, 288, 292, 294, 297, 299, 304n20, 305n26, 325–37. See also literature
reception, 6, 57, 65n4, 117, 233–52, 267, 296. See also readers and readership
Red Army, 4, 9–11, 22, 112n5, 113n47, 237, 239, 249n47, 257n1
rehabilitation, 3–14, 47–48, 58–59, 70, 87–88, 105–6, 119–21, 133–34, 148–52, 233–34, 240, 253–54, 261–63, 276–77, 283–84, 300–302, 325–28; contested, 19–30, 54–58, 70, 166–69, 283–312, 315–24; "from above," 70, 94, 157–89, 193–95, 205, 207, 214–19, 235, 244–46, 328–36; "from below," 241–44, 246, 328–36; repeated, 59–64, 131; reverse, 7, 261–75
Repin, I. E. (1844–1930, painter), 158, 173n10
resistance. See Blium; dissent
Revolution (October 1917), 4–5, 17, 19, 24, 31–33, 35n20, 37n38, 42, 51, 65n8, 80, 96n16, 117, 132n1, 165, 194, 215–16, 219n12, 234, 236, 246, 255, 257, 257n4, 262, 284, 287, 297, 328, 331, 333, 336

Rozental', M. M. (1906–1975, critic), 297–301, 306n35, 306n37, 307n41, 307n46
Rus'. See Kievan Rus'
Russian chauvinism, 67n23, 84, 205, 319
Russian Orthodox Church, 21–22, 29, 34n9, 89, 106, 161, 180, 183, 236

Samosud, S. A. (1884–1964, director), 103, 270, 278
Second World War, 6, 13n8, 53, 59, 68n37, 143, 164–65, 174–75nn26–27, 178n51, 180, 205, 218, 233–34, 238, 242–46, 251nn48–49, 251n55, 255, 257n7, 258n11, 258n15, 263, 267–68, 271–72, 300, 330–31
secret police, 9–10, 99–100, 201–4, 326. See also purges
Sergeev-Tsenskii, S. N. (1875–1958, writer), 248n15, 315
Shamil' (1797–1871, Caucasian rebel), 4, 10
Shcherbakov, A. S. (1901–1945, party hierarch), 160–62, 166, 170, 173n6, 174n26, 175n27, 177n46, 179–89
Shestakov, A. V. (1877–1941, historian), 14n15, 55–57, 158, 233, 241, 250n40, 316, 320. See also Short Course on the History of the USSR
Shklovskii, V. B. (1893–1984, critic), 20, 250n31
Short Course on the History of the USSR, 14n15, 55–57, 158–59, 173n10, 188n11, 233, 250n40. See also Shestakov
Shostakovich, D. D., (1906–1975, composer), 162, 174–75n26; Lady Macbeth of Mtsensk District, 7, 111–12n1, 112n15, 117–39, 146, 333, 334
"social commission," 54, 161–67, 170, 174–75n26, 178n56, 179–80, 183, 196, 318
socialism. See ideology

Socialist Realism, 11, 14n17, 32, 119–21, 131, 132n7, 135–39, 194, 242, 255, 268, 271, 305n22, 326, 328–29, 333; defined, 8–9, 74n3; the positive hero, 9, 120, 133n11, 270; catered to mass readership, 9; relationship to the "classics," 8, 117–18

Solov'ev, S. M. (1820–1879, historian), 148, 182, 188n13

Solov'ev, V. A. (1907–1978, playwright), 143, 164, 167, 177n49

"Soviet patriotism," 5, 9, 67n23, 77, 81, 86–88, 94, 95–96n14, 150–52, 167, 234–46, 251n54, 255–56, 263, 277–79, 288, 316–20, 322n13

Soviet Writers' Union, 32, 73n2, 74n3, 88, 94, 101, 149, 158, 173n6, 196, 199, 210n23, 211n38, 283, 293, 295, 298, 303n13, 304n15, 316, 319, 320, 323n25, 332, 334

Sovnarkom (Council of People's Commissars), 88, 93, 95n8

Stakhanovite movement (labor heroism), 10, 288n15

Stalin (Dzhugashvili), I. V. (1879–1953), 8, 10, 19, 23, 32, 58, 70, 72, 77, 80–84, 87, 96n20, 96nn25–26, 121, 135, 138n2, 144, 151, 154n34, 155n49, 167, 177n46, 180, 187n2, 188n6, 195–96, 218, 234–35, 242, 244, 251n54, 252n59, 257, 325–30, 334–36, 337n2; as critic, 3–5, 11n1, 12n2, 74n3, 74n8, 84, 94, 96n16, 170–71, 174n25, 175n32, 177n50, 219n12, 265–66, 315–20; cult of personality, 4–5, 53, 169, 234, 246; and Ivan the Terrible, 143, 147–49, 152, 157–58, 161–66, 168–71, 175n27, 177n47, 178n59, 326, 329; and Peter the Great, 3–4, 54, 66–67n20, 176n41, 326

statism. *See* ideology

Stavskii (Kirpichnikov), V. P. (1900–1943, writer), 77, 88–92, 101–2

Susanin, Ivan (peasant partisan of legend, 1612), 5, 10, 261–80, 320, 322n16. *See also* opera; Poland; Time of Troubles

Suvorov, A. V. (1729–1800, generalissimo), 5, 10, 242, 251n54

Tairov, A. Ia. (1850–1950), 88–92, 97n33, 99–114, 332. *See also* Bednyi

terror. *See* purges

Teutonic Knights, 165, 234–40, 245, 248n11, 248n13, 249n26, 254–57, 267–68, 277, 330–31. *See also* Battle on the Ice

textbooks and school curricula, 5, 14n15, 18, 29–30, 37n42, 55–57, 74n8, 88, 94, 148–51, 156n63, 158–59, 170, 173n10, 174n17, 196, 199, 210n23, 222, 223, 233, 235, 238, 241–46, 250n40, 325, 326, 329, 330, 332, 334

theater, 5, 7, 29, 48, 52–61, 67n21, 87–95, 97n33, 97n37, 98n58, 99–114, 124, 137, 143–56, 160–70, 175n31, 177nn46–47, 177n49, 178n56, 179–89, 196–205, 212n51, 254, 256, 315–24, 326, 328, 335. *See also* mass culture, opera

Timasheff, Nicholas. *See* "Great Retreat, the"

Time of Troubles (1605–1613 interregnum), 7, 81, 165, 182, 188n7, 189n23, 262, 266, 329. *See also* Minin; Poland; Pozharskii; Susanin

Tolstoi, A. K. (1817–1875, playwright), 182–83

Tolstoi, A. N. (1873–1945, writer, playwright), 6, 47–74, 88, 158, 165 169, 173n7, 174–75n26, 176n35, 176n41, 248n15, 328, 334, 336; *Ivan the Terrible*, 143, 160–63, 166–67, 175n31, 177nn46–47, 177n49, 179–89; *On the Rack*, 54, 147; *Peter I* (film), 48, 50, 57–58, 62, 67n33, 69–74, 315; *Peter I* (historical novel), 48–54, 59–64, 65nn2–3, 66n9, 67–68nn36–37;

Index   355

Peter I (play), 48, 52, 54–55, 59, 62; "Peter's Day," 48–49, 51, 59–61, 65n1, 65–66n7–8
Tolstoi, L. N. (1828–1910, writer), 6, 17–43, 118–19, 156n63, 196, 222, 284, 327, 330–31, 333, 336
Tolstoianism, 17, 18, 21–24, 29–32, 34n4, 34–35nn16–17, 36n33, 38n51, 39–40
Trotskii (Bronshtein), L. D. (1879–1940, revolutionary), 19, 78, 329, 331
Trotskyism, Trotskyites, 11, 31, 70–72, 199–200, 214, 217
Turgenev, I. S. (1818–1883, writer), 119, 222

"usable past." *See* history

VAPP (All-Union Association of Proletarian Writers), 8, 41, 43n6
Vasil'ev, D. M. (director), 254, 257n9
Vertov, Dziga (D. A. Kaufman) (1896–1954, film director), 195, 253
Vipper, R. Iu. (1859–1954, historian), 143, 148, 164–65, 169, 174–75n26, 176n34, 176n38, 182, 188n9
Vishnevskii, V. V. (1900–1954, writer, playwright), 105, 107, 112n6, 113nn29–30, 168, 178n53, 234–36, 243, 248n16, 248–49n19

Vladimir I, "the Great" (d. 1015, grand prince), 89–92, 97n40. *See also* christening of Rus'
Volin (Fradkin), B. M. (1886–1957, party official), 36–37n36
"vulgar sociology," 33n2, 55, 98n59, 219n7, 283, 298, 302n1, 309, 312n9. *See also* Pokrovskii

workers, working class, 4, 9, 10, 22–23, 27, 29, 32, 33n2, 35n20, 37n40, 40–41, 43n6, 69, 74n8, 79–85, 95–96n14, 148, 288n15, 238, 240, 241, 244, 251n48, 255, 289, 295, 305n25, 318, 333. *See also* class consciousness

Zamiatin, E. M. (1884–1934, writer), 122–30, 134n20, 134n25
Zhdanov, A. A. (1896–1948, party hierarch), 14n15, 55, 72, 74n3, 74n8, 93, 138n2, 148, 158–59, 161, 168, 170–71, 174–75n26, 177n50, 181, 228n4, 234, 248n15, 303n13, 317, 320, 323n26
Zhukovskii, V. A. (1783–1852, poet), 201–3, 278
Zoshchenko, M. M. (1895–1958, satirist), 193, 197–98, 205, 210n31, 220–29